Political Ecology of Deforestation and Tribal Life

About the Author

Bhupendra Nath Goswami (*b.* 1961) received his M.Sc. (1989) and Ph.D. (2015) degrees in Geography from Gauhati University, Guwahati. He has to his credit three edited books and more than two hundred and fifty articles published in various Newspapers, Journals and Megazines. He is presently an Associate Professor in the Department of Geography, Mariani College, Assam.

Political Ecology of Deforestation and Tribal Life

A Study of Assam-Nagaland Border Areas

Bhupendra Nath Goswami

CONCEPT PUBLISHING COMPANY PVT. LTD.
NEW DELHI-110059

ISBN-13: 978-93-5125-190-3

First Published 2017

Published and Printed by:

Concept
Since 1974

Concept Publishing Company Pvt. Ltd.
Regd. Office:
A/15-16, Commercial Block, Mohan Garden,
New Delhi-110059 (INDIA)
T : 25351460, 25351794, *F* : 091-11-25357109
E-mail : publishing@conceptpub.com,
Website: www.conceptpub.com

Cataloging in Publication Data--Courtesy: D.K. Agencies (P) Ltd. <docinfo@dkagencies.com>

Goswami, B. N. (Bhupendra Nath), author.
Political ecology of deforestation and tribal life : a study of Assam-Nagaland border areas / Bhupendra Nath Goswami.
pages cm
Includes bibliographical references and Index.
ISBN 9789351251903

1. Deforestation—India—Assam. 2. Deforestation—India—Nagaland. 3. Tribes—India—Assam. 4. Tribes—India—Nagaland. 5. Political ecology—India—Assam. 6. Political ecology—India—Nagaland. I. Title.

SD418.3.I4G67 2017 DDC 333.7509541 23

Foreword

On 27th October, 1993, I had an informal meeting with Dr. Raymond Bryant in the Department of Geography, King's College, London. Dr. Keith Hoggart of the same department very kindly arranged my meeting with Dr. Bryant. Dr. Andy Collision, a young faculty member of the College also participated in the discussion. Dr. Bryant had already completed his doctoral research on political ecology of deforestation in British Burma (present Myanmar) and in course of discussion, he interestingly referred to my native land—Assam, a State of India. I was delighted when he handed me over some of his recent publications including the one entitled Political Ecology: An Emerging Research Agenda in Third World Studies. The friendly and enlightening discussion and the papers he presented influenced me so deeply that I made up my mind to do some work in this direction.

Dr. Bhupendra Nath Goswami, the author of this book is known to me since his student days. I found in him required urge and intellect to carry out a work from political ecological perspectives on a relevant area within India's North-East. I discussed the matter with him and he came forward to take-up such a study as a part of his Ph. D. programme. As he is from Mariani College, Mariani, Assam, he already had first hand knowledge about the process of deforestation in the Assam-Nagaland border area, which is not far from his working place. He thus finally came out successful in unfolding the long process and complicated pattern of deforestation in a highly sensitive area like the Assam-Nagaland Border. He had to take lot of pain in carrying out field work in the area and also in collecting information from the secondary sources on the issue. His study, which I supervised, was basically an attempt to develop an integrated understanding of the ecological and political forces that interact to cause environmental and social changes in the area.

The study systematically explores the changing nature-culture relation in a hill-plain contact zone of immense ecological and socio-political importance and points to the processes operating and the overall impact of massive deforestation on the tribal life in particular and the society in general. Importantly, Dr. Goswami is successful in finally coming out with certain workable strategies and action plans to resolve the border conflict and to ensure sustainable environmental and socio-economic development in the area.

I would like to express my boundless thanks to Dr. Goswami for bringing out such a valuable book and also to the Department of Geography, Gauhati University, Guwahati, Assam, my intellectual green-house for almost twenty six years, in which he carried out the work, and specially to my teachers and students, who epitomise the values of geographical enquiry, high ideals and creativity. Lastly, I hope that the book will receive wide acceptance among scholars of our country and abroad.

7, Gauhati University Campus
Guwahati, Assam, India
24th August, 2015.

A.K. Bhagabati

Acknowledgements

At the very outset, I would like to express my heartfelt gratitude to Dr. A.K. Bhagabati, an eminent scholar in the field of Ecology for his guidance, encouragement and overall inspiring support, which enabled me to complete this work. His thoughtful and practical suggestions have definitely enhanced the quality of this book.

I am greatly indebted to all the faculty members of the Department of Geography, Gauhati University for their valuable suggestions and encouragement at various stages of this research work. I am also thankful to all the employees of the Department for their spontaneous co-operation during the research period.

I am specially grateful to Professor A.K. Bora and Dr. P. Bhattacharya of the Department of Geography, Gauhati University for going through the manuscript and suggesting necessary corrections to be made particularly in some of the tables and maps included in the book.

I must acknowledge the moral and spiritual support which I received from my uncle, Dr. G.C. Sarmah, Ex-Principal, Arya Vidyapeeth College, Guwahati and S.K. Barthakur, Ex-Principal, Mariani College, Mariani. I would also like to thank Samaresh Chakravarty, Librarian, Mariani College, Sada Tanti, Rupjyoti Dutta and Phatik Borah for their help and co-operation. I also owe special thanks to Rana Borah and Madhurya Mili for preparing maps included in the book. Interactions with Hem Phukan of Brihattar Tengani Unnayan Parishad, Dibyajyoti Sarmah, Secretary, Jorhat District Krishak Mukti Sangram Samittee, Freedom Fighter Mani Basak and late Bhuban Mohan Burhagohain, Bhaben Saikia, Gaonburha of Bochagaon, Indramoni Singh, Binoy Saikia, Dambarudhar Sonowal and Dulal Borah have been highly productive for me. I owe a special debt to Wati Ao, Khatowang Kanayak, Nomal Shyam and Arjun Kardong for the benefit I reaped from the long interactions with them. My thanks go to Dibyajyoti Borah, Purnananda Phukan (Pona), Atul Chetia, Dhrubajyoti Bordoloi, Rana Gogoi, Ranjit Das and Kanak Dey for their help during my survey work. I would also like to express my indebtedness to Bijoyendra Chakravarty, Ransen Jamir, Achumi Chumi, Dr. V. Macro and Thiakhapa Ao for their help and guidance in conducting survey in the hill areas. I am also indebted to the teaching and non-teaching staff of Mariani College for their encouragement in pursuing my work.

I am thankful to Kali Charan Das and his son Raja for taking all troubles and pains in typing the text of the book. The entire research endeavour owes a great deal to my family members for their profound caring and forbearance. My family had to suffer due to my long absence from all responsibilities. Puspanjali, my better half, inspired me a lot shouldering all burden of the family. My son Paul more often complains of his loneliness but never fails to encourage me.

Last but not the least, I express my gratitude to Mr. A.K. Mittal, the Managing Director, Concept Publication Co. (P.) Ltd., New Delhi for his encouragement and enthusiastic co-operation on the way of publication of this book expeditionaly.

Place : Mariani, Assam **Bhupendra Nath Goswami**
Date : 29th April, 2017

Contents

List of Tables, Figures and Maps

LIST OF TABLES

LIST OF FIGURES

LIST OF MAPS

1 Introduction

1.1 The Problem

The most alarming ecological crisis and the degradation of biosphere resulting from the impact of growing human activities have compelled the world scientific community to search for a way out of the situation. It of course remains an unresolved problem for the world conscious community. Some are suggesting partial solution, while others believe in establishing norms on pollution of air and water and imposition of high taxes on polluting agencies. Utopian groups suggest to 'back to nature' and reject consumerism. Examining the global ecological crisis from philosophical perspective, it can unequivocally be recognized that the key to the solution of the ecological problem lies in a social reconstruction through the principle of collectivism, rational development and sustainable interaction with nature.

Today's ecological problem practically imbued from continuous human intervention in the natural processes through industrialization and urbanization, exhaustion of conventional energy sources and natural resources, disposal of wastes, etc. Steady scientific and technical progress has led to unprecedented growth of manpower in relation to nature. The technical civilization has started encroaching heavily on nature. Scientific and technological know-how has now literally enabled people to move over to the mountains, control rivers, and transform desert areas into fertile agricultural lands. Limitless encroachment on nature gives rise to uncertainty and instability in the ecological systems. Such consequences have demonstrated that human interference with nature cannot be allowed to continue unabated. In the preface of the book *Philosophy and the Ecological Problems of Civilization* (Ursul, 1983), it is mentioned that

"It is not only possible to convert a wild, natural environment, often disastrously affecting mankind (earthquake, typhoon, hurricanes, storms, floods, droughts, winterkilling etc.) into a safe, humanized one adapted to human needs, but it is necessary to do so. Such a transformation can only be carried out, however, according to the laws of the functioning, development and evolution of the biosphere as an integral, self-regulating, living super-organism, which means that the ecological problem is now becoming not just one of pollution of the environment and other deleterious effects of our economic activity on earth but also one of transforming our anarchic impact on nature into a conscious, purposeful, systematically developing interaction with her." The works by Blaikie (1985), Blaikie and Brookfield (1987), Rees (1985) and Redcliff (1984) bear great significance in the development of linkages, among resources, economics, institutions, individuals and societies. These works emphasize on the social, political and economic origins of environmental problems and the consequences of overall deterioration of the natural environment. Redcliff (1987) pointed out the role of technology in accelerating the pace of relationship between man and environment. Rising against the overestimating potentials of science and using technology he says, "We must be proactive rather than reactive to production process. We must make explicit needs and the historically determined interpretations of these needs. Finally, any attempt at resolution of resource issues must recognize the importance of the local knowledge of those actually making decisions, the political-economic conditions underlying that knowledge and constraining decision, and the many implications of state intervention" (Emel and Peet, 1989). Although the necessary relationship between any specific form of political economy and ecological production is not traceable, it is quite rational to innovate and find form of articulation in order to address the contradictions inherent in the development of the ecology. A contemplation to formulate a way out from the probable disaster of nature is the need at the threshold of this century.

Before having a discussion on political ecology it seems rational to understand what political economy is. Political economy studies the basis of the development of the society. It studies production only from the point of view of the economic relations between people in the production process. "It is not with 'production' that political economy deals, but with the social relations of men in production" (Lenin, 1977). The method of political economy is that of dialectical materialism which presupposes (i) investigation of the production relations in the process of their emergence and development; (ii) consideration of this process as an objective reality; and (iii) relation of the internal contradictions of development inherent in social production.

Politics and environment or ecology in a straight sense seem to be non-related as the traditional analyst thought and very little attention was put to co-relate both politics and ecology in the analysis of the problems. "The dynamic interaction of environmental and political forces has but recently received scholarly attention. It was only in 1980s, that third world political ecology emerged as a research agenda" (Bryant, 1992).

The term 'political ecology' was first coined by Frank Thone in an article published in 1935. It has been widely used since then in Human Geography and Human Ecology, but with no systematic definition. Anthropologist E.R. Wolf gave it a second life in 1972 in an article entitled "Ownership and Political Ecology" in which he discussed how local rules of ownership and inheritance "meditate between the pressures emanating from the larger society and the local ecosystem" (Wolf, 1972).

The origin of the field in the 1970s and 1980s was a result of development of radical geography and cultural ecology (Bryant, 1998). Historically, political ecology has focused on phenomena in and affecting the developing world; since the field's inception, "research has sought primarily to understand the dynamics of surrounding material and discursive struggles over the environment in the third world" (Bryant, 1998). Political ecology may be defined as the attempt to understand the political sources, conditions and ramifications of environmental change. Blaikie and Brookfield (1987) defined political ecology as—"The phrase political ecology combines the concerns of ecology and a broadly defined political economy, together this encompasses the constantly shifting dialectic between society and land-based resources and also within classes and groups within society itself". Adams and Hutton (2007), on the other hand, defined political ecology as a field of study that embraces the interaction between the way nature is understood and the politics and impacts of environmental action. The goal of the political ecology is to analyse ecological condition as the product of political and social processes in a way from local to global concern since events over the globe are inseparable and directly or indirectly related to one with the other. In nature, nothing takes place in isolation, everything affected and is affected by every other thing (Engels, 1881). The *Journal of Political Ecology* (1994, Vol. 1) has been consistently working to expand the horizon of a systematic approach, pin pointing the essence of political ecology by saying that Karl Marx, perhaps came closer to define the dialectic between individuals and nature that political ecology seeks to address by his insistence that one must begin not with abstract premises or dogmas, but with the productive activities of real individuals. Greenberg and Park (1994) commented—"political ecology expands ecological concepts to respond to the inclusion of cultural and political activity within an analysis of ecosystems that are significantly but not always entirely socially constructed." However, being a component of nature and dependent on nature by many ways for survival, human beings cannot be seen separately from nature. Moreover, by nature man is a product of ecology; the question of his survival, mode of activity, livelihood, cultural attitude, mental make-up etc. have close relation with ecology. Hence, human decision-making processes cannot be independent of the prevailing ecological conditions.

The definition of political ecology as advocated by Blaikie and Brookfield (1987) strictly adheres to not only the land but also the entire environment. One should be very careful in accepting the inherent meaning of the definition so that the shadow of economic reductionism in no way enters into the analysis. Bryant very cautiously warned "Economic reductionism can weaken research in third world political ecology in at least three ways. First, reductionism fails to attribute explanatory significance to ecological factors. Secondly, economic reductionism neglects other sources of environmental change. By equating social factors with capitalist development, it not only neglects ecological factors, but also devalues the role and importance of state and inter-state forces. Finally, economic reductionism also excludes from serious consideration those 'without power'—peasants and other socially disadvantaged groups. And yet, such premises are ill founded—those "without power are not always incapable of resistance as reductionist accounts might imply". However, the presence of economic reductionism in any form might divert the whole endeavour in establishing the ecological problem really persists over the globe. It is, therefore, often advised to avoid such instinct in the process of analyzing the ecological problems. A set of relationship fundamental to conservation, political ecology typically engages in field-based empirical research (often case study research), a local or regional approach with roots in geography, anthropology, sociology and environmental history (Yong, 1998). The general trend of social sciences is not only to focus on either local cultural dynamics or international exchange relation but also it seeks to address the past and present relationship between policy, politics or political economy and the environmental needs. From the perspective of political ecology, the environment in question may range very largely from cultural (e.g. that of the epidemiology of disease in urban settings or even the cultural corpus about health or disease), through the intensely political (e.g. resource endowments for strategic materials) to the fairly significantly natural (e.g. rainforest in remote areas of New Guinea or climate itself) (Greenberg and Park, 1994). Considering the whole set as a closed system, no single minor component seemed to be insignificant, can be ignored or disqualified and the logic that stands on the way is the incorporation of political and economic system to substantiate the field observations and to formulate an acceptable solution on the basis of the ground reality.

Colonization is often regarded as the watershed of world ecology and scholars including the recent researches have clearly established a close relation between colonial expansion and declining world ecology. Indian ecological history is characteristically indifferent in view of the fact that British colonialist played a very crucial and pervasive role in transforming the ecology into a deplorable state. Gadgil and Guha (1992) pointed out—"The ecological history of British India is of special interest in view of the connection that recent researches have established between western imperialism and environmental degradation. World ecology has been profoundly altered by western capitalism, in whose dynamic expansion other ecosystems were disrupted, first through trade and later by colonialism". Motivated politically to govern the world resources, the colonialist intruded in the areas of virgin land and established their overall control on both human and natural resources. "Ecological Imperialism", a term coined by Alfred Crosby (1986) who wrote on the impact of their attitude—"the fire power of European vanguard, and the complex of weeds, animals and diseases it brought, devastated the flora, fauna and human society of the new world. However, the extermination of the native ecosystems and populations only paved the way for the creation of "Neo-Europe's extensive and enormously productive agricultural system that dominates the 'New-World' today." Very interestingly and of course practically, Crosby's observation on the ecological imperialism of Europe was based on the reality which could well be understood from his comment on the nature of the European expansion—"the areas that he believes were 'within reach' and 'beyond group'—the complex old world civilizations in the Middle East, China and India." He argues that density of population, resistance to disease, agricultural advancement and a strong base of socio-political set-up—all made these areas more resistant to the ecological imperialism of Europe. It is referred to as—"although the European conquered the tropics but could not Europeanize the tropics". It would be over simplistic and quite misleading if one twisted the coin in favour of the Crosby's observations. The European imperialist, at least, left the imprints of how to dismantle the settled ecological order and, in most cases, they completed the initial works of dismantling the ecological settings of the areas they conquered.

Gadgil and Guha (1992) summed up the imperialist's activity in the countries they owned. By around 1860, Britain had emerged as the world leader in deforestation, devastating its own woods and forest of Ireland, South Africa and North-western United States to draw timber for shipbuilding, iron-smelting and farming. Instances are there that the destruction of forests was used by the British to symbolize political victory. Handique (2004) observes—"Before the establishment of British rule, there was limited use of forest resources in Assam. There were practically no proper forest laws and the state's role was limited to the collection of revenue from a few forest products. Forests became a resource to which the colonial policy of revenue extraction and revenue maximization got extended to offer the advent of the British rule. With that end in view, the British forest policy was formulated and laws and regulations were enacted to give legitimacy to the exploitative operation." Henry Cleghorn (1860), one of the British conservators of forest in India very nakedly commented—"the English have been most regardless of the value of the forests, partly owing to their climate, but chiefly because England has been so highly favoured by vast supplies of coal; and the immigrants to the United States have shown their indifference to this subject by needless destruction of forests in that country of which they now feel the want." For many years it had been the opinion of a section of the inhabitants of Assam including many officials that the province had limitless forests and the tendency had been to regard them as a nuisance to be cleared away as rapidly as possible in order to make room for crops and tea gardens. The Nambor experiment of colonization had given the forest department ample experience of the destruction of forest resources (Saikia, 2011).

It is an established fact that even after the British annexation of Assam the entire state was covered by dense forests and few patches along the Brahmaputra plains witnessed settlements here and there. The hills and the mountains, on the other hand, were spectacular with dense green cover and well spread out hamlets where the hill tribes practiced shifting cultivation, maintaining a kind of co-existence with the forest environment. "But near the hills cultivation again falls off, and grassy plains and forests stretch to their feet. Even here, however, rice is grown on fields irrigated from the hill streams, and European enterprise has in many places felled the forests and opened prosperous tea gardens. Little of this is seen by the traveller on the river steamer, and he is apt to receive the impression that Assam is a wilderness of impenetrable jungle, the home of nothing but wild beasts" (Allen, 1979). The large numbers of reserved forests along the Assam-Nagaland Border areas still bear the imprints of the existence of dense forest cover in the recent past, i.e. prior to the British annexation of Assam. Large number of tea gardens in the area came up probably at the cost of forest cover. Most of the lands available in this part particularly were allotted for tea cultivation. The makers of the Assam Forest Regulation, 1891 kept provision for deforestation and, accordingly, under the provision of section 28 of the regulation, deforestation was permitted with the sanction of the Government of India. Soon the colonial Government went ahead with the policy of deforestation to maximize revenue. Initially, lands lying fallow or without any commercially productive timber were deforested or disposed to meet the requirement of the tea companies. The best example of such deforestation was the Nambor colonization scheme (Saikia, 2011).

It is, of course, clear from the discussion so far made that most of the forest land came under non-forest use as a consequence of the policies framed by the policy-makers to serve their economic interest. Deforestation is a world-wide phenomenon which is now-a-days a matter of great concern for the environmentalist in particular. However, the definition of deforestation is yet to get a common meaning. It therefore requires a generic scrutiny of the views forwarded by the concerned experts to arrive at a consensus.

In the common verse, deforestation means the removal of forest or stand of trees of an area, which is thereafter converted to non-forest use. However, controversies exist in using the term deforestation. Scholars argue in different tunes and most of them do not consider the two terms as synonyms. In the case of degraded forest, it is quite impractical to say that the non-existence of forest and certainly degradation of forest can be a precondition or previous state of deforestation. On the contrary, deforestation normally stands for a total removal of forest cover. The Oxford Dictionary and Thesaurus of Oxford University Press mention the meaning of the two terms as "Deforest/di:forist/verb clear of forests, and degrade/di:greid/verb(-ing), reduce to lower rank. The two terms as synonym of each other can be out right rejected."

Deforestation has already posed a serious threat to the survival of mankind as a whole by pressing the pace of global warming and accelerating the advancing grip of climate change. Apart from this overall global scenario, deforestation has already made sufficient inroads in the areas where the interaction between man and forest is very deep. The forests are critical ecosystems for the peoples who depend on them, but also for global regulation of climate, and, of course, biodiversity (WRM's bulletin, 2010). However, the forests are disappearing at a faster rate with the advancement of science and technology and concomitant human needs and pressure. Deforestation is mainly caused by subsidized commodity production, a problem compounded by growing demands for agro-fuels/bio-fuels and meat, among others. The forest, in particular, has never been still. Not only is it a living, ever changing entity that is affected directly by both short-and-long term environmental changes, particularly climate, but it is also severely affected by quite minor human disturbances. Agriculture, domestication and the control of fire have all been roughly coincident with the formation of the modern forests during the last 10,000 years, and their interaction is inseparable (Michal, 2006).

Deforestation as defined by FAO—"is a non-temporary change of land use from forest to other land use or depletion of forest crown cover to less than 10 per cent" (www.wikipaedia.com). Whatever may be the ground of the rational view, it can be substantiated that degradation as a process evolved or surfaced prior to deforestation, i.e. elimination of forest cover. Apart from the various natural processes like forest fire, volcanic eruption, flood, landslide, tsunami etc. human civilization from its very inception has been ceaselessly involved in changing the forest cover over the earth's surface. Deforestation is a human-induced process of environmental change. The human impact on the forest has always followed the prevailing way of life (*genre-de-vie*) of human society in a given time and place.

The Structures of everyday life, a genuine discourse on man-environment relationship in which Braudel (1981) states—"the need for food, for fuel to keep warm, to smelt metals and to cook, the demand for wood for construction, utensils, tools and ships and the use of forests for making new land to grow food have not changed much since humans have been on earth, except in as much as the number of people utilizing them has grown inexorably. This process might well be termed the 'driving force' or courses of change in the forest environment". It is obvious and of course, a decisive postulate that the forest cover experiences a cumulative decreasing effect with the increase of population and indubitably that occurs due to the material cause alone. Considering all consequences, it can be concluded that there exists a strong negative correlation between the extent of forest cover and the population size indicting a decline in the former with the increase in the later.

It is a common notion that the world was stable, ecologically pristine before the industrial age. Rainforests will have disappeared by the end of twentieth century. The World Resources Institute (1990), estimates that 12 million hectares of tropical forests were lost in eight countries in 1987. Perkins Marsh identified man as a disturbing agent since there is no denying that the world forest cover has drastically been reducing as a result of disruptive human intervention (William, 2006). The adverse effects of deforestation include the loss of habitat for countless animals and plant species; the destruction of homes and livelihood of native tribes; providing an easy path for soil erosion and rain to flood valleys below; uncertainty of normal climatic events and many more environment related global problems. It is quite difficult to measure exactly the extent of deforestation world-wide partly because of difficulty of defining what deforestation is. Apart from this, the type and form of forest cover varies from region to region and from place to place which, in turn disowned a generic definition of deforestation. C.F. Jordan, however, estimated that at present the level of destruction in the world is four times more than the rate calculated by the FAO in 1980. Further RS data shows that the tropical forests are getting vanished at a rate of 16 to 20 million hectares a year, much higher than the U.N. estimates of 11 million hectares (Karmandy, 2004).

The Indian scenario of deforestation is quite illative from the viewpoint of its forest cover existing today. Under the high pressure of population and consequent expansion of agriculture at the cost of forest it is not much difficult to excogitate the pattern of forest cover in the country as a whole. The scenario is said to be a bit devastating when the forest cover of the country came down to a mere 12 per cent from 22 per cent within a period of just 36 years from 1952 to 1988. The latest satellite data also reflect a very tragic picture showing the annual rate of loss at 1.3 million hectares. At present, India has only 1.0 per cent of the total forest area of the world. The per capita availability of forests in India is 0.08 hectare as against the world average of 0.8 hectares. According to a survey conducted by Ministry of Environment and Forests, the country's forests have got reduced by 5,482 sq.km. between 1995 and 1997 of which dense forests have been a major causality. As against the rural populations' annual requirement of 157 million tons of firewood, the production is only 58 million tones. The balance is met by illegal felling of trees. In addition, indiscriminate felling of trees is done for fulfiling commercial interests, for quarrying and construction (Sharmah, 2006).

The devastation caused to the Indian economy by continued and excessive deforestation is indeed anomalous. Apart from the general consequences of deforestation like increase of flood frequency, soil erosion, heavy siltation at the dam site, changes in rainfall regime, loss of habitat of both plants and animals, and some other which indirectly generate a threat to the dwellers of forest and fringe areas. Accurate estimation in this respect is not yet possible since no such records have either been officially registered nor has any organization or individual done such works to excogitate any specific and authentic information relating to the matter. It is the irony that out of total displaced persons in the country only one-fourth could be rehabilitated and even tribal could not be rehabilitated according to their natural settings. Instead of a forest which provided them food, fuel, medicine, housing materials, they get a few rupees. Instead of a river they have a hand pump, not to speak about the easy access to other natural resources. A majority of the displaced end up in ghettos on the peripheries of big cities (Singh, 2006).

Being an integral part of the country and having one political and economic set-up, the North-East India, a region known as the land of jungle, invariably witnesses the same fate of the forest destruction especially from the onset of the British colonial rule in 1826. Prior to that period no significant interest was on the forest as a source of economic importance. The possession of the Brahmaputra valley of Assam by the East India Company and the subordination of Manipur as a 'Native State' in the early nineteenth century brought the British into contact with the intermediary hill tribes. Some of them were brought into their control by conquest. Yet, the British claimed the entire region west of Burma as theirs. Having stepped into the shoes of the erstwhile Ahom Monarchy, the British also inherited all rights enjoyed by the Monarchy in the hills in the immediate proximity of the Brahmaputra valley. Despite this claim, the East India Company brought under its direct rule only those territories which were identified as economically and strategically important (Bezbaruah, 2010). Plenty of forest cover was by any means a lucrative and a viable means of economy for the colonialist which encouraged them to bring the entire North-East India under their administrative cover. Before the advent of the British, the forest of N.E. India virtually was virgin and remained almost unexplored. Revenue was only collected from few selected items like ivory, aloes wood, resign, etc. But, after Assam was colonized, every bit of available land was sought to be brought under imperial control. The development of the idea that the forests could be a source of revenue and that the forest produce could be commercially exploited, changed the very outlook of the government as well as the people towards the hitherto unexploited virgin forests of Assam (Saikia, 2011). This change of outlook marked a radical departure and resulted in drastic change in the overall development of Assam as the province was full of forests at the time of British occupation (McCosh, 1975).

Assam came under the British rule earlier than all other hill states of N.E. India. Assam was targeted for its easy accessibility by the colonialist to exploit its natural resources. The Brahmaputra valley as a whole was better penetrated by the British than the other areas of the province. Therefore, the effects of British forest policy and its implementation manifested badly in that area (Handique, 2004). Palpably, it was the dawn of the process of forest clearance in the State of Assam and except few constitutional enactment and revision no any significant change in the forest policy of the post-Independence government was made either to protect the rich forest cover of the region or to relieve the people living in the forest and fringe of their poverty and backwardness.

The situation till remains more or less unchanged. It is said to be more aggravating even after the enactment of the new forest policy, 1988 by the Ministry of Forest and Environment, Government of India. Forest cover of N.E. India has been assessed by Forest Survey of India every after two years. According to the assessment report of Forest Survey of India, the total decrease of forest cover during a period of just eight years (1989-1997) was 1225 sq.km. However, the National Remote Sensing Agency (NRSA) estimated from their study that the region has lost its forest areas at the rate of 2418 km^2 per year during the period.

Statistical Account of Assam by Hunter gives some valuable statistics pertaining to the distribution of land and people where he showed that the total area of the then Sibsagar district was 2855 sq. miles (4596.55 sq.km) in 1872 with a total population of 2,96,589 (The then Sibsagar district covered the present Sibsagar, Jorhat, Golaghat and parts of Karbi Anglong districts). The total area under tea plantations was just 2500 acres in 1852 which increased to 108,050 acres in a period of twenty years (1852-1872) which now stands at 71,357.68 hectares or 713.58 sq.km. It is quite clear that the toxicity of deforestation took place during the progression of tea cultivation to serve the colonial interest. Merciless uprooting of plant cover was accomplished with no opposition from any corner to expand their tea cultivation which victimized large forest patches. The total area covered in Sibsagar under the Assam Wasteland Rules for tea cultivation amounted to 108,050 acres at the end of 1894 (Hunter, 1879).

The episode of deforestation in N.E. India is different from the state of deforestation in the country as a whole. The situation is said to be worse in the region where deforestation is continuing even after the enactment of the New Forest Policy, 1988. Moreover, the decision of the Central Government to generate a total of 50,000 MW hydroelectric powers from the rivers flowing down through Arunachal Pradesh will aggravate the situation by submerging fresh forested areas.

The foothills of Assam-Nagaland Border areas, a tract measuring about 310 km in length and 20 km in width are inhabited mostly by tribes like Thengal Kachari, Boro, Sonowal Kachari, Ao, Kanyak, Rengma, Angami, Mishings, Karbi, Tai-Shyam etc. The process of forest depletion in this part of the region is so severe that a large number of reserve forests have already been cleared and put to non-forest use and the tribes in many places are displaced. From the southern end of the foothill tract at Diphu to the northern end there exist 11 reserved forests running parallel to the Assam-Nagaland Border areas. Enriched with shallow black brown and alluvial soil of ochrepts type and red loamy soil of ustalfs type, the entire border patch enjoys a congenial monsoon climate to favour luxuriant growth of vegetation. The forests in this belt of N.E. India are normally of mixed semi-evergreen, deciduous and dry miscellaneous type in areas where annual rainfall seldom exceeds 150 cm mark.

Large-scale deforestation resulting from multiple causes has already put a threat to the tribal mode of life. The growing population pressure and absence of alternative living means other than agriculture have forced the people to encroach the forest land and as a result the forest and forest-fringe dwellers have started facing problems in their traditional practices. The needs of the tribal people inhabiting the forest tract are very limited. They collect fuelwood to cook food and to keep them warm in winter, they collect materials like bamboo, wood, thatch etc. for constructing their small huts, life-saving medicines of all types, fruits and leaves from the forest. Social and cultural functions performed by them have close attachment with the forest environment. They never practice over harvesting of resources from the forest. They strictly observe local ecological ethics in all kinds of their activities. Worshipping of wild animals and certain plants is an integral part of their tradition. The tribes living in the foothills of Assam-Nagaland Border areas are no exception to these traditional practices and habits. Forest remained undisturbed for long as they co-exist with them. A kind of give and take relation persists between the tribal people and the forest resource from time-immemorial. Deforestation leads to depletion of forest recourses, which along with population pressure and increasing greed for forest resources from outside has caused a disastrous situation for the tribal people living in and around the forest.

Mining, quarrying, construction of roads, ill practices of the timber merchants, malpractices of the forest officials, shifting cultivation, pressure from neighbouring hill states for more fertile agricultural land, non-implementation of the policies made towards the improvement of the forest environment by the Government etc. may be held responsible for the deforestation in the foothill tracts of Assam-Nagaland Border. With an area of about 6213.35 km^2, the zone was covered by thick forest cover, which remained conspicuous up to the last part of 1970s. Taking into account the population of the revenue villages in the forested tract as per 1971 census, the population density stood at 52 persons. The 2001 census on the other hand, displays a substantial increase in the population density (94 persons/km^2). The Forest Survey of India in its latest survey conducted particularly in the reserve forests of the state border areas confirmed the destruction of forest by about 60, 000 hectares alone in the Assam-Nagaland Border during last thirty years.

The manifold problems of the tribal people residing in the forested foothill areas of the Assam-Nagaland Border can be summarized as—(i) the tribal people accustomed with their forest environment and traditional ethics, have started gradually losing their habitats, traditional practices and the mode of co-existence with nature, (ii) ruthless deforestation coupled with frequent inter-state boarder conflicts pushed the tribes from the forest areas, (iii) in the absence of timely intervention, and efforts for population control, the door for reckless exploitation of forest wealth remains open which has created congenial ground for the extremist outfit to operate from the forest belt of the border areas, (iv) the forest-based socio-cultural and economic foundations of the tribes, which generally do not go against the forest environment, are presently in crisis and (v) consequently, there appears to be emerging long-term ecological disorder, which may eventually uproot the existing ecological society in the area.

An analysis of the problem of deforestation and its impact on the tribal people in the foothills of Assam-Nagaland Border areas is, therefore, imperative before introducing any alternative to those who have been pushed back by the process of deforestation. It is, at the same time, very important to look back to the causes of racial uprise and the ethnic clashes in Assam. Last but not the least is the growing trend of grabbing arable land within the forest areas by a section of people of immigrant origin, which has become a very sensitive issue of political ecological concern. Thus, it calls for a thorough investigation from appropriate perspectives to contribute towards bringing ecological and social stability in the area.

This study, therefore, attempts to carry out socio-ecological analysis covering some aspects of political ecology to derive a judicious and humanitarian solution to the problem of deforestation and its impact on the tribal people in the foothills of Assam-Nagaland Border areas.

1.2 Objectives

The main objectives of the study are to—

(i) analyse to the extent of deforestation in the study area and to depict the nature and pattern of deforestation;
(ii) identify the principal causes of deforestation and change of settlement of the tribal people in the Assam-Nagaland boarder areas;
(iii) analyse the socio-economic structure of the tribal people and their forest-based tradition and activities;
(iv) find out the nature of change in the tribal mode of life arising out of continuous deforestation;
(v) analyse the government policies concerning the forest-dwellers and their impact on the tribal people;
(vi) analyse the crisis developed in the forested foothills of Assam-Nagaland Border and to formulate workable measures to resolve the problems sustainably; and
(vii) suggest measures towards rational upliftment of the forest areas and the people sharing the forest environment.

1.3 Hypotheses

In order to achieve the above objectives, the following hypotheses are proposed and attempts are made to test these hypotheses in the course of the work:

(i) Continuous destruction of forest cover in the foothill zone of Assam-Nagaland Border has been creating an ecological disorder affecting the living and non-living components of the concerned environment.

(ii) Depletion of forest is not a result of the ill exercise of some individuals, it is primarily a combined effect of multiple causes including the failure of the government agencies.

(iii) There exists a strong positive relationship between the magnitude of forest depletion and the ecological instability in the region.

(iv) The relation traditionally maintained between the natural environment and the tribal life is mutually effective and helpful for protecting the forest from depletion caused by the greedy outside agencies.

(v) A strong positive correlation appears to exist between the extent of deforestation and the deterioration of tribal mode of life in course of time.

(vi) Encroachment in the forest areas is accelerated by increasing population pressure, absence of alternative living means and indifferent attitude on the part of the government towards uplifting the quality of life among the forest and fringe-dwellers.

(vii) Loss of biological and cultural diversity leads to a decline in the traditional knowledge base concerning particularly, the traditional food and health care systems.

1.4 Database and Methodology

The Assam-Nagaland Border region, the study area of this work, is a belt formed of parts of the state of Assam and a part of Nagaland. It is delimited on the basis of—(i) terrain characteristics, (ii) forest cover, (iii) vegetation, (iv) climatic characteristics, and (v) human factor. The entire border region can be regarded as a single geographical unit with all its natural and human elements.

The area so demarcated is then divided into three major physiographic divisions depending on the relief and topographic similarities. These are: (i) the plains, (areas within 110 m contour), (ii) the mid-altitude zone (areas lying between 110 m and 300 m contours), and (iii) the high altitude zone (areas between 300 m and 600 m contours).

The data pertaining to the study are of both primary and secondary type. Secondary data relevant to the study are not readily available and accessible as the study area is neither an administrative nor a politically integrated unit. By applying statistical method of estimation required data are extracted to feed the analysis of the problem under study. The area is delimited on the basis of few selected criteria and then the census report of India is consulted to procure data on land and people. As such, data on forest cover, extent of deforestation, terrain characteristics, encroachment on forest land etc. are collected and computed from the sources mentioned below.

(i) Information pertaining to forest cover in the initial stage and the mode of deforestation are collected from the early writings of historians like J. Mckoch, E. Gait, H.K. Borpujari, W.W. Hunter, J.M. Mills, A. Butler and others. Other sources include Assam archives, various departments of Government of Assam (Forest, Revenue, Agriculture, Directorate of Statistics and Economics), and the Gazetteers published from time-to-time.

(ii) It is noteworthy that there is no clear information or data base on the extent of deforestation in the Assam-Nagaland Border area at specific interval which deters one from having a clear understanding of the changing situation. The topographic sheets of Survey of India with 1:50,000 scale, are used to study the nature and extent of forest cover particularly in the post-Independence period. The forest cover is measured and mapped for an effective analysis and to make comparison with the forest cover of pre-Independence period. The settlement pattern, population size, land use pattern etc. are studied in a generic way to relate them with the process of deforestation. This task is essential in order to make a breakthrough in the study of the nature of involvement of the political, social and economic factors and institutions in deforesting the area. To develop an authentic map covering the entire study area several topographic sheets (83 J/13, J/3, J/9, J/2, J/7, J/6, J/5, G/9, N/1, I/16, F/15, M/8) have been consulted.

(iii) Furthermore, these parameters are used to analyse the mode of living, social ethics, cultural behaviour and the economy of the people of the region. A comparative analysis in between the tribal life and the reducing forest cover is also made to achieve the objectives of the study.

(iv) To accomplish the study on deforestation, data from Department of Forest and Environment, NGOs and other relevant sources are collected and for authentication satellite imageries produced by Indian Remote Sensing Organization, Hyderabad (ISRO) representing the study area are considered specifically with respect to the Assam-Nagaland Border region. The imageries to cover up the whole area of Assam-Nagaland Border are consulted accordingly. The imageries selected include—row/path: 54/112, 54/113, 54/114, 54/115.

(v) A large number of books, journals, magazines, periodicals, leaflets, pamphlets, newspapers published from time-to-time are carefully consulted to ensure a comprehensive analysis of the problem. Informations are also procured from individuals who have ample knowledge on forest, forestry and environment of the area through direct interaction in the field.

Primary Data

A substantial part of the study is essentially based on primary data collected from selected areas of the Assam-Nagaland Border region. In view of the paucity of secondary data relating to the impact of deforestation on the tribal life, primary data are mainly used to support the analysis. It is quite problematic to cover up the entire border region for collecting primary data due to administrative, social and accessibility constraints. Therefore, sampling technique has been purposively applied in appreciating the ground situation of deforestation and its impact on the tribal life. As the tribal mode of life is closely associated with forest, the emphasis is given on the changing mode of tribal life with the change in the forest cover scenario in the area. To achieve the objectives of the study, villages for survey are selected from the areas located either within the forest or at the outskirt of the forest. Accordingly, stratification of the area is made by consulting the topographic sheets of Survey of India published in 1974. Two categories of village from the topographic maps are identified and traced their location in such a way that the villages irrespective of community and accessibility enter into the sampling network to serve the purpose of the study.

The villages selected for collecting data are stratified into two: (i) forest village, i.e. villages within the notified forest area; and (ii) forest fringe village, i.e. villages located outside the notified area but with a forest-based culture and economy. Looking into the variability of impact of deforestation, a schedule is prepared to know the extent and magnitude of change caused by deforestation. The schedule pays attention to: (i) family structure, (ii) occupational pattern, (iii) landholding structure and cropping pattern, (iv) family income, (v) means of hunting and collecting forest products, (vi) nature and cause of forest depletion, (vii) use of medicinal plants, (viii) loss of biodiversity and its impact, (ix) food habit, (x) food items collected from forest, and (xi) role of forest officials and

NGO's and so on. For acquiring further knowledge of the situation some experienced elderly people are interviewed.

The data so obtained are processed, classified and summarized and then analyzed through statistical and cartographic representation. Models and diagrams are also developed, wherever possible, to enhance the quality of explanation.

1.5 Review of Relevant Works

The age of *Upanishad*, (6th or 7th Century BC) grasped well the importance of forest (*oshadhi*) products and made several explanations on the life supporting capability of *oshadhi* by the Saints, Brahmanas and the kings. *Chhandogya Upanishad* is undoubtedly one among several *Upanishads* which deserve all credit for its volumetric explanation particularly on *oshadhi* (Goswami, 1975). Accentuating on the effectiveness of the *oshadhi* it was emphasized that "the person who makes use of plant products in their daily diet, they can give birth a good child". The *Aranyaks* were specially written for the forest-dwelling saints with all directives primarily concerning the coexistence of forest and nature and fixed rules for such a living. It is clearly stated that deforestation was quite extensive. Chattopadhyaya (1959) narrated in his *Lokayata Darshanaas*—"There is a considerable progress in the control of nature, thanks mainly to the introduction of iron implementation on some scale and the improved technique of agriculture and handicrafts." Describing the ideal mode of living of the king or noble he says "He shall live on surplus." The importance of forest was understood by the ancient kings and the rulers which is well illustrated as "the king declared some forest as his won for protecting capturing and taming elephants, he had his own land for his herds of cattle, his own branch of agriculture as well as in "kings field" as in great clearing of forests where he settled peasants and herdsmen in villages which were not so quite independent (Chattopadhyaya, 1959).

Deforestation is "the thinning, changing and wholesale clearing of forests for fuel, shelter, and agriculture is among the most important ways humans have transformed the environment" (William, 2006). Surveying ten thousand years to trace human induced deforestation, effect on economics, societies and landscapes around the world, the book *Deforesting the Earth* (William, 2006) is undoubtedly a prominent history of this process and its consequences. In the same tune of Michel Williams, the Encyclopedia published by Wikipedia investigates the process of deforestation in the prehistoric age. The one excerpt from Wikipedia's encyclopedia relating to such process is—"The rise and fall of Roman Empire encompasses the time when Rome was the leading contributor to deforestation in the Mediterranean. Whereas the Mediterranean was largely 'prehistoric' in 1000 BC, it was definitely 'historic' by 500 AD. Roman geographical and population 'expansion spread methods' of agricultural and economic development which encouraged the clearing of forested land. The spread of Roman practices had unintended devastating effect on the environment". The Wikipedia's encyclopedia denominated the causes and consequences of deforestation where causes were identified mainly as housing and building, use of fuel, agriculture, overgrazing, military practices, ship-building, urbanization and on the contrary, the consequences were in the form of soil erosion and flooding the ports and harbours. White (1967), an eminent scholar of ecological history, described the human-nature relationship from historical point of view. The perspective of the human-nature relationship holds that humans have dominion over nature. A quote from the Old Testament—"Let us make man in our image, after our likeness: and let them have dominion over the fish of the sea and over the fowl of the air and over the cattle and over all the earth and over every creeping thing that crept upon the earth." It is clear enough to understand the very root of the crisis of nature which, in fact, is a product of religious philosophy.

Carl Linnaeus emphasized the human dominion over nature in his *Discovery of Nature* published in 1749. He said—"All the treasures of nature, so artfully contrived, so wonderfully propagated, so providentially supported ...seem intended by the creator for the sake of man". English naturalist Gilbert White (1798) opposed the self-emancipating concept of Linnaeus. His *The Natural History of Shelburne* epitomizes on Arcadia of idyllic contentment reaching back to Greek animism and pantheism, the very quintessence of harmony of human and nature. This tradition of thinking developed as a reaction to the growth of industrialism. Torry (1906) writing on Thoreau mentioned that Thoreau carried forwarded this tradition of men-nature harmony and interpreted that the nature was an extension of the self, nature being best understood and appreciated by acknowledging correspondence and kinship with it. George Perkins Marsh (1864), in his *Man and Nature or Physical Geography as Modified by Human Action* put this point well as "Man has too long forgotten that the earth was given to him for usufruct alone, not for consumption, still less for profligate waste." Contrary to this Karl Ritter viewed the nature in a different way. In '*Erdkunde*' (the science of the earth) Ritter wrote—"the earth and its inhabitant stand in closest reciprocal relations and one cannot be truly presented in all its relationship without the other. Land influences the inhabitants and in turn inhabitants transform the landscape." Through his writing he tried to prove that the earth is made for man: "As body is made for soul, so is the physical globe made for mankind."

Darwin's (1958) theory of the "Origin of Species" and "Descent of Man" almost volcanized the philosophical base of the world. German and American scholars, working in the fields of "man and nature" immediately grasped the Darwin's concept and tried to explain the man-environment relationship from a new perspective. The uprise of the philosophy "Environmental Determinism" thus got feedback from all concerned which in turn, highly influenced the work of Ellen Churchill Semple (1911) and Huntington (1924). The extreme generalization of environmental determinism subsequently led to a counter thesis. This antithesis of environmental determinism known as possibilism, presents the individual as an active agent to act upon the earth's environment.

Darwinian view almost overwhelmed the works of the then thinkers and philosophers of the western world which could be regarded as a turning text of the entire socio-political setup of the western world. Ratzel, an eminent German philosopher coined the term 'Lebensraum', meaning the living space. Ratzel compared a nation with a living organism. He argued that a country's search for territorial expansion was similar to a growing organism's search for space (Dikinson, 1969). The struggle and survival of the fittest theory of Darwin got wide acceptance from scholars of different fields which influenced the scholars, specially the German political philosophers. Conflict between the nations for territorial expansion became a matter of contest in the western world with the motto—'survival of the fittest'. Ratzel stressed that "just as the struggle for existence in the plant and animal world always centres about a matter of space, so the conflicts of nations are in great part only struggle for territory" (Hussain, 2004). It was the period 1880-1914, which witnessed a turn in the approach of the British Geographers where their major concern chiefly concentrated in studying man-nature relationship. It was pointed that nature itself has all capability to control and determine the human activities over the earth's surface and thus human activities vary from one natural region to the other depending upon the varying natural scenario. *Habitat, Economy and Society* of Forde (1934) discussed at length the role of primitive society and the influence of environment on the occupation and mode of life of the people. He primarily emphasized on cultural groups in their areal context. The principle of environmental determinism as a central theme has been defied in his studies. The works of Semple are considered prominent among the geographers of America of her period which are reflected in her voluminous book *Influences of Geographic Environment* and *American History and its Geographic Conditions*. Notably *Influence of Geographic Environment* is an authoritative work in the field of human-environment relationship and can be regarded as an anti-thesis of environmental determinism. The first line of the opening Para of her book—"Man is a product of the earth's surface, this means not merely that he is a child of the earth, dust of her dust, but that the earth has mothered him, fed him, set him tasks, direct his thought. Confronted him with difficulties that have strengthened his body and sharpened his wits, given him his problems of navigation or irrigation and at the same time whispered hints for their solution." Being a strong follower of environmental determinism in the early part of his career Bowman (1911) turns his back and started giving adequate importance to the role of man in transforming his natural environment. In his own words—"man is changing himself as well as the world as he goes along".

Friedrich Hegel (1817), the pioneer of dialectical logic almost moulded and beset the world of philosophers by formulating a new way of thinking, analyzing and explaining the phenomena those exist and develop over the globe. Recognizing the ever existing continuity Hegel emphasized particularly on the way of explaining the prevalence of dialecticism everywhere. In his words—"continuity stands forth as one of the most essential facts of the law of the negation, manifesting itself in nature, society and thinking as an objectively indispensable link between the new and the old in the process of development". Continuity always can either be progressive or in specific cases regressive. Biology, for instance, has witnessed a number of phenomena of regressive evolution of plants and animals. Following the universality of continuity of the process of development it is said that continuity is strictly specific in cases of negation. For example, continuity is unerringly specific in the development of living nature, as distinct from continuity of lifeless nature. Referring Hegel, Maurice Cornforth (1968) argued that the numerous changes on the world of nature are the repetition of careless process of changes. No totally new usually happened in nature. It is only in the conscious world where the new came up in the system of change. All the changes in the nature are dependent on the natural processes and the existing environment. Man-nature relationship is seen well scrutinized from a materialistic point of view by Simonov (1983). Accentuating the socio-economic causes he mentioned "the aggravation of the contemporary ecological situation is due primarily to socio-economic causes." But an ecological problem is by no means simply pollution. In fact, it is a problem of optimizing society's interaction with nature, the conversion of human material production into an 'organ' of the biosphere. The critical state of society's interaction with nature today is largely caused by the ecological imperfection of the mechanized technological mode of production. He pointed out that in a traditional mode of production society could only have a local effect on nature. Responsibility for the aggravation of relations between society and nature that is seemingly caused by the transition from hand tool and large-scale, industrialized, mechanized production rests wholly on capitalism. To maintain the balance between man and nature he advocated the concept of Bio-nation which according to him is found to become the technological foundation, theoretical basis and practical method of dealing with the ecological problem (Smirnov, 1983).

The "Dialectics of Nature", a great philosophical work of F. Engel (1974), elaborates the man-nature relationship from a different view point. He tried to establish a link between the nature, natural events and the related changes with the law of science by applying the dialectical logic. He remarked in a grieved tone—"Let us not flatter ourselves over much on account of our human victory over nature. For each such victory nature takes its revenge on us. Each victory, it is true in the first place brings about the results we expected, but in the second and third places it has quite different, unforeseen effects which only too often cancel the first". Marx pointed out the distinguishing feature inherent only in human production as a whole, i.e. its universal character founded on development of production and means of production. Birds, for example, produce a nest in the course of their life activity, but not radiators and are unable to produce many other conditions of their lives. Men universally produce themselves not only as living, natural creatures, but also as social one belonging to a system of social relations and this universality of production constantly progresses throughout history (Marx, 1975).

Losing ground environmental stress and world food prospects of E.P. Eckholm (1976) and "The Twenty Ninth Day, Accommodating Human Needs and Numbers of the Earth Resources" of L.R. Brown (1978) are two prominent works where detailed and innovative discussions were made on how the socio-political system misappropriated the nature and the ecological situation over the earth's surface. It is mentioned that the contemporary ecological degradation is, to a considerable extent, a derivative of the economic, social and political disproportions and imbalances inherent in capitalism. Many liberal minded scientists and scholars have even been forced to recognize that the value of natural resources has acquired a consumer expression under the economic domination of capital. In their view many western writers of course still hope that the transformation of socio-economic and political structure will be possible within the context of traditional bourgeois capitalist values. Regarding the capitalist system, it is mentioned that capital is a universal relation of exploitation. For it, man, science and nature all becomes an object of exploitation and of extracting profit. Nothing is sacred for it, except profit (Eckholm, 1976). Colonialism, an aggressive off spring of capitalism, however, more often is caught responsible for large scale elimination of forest cover in many parts of the world in the name of so-called development, a way to generate more profit from more exploitation. Examining the political economy of nature tourism Eddie Koch (2006) narrates—"At the same time Africans were subjected to a range of harsh and discriminatory legal restriction. They were not eligible for hunting licenses, not allowed to kill wildlife that damaged their crops, curbs on fishing were imposed and depriving people of an important source of protein. Many of these restrictions were part of ruling classes' efforts to create a cheap labour force for the mines and other industries that mushroomed after the discovery of gold." Excerpt from the local added in the article reads: "Older villagers recall a time when the land, now enclosed by park boundaries, was theirs to use for agriculture, grazing their livestock's, collection of firewood etc. But during the colonial era, the best agricultural lands in Zimbabwe were appropriated for small elite of European farmers and communities were evicted from their traditional homes to make way for recreational reserves and safari hunting areas that benefited only the small European population in the country or visitors from abroad". Condition is also totally different in the case of Costa Rica where large scale deforestation was due to the expansion of coffee plantation by the European colonialist. Conducting a detailed survey on the process of deforestation Boza and Mendoza (1981) describe—"... there were about 65000 inhabitants, living mainly in the central valley. Most of the country remained under dense forest cover. However, the expansion of coffee production during the nineteenth century to initiate a process of agricultural colonization, the then rulers supported this process with several incentives and a railway connection was established connecting the agricultural field with the Atlantic harbor of Limon which in turn cleared the extensive forest cover from the area. The process continued and the region started suffering from the odds of forest clearance." P. Utting (1993), Rackham (1989), Kemf (1993), Colchester (1994) and many other scholars rendered significant contemplation regarding the removal of forest, its adverse effect on society, people and development from different perspectives and finally tried to draw conclusion in common with a mere holistic attitude to maintain the balance of man-nature relationship.

The works relevant to the scenario of deforestation in India are however, not extensive. But there is no dearth of references of deforestation in literatures since the pre-historic period to the modern research initiatives. Although agriculture had brought a drastic change in the pristine forest cover, the actual damage caused by it was severe during the post-colonial period with the introduction of modern machines and commercial farming in many parts of the country. Guha (1989) mentioned the role of colonialism in declining ecological condition in India in a very logical and dulcified way. He tried to bring out an ecological perspective in sociology by an in-depth study of agrarian history and peasant resistant movements. He remarked that the historians intentionally neglect the relation between colonialism and ecological decline and pointed out that the important consequences of colonial rule were the introduction of commercial forestry in the name of reserved forest. Roy (1911), who was invited by the eminent historian E.A. Gait to conduct a study on the nature and the customary law of the Mundas and other tribes, high-lighted the genesis and proceeding of the customary law and its impact on the socio-cultural system of the tribes. Discussing various issues pertaining to the tribal society it focused on the efforts for making direct contact with the tribal settings by the alien rulers and their Indian agents for commercial benefits and the tribal people became the victims of exploitation in the long-run. The free access of the Christian Missionaries to the forest loving tribal villages promoted some welfare activities under the patronization of alien rulers which in turn, insisted the entry of contractors, *zamindars*, revenue and police officials as well as some middle man and money-lenders. In numerous ways, these intruders of various classes started fulfiling their own interests and the benefits from these tribal people. Characterized by simplicity, ignorance and illiteracy, these tribal people have been exploited in various ways in due course. *The Cambridge Economic History of India*, a two volume history book edited by Kumar and Roychaudhury (1982) traces the economic evolution of the sub-continent from the thirteenth century onwards to twenty first century where several references are made regarding deforestation, forest people and the economy of the country. One reference from among numerous is quoted here—"The process of decline in the western parganas of Midnapur, as evident from the reduction of cultivation by 5 per cent between 1870-75 (the period of revenue survey) and 1911-17 (the period the detailed cadastral survey) was mainly due to indiscriminate deforestation, as a result of which "the soil deprived of the binding force of the tree roots tends to get washed off the slopes into valleys by torrential rains". The process of slope-wash was checked only with the opening-up of the country by railways in creating the demand for timbers. The initiative behind a similarly reckless deforestation in Bankura came mainly from the charcoal burners, where product was used for smelting iron. Oldham (1852) found how in the districts the forests and jungles are disappearing before the axe of the charcoal burner. The role of British Government in agrarian reform was also discussed in detail. The results of the disrupted agricultural policy of the alien rulers indirectly push the tribal for reckless deforestation as means of alternative livelihood. It is also mentioned that "Foodgrain output per head was 30 per cent lower in 1945 than in 1966. The forests were eroded to vanishing point and disputes over forest products became bitter. The Yanadis and other tribals who had lived by hunting were forced into agricultural labour" (Kumar and Roychaudhury, 1982). Sarkar (2006) observed—'The tradition-oriented rights of the tribal people of India on lands and forests are not only the indigenous issue developed long ago, but in most of the cases these surpass the frontiers of history. After their many sided confrontations with the contemporary questions, the question of National rights and their feasibility has raised a lot of queries and counter queries in the sphere of safeguarding the indiscriminate destruction of the forested environment and unusual utilization of the lands in nature". He writes—"the tribal people living in and around the forests are not the destructor but the conservers of the forest and related natural resources. Their love and sympathy for the natural resources have been processed characteristically in their cultural patterns and ultimately these have oriented the all-embracing tribal philosophy. A total of nineteen research papers discussing the numerous issues of the tribes of India have attempted to focus the way of solution to the problems faced by the tribal societies in and around the country. However, few of the papers are lacking a genuine and reasonably strong philosophical base."

Forest, Government and the Tribe, a compendium of fifteen papers edited by Paty (2007) examines the symbiotic link between the forests and the tribal life in India. Arguing that the Government should not ignore such close link while framing forest rules and initiating development programmes. It addresses the issues pertaining to forest laws, ecological ideologies, social protest, forest protection and development.

The vanishing scenario of wildlife ecology is particularly reflected in a book edited by Sharma (1999). It offers discussions on conservation and developmental aspects of the wildlife. Experts from different specializations have made their contribution in these books which throw lights for further study in the field of Indian wildlife. Of special interest are the contributions on the eco-diversity of wildlife resources, habitat conservation and management, birds of prey, barn owl ecology and conservation. It also includes contributions on wildlife pest, predators, parasites ecology and eco-tourism. Mukherjee (1994), a pioneer in Indian social science, tried to link up the two aspects, man and its habitat by a mere explanatory tool which is undoubtedly a landmark in the study of social ecology. He says that the symbiotic relationships between different groups of people with their different modes of exploitation of natural resources and social habitats develop so that the region becomes an assemblage of a specific ecological pattern. The major issues primarily dealt here include the study of human reactions to the environment, physical and organic; his adaptation to soil and climate as well as his structural and behavioural responses and the relation with other individuals or communities. Elaborating this close relationship between man and nature, examples are cited from crowded plains of India and South-east Asia as these are subjected to intensive one-sided exploitation resulting in the fast depletion of nature.

Bhasin (1989) undertook two tribal groups-Lepchas and Bhutiyas to study their relationship with nature. The author is not at all illusive by their sharp similarities in nature, behaviour and habit rather more inquisitive to know their adaptability in different environmental conditions. The location of their habitats in distinct physical environment may lead to an understanding that the geographic factors play a vital role in their distinctiveness. Hilly forested terrain of the Lepchas and the high altitude zone of low vegetation for the Bhutiyas are distinct enough for the two groups living in different conditions. With a clear analysis on the life style characteristics of the two groups he argued that isolation of a region, community or individuals promote self-sufficiency, which in his view, is a normal urge of the living creature. Isolation is therefore, a feature of environmental political subjugation and a matter of choice based on these considerations.

No organism lives in isolation, nor is the behaviour of any organism understandable without reference of others. Malik (2004), conducted a thorough investigation to develop a deterministic approach to understand the facts of tribal life and culture. How far the dependence of tribal on forests has been affected by deforestation and modernization? Has it disturbed their social and ecological settings? Whether they themselves perceive forests as source of livelihood? How far the tribals understand the environmental processes and in the way they manage their scarce resource? To what extent the environmental degradation and deforestation have impacted the autonomy of the local people? Are they still dependent on forests? These vital questions are examined with the help of a set of both primary and secondary data. Malik studied these aspects of tribal life using new theoretical developments in the study of social ecology and forest. Suryanarayan and Kothari (1999) very carefully present the story of how a community organized itself to conserve precious forests, achieve equity in irrigation and revives agricultural traditions which conserve and develop a range of crop diversity. Jardhargaon is a typical hill village with a picturesque surroundings. The higher ridges of the village consists of dense forests of oak, apricot and rhodendron trees with 17 of hamlet locating at considerable distance from each other. They started facing problems generated as a result of large scale deterioration of the natural environment. The people of the hamlets came out to restore the environment for their survival. It is obviously an instance of collective effort towards conservation.

A sizeable number of research papers published in the *Economic and Political Weekly* expressed concern on the problems of forests and forest people. Among these, the one by Hebbar (2006), is remarkably a thought-provoking one which opens up a new line of thinking against the viability of Forest Bill 2005. The basic question regarding the forest bill is whether the Tribal dwellers of the forest and forest fringe areas could continue their age-old traditional eco-friendly practices or could they enjoy their rights to conserve the forest to procure their needs? Apart from these, the paper also seeks to address the discernible and clear contradiction between the intention of the bill and the ground realities in Jharkhand as well as its implications on the tribal struggle for self-rule. Roseneranz and Lele (2008), supporting the case of Godavarman and the role of Supreme Court as the top judiciary of the country also criticized the court for the act of over stepping its constitutional mandate, where it, to some extent, becomes policy-maker by taking over the Governance of Indian Forests leading to negative social, ecological and administrative affect. However, very positively he pointed out that indiscriminate felling of tree elsewhere in the country came to a halt only after the strict implementation of this law. In North-East India also, some positive results of this law can be observed with respect to forest conservation in the region.

Works on N.E. India

The epics and *purarnas* and some other religious and mythological books have made references of the forest and trees apart from ethical and religious aspects, *Yoginitantra, Vishnupurana, Mahabharata*, etc. outlined the nature of highly dense forest cover of Pragjyotisha and Kamrupa. Intensive use of herbal medicines in ancient Kamrupa to cure diseases substantiates the close relationship between man and the plants. However, no specific writings of pre-historic period solely on forest, ecology and man are found. Borpujari (1992) of course provided some clues regarding the beginning of deforestation in parts of the state of Assam. He threw some light on the forest economy of the state where people were mostly dependent on the forest products for sustenance and to cure diseases. Collection of fire woods, housing materials, trees for making boats and also food items were all forest-based works. Knowingly or unknowingly people did all these in an eco-friendly manner. No significant damage to the forest cover was made during that period. Hill people practiced *jhuming* as an age old tradition which caused no significant change to the forest cover since population was extremely sparse.

Expansion of agriculture, construction of roads, increasing population pressure and other development works are identified as the prime factors responsible for deforestation in Assam. *Ahomar Din* of Hiteswar Barbaruah (1981), *Assam Buranji* of Harakanta Baruah Sadar Amin (1930), *Purani Assam Buranji* of Hem Chandra Goswami (1922), *Kamrupar Buranji* edited by S.K. Bhuyan (1958), *Assam Buranji* of Kashinath Tamuly (1845), *Assam Buranji* of Padmanath Gohain Baruah (1937) the *Arunodoi*, a monthly magazine published by American Baptist Mission (1850) etc. portrayed such several references of deforestation witnessed during that period. Changkakati (1986) discussed the status of forestry and the problems it had been facing. The major causes of deforestation according to him are—(i) construction of hydel project; (ii) use of forestland for agriculture; (iii) encroachment and illegal felling of trees; (iv) *jhuming* in hill districts; (v) drilling of oil; (vi) colliery; (vii) flood damage; and (viii) military exercise etc. John Butler's travelogue *Travels in Assam* (Reprinted, 2004) provides a vivid account of the State of Assam. Butler spent long fourteen years among the tribal people of the state during the first half of the nineteenth century. He described his long and horrible journey through the dense jungle and hostile topography starting from Nowgong *via* Dimapur to N.C. Hills. During the journey he collected ample information about place, people, climate, topography, history, administration and many more. To derive a clear understanding on the status of the then forest cover, Butler's book could be very useful.

A Statistical Account of Assam (Reprinted 1975, vols. I and II) by W. Hunter continues to be almost indispensable for the scholars and researchers who are interested in historical accounts on the state. Specific statistics along with all other accounts including people, climate, soil, economy, agriculture etc. are available in the book. The book contains discussion on the forestry condition of the then districts of the state which provides a genuine guidance for further investigation and research on the problem. *A History of Assam* by E. Gait (1926) has been in great demand for both students and researchers. This book is a milestone where a total general picture of various aspects including social condition, economy, literature, laws and customs etc. from the pre-historic period to British regime has been presented carefully. Gait was also equally concerned with the varying modes of tribal life which he specified along with descriptions of other related matters. The four pioneer administrators of Indian Civil Service B.C. Allen, E.A. Gait, C.G.M. Allen, and H.F. Howard compiled "Gazetteer of Bengal and North-East India" with all authentic materials collected in the initial stage by the District Officers of the concerned areas. The Gazetteers covered the physical features including mountains, lakes, rivers, forests, population, agriculture, the tribes and castes, the social morals and customs etc. and the problems relating to day-to-day life of the people in those days.

The most outstanding contribution specifying the political motives of the British to rule over the forest wealth of Assam, however, was made by Handique (2004) in his book British Forest Policy in Assam. It is a remarkable endeavour where attempt was made to analyse the British forest policies from 1864 to 1947. Tracing out the genesis and development of British forest policy, it examines the socio-economic and environmental impact of the policies. In the preface, the author distinctly mentioned—"At the time of British occupation of the province, Assam was mostly covered with forests. After the coming of the British the forests of Assam, which did not have wide commercial use till then, came to be regarded as a source of revenue and resource extraction, which totally revolutionized the outlook of the Government and the people towards forest. In fact, the advent of the British marks an ecological watershed in the history of Assam." Mazumder (1988) illustrated the deep rooted faith of the people on curability of the medicinal plants found elsewhere in abundance. He describes—"Various age old traditions, customs and socio-economic behaviours are still prevalent in the area. The land seems to be the meeting ground 'Sangam' of aryan and mangolian faith, traditions and culture. Naturally there is a wide range of scope of collecting information about traditional medicines and so also the folklore on medicine in traditional treatment. It opens up a great scope for ethno-botanical studies at different strata of population and people in geographical isolation". The quoted lines upheld the importance of medicinal plants which were once used all throughout the State of Assam as very effective health care measures. Medhi (1993) studied extensively the traditional practices and mode of life of various tribes and sorted out a list of medicinal plants commonly used by the people. *Forest Resources in North East India*, edited by Duttaray and Alam (2002) highlights the issues like population pressure on forest land and stresses on the need to regulate inflow of people to the forests. The book suggests for formulating special and new policy solely for the conservation of forest in N. E. India in the context of its diverse physico-climatic situations. Guha and Chattopadhyaya (2006) examined the linkage amongst the development parameters, population dynamics and forestry in North East India. Though they could not present a clear discussion on the forests and forest rights of the tribals, it has still relevance to the tribal people who have been mostly depending on the ecological settings. The increasing population pressure has resulted in the shrinkage of forest cover which has put a severe blow on the forest based tribal economy. While analyzing the population dynamics and environment, the authors have noted that large scale tree felling has been operated here mainly because of greater demand for food from agriculture. Pointing to the increasing population pressure the authors support the need of a broad based mass movement for the protection of forests from further degradation.

Biodiversity of Assam, edited by Bhagabati, Kalita, and Baruah (2010) is a book with an illustrative account of plants and animals found in the jungles and open patches of Assam. The checklists of species of both plants and animals pro*vide* wide ranging information about the rich biodiversity base of the state. From microbes to giant mammalian species and from plankton to the loftiest dicotyledonous plants are documented here in a well-organized and orderly manner which may be a useful guide for the researchers, students and wildlife experts.

1.6 Organization of the Study

This study contains seven chapters altogether including the introduction, summary and conclusion. The introductory chapter includes the research problem and the data source and the methodology of the study. In this chapter literatures relevant to the research problem are reviewed in order to develop a theoretical base for the work. The study of deforestation from political ecological perspectives is vital to understand the dwindling ecology in the third world countries as the impact of deforestation on the livelihood practices of the tribes is all pervading. In this chapter, a discussion on the data base and methodology followed in the study is also provided to streamline the analysis.

The second chapter provides the background of the study area i.e. the Assam-Nagaland Border region and the tribes living there. The study area is delineated on the basis of some selected criteria following Hertshrone's concept of unity of organisms in subordination of non-organic components. This chapter highlights the physical parameters of the study area along with dynamic attributes which focuses on the specific character of the area.

The analytical part contains four chapters. The third chapter gives a detail discussion on forest cover, forest ecology and status of the forestry which are taken into consideration for a critical analysis of the political ecology of deforestation in the study area.

The fourth chapter is devoted to discuss the pattern and nature of the forest tribes with special reference to those living in the Assam-Nagaland Border. It examines all the variables and attributes of the tribes of Assam-Nagaland Border areas.

"Analysis of the Impact of Deforestation"—is the chief content of fifth chapter of the study. In this chapter, attempt has been made to find out the overall impact of massive deforestation on the tribal life and the society in general in the border region. Here, the main thrust is on the livelihood and behavioural change among the tribal people resulting from rapid depletion of forest resources in the area.

The sixth chapter, however, tries to formulate measures towards sustainable development in the changing ecological context of the region. The problems arising out of the changes caused mainly by external forces and strategies to be adopted for their mitigation are focused in this chapter.

The last chapter summarises the work and presents the major findings. Some generalizations are also made here on the basis of the results of the study.

2
Background of the Study Area

2.1 Physical Aspects

2.1.1 Location

The study area, the Assam-Nagaland Border, lies between 25°17′53.57″ N to 27°03′46″ N latitude and 93°20′32″ E to 95°18′03″ E longitude.

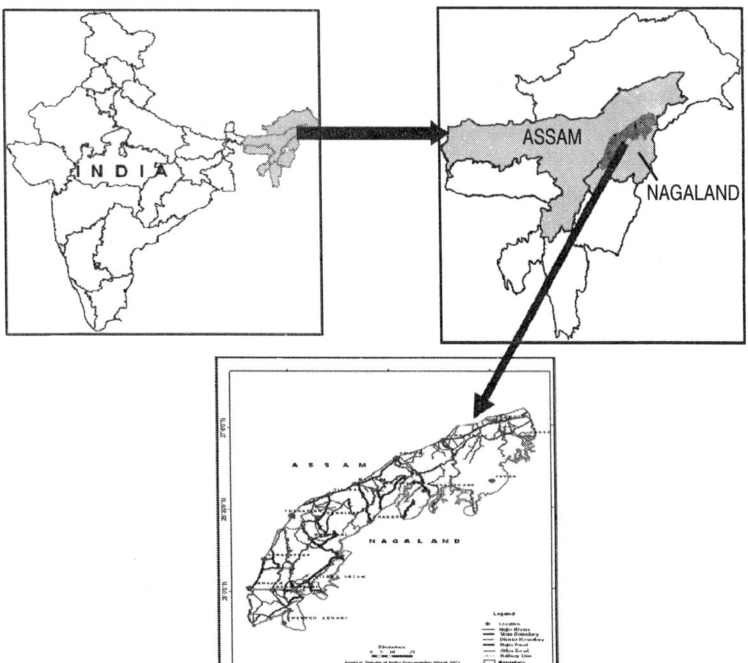

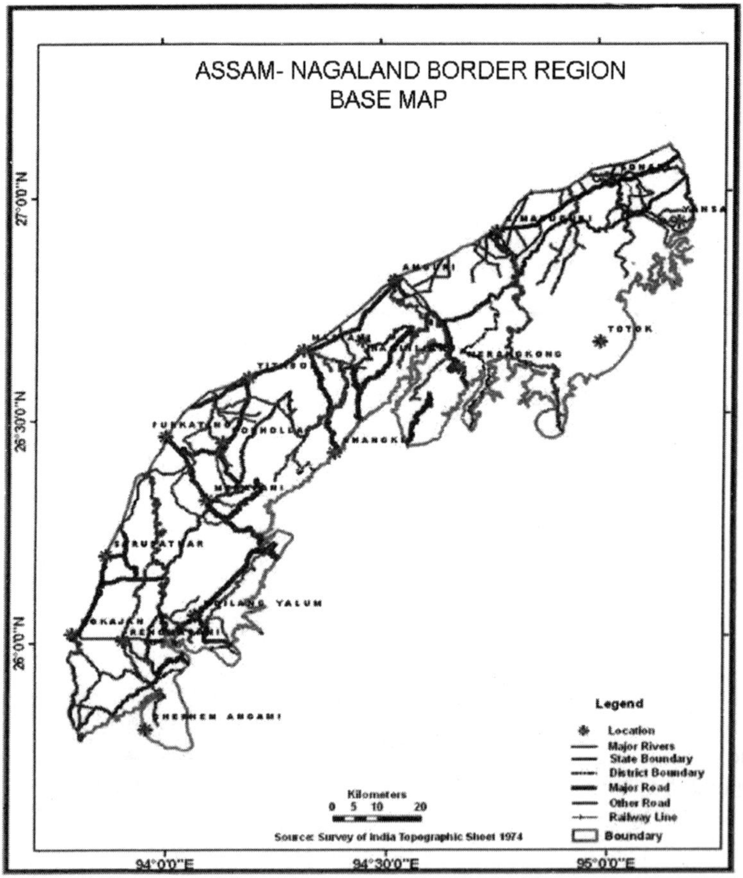

Map 2.1: Location of Assam-Nagaland Border Region

Predominated by transitory nature of both hills and plains the region exhibits tortuousness where the rivers are there. Diverse topographic forms and a humid meso-thermal climate provide favourable environment for rich floral diversity with a dense canopy cover in the region. Facing old crystalline Karbi Plateau and the Brahmaputra Valley of Tertiary sediments on its west and north-western margin, the scarp line of the Naga Hills with spectacular ups and downs exhibits a rich green cover

As a whole, the study area encompasses the parts of the state of Assam and Nagaland and hence delimitation criteria are taken into consideration to specify it. Extending NE-SW the area is 310 km in length and only 20 km in width. Tortuousness of the hilly outskirt and the river valleys between the hills give the entire border line a zigzag course with the plains on its base. Nagaland, a hilly state with a relief ranging from 115 meters to 1200 meters on an average keep the Brahmaputra Plain distinctively separate (Map 2.1).

2.1.2 Delimiting the Study Area

The study area, the Assam-Nagaland Border track, extends along the boundary between the States of Assam and Nagaland. Although mention has been made specifically as the Assam-Nagaland Border, it will be practical to avoid all tortuousness of the border areas lying between the two states. In order to avoid all complicacies, forest is considered to be the central attributes in the process of delimitation of the study area. Not only in the uphill slopes, in the foot hill areas also the forest cover is spectacular and well exposed all along the border. Presence of quite a large number of reserved forest along the border areas namely—Abhaypur, Singphan, Geleki, Tiru Hills, Desoi, Desoi valley, Dayang, Diphu, Rengma, Rangapahar reasonably suggests its richness in forest cover.

The other attributes of the study are the human aspects which are highly dynamic both horizontally and vertically. However, the human aspects are found to create complexities in delimitating the study area. In the words of Hartshrone (2005)—" Once man enters, he and all his works, whether or not they become a part of the new unity—which without them is not a unity which we could never study directly, has in any case long since ceased to exist." Referring Bluntschli's (2005) works on Amazon lowland Hartshrone emphasized more on the aspect of climate and relief in the process of delimitation of a natural region. He noted that "Areas where perhaps two natural elements are fairly uniform throughout and one is of such an extreme character as to dominate most other elements, the area may appear to have such a degree of interlocking and indivisible harmony that we are led to think of it as a unit, indeed as an organic unit." This essence of areal zoning is well reflected in the dense forested patch of the foothills of Assam-Nagaland Border. The human intervention has, however, made some discontinuity in the relief pattern in addition to the type of vegetation by extending their activities to the foothill zone. Except for the horizontal and vertical mobility of the inhabitants of this forested patch, all other natural and environmental factors demonstrate the unity of form and content of the zone and thus it can be regarded as a unique entity for study. Thus, in the process of delimitation of the study area the following considerations are taken into account: (i) terrain characteristics, (ii) forest cover, (iii) vegetation type, (iv) climate and (v) human aspects.

Terrain Characteristics

A foothill can be defined as the outward limit of a mountain characteristically composed of low hills culminating in the plains. Assam part of the border region is broadly comprised of plains while the Nagaland part is solely on the hilly patch, which is structurally a southward extension of the Himalayan system. The height all along the border track therefore varies from 165m to 275m in areas and most of the forested patches are seldom seen climbing past that height. Numerous rivers, tributaries, rivulets are draining down the hills to kick off the augmentation of headward development of slopes. It makes the foothill zone more tortuous and irregular. In places, foothills close to the plains have a cliff like structure and in others it is too gentle and shows long intrusion of valleys inside the hills. The tributaries of Dikhow, Namdang, Dwarika, Jhanji, Puthi, Bhogdoi, Kakdonga, Dhansiri, etc. develop broad headward valley with numerous broad waterlogged, swampy areas and thus provide a congenial ground for the growth of lentic ecosystem in the area. However, the most noticeable aspect is the pattern of distribution of forests which usually exhibits a distinct line of greenbelt sloping down approximately from the 200m contour to downhill slope and the plains. Therefore, delimitation of the forested track in the Assam-Nagaland Border is quite clear.

Forest Cover

Extent of forest cover, type of vegetation, density of forest, canopy cover, etc. are more often used as effective indicators in the process of delimitation of any area. Plants are also deterministic component of climatic behaviour of a region since both are reciprocal to each other. Plant growth and its type could easily reflect the nature of climate of a region. The Assam-Nagaland Border can be identified as a distinct zone on the basis of forest cover alone. Deciduous and mixed deciduous vegetation are predominantly there in the outer low hill areas as well as the river plains at the foothill patch. On the contrary, semi-evergreen vegetation dominates the upper mountainous parts stretching from 270 m to 900 m. Except for the semi-rain shadow belt at the north of the

Barail range, no other areas exhibit any difference in the form and extent of vegetal cover. However, the present forest cover in this belt displays a somewhat eratic nature which is identified as a product of deforestation for settlements and *jhum* cultivation. But, by and large, a region of uniform vegetal cover can be demarcated in the border region on the basis of this criterion.

Vegetation Type

The vegetation of this belt is invariably the same as the vegetation type of the whole of North-East India. The entire border range is dominated primarily by tropical type of deciduous, evergreen, semi-evergreen and grassland vegetation. Moreover, the riparian forests are common along the river banks of the Assam valley and the tributaries invading the hills of the Assam-Nagaland Border. Deciduous forests occur in the plains and foothills while the semi-evergreen and evergreen type of vegetation is found in the wet hilly scarp within the range of 300m to 600m.

Climate

Tropical monsoon climate is the characteristic climate that prevails all along the Assam-Nagaland Border. Warm and humid nature of this type of climate favours the healthy growth of plants. The mean annual temperature for the whole region stands at 19.42°C, while the average annual rainfall varies between 200 and 250cm and occasionally in places it reaches 300 cm. This variation exists because of the topographical set-up and density of forest. The east-west perturbation of Barail range acts as a barrier to the free cross over of the monsoon wind which creates a rain shadow zone at its northern proximity extending from eastern Karbi plateau to the Dhansiri valley of Golaghat district. The rainfall therefore is less in this part compared to the other areas of Assam-Nagaland Border. The rainfall, however, increases northward and even crosses the 300 cm marks in north-western margin of the Naga Hills.

Human Factor

Human factor is seldom considered as a criterion in the delimitation of a region. Assam-Nagaland Border, a unique area from the viewpoints of location, climate and vegetation is inhabited mostly by the tribal people of mongoloid origin, with distinct variation in behaviour, tradition, society and economy. The commonalities that may be observed among them lie in their way of life, practice of herbal medicines, belief systems and dependency on nature. On the basis of all these, the region may be considered as a single entity (Map 2.2).

2.1.3 Geological History

The geological evolution of this part of Assam is very complicated. The area is located at the tri-junction of three separate tectonic belts: Tibetan belt on the north, Burmese belt on the east and Indian belt on the south west. The Tibetan plate, although is not in attached to the Assam-Nagaland Border, the geological evolution of this part has a close link with it. The entire border region can better be called a resultant landform of the interplay among the Indian Plate, Burmese Plate and the Tibetan Plate where upon both tectonic and geomorphic activities occurred to generate the geological structure of this zone.

Prior to the appearance of Tethys, the great geosyncline, extending from Central Europe to East Asia, the Indian landmass including N.E. India was virtually non-existent. Deposition of Archean rock-groups of

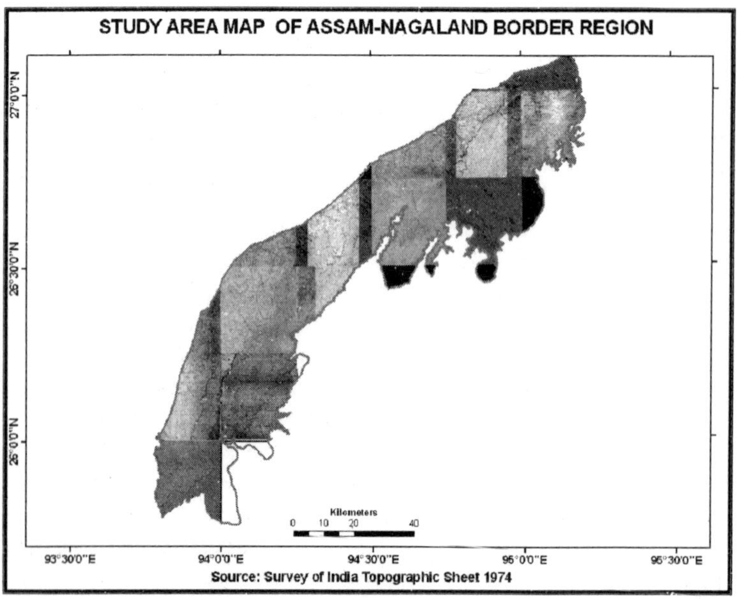

Source: Survey of India Topographic Sheet, 1974.

Map 2.2: Study Area Map of Assam-Nagaland Border Region

Dharawar system during Lewisian and Anglokian age formed the basement rock of this region. Archean fundamental gneiss and intrusive granite were the major component of this system while the Mijo series of rocks belong to the Cuddapah system. Speckled sandstone, a deposit of Lower Gondowana system belonging to barker stage gave the shape of the Subansiri beds of Assam. It is not widespread and deep rooted; only a shallow seam of rock system formed the basement rocks of Subansiri basin. On the other hand the Disang series of rocks, mainly composed of intrusive granite, gabbros and serpentine formed during the Cretaceous are well exposed and formidable in the adjacent part of Assam-Nagaland Border. As such, numilitic limestone deposited during upper Eocene age constituted the Barail series of rocks extending from East Karbi plateau through the Naga Hills region of Assam border to the Eastern Burma region (Wadia, 1916). Moreover, Disang series of rocks continued to deposit from Cretaceous to Eocene period where Eocene rocks have a succession of sandstone over clay stone resembles the Barail series of rocks. Rocks of Shillong series composed of metamorphosed gneissic and granite constitutes the Karbi plateau which has a great bearing over the geologic configuration of Assam-Nagaland Border Region.

Tertiary rock succession, however, is dominant over eastern and southern part of the state. Deposition of Tertiary sediments took place in two separate faces, i.e. the shelf faces in parts of Upper Assam, and Karbi plateaus and the geosynclinals faces of the Nagaland and Manipur. Disang series of rocks in the east and Jayantia series in the west are distinct formations which demarcate the two facies from other formation.

Jayantia and Dichang rock formation are overlaid by the Barail series and is characteristically a fossil bearing conformable rock series. In the upper Assam part, its thickness ranged from 1000 to 6000m which is a source of coal and oil. The Tipam series of rocks are rich in fossil and is extensive and exposed all over the Assam-Nagaland Border with a thickness of 2300 m. The Mio-pliocene period witnessed a series of deposition over the Tipam formation, specially composed of sandstone with a little mixture of conglomerate, grit, coal etc.

Deposition in a river born facies took place during Pliocene period and out crops are conspicuous along the Dihang river and accordingly called Dihing series of rocks. Quarternary deposits over the Dihing rock series are formed of yellow and radish soil. Sand, pebbles, cobbles are found in mixture. The entire Brahmaputra valley and the Surama valley along with the foothills of the Nagaland are covered by this formation.

The Assam-Nagaland Border tract invariably shows the similar rock succession except for the elongated Naga Thrust which opens up at the broad alluvial plain of the Brahmaputra.

Table 2.1: Geological succession of Assam-Nagaland Border Region

Epoch	*Period*	*Time (million year)*	*Terminology*	*Rock Type*
Recent	Holocene	10,000 years till date unconformity	–	Clay, sand, silt, boulders, gravel and alluvium
	Pleistocene	10,000 years unconformity		Consolidated clay, sand, silt boulders, gravel and alluvium
Tertiary	Pliocene	65-1.7 unconformity	Dihing formation	Pebbles beds, coal, clay etc.
	Miopliocene		Dupitila	Sandstone, coal, conglomerate, sand pebbles
	Miocene		Tipam formation	Conglomerate, sand pebbles, shales, ferroginous, molted clay
	Oligocene		Barail formation	Shales, sandstone, limestone, coal clay, Fossiliferous, sedimentary rocks etc.
	Eocene		Disang formation	Shales and sandstone
Mesozoic	Cretaceous	70-65 Unconformity	Disang formation	Sandstone, clay limestone and coal
	Permian		Gondowana series	Sandstone, shales etc.
Archean	Dharwar		Shillong series	Archean, gneiss and intrusive granite

Source: *Geology of India and Burma*, M.S. Krishanan, 1982.

2.1.4 Relief

It is quite natural that an area facing a long folded mountainous chain at one side, an old plateau of Achaean origin at the other and a younger river valley in between certainly portrays diverse relief features. Bifurcating the two extremes i.e. the folded mountain system of Nagaland and the great river valley plain of the Brahmaputra, the entire Assam-Nagaland Border area is very complex and highly diverse in terms of terrain characteristics and relief (Map 2.3A). The border area can be divided into three major physiographic divisions: (1) the zone of low hills, (2) intervening built-up plain of the foothills and (3) the open river valley plains (Map 2.3B).

The Zone of Low Hills: It is a continuous but irregular patch stretching all along the Assam-Nagaland Border. Characterized by low altitude ranging from 110-900 m and gentle gradient, nowhere exceeding 45°, this belt possesses a number of hills extending down to the broad plains. This low hill zone has a gentle rising trend gradually from south-west to north-east except the intervening point of the Barail range. This

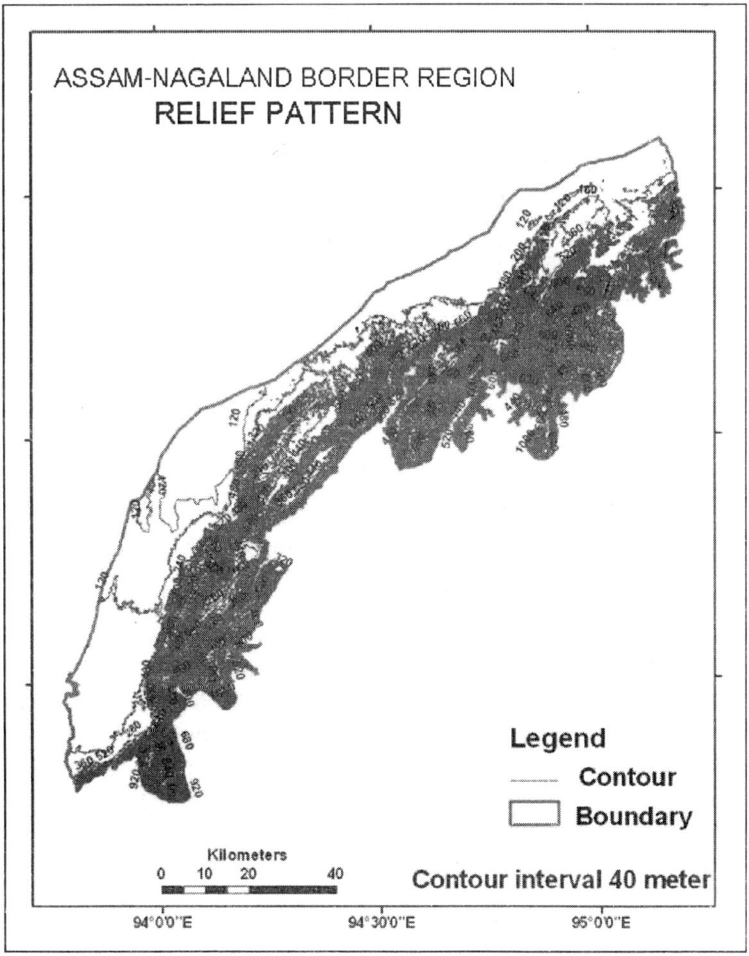

Map 2.3A: Assam-Nagaland Border Region : Relief Pattern

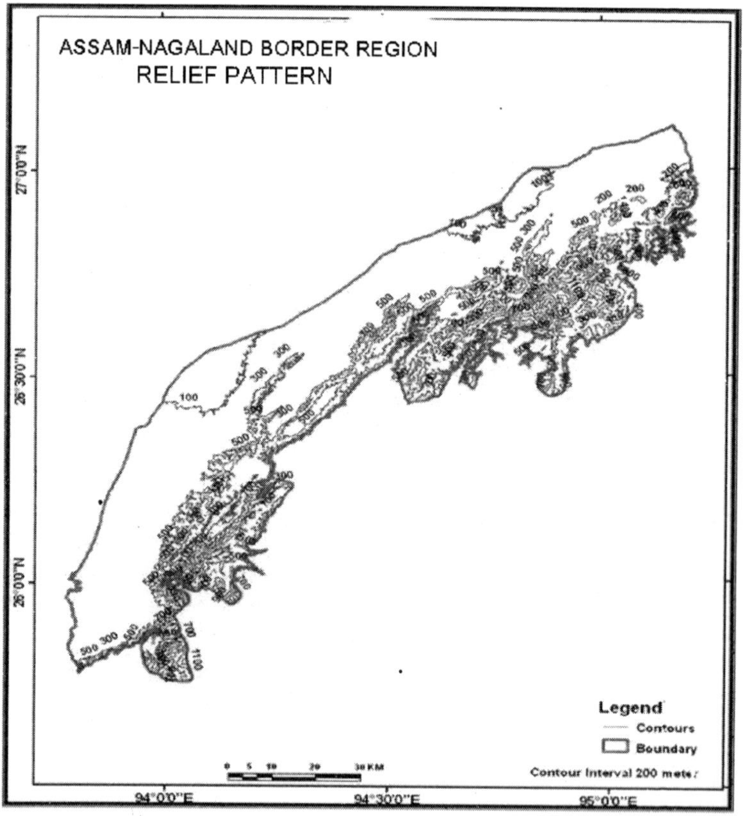

Map 2.3B: Assam-Nagaland Boarder Region: Relief Pattern

range enters into Nagaland from North Cachar and after crossing Kohima it turns northward to Wokha. Few conspicuous dissected hills are formed as a result of denudational works of the rivers which give a distinctive view of the outlying extension of Naga mountain range. Dwarika and Sufrai, for example, have cut the mountain chain to separate the Charideo hill extending from Charideo with an elevation of 152 m to Sola reserved forest. Towards the south of Abhaypur reserved forest an isolated hill is produced as a result of the degradational works of the river Tizit and its tributary Taokak. A broad river valley plain in between the Naga mountain range and the Phoihoa hills with an altitude ranging from 300-500 m forms a congenial ground for the growth of healthy forest. This plain is

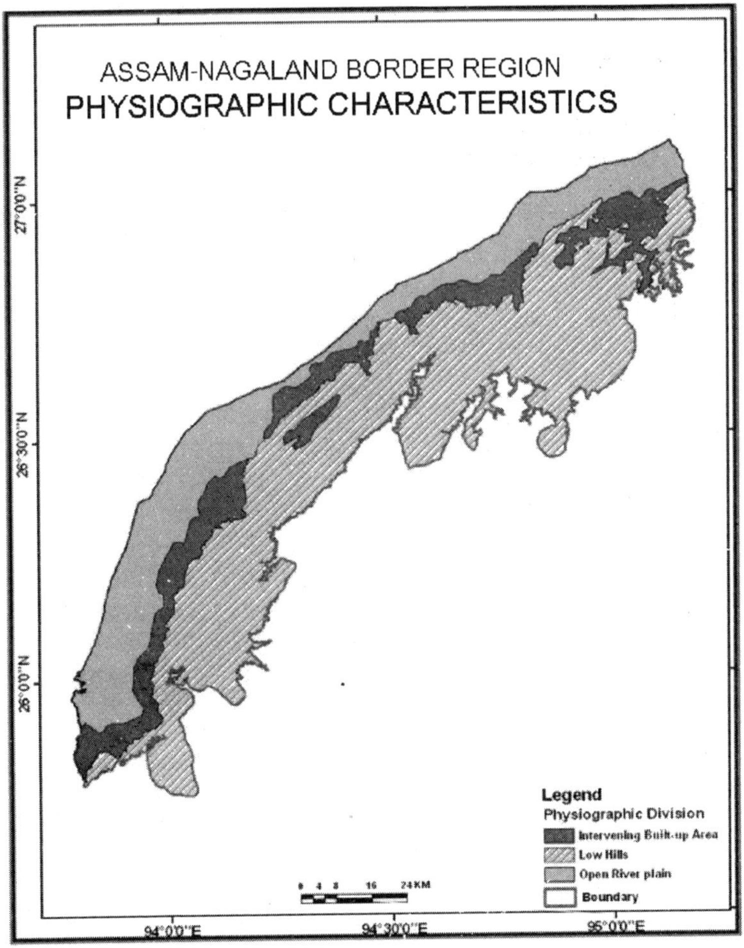

Map 2.4: Assam-Nagaland Border Region: Physiographic Characteristics

basically a product of the headward erosion of the Taokak river. Several monadnocks are found scattered in this plain. This foothill zone consists of piedmont plain, anticlinal ridges and synclinal valley with terraced alluvial fills.

The southern part of Assam-Nagaland Border area is almost hilly except for the Dimapur plain which is a denudational valley produced by the river Dhansiri and its tributaries chiefly the Khova, Disagaphu, Longlong, Balijan, and Singrijan. Rangapahar reserved forest at the south of Dimapur and Daldali reserved forest is distinct for their topographic dissimilarity. Dimapur plain is the last guard separating the young folded mountains of Nagaland and the Precambrian Karbi plateau. From Rangapahar the border is merged with the North-Cachar hills. However, most of the slopes of gentle gradient, up to a height of 1200 m, have been cleared for cultivation (Allen, 2002).

Intervening Built-up Plains: The outer foothill areas which rises from the Brahmaputra plain in the western part of Nagaland are the lowest part ranging from 110 to 300m in elevation. The parts bordering Assam are intervened by few plains like the Dimapur plain. Extending from Chumukedima to Golaghat district it covers an area of about 150 sq. km within the State of Nagaland. It is the only great plain of Kohima district. Another with a total area of about 50 sq. km is lying in and around Naginimara in the mid-west of Nagaland. Starting from the foothills near Kongon village of Mon district it extends up to the lower-middle courses of the Dikhow river. Although, once it was rich in biodiversity, but due to increasing encroachment, specially by the people of Nagaland, it is now a plain with high human interference. Tizit plain is another such plain in the Mon district with a surface area of about 75 sq. km. In the outer hilly tract, a number of broad valleys, resulting from the degradational works of the rivers are found even at a height of 300 meters. Few of them are intermontane in character. These are: (1) Ghaspani valley, (2) Bhandari valley, (3) Merapani valley, (4) Tsurang valley, (5) Lakhuni valley, and (6) Tiru valley. All these valleys are elongated and provide a favourable ground for the growth of flora and fauna.

Ghaspani valley, Bhandari valley and Merapani valley are located in the southern part of Assam-Nagaland Border while the Tsurong and Lakhuni valleys occupy the middle part of the border land. The northernmost is the Tiruvalley which is widely known as Tirupathar. All these valleys seem to be the extending limb of the great Brahmaputra plain. In these valleys, people practice intensive cropping since the hills lack sufficient cultivable land.

The Open River Plain

It is the largest and continuous plain covering large part of the Assam-Nagaland Border. Except the southern part, the areas from Golaghat to Sibsagar district are composed of alluvial soil. The river banks of the Dayang, Kakadonga, Bhogdoi, Jhanji, Teok, Dwarika, Dikhow and Taokak are filled heavily with recent alluvium transported from the Naga Hills.

Most of these rivers have their plain embayment in the foothill regions partly through their headward erosion and partly through subsequent deposition. This gently sloping plain adjoining the foothills provide congenial ground for tea cultivation. The old alluvial soil mixed with residual soil makes the plain fertile. In absence of any free face slope at the juncture of the river plain and the hills, the region provides a genuine stock of man-nature interaction. Slightly acidic in character, the piedmont zone of Nagaland provides all topographic facilities for cultivation.

2.1.5 Drainage

The Assam-Nagaland Border areas have innumerable drainage links over its topography consisting of both plains and mountains. The rivers flowing downhill for a longer part have countless tributaries from both thrust belt and highland of eastern scarp. The thrust belt has established a great control over the drainage system of the region. The major rivers in the region are Desang, Dikhow, Dwarika, Jhanji, Teok, Bhogdoi, Kakadonga, and Dhansiri or Dayang. Except Desang and Dwarika, the other rivers spectacularly exhibit the control of the Naga thrust. They, for several kilometers on the mountainous part, run parallel to the Naga thrust before meeting the plain through narrow gorges. On the other hand, the Barail range (1100 m in average) on the south stands as the zone of water divide in between the two major river systems, i.e. the Brahmaputra system and the Barak system (Map 2.5).

Bifurcation ratio computed for a few selected rivers of this zone is found to be high in the upper reach (where the ratio exceeds 5.0 mark) and hence the number of tributaries is maximum in the mountainous part of the rivers. Except the river Dhansiri, the ratio for other rivers changes drastically indicating the changing pattern of hydrological behaviour and geomorphic character of the rivers. Most of the rivers are rain-fed and therefore peak flow period falls in the rainy months from May to September. At the same time it is observed that higher the bifurcation ratio higher is the volume of discharge which is a common characteristic of the rivers found in this belt.

On the other hand, most of the reserved forests are located at the points where the rivers debouch to the plain. Topographic diversity in combination with tropical monsoon climate favours a dense forest cover in these patches of the Assam-Nagaland Border. The small rivers like Dwarika, Teok, Kakajan etc. originate at the base of the mountain and hence hydro-morphological significance is less compared to the big rivers.

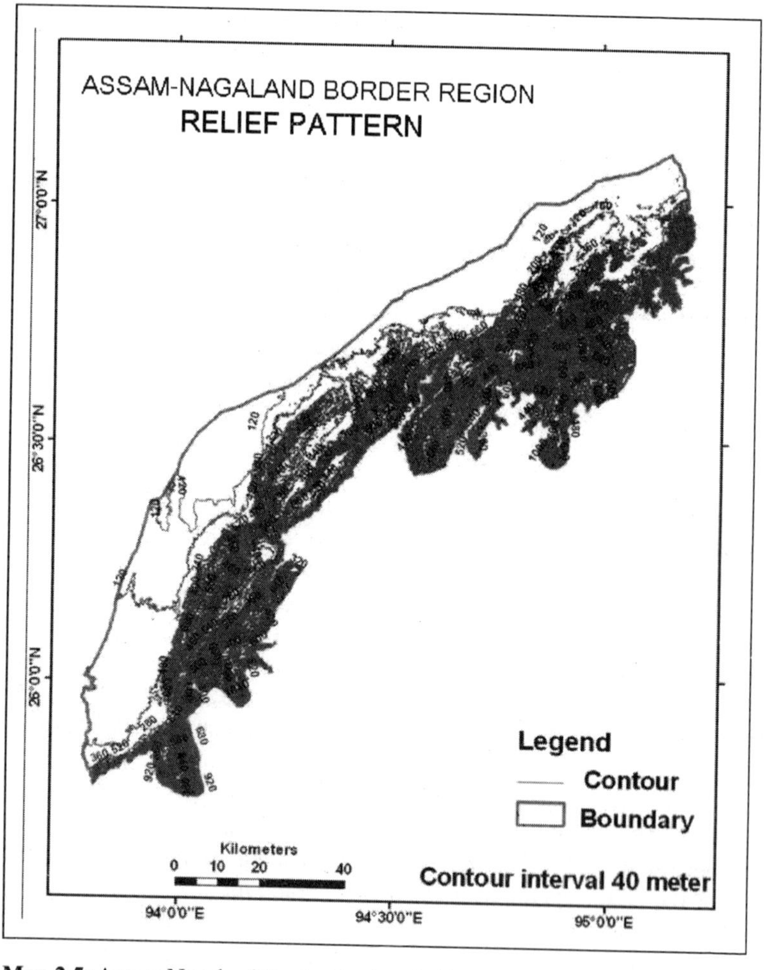

Map 2.5: Assam-Nagaland Border Region: Relief Pattern

Dikhow, Jhanji, Bhogdoi, Kakdonga, Dayang and Dhansiri have been playing vital role as important trade routes since historic past and maximum supply of forest products were carried through these rivers. In other words, these rivers are the prime witness of wanton destruction of forest during the British period (1826-1947).

Table 2.2: Drainage and their attributes

Rivers	*Length (km)*	*Catchment area (sq.km)*	*Sediment yield (Meter/ hectare/Year)*
Desang	230	3950	219
Dwarika	45	—	—
Dikhow	200	4372	254
Jhanji	107	1350	37
Teok	40	470	—
Bogdoi	160	942	83
Kakadonga	100	1100	—
Dhansiri	350	12584	62800
Dayang	218	7347	—

Source: Sharmah, J.N. (1993).

2.1.6 Climate

Climate influences the morphogenetic processes indirectly through (i) vegetation and (ii) soils. Climate and vegetation, and climate and soil are so intimately interrelated that these greatly influence each other. For example, vegetation determines pathogenesis (soil formation), while soils determine vegetation type which is again dependent on climate (Singh, 2005).

According to the classification made by J. Tricart and A. Cailleux (1972) on the basis of major climatic and zoogeographical regions, the Assam-Nagaland Border area falls in the Humid Tropical Morphogenetic region. Subsequently two sub-groups are identified as (i) savanna region and (ii) forest region. Another classification of morphogenetic regions was developed by R.J. Chorley, S.A. Schumn and D.E. Sugden in 1985. As per the classification and the criteria affixed the climate of Assam-Nagaland Border can be identified as humid tropical which is again subdivided as Af and Am. However, keeping the climatic characteristics of the Assam-Nagaland Border tract in view the climatic type can be identified as Amg. i.e. monsoon climate gangetic type (Chorley *et al.*, 1985).

The Assam-Nagaland Border region is physiograhically transitory with a combination of plains, river valleys and hills and mountains. Presence of broad plain bounded by lofty Himalayas on the north, the Naga Hills on the east and the Karbi plateau on the west and south provides a complex form of orographic control over the rainfall regime of this region. Marked variation in rainfall therefore is observed in southern end of the region. As such wind movement shows a marked difference in between the two end parts of the region, i.e. north-east and south-west. Distinct spatial variation in the distribution of rainfall within the region can, therefore, be observed (Table 2.3).

Table 2.3: Distribution of rainfall and number of rainy days (2001-2011)

Station	*Annual rainfall (cm)*	*Average no. of rainy days*
Dimapur	160.20	131
Golaghat	192.30	142
Sibsagar	250.90	146
Jorhat	227.25	144
Hilly tracts	366.90	149

Source: Respective tea gardens and Statistical Handbook of Nagaland, 2011.

Rainfall recorded so far reflects a unique spatial variation within the region where northern part receives more rainfall than the southern part. Again the low hill tracts have more rainfall than the plain parts. The distribution of rainfall is in fact, controlled by the diversity of physiographic structure. On an average, the entire region received an amount of 200-250 cm rainfall annually. On the other hand, the low hill tracts of Nagaland usually receives 280-300 cm rainfall per annum, while the rainfall in the plains ranged between 220 cm and 250 cm. Again the southern part of the region experiences relatively low rainfall (150 cm/ annum on average). A look into the number of rainy days provides a very comprehensive picture about the rainfall variation in the region. During the last 10 years from 2001 to 2011 the average number of rainy days was 131 days at Dimapur, 142 days near Kakadonga reserved forest and 149 days at Sibsagar. The number of rainy days and the amount of rainfall are found to be higher and higher from south to north which substantiates the physiographic control over the rainfall distribution.

So far the temperature is concerned, the southern part, being located in the leeward side, experiences a higher summer temperature than the areas located in the northern part. Again the low hill tract which, although is highly degraded, has still a green shade to make the temperature moderate. The summer isotherms therefore, show three distinct thermal zones viz: (i) the southern zone of high temperature; (ii) the northern zone of moderate temperature; and (iii) the low hill tracts of low temperature.

Over the foothills the range of summer and winter temperature is between 12°C-32°C on average, while it is 10°C-36°C in the southern plain and 10°C-34°C in the northernmost plain (Table 2.4).

Table 2.4: Mean monthly temperature in °C (1920-2005) in Mariani, Assam

Year	January	February	March	April	May	June	July	August	September	October	November	December
1970	15.55	17.8	21.65	24.10	25.15	27.85	28.50	28.95	27.95	25.0	21.40	17.15
1980	15.85	17.45	21.65	24.25	25.90	28.90	29.85	28.80	28.25	25.00	21.15	18.50
1990	17.65	18.50	20.00	21.70	26.50	28.45	28.75	28.60	27.50	25.15	22.00	17.90
2000	15.75	17.40	20.55	23.30	26.75	28.30	28.95	28.20	27.50	26.00	21.35	17.50
2005	16.20	1985	21.50	23.50	25.30	28.75	27.55	29.30	29.80	26.10	21.80	17.15

Source: Meteorological Station, Sonowal Tea Estate, Mariani.

2.1.7 Soil

A number of soil classification schemes have been developed among which the classification made by U.S. Soil Conservation Service of the Development of Agriculture (1975) is accepted widely. The Assam-Nagaland Border, being located at the juncture of three distinct physiographic structures viz. (i) the eastern Himalaya (Naga Hills), (ii) the Karbi Palteau, and (iii) the plains of recent alluvium, exhibits different soil formations in different parts depending upon the character of the parent rocks. Following the classification of U.S. Soil Conservation Service, the soil of this region can broadly be grouped under four major types, i.e. entisols, histosols, oxisols and ultisols. The banks of the rivers Taokak, Dikhow, Jhanji, Teok, Bhogdoi, Kakadonga, Daynag, Dhansiri etc. represent the soils which are weakly developed, very young in formation, and hence lacks definite soil horizon. Often called alluvial soil, this type of soil is composed of sand, silt, pebbles, cobbles etc. Loose formation, rich in humus content and high moisture level of the soil provides a congenial ground for the rapid growth of vegetation. Dense forest cover is mostly found in this part of the region.

Histosols are profound particularly at the base of the hills mostly associated with the river channels. This type of soil is rich in organic matter. Maximum peets, bogs, bills, swamp and marshy lands are found well spread all along the low hill zones which are formed as a result of frequent shifting of channels. The histosols, as seen in the region except for the highly degraded forest area, favour the healthy growth of hydrophytic plants and trees.

Oxisols are characteristically well-weathered tropical soils rich in iron oxides and humus. Maximum accumulation of oxisols or lateritic soil is observed in the southern part of the Assam-Nagaland Border area, i.e. the eastern part of Karbi plateau and N.C. Hills. These soils are dark in colour and fine textured with heavy loams and deficient in nitrogen, potash, phosphoric acid and lime. Oxisols are primarily composed of hydrated oxides of aluminium and iron with small amount of manganese oxide. Oxisols are poor in nutrients and therefore do not support the growth of a dense lofty forest.

It is however, seen that the vast plain part of the region is fairly composed of ultisols which are old in formation, strongly leached and with low alkaline content. All the interfluves of the rivers are characterized by the presence of this type of soil. Although in comparison to the histosols, the ultisols have low pH value but because of occasional inundation by river water the supply of humus is balanced to support the growth of minor plants and trees. On the other hand, high rainfall and higher temperature provide grounds for rich plant cover in this part of the Assam-Nagaland Border region.

As the region is dominated by mountains particularly its eastern part, variation in soil type is well marked. Soils here are characterized by a surface layer of organic matter rich in nitrogen. Their base status varies depending on the degree of leaching. This type of soil is extensive in the southern Naga Hills of low gradient. Steepness of the mountain slope in the humid tropics does not favour the formation of this type of mountain meadow soil (Map 2.6).

Trees show wide variations in their soil preference. Most plant species avoid shallow, stiff, heavy clays, precipitous slopes and saline alkali soils. Semi-evergreen and deciduous forest casually prefers soil containing high organic matter, have continuous supply of moisture, characteristically fertile and well-drained soil. The ability of bamboo to grow on a variety of soils is indicative of their hardy nature and perhaps for that bamboos are found extensively in the region at different altitudes and soil types. The soil map of the Assam-Nagaland Border areas prepared on the basis of investigation, observation and analysis can be considered to have a close relation with the nature of forest cover in the region.

2.1.8 Plant Cover and Wildlife Diversity

Keeping in view all the criteria of tropical forest biome, it can be stated that the Assam-Nagaland Border area is an integral part of this biome. The latitudinal extension, climate, soil, topography, species diversity and the ecosystem of the area are invariably same with that of tropical forest.

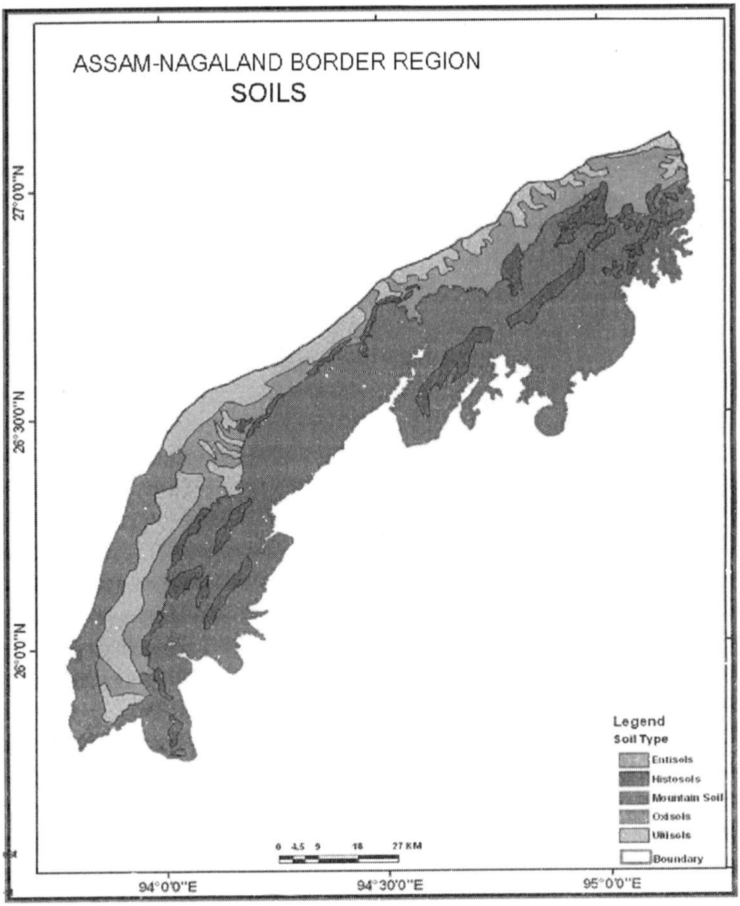

Map 2.6: Assam-Nagaland Border Region: Soils

However, several types of forests ranging from deciduous to evergreen type are seen in the region because of altitudinal, climatic and edaphic variations. In 1936, Champion forwarded a classification of Indian vegetation type. He along with Seth (1968) conducted a survey of Indian forestry. On the basis of the classification, the forests of Assam-Nagaland Border can be grouped primarily into four types: (i) tropical wet evergreen forest, (ii) semi-evergreen forest, (iii) tropical moist deciduous forest, and (iv) bamboo forest.

Tropical wet evergreen forests are seen in the areas having rainfall more than 210 cm annually with short dry season. Moisture content of the soil is the chief determining factor of tropical forest and thus maximum concentration of this forest is found along the downhill slope which receives continuous supply of water leaching through the rock joints even in the dry winter months. Evergreen forests occur in the northern part of the region because of higher intensity of rainfall in comparison to the southern belt except the border areas of N.C. Hills district with more than 250 cm rainfall on an average. The Barail range acts as a *divide* in between the N.C. Hills and the Karbi Hills. However, large scale removal of forest cover has significantly reduces the areal coverage of the evergreen forest in the Assam-Nagaland Border areas.

A line of demarcation, although not regular and continuous, can be drawn separating the evergreen forest from the moist deciduous forest by a belt of semi-evergreen forest that exists in between. Presence of this belt is seen at the foothills within the altitude of 200-300 meters along the border. Bank of the rivers namely Taokak, Dikhow, Bhogdoi, Dayang etc. had also been occupied by the semi-evergreen forest up to the 1970s. Tropical rainforests were also there in the reserved forests viz. Desoi, Desoi valley, Abhaypur, Galeki, Rengma etc. The remnants of the semi-evergreen forest cover are now seen scattered in the area.

The tropical moist deciduous forests are extensively found mostly in the plain parts of the Assam-Nagaland Border region. Areas having dry winter month and summer rainfall of 150 cm to 200 cm usually possess deciduous forests. About 60 per cent of the forest area of the Assam-Nagaland Border is occupied by deciduous forest. The dominant trees found in this belt include Hollock, Khokon, Ban Bagari, Bahat, Samkathal, Rudraksha, Champa, Gamari etc.

The bamboo forest has a wide range and spreads even up to a height of 2000 m. From deciduous to the evergreen forests, everywhere the presence of varieties of bamboos is conspicuous all along the Assam-Nagaland Border region. The bamboo species found in this belt, are *Bambusa balcooa* (*Holuka), Bambusa vulgaris Schrad* (*Jati), Dendrocala mushamiltonii Nees* (*Kak*), *Melocanna bambusoides* (*Muli), Bambusa nana* (*Doluo*), *Bambusa tulda* (*Bijuli*) etc. It has high demand among the villagers for its utility, cheapness, availability, and easy access. These are widely used to make huts, furniture, fencing, basketry, mats, sticks, numerous household items and agricultural implements. Because of the growing importance of bamboo, the Department of Forest and Environment, Government of Assam has taken some effective measures for bamboo plantation. Accordingly, the Forest Department started bamboo plantation scheme in the highly degraded forest areas of the Assam-Nagaland Border in 2009-2010.

The department, for easy access and management, has divided the whole forest area of the Assam part of the border into six sectors. Table 2.5 shows the reserved forests under each sector along with their sizes.

Table 2.5: Sector-wise distribution of reserved forests

Sector	*No. of reserved forest*	*Name of reserved forest*	*Total area (in hectare)*
A	1	Diphu R.F.	18,365.71
B	1	South Namabor R.F.	27,057.55
C	1	Rengma R.F.	13,921.60
D	2	Dayang R.F. Kakadonga R.F. (dereserved)	24,635.37 —
E	3	Desoi R.F. Desoi Valley R.F. Tiruhills R.F.	2797.148 16381.446 5858.552
F	2	Galeki R.F. Abhaypur R.F.	5927.000 6738.000

Source: Forest Survey of India, 2010.

Lack of proper management and malpractices of the forest officials as reported encourages deforestation followed by encroachment for non-forest use. For instance, Kakadonga reserved forest at present is non-existent, Tiru hills reserved forest is virtually degraded by the encroachers. The Dayang reserved forest is lately brought under rehabilitation measures to settle the people evicted by flood and river bank erosion. Thus, the scenario of forest cover in the Assam-Nagaland Border region is quite dismal and devastating.

Wildlife Diversity

Wildlife diversity is primarily a product of the variety of habitats. As such, it is also regarded as the function of soil, topography, climate and vegetation. In other words, diversity in topography, soil type, climate and vegetation is directly proportional to the diversity in wildlife, i.e. the higher the diversity of the wildlife building components (topography, soil, vegetation, climate) higher is the wildlife diversity.

Being the core zone of North-East India, the State of Assam has the Indo-Mallayan and Indo-Chinese bio-geographical characteristics contributing to its biodiversity. Its altitudinal variations and climatic individuality offer diverse ecosystems ranging from different forest types like wet evergreen forests, moist deciduous forest, wet savannah, riparian forests, swamps, marshes, and the river systems that can maintain the rich gene pool of a wide variety of fauna. Moreover, Assam serves as the faunal gateway through which the oriental and palaearchtic fauna could spread and colonize the country. It is the westernmost boundaries of many Indo-Chinese mammals like primates and easternmost limit of many peninsular mammalian species (Bhagabati, *et al.*, 2006). The ecosystem of the Assam-Nagaland Border is invariably dominated by forest ecosystem with occasional presence of aquatic ecosystem of both lotic and lentic type. On the other hand, no specific grassland ecosystem can be strike out for zonation since bamboos of different varieties are wide spread all along the forest area of the region. Works on forest and vegetation of North-East India done by Griffith (1847), Hooker (1849), Clarke (1889), Fisher (1938), Kingdom and Ward (1960), Naik and Panigrahi (1961), Rao and Joseph (1965), Baishya and Rao (1982), Rao and Hazara (1986), Handique (1992), Chaudhury (2005) etc. are important. On the basis of these works and the existing pattern of the ecosystem of the region, the wildlife diversity of the Assam-Nagaland Border region can best be illustrated under two main categories. These are (i) forest ecosystem and (ii) aquatic ecosystem.

Forest Ecosystem

The wildlife sanctuaries, reserved forests, unclassed state forest etc. are the legitimate constituent part of forest ecosystem of the region. Several reserved forests, in fact, constitute the backbone of the forest ecosystem which is endowed with diverse flora and fauna. The floristic diversity is conspicuous having numerous species ranging from evergreen type to wet savannah type of vegetation. The outstanding features especially of tropical wet evergreen forest are their high species diversity, complex stratification and large standing biomass. The following species are representative and typical to the region.

The tree species usually found include *Kayea assamica* (sia-nahar*),* *Shorea assamica* (Makai*), Dipterocarpus* (Hollong*), D. turbinatus* (Gurjan), *Mesoa farrea* (Nahar), *Guruga pinata* (Kahimala), *Palaquium polyanthum* (Kurta), *Hibiscus macrophyllus* (Chemia), *Carallia bracheata*, (Lateku), *Sapium baccatum* (Chelleng), *Dysoxylum binectariferum* (Bandardima), *Michelia champaca Linn.* (Titachapa), *Artocarpus chaphasha* (Cham), *Eugenia jambolana* (Jamu), along with several other tree species. The shrub layer is quite prominent and often merges with the tree layer of smaller variety. Innumerable species of tree ferns, angiopteris, other ferns and fern allies, many lianas are common in these forests. Multiple species of bamboo and cane are found in the wet foothills and valleys.

Tropical deciduous forests have a larger concentration in the long Assam-Nagaland Border region. This type of forests mainly occurs in the areas where the average annual rainfall is normally over 150 cm. in These forests are dominated by *Shorea robusta* (Sal), *Gmelin aorbora* (Gomari) *Schema wallichii* (Makarisal), *Tetrameles nudiflora* (Bheleu), *Artocarpus lakoocha* (Bahat) etc. During rainy season the forests become almost impenetrable due to the gregarious shrubby layer. Bamboos of various species are conspicuous. The forests serve as the source of livelihood for a major section of people living in the forests and forest fringe areas. Trees found in this belt are primarily used for timber, production of medicine chiefly the herbals, production of gums and resigns, paper and pulp, bamboo-cane products, fodder for domestic animals etc. As a result, mounting pressure is there on the forest areas leading to severe deforestation. Government management authority is there, but they are there only to witness the merciless destruction of forest by sections of vested interest.

Aquatic Ecosystem

The region is also endowed with a dense network of rivers, streams, streamlets, along with a number of beels, swamps and marshy lands. Aquatic ecosystem of both lotic and lentic types are there that harbour diverse forms of life. By virtue of the quality and behaviour the aquatic community has been maintaining their presence in the beels and marshy lands of this region. The lotic system constituted by numerous rivers and streams possesses periphytons which include attached clumped and filamentous green and blue green algae and various sessile invertebrates. Farther downstream floating and emergent vegetation along with sessile invertebrates and a number of snails, crabs and fishes are abundant. The banks of the rivers in the plains are enriched by the presence of thick cover of reeds, Jhau, Khagari, Nal etc.

Lentic ecosystems on the other hand are amassed in large particularly along the transitory belt between the hills and plains. Most of the lentic systems i.e. beels, swamps, marshy lands, bogs etc. are the product of the shifting of river course and scattered depositional works at the point where the rivers debouch. The bowl-shaped beels and marshes provide a genuine el-dorado of fresh water organisms of tropical variety. The limnetic zone mostly contains phyto-plankton that consists of diatoms, green and blue-green algae and variety of zooplanktons. Fish, amphibians, reptiles, insects are abundant in this zone.

It is however, seen that in terms of areal coverage, the aquatic ecosystems are sporadic all along the border but play a pivotal role particularly in maintaining a rich wildlife-diversity.

2.1.9 Account of Dwellers

The region has been under human influence since time immemorial. From all the records of historic events it appears that the entire region, particularly its river valleys were the centre of human activities—economic, political, social and cultural. Prehistoric presence of human may be traced to the time of *Mahabharata*, where there was reference of the Hidimba Rajya probably near present Dimapur and the Kachari Kingdom who ruled this greater eastern part of Assam before the advent of the Ahoms in 1228 A.D. The sporadic conflict with the Nagas also reflects the existence of the Naga tribes in nearby hills of the Kachari Kingdom. The Ahom established several army camps along the foothills of the Assam-Nagaland Border during their regime to combat and subdue the Naga hooliganism (Borpujari, 1992). Such camps were fortified in places like Disoikoth, Bacha Bahar, Marangi etc.

The Assam-Nagaland Border, as sketched in the foregoing discussion, was not at all an attractive area for human settlement since most parts were covered with dense jungles with various wild beasts like tiger, bear, wild dog, wild boar, elephant, snakes etc. Settlement pattern was of hamlet type in the areas having life support amenities like water, fertile land for agriculture, security, shelter etc. Settlements were extremely scattered and was mostly confined to the fertile river valley areas. Barpujari (1992) made several references about the settlement pattern of the ancient period particularly from various historical records of the then rulers of the region. Robinson (1840) gave a rough estimate of the total population of Sibsagar district during the early part of the British rules. According to him the total population of Sibsagar districts was 2,00,000 in 1840. As per the census conducted by the British in 1853-54, the total population of Sibsagar district (the old Sibsagar district included Sibsagar, Jorhat and Golaghat Sub divisions), stood at 2,11,477. Similarly the total number of villages was only 203 (Jorhat—93, Sibsagar—56 and Golaghat—54).

The population of the Jorhat, Sibsagar and Golaghat divisions was respectively 116,856; 103, 247 and 76,486 (Mills, 1855).

The most important aspect of the settlement pattern of the entire Assam-Nagaland Border region has been its dispersion. This is because of the fact that (i) most of the villages in Sibsagar district were concentrated in the highland plains; (ii) the dense forests, hostile nature and unhygienic conditions of the Assam-Nagaland Border do not favour smooth living; (iii) the presence of Naga recalcitrants and their frequent rebuff to the plains causing disturbance; and (iv) the wild animals make the area hostile for human habitation. On the contrary, the western low hill zone is the largest part of Nagaland in terms of population size. From accessibility point of view, the entire Nagaland can broadly be divided into three physiographic divisions: (i) easily accessible area; (ii) moderately accessible area; and (iii) hardly accessible area. Naturally, the western part of the state facing Assam, where the land is characterized by relatively low altitude, forms the easily accessible area. Here the terrain does not pose much problem to the movement of people from one place to another and to the implementation of developmental programmes (Lannusosang, 1987). As per the Census of 1981, this western zone (part adjoining Assam) has a population of 44,219 or 18.61 per cent of the state's total. The past population scenario of Nagaland, reflects certain complicated social and traditional customs of the Naga tribes and sub-tribes. Relatively high concentration of human habitation in the areas of high altitude had been there mainly for security reasons. The Nagas whose society was stained with head hunting practice in the olden days preferred to set-up their settlements on the hilltops basically for strategic reasons. Their dislike for settling down in the low hill areas is repudiated in course of time as the days of head hunting are over.

It is clearly evident from the recent migration of the people from the hilly areas and the spurts of settlements in the foothills of the western part which is not only good for agriculture but also for pursuit of other economic activities (Lannusosang, 1987). The districts facing the westernmost boundary of the state, namely Dimapur, Wokha, Mokokchung and Mon, record a higher growth of population where the average density of population increased from 82 in 1991 to 180 in 2001. It is excessively higher compared to the state average and other districts located in the eastern most part. Contrarily, the initial peopling stage in this hilly region was marked by very low population density towards the westernmost part compared to the eastern high altitude areas. The surveys conducted by the British Government in 1881, 1891 and 1901 estimated the total population of the entire hill section of Nagaland at 95,570; 96,637 and 102,402 respectively. In 1901, there were only 85 children under five for every 100 married women between the age group of 15 to 40, as compared to 115 and 110 in Nowgong and Kamrup (Allen, 1905). The causes behind this low birth rate particularly among the hill tribes, although was not explained, are assumed to be the food habit, extremity of climatic hazards (storm, intense rain, coldness, etc.), excessive labour in the rugged hilly terrains, social customs etc.

The Assam-Nagaland Border, even at present, has been a zone of low population density since most of its areas are covered either by forests or by rugged terrains causing difficulties for economic activities. Apparently, though the scenario of population pressure seems to be not so countable, the growth of population in the region shows a higher rate (Map. 2.7). The conclusion that may be drawn from a comparison of decadal growth rate of population for the period 1981 = 1991 and 1991= 2001 as per Census of India at Circle level for the region as a whole, is that there is a growing population pressure in the region. The decadal growth of population was 60.05 per cent and 71.30 per cent respectively for 1981-1991 and 1991-2001.

Spatial Distribution

Distribution of population in a rural region with topographic diversity and ethnicity is always found to be heterogeneous. On the other hand, a region largely inhabited by people of varying ethnic groups in combination of multifarious cultural landscapes reflects diverse attributes of population distribution (Grover, 2004). On the other hand, ecology as a revolutionary force of life (Marcuse, 1972) is seen as one strong determinant of distribution of population with distinctive social and cultural imprints. The prevalence of tribal people in this belt of Assam-Nagaland Border therefore, acts as a critical element in the distribution of population. For instance, a specific tribe with strong traditional and cultural identity prefers to settle in places where they found their available ecological condition favourable to detach them from other tribes. This typical character of distribution of population governs the spatial distribution from one end to another within the region. In the hills, the *jhumiyas* representing different Naga tribes exhibit a typical character which can be used as a tool to describe the nature of spatial distribution.

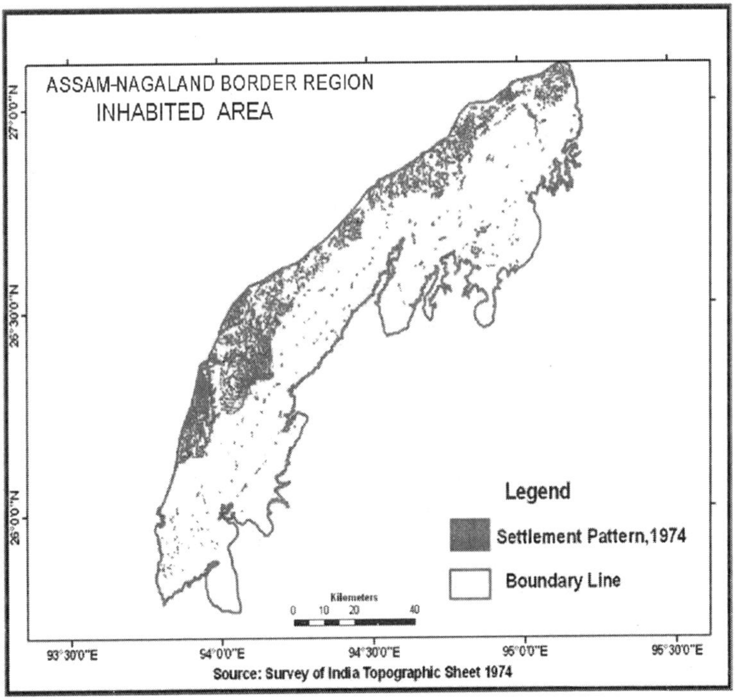

Source: Survey of India Topographic Sheet, 1974.

Map 2.7: Assam-Nagaland Border Region: Inhabited Area

Eastward and north-eastward, from the Assam Bengal railway line up to the Naga Hill range, three culturally distinct settlement zones can be identified on the basis of racial, ethnic and cultural attributes. These are: (i) the non-tribal settlement zone; (ii) the plain tribes settlement zone and (iii) the hill tribes settlement zone (Map. 2.8). The non-tribal zone is the westernmost zone extending from Assam-Bengal railway line to a distance of about 10 km eastward. Characterized by small size of agricultural fields, mixed occupational pattern and better economic development, this settlement zone exhibits high population density (352 persons per sq.km as per 2011 census). As this belt has large number of tea gardens and several urban centres, hence it can be regarded as the focal economic zone of the greater border area. Nazira, Simaluguri, Amguri, Mariani, Titabor, Forkuting, Bokajan, and Sarupathar are the focal urban centres of this zone. The total urban population of the area as per 2001 census is 3,31,038.

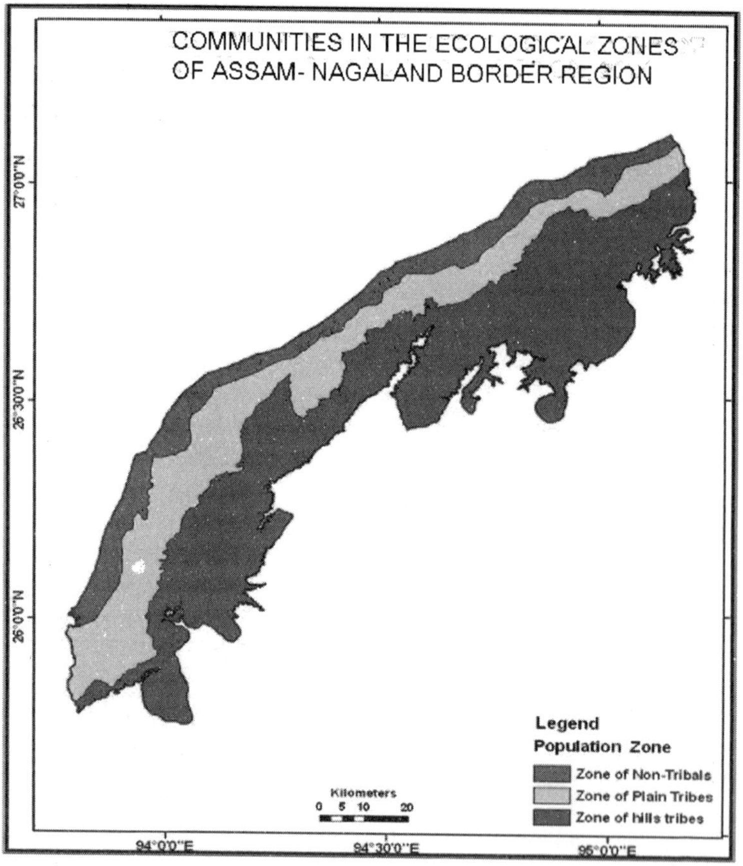

Map 2.8: Communities in the Ecological Zones of Assam-Nagaland Border Region

Next to this zone lies the zone of plain tribes. Extension of Assam-Bengal railway, urban growth and the expansion of tea plantations to the forests of the plains pushed away most of the plain tribes to the interior of the region. Ecocentrist tribals, who are intended to develop an economically informed base of life that is able to value (for their own sake) ecological entities at different levels of aggregation, characteristically and also identically are united by biological links or by common culture, tradition and (Hart, 1984). They are purely the eco-system people (Guha, 1994) who love to leave with nature. Occasional intervention of immigrant people from Bangladesh and Nepal, ex-tea garden workers and Naga tribes create disturbance in the area. The density of population in this zone as a whole is estimated at 220 persons per sq.km. Large agricultural fields along with plantation crops are seen everywhere and rearly an urban agglomeration is seen in this belt except the weekly markets like Merapani, Changkhati, Dayang Tarani etc. The major groups of plain tribes found in this belt are Thengal Kachari, Sonowal Kachari, Bodo, Miching, Khamayang, Tai, Turung etc.

The third zone spreading over the hilly areas of Nagaland is dominated by the hill tribes, such as Rengma, Angami, Ao, Lotha, Kanyak, Sema etc. *Jhum* cultivation is their mainstay of life. They are occupying most of the outer low hill areas of Nagaland with their hamlets called 'Basti'. A general tendency among them, to occupy more low land areas of the foothills is growing vigorously which imputes disputes in the interstate boundary. They are, in fact, the ecosystem people depending on the forest resources for their livelihood. The density of population here is low (145 persons/km^2) compared to the other two zones (Table 2.6).

Table 2.6: Population in the ecological zones of Assam-Nagaland Border region, 2001

Ecological Zone	*Area (sq.km)*	*Total Population*	*Population Density (person/km^2)*
1. Non-tribal zone	1425.07	5,01,625	352
2. Plain tribal zone	2,448.81	6,04,739	220
3. Hill tribal zone	3,041.06	4,40,953	145

Sources: (i) Area delimited from topographical sheet of 1:50,000 scale.
(ii) Population compiled from Village Directory, Census of India, 2001.

Apart from this, the circle-wise distribution of population in the region presents a substantial growth of population during the last three decades. Against the decadal growth of 64 per cent in the state during 1991-2001 period, the growth for this border area was as high as 81 per cent. Labourers of immigrant origin hired to work in the *jhum* fields and the growing trade and commerce in the recent decades contributed to the population growth in this part as stated by the local people. The hired labourers instead of leaving the work place after completion of the allotted works search for areas of their convenience in the degraded forests to open up a new settlement for them. Upper Merapani foothill, Bheleguri Muslim, Lukto Nepali etc. are such villages resulting from the influx of people of immigrant origin.

Lader Parde, an eminent social worker of Nagabat, describes that their ancestors were brought here to clear the forest for tea plantations by the British officials. Some of their fore-fathers were killed either by the wild animals or by snake bites. They fled away from their work place and took shelter in this inaccessible forested part of the border region. In later periods, many more retired tea tribes and the hired labourers to cut trees for timber brought by the traders established their settlements as time passes (Kikon, 2008). It is a unique situation where the tea tribes reside in the village without any tea plantation. Presence of a sizeable number of tea tribe population, approximately 12,000 distributed in 15 villages in the zone of plain tribes adjoining the foothills of Nagaland, is remarkable from the viewpoint of ecological sustainability.

It is necessary to mention about the distinctiveness of the distribution of population in between the hills and the plains of the border areas. The forested organic unit as demarcated on the basis of few selected criteria, is primarily comprised of parts of Dimapur, Wokha, Mokokchung and Mon districts of Nagaland and Sibsagar, Golaghat, Jorhat and Karbi Anglong districts of Assam. A marked difference in the decadal growth of population between the hills and the plains of the region can be observed. The population growth during 1991-2001 was 16.88 per cent in the plain zone against 65.73 per cent in hills districts (Table 2.6).

A comparative analysis of the growth of population in the two parts of the border area is made to reveal the trend of population growth during 1991-2001. The trend lines for the two inter-state units, i.e. border adjoining parts of the districts of Assam and Nagaland, are drawn on the linear equations $Y = -0.324 + 2.6748x$ and $Y = 0.0598 + 1.1222x$. The trend of population growth, however, is marked by a sharp rise in the part of the districts of Nagaland border while the same is comparatively steady in part of the plain districts of Assam border. Regression coefficient (b) for Nagaland part is 2.6748 or $\tan^{-1}69.50$ which is significantly high in comparison to the part of Assam border. The regression coefficient (b) for Assam part is 1.222; hence the growth of population is almost uniform during 1991-2001 decade. If this trend persists in part of the districts of Nagaland border, in an irrecoverable ecological crisis in the region will emerge. A critical situation in the border belt is already developed especially for appropriation of more agricultural land in the area. Agriculture being the mainstay for 90 per cent of the inhabitants of the border region, and as *jhum* areas have low efficiency level to support the people, the *jhumiyas* often want to resolve their crisis arising out of increasing population pressure by acquiring more productive agricultural land from the plain districts of the neighbouring state.

Table 2.7: Growth of population of areas belong to Assam-Nagaland Border region (1991-2001)

Parts of the districts	*Total population*		*Decadal growth (in percentage)*
	1991	*2001*	
Parts of hill district of Nagaland:	215281	440953	65.73
Dimapur	1,37,854	3,36,363	144.01
Wokha	9,541	14,695	54.02
Mokokchung	32,511	43,239	33.00
Mon	35,375	46,656	31.89
Parts of the districts of Assam:	9,58,651	1,106,365	16.88
Sibsagar	4,20,902	4,87,531	15.83
Jorhat	2,19,078	2,51,261	14.69
Golaghat	2,78,104	3,17,790	14.29
Karbi Anglong	40,567	49,783	22.72

Source: Census of India, Series 19, Statistical Handbook of Nagaland, 1991-2001.

So far the population density in the region is concerned, the accessibility attribute is much active and effective. The density of population is found highest in the non-tribal zone with nearly 352 persons/km^2. On the other hand, the hill slopes of Nagaland where *jhuming* is practiced show a density of 145 persons/km^2 while the moderately accessible belt of the plain tribes show 220 persons/km^2. The most important point to be noted here is the growing ethnic violence between the hill tribes and the plain tribes for acquiring fertile cultivable land of the plain. As the lands are the basic resource in an agrarian economy, encroachment of farm land is a serious problem. The failure to provide acceptable option to the *jhum* cultivators by the concerned government on the one hand and the increasing population pressure on the other seem to be the prime causes of unrest in the border area.

Religion and the Ecological Ethics

Religion in all simple societies is a very important aspect of social life. Social, economic, cultural and psychological aspects of the life of the primitive social groups are intricately intertwined with their religious belief system (Malik, 2004). To understand the tribal religious system comprehensive exploration of life cycle is essential.

Animism in tribal religion in this context becomes more and more vital and important. Being a belt of tribal dominance of diverse tradition and religious culture, Assam-Nagaland Border region bears immense potential to manifest a common agenda for the sake of nature's conservation. The tribes namely Tai Turung, Tai Khamayang, Sonowal Kachari, Thengal Kachari, Mising, Ao, Kanyak, Rengma, Lotha, Angami, Karbi, etc. are endowed with specific religious culture, traditions and rituals mostly centering animism, mythism and totemism. The basic idea of totemism lies in the fact of "like produces like" (Froyed, 1953). "Similar works results similar"—following these believes, most of the tribes exercise it in different form and style. For instance, the thorny palm tree is believed to be a symbol of puzzle and disturbance by most of the tribes of the region. To avoid all kinds of disturbance, constraints, puzzle etc. in the future life of a child, the Sonowal Kachari tribe believes that it is necessary to pass a branch of palm tree through the two legs of a new born baby. Gacko snake is the fortune teller for Karbi tribes and therefore they never kill it. Mishing tribe performed 'Kachan' within dense forest praying for a successful hunting in the forest. Similarly certain Naga clans identified their communities with certain animals. Such totem animals were perceived either as group ancestor or as guardian spirit. Among the northern Naga groups, there exists lizard, tiger and frog clan (Stirn and Van Ham, 2003). Hornbills are seen as representing warfare bravery (Saul, 2005). A long note on the practice of animism among the tribes of the region can be appended and mention of such a few components is apprehensive to examine the close relationship between tribal religion and the nature. A brief account, however, is attached here to authenticate and to supplement the dominance of animism among the tribes of this border region (Table 2.8).

This brief account of the animistic practice of the tribes of Assam-Nagaland Border is only a simple representation to make the thing comprehensive which obviously substantiates the dominance of animism in the traditional tribal religion. Any attempt to disassociate the animistic instinct in tribal religion may lead perhaps to a total collapse of tribal mode of living and the forest ecology symbiotically sustained there in. The Karbi tribes, for instance, regularly worships animals like *Engnar* (Elephant), *Thakbam* (Bear), *Teke* (Tiger), *Dor* Thelon (Snake) *Bhutadi* (Forest). This kind of mutualism is one sided since all the wild animals mentioned are characteristically and behaviourally ferocious and hence the relationship is antagonistic. In the tradition of tribal society's commensalism acts in an effective way to sustain ecological stability in the areas they live. It was presumably well maintained and continued until the advent of the British (Saikia, 2011) who started damaging the forest ecology for cheap revenue earnings.

Table 2.8: A brief account of animistic attributes in tribal religion of Assam-Nagaland Border Region

Tribes	*Religious practice*	*Animistic attributes*
Karbi	(i) Denza Puja (ii) Thakbam (iii) Ingnar puja (iv) Bhutadi puja	(i) Worship performed in the forest to keep safe from wild beasts (ii) Worship bears of the jungle (iii) Prayer performed to protect them from elephant depredation (iv) Performed worship for the growth of jungle
Sonowal Kachari	(i) Khring Khring Puja (ii) Baghdew puja (iii) Bali Sabah (iv) Jalkhai	(i) Performed in the forest under a big tree (ii) Rituals observed in the forest for protection from tiger attack (iii) Worship cyclone, storms to protect their dwellings and the fields (iv) A prayer performed on the river bank to satisfy the God of water
Bodo Kachari	(i) Zwmwn Zwla, Zwmwn Buri (ii) Baichagu	(i) Worship the God of hunting performed during hunting operation (community hunting) (ii) Cows are nursed and prayer and dance performed for a healthy production of crops and for a calm and quite nature (iii) Observed for seven days during which nobody cut trees, perform hunting, harvest crops, plough their land, climb trees etc. If done, they believe, will affect adversely.
Naga	(i) Naknya Lum (ii) Tsokum	(i) Observed in August before harvest. People decorate houses with a kind of tree called 'Ngunam' and prayed to keep away thunderstorm, cyclone etc. (ii) People gathered in the open field and dance and pray for a good return of their works done in the field and forest

(Contd.)

Tribes	*Religious practice*	*Animistic attributes*
Mishing	(i) Kachan (ii) Dailung Dabur	(i) The hunters perform this rituals in the forest to have all legitimate hunting in the forest (ii) Idol of two dragons is made using 'Ruktag' and 'Tabujong' grass and worship for the welfare of the people. Similar to snake worship.

Source: Pegu, N.: *Mishing sakalar Itibritta aru Sanskriti*, Lakhimi Press, Dibrugarh, 2000.
Narzi, B.: *Bodo-Kacharir Samaj aru Sanskriti,* Bina Library, Guwahati, 2009 (Reprint).
Terang, R.B. (Ed.): *Karbi Sanskritir Ruprekha,* Asom Sahitya Sabha, Diphu, 2010.
Kachari, N.: *Sonowal-Kachari Samaj Sanskriti Aru Bhashar Parichay,* Tribal Research Centre Culture, 2011.

It is now an established fact that large scale intervention in the tribal areas exclusively for capital earnings by various government and non-governmental agents and agencies disestablished the whole setting of tribal mode of life and living means. From the perspective of political ecology, the cultural characteristics of indigenous life, those directly related to ecology, are currently marginalized. Indigenous people are often the soft target of external economic domination by multinational business which seeks to exploit indigenous culture areas often with the help of nation-state machinery (Godicks, 1993). The destruction of indigenous homeland and excessive exploitation of resources create a situation for the indigenous to submit themselves in the mainstream which however, dismantles the traditions and ritual practices (Grinde and Johanon, 1995). Colonialist interference in the resources especially the forest areas in which most tribes live gives birth to a new situation. This new situation pushed them from their original status of environmental wisdom, David Sujuki named this group of people as 'first ecologist' (Sujuki, 1993). This 'first ecologist' antagonized by intensive colonial intervention compelled to adopt and adjust themselves with the changing situation under erroneous resource base. Lynn White (1967) has suggested that the emphasis in Judaism and Christianity on the transcendence of God above nature and the dominion of humans over nature had led to a devaluing of the natural world and a subsequent destruction of its resources for utilization ends.

Large-scale destruction of forest and forest based livelihood of the tribes of Assam-Nagaland Border by intensive exploitation during the colonial and post-colonial periods brought a wave of change among the tribes of the region and opened the pave for world religion like Hinduism, Christianity and Islam etc. Christianity had made its inroad in the areas of tribal dominance particularly in the hills during the period of colonial rule. From then most of the hill tribes started adopting Christianity. Hinduism, particularly Vaishnavism, made its ways among the plain tribes of the region. The process of religious conversion and replacement has been still prevalent in this part of the border. Under compulsion of the changing ecological situation and continuous insisting from religious priests most of the tribes of the region changed their religious practice from traditional to world religion. The linkage between cultural and natural systems is dialectical in nature. As changes start in nature, they provoke related changes in the other (Dove, 2004). Religion being an integral component of tribal culture faced changes as the nature turned to be changed with the invasion of capitalist economy into their habitat and livelihood practice. Under this perspective of irresistible conflict between the modernity and primitive, animistic tribal religion gradually faced replacement and thus the door for the modern world religion got opened in the areas of tribal dominance.

Thus, the scenario of religion in this border region has witnessed a sea change from colonial period onwards. The concept—"the human race and nature are interdependent"—greatly changed with the coming of Christianity and modern development. Christian missionaries considered the beliefs and practices of the people as superstitious and meaningless. As a result, as time passes, people gave up their belief evolved in association with the spirit of forests, trees, animals, rocks, rivers etc. They surrendered their close attachment to nature. They now look at nature as profitable resources for manipulation and exploitation as they cultivate new land, cut big trees, clear jungles, encroaches forest land and hammer big rocks (Wezah and Casino, 2011). Enriched with ecological ethics, Hinduism particularly spread among the tribes of the plain region, while Christianity embraces the areas of hill tribes more especially among the Naga tribes. Areas of indigenous Muslims and immigrant Muslims are the core areas of Muslim dominance, while Buddhism is confined to the communities like Tai Khamayang, Tai Turung and Tai Shyam. Religion-wise break-up of population is shown in table 2.9.

The change in the religious structure is quite illative from table 2.9 as it reveals the dominance of the modern world religion in a region of primitive tribes. Against 10,93,198 Hindu and 3,98,914 Christian population there exist 5,46,096 persons practicing traditional tribal religion and most of them are scattered in the plain part of the region.

In the hills, particularly in Nagaland, except for a few scattered and isolated remote pockets of settlement, the entire population has adopted Christianity after the whole territory was brought under British occupation. The colonial power subjugated the Nagas, the ecosystem people, by their mightier fire weapon after a long battle and the activities of Christian missionaries started thereafter to subdue the Nagas by modern world religion. It totally changed the ideas, views, beliefs and tradition of the Naga tribes. The catastrophe to the nature and to the forest of the region as well as to their mode of living came down after their conversion into Christianity.

Table 2.9: Religious composition of population in the Assam-Nagaland Border Region, 2001

Religion	*Plain Areas*		*Hill Areas*	
	Total population	*% of total*	*Total population*	*% of Total*
Hindu	10,93,198	49.41	8,847	1.04
Christian	3,98,914	18.03	8,18,482	96.21
Muslim	78,543	3.55	5,274	0.62
Buddhist	36,285	1.64	—	—
Tribal	5,46,096	24.68	—	—
Others	59,516	2.69	18,121	2.13

Source: Partly compiled and partly projected from Census of India, Assam and Nagaland Series (Village Directory), 2001.

On the other hand, Hinduism, however takes hold all well from ecological point of view as it believes that tree, snake, other animals, rocks, rivers, and lakes etc. as supernatural features and therefore these should be worshipped. Similarly Buddhism also has few such belief systems which are effective to uphold the ecology with all their living beings. These types of beliefs in Hinduism perhaps have been positively working among the plain tribes to keep the traditional tribal religion active. Some Muslims villages are there from the period of Ahom kings who were settled as war captive. But, lately after 1980's, immigrant Muslim settlers rushed into the area in a substantial number and they have primarily selected areas of dispute between the Governments of Assam and Nagaland for settlement. In 1985, Nagaland and Assam decided to maintain a *status quo* on border line after the Merapani masscre by Naga underground outfit. However, an increasing number of Bengali speaking Muslim and Nepali settlers have settled in the area. Since these settlers occupy the buffer zone in the foothills, the situation often becomes volatile (Kikon, 2008). The religious structure in this border region has been changing fast with the increasing intervention of modern world religions like Christianity, Islam, and Hinduism etc.

2.1.10 House Type

An areas dominated by ethnic groups usually expose traditional attitudes representing their response to ecological, economic and cultural factors. The traditional dwelling is not simply an isolated element within the existing culture but is an integral component of a system which normally bears immense importance from ecological point of view. The dwellings thus appear as a major ingredient of ethnographic and ecological study. A house or a dwelling in the traditional society is manifestation of the intimate relation between man and his immediate environment. A house, in true sense, is an important ingredient of a society that presents the changing nature of interaction between human and environment in an area. At the same time, it also tells the story of man's struggle for shelter through time and space.

Enriched by ethnic diversity, the Assam-Nagaland Border region harbours three distinct types of traditional dwellings representing three major ethnic groups, namely Naga, Karbi and the Assamese. In presence of intra ethnic diversity, this generalization is somewhat an abrupt coincidence but in a wider sense this categorization on the basis of some characteristics such as outdoor decoration, structural configuration and use of the dwellings stands to exhibit the commonness and thus provide the base of the generalization.

The traditional houses of Nagas are of primitive archetype characterized by rectangular courtyard, slanting roof and a decorated frontier. The materials used are chiefly collected from the immediate environment. Thatch, asoka leaves (takau pat), bamboo and ground ports of wood are the chief building materials. It is, however, seen that among the various tribal groups a marked difference is there in decorating their houses. The traditional Naga house normally measures about 25 feet long and 14 to 20 feet width with a platform at the back, a small room towards the front at ground level, a big room on pile and also a sitting out platform at the back. The big room is used as the main functional serving as all purposes of the family. Cooking to sleeping and associated house works are performed in this room. The floor of the room is designed by interlaced split bamboos supported on piles. In one side of the room the hearth of heated earth is kept to provide cooking facilities and warming. The sitting out platform is used for washing and bathing purposes along with the provision of relaxation to get relive and pounding the paddy crops. The room at the front is used for keeping domestic animals, firewood, the rice pounding table and other accessories of their day to day life. On the other hand, Angami Nagas construct a separate porch attached to the front of the house to use for the same purposes.

Ashoka (*takau*) leaves and thatch for roofing are collected from nearby forest areas. To make the roof weather resistant thatch or ashoka leaves are firmly attached in the roof using cane or bamboo threads. The front of an indigenous Naga house is systemically decorated with animal horns, skulls and beaks of game. The decoration of the front, however, is more in vogue among the tribal groups like Ao, Lotha, Angami etc. and of course, variations are there depending upon the social status of the family chief. Rich people with high social status and the village head (*Gaonbuhra*) construct their houses normally bigger in size than those of common people. The traditional practice of decorating or adorning the front of the house with those games has thus social implications which, in turn contribute to the general social ethos of the people (Lannusosang, 1987). It is observed that with the chronic deterioration of the forest resources in Nagaland, changes are there in house type and the housing materials used. People of different tribes have already put preferences for alternative building materials like C.I. sheet, asbestos, bricks, cement, sand, gravel etc. and partly wood and bamboos.

The Karbis are the second largest hill tribes living at the southern part of Assam-Nagaland Border. The house type of the Karbis can basically be grouped into two on the basis of the archetype of the house. These are: (i) traditional type and (ii) common rural Assam type. In between these two, another type of house is seen here and there in the district which is built with some modification of the traditional type. Another spectacular change in housing materials is observed that thatch, gradually being replaced by C.I. sheets which indicate the decreasing supply of local natural resources and the growing ecological disorder. Significantly, most of the people expressed that from climatic point of view C.I. sheets in no way can be a compatible alternative to the thatch which we enjoyed till few years back.

Traditional Type

The most common building materials of a traditional Karbi house are thatch and bamboo. The house is built on bamboo posts and the floor of the house is raised on a platform usually varying in length from 5 to 7 feet as per the need and the quality of their surroundings. The floor and the fences of the house are made of flattened out bamboo splits and the roof is knitted with thatch. The roof normally has four parts, two are placed lengthwise and other two placed at the back and the front of the house.

The house is divided lengthwise by a partition called *Arpons*. The part of the right side is called *Kam* and the left side is called *Kut*. All the family members stay in the *Kut* while servants, guests etc. stay in the *arpons*. A narrow chamber attached to the *Kut* on the outside of the wall called *Vo-roi* is constructed to provide shelter to goats and poultry. Attached to the *Vo-roi* and *Kut* is the fire place and between the *Vo-roi* and fire place provision is made to keep husked rice which is known as *Sangrangtik*. Pig-site is usually common everywhere and is kept under the platform which in Karbi dialect is known as *Phak-voi*. Families having permanent and wet cultivation rear bulls and these are also kept below the platform in a separate enclosure.

It, however, appears that during the last few decades the house type has been changing at a faster rate and apparently it is due to the fast disappearing housing materials from the forest. At present, nearly 60 to 65 per cent houses are of modified type. The causes of change in house type can be summarised as:

(i) The construction of traditional house is complicated and it needs a large amount of bamboos and woods which are now costly and not available as per requirements.
(ii) With the disappearance of forest cover the housing materials have become locally scarce to meet the growing demands.
(iii) Change in the mode of living from shifting to permanent and shifting of sites from hills to plains or foothills, more precisely from forest to the open areas, have rendered the platform houses increasingly clumsy and avoidable.

Common Assam Type House

The common Assam type house is a house of thatched roof with mud-mixed-cow dung plastered wall. Two long sheets of roof placed on bamboo or wooden post giving the house top a triangle shape. The house is partitioned into several rooms in order to provide various functions like cooking, sleeping, storage, resting etc. All the rooms have doors and windows for easy access of light and air. A *verandah* at the front facing the courtyard usually is built for various household works as sitting place for both family members and visitors. In some family, cook shed are constructed under separate roof attached to the main house. Again, well-to-do families construct the same type of house using costly materials instead of thatch, bamboo and wood. A new trend is seen gaining ground where the house is totally built on reinforced concrete. A common Assam type house is most popular among the Karbis living in the plain areas of the district.

The third and the big contingent of the population comprised mostly of numerous small racial groups belong to Assamese community live in the plain districts of the Brahmaputra valley namely Sibsagar, Jorhat and Golaghat. The dwelling houses in this part of Assam-Nagaland Border range from thatched cottage to reinforced concrete type. The main types are: (i) thatched house (*kutcha* house), (ii) semi-*pucca* Assam type, (iii) *pucca* Assam type, and (iv) reinforced concrete type (Table 2.10). The thatched houses are traditional Assamese dwelling which are well designed to match up the prevailing climatic conditions. Protection from rain and sun is important consideration in the construction of the houses. For free run over of rain water the roofs are made slanting approximately by 40-60 degree. The dry thatches work as a strong sun screen to protect from excessive heat particularly during the summer days. *Verandahs* are added at both front and back of the house for works and resting place for the family members and guests. who comes to visit. On the other hand, these *verandahs* keep the house cool by obstructing sun shine. The arche types of the houses are rectangular made of thatch and bamboo and in cases made of wood. The walls are made of crushed bamboo splits and reeds and plastered with a mixture of mud and cow dung.

The cowshed and granaries are constructed separately keeping a considerable distance from the main house. The place for cowshed and the granary is usually at the side of the courtyard subject to the availability of space, otherwise these are transferred to the back of the main house.

The Assam type buildings are primarily the results of the initiatives taken by the British with some elements of European architectural design. These houses were designed so as to suit the local environmental condition by tuning a little change in the setting of the roofs. The rural areas of the

Table 2.10: House types by dominant roof materials, 1980

Sample Village	*Assam Type Thatch/Bamboo Cottage*		*Assam Type Building GI/asbestos/Metal Sheet Roof*	
	Number of Household	*% of Total*	*Number of Household*	*% of Total*
Aochendung	58	93.55	4	6.45
Akatitto	46	97.87	1	2.13
Than Pathar	179	90.86	18	9.14
Nagaadi	109	94.78	6	5.22
Golakpar	145	94.77	8	5.23
Gamariguri	102	90.27	11	9.73
Betbari	87	89.69	10	10.31

Source: Gaonburah or Village Head of the Respective Villages and Sample Survey, 2011.

region is mostly characterised by Assam type houses of varying size and style. The housing scenario of the rural Assam is fast changing where the ratio between Assam type thatched cottage and Assam type building has been increasing almost by three times within a span of just ten years. Data collected from the sample villages indicate that the ratio has changed from 1:20 to 1:6 during the period 1980-2011 (Figs. 2.1, 2.2). However, multi-storied building (maximum two storied) has emerged here and there within the rural landscape of the area, but in number these are quite insignificant (Table 2.13).

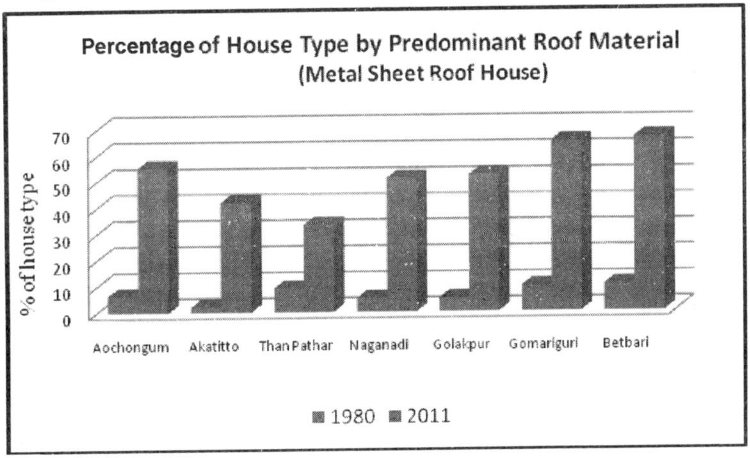

Fig. 2.1: Percentage of House Type by Predominant Roof Material (Metal Sheet Roof House)

Table 2.11: Number and percentage of house type by dominant roof materials, 2011

Sample village	Assam type thatch/ bamboo cottage		Assam type building GI/ asbestos/ metal sheet roof	
	Number of House-hold	% of total	Number of House-hold	% of total
Aochendung	32	44.44	40	55.56
Akatitto	40	57.97	29	42.03
Than Pathar	160	66.67	80	33.33
Nagaadi	97	48.99	101	51.10
Golakpur	109	47.60	120	52.40
Gamariguri	70	34.83	131	65.17
Betbari	35	33.33	70	66.67

Source: Personal Survey, 2011.

An analysis of the house type of the region would provide an interesting instance of human response to the physical environment. A house is an element of cultural landscape which expresses the physical condition of the region and cultural heritage of the people. The type of roofs, the walls, frames etc. show a remarkable adjustment of man to nature (Bhattacharya, 2010). The second important aspect which is exclusively conspicuous is the people's dependency on the immediate environment. As the dwelling houses are considered as the vital basic needs of man, any change in it is in fact a genuine product of the ecological changes.

Table 2.12: Houses by dominant roof material, 2011

District	Total No. of household	Thatch/grass/ bamboo cottage	GI/asbestos/ metal sheets	R.C. concrete	Others
Sibsagar	97,500	18,037	72,638	4,602	2,223
Jorhat	50,252	10,568	35,619	2,145	1,920
Golaghat	63,558	13,023	48,774	877	883
Karbi Anglong	9,957	3,790	5,825	126	216
Dimapur	67,272	12,525	51,570	1,950	1,227
Wokha	2,939	1,249	1,446	112	122
Mokokchung	8,647	2,105	5,542	320	680
Mon	9,331	3,245	5,801	140	145

Source: Census of India, 2011.

In 2011 there were 3,09,456 households in the region and of these 2,39,176 were rural and 70,280 urban. The houses of each family are used for different purposes. Tribal people, in general, construct one or two houses with the provision of their bare necessities of space to perform various household functions. On the other hand, the hill tribes usually possess a single house, with provisions for conducting their day to day household works. A family having a higher income and with joint family system builds more than two or three houses to make room for all the family members and all their household works.

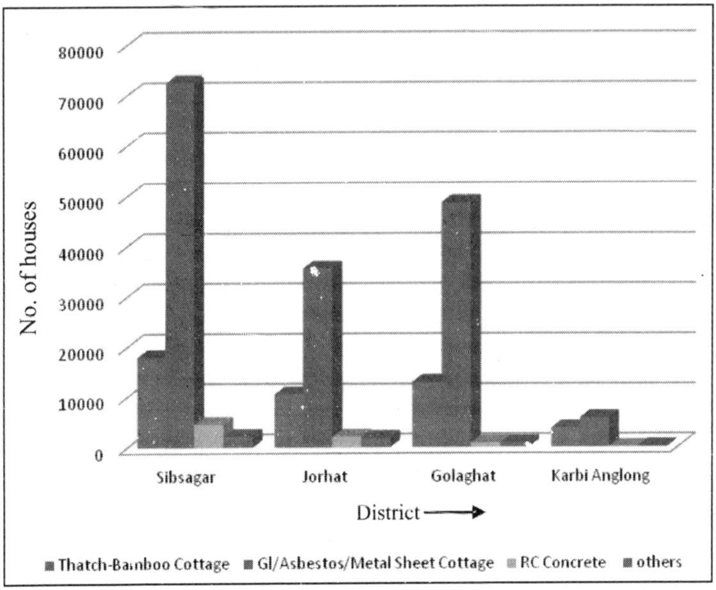

Source: Personal Survey, 2011.

Fig. 2.2: Present Status of House type in the Assam-Nagaland Border Region, 2011

2.1.11 *Food Habit and Diet*

It is quite illative that the tribes living in the forest and forest fringe areas are largely dependent on so far nature as food habit and diets are concerned. Characteristically the tribal society is habituated in food gathering practices since time immemorial. It is a common practice everywhere among the tribal groups.

It is seen that all the tribal communities except those depending primarily on institutional pursuits have a land based strategy of livelihood. A large number of tribal communities having settled or shifting agriculture draw their secondary, tertiary or even lower level economic support from 'food gathering' (Saksena, 2006). Except staple food which they produce from settled or shifting agriculture, they mostly depend on the forest for other dietary items such as vegetable, fish, meat, medicine and so on.

The symbiotic relationship in the forested Assam-Nagaland Border was acknowledged until the enactment of forest policy by the British after 1826. The mutual relation between people and forest was well maintained through traditional practices as there had been limited alternatives of living means. Timber yielding trees and trees used for paper pulp came under the category of major forest produce. The British government had put a ban on felling of those trees which came under major forests produce. However, they themselves were interested in cutting the trees for their own purposes like building ships, furniture, construction of buildings and pulps and papers. They left the tribes for collection of roots, leaves, flowers, honey, wax etc. which they considered as produce with no value. They used the term MFP, i.e. minor forest products. The British rarely collected the MFP but these forest products were of great value for the tribes since time immemorial. Tribals have enjoyed the right of collection of MFP by tradition. This tradition also indicates the symbiotic relationship since prehistoric times (Srivastava, 2006). In *Tribal Demography in India*, among various characteristics of tribal, the notable one concerning the food habit is noted as—"they follow primitive occupations such as hunting, gleaning etc. and are largely carnivores or flash or meat eaters". Meat, of course is an important dietary item of the tribes living the Assam-Nagaland Border. Moreover, there had been a substantial change in the food habit caused by changing socio-economic situations.

Rice, for the entire region, is the staple food and is produced either by shifting or settled cultivation. Naga and Karbi people in general depend on maize and millet at the time of scarcity of rice. Meat constitutes an important ingredient of the dietary staff of the tribal group of the region. Choices of meat, varies from tribe-to-tribes. Nagas in general relish pork most, while the plain tribes, such as Sonowal Kachari, Thengal, Khamti, Miching etc. prefer both pork and chicken equally. But, beef which includes meat of Cow, Buffalo and Methun etc. is by far the most common meat for Nagas as it is cheaper and easily available. Other tribal groups of the region out right repudiate beef since they are not accustomed and have religious restriction. To be frank, tribal groups belonging to Hinduism usually rescind meat of cow as they worship it as a totem of God. Nagas do take meat of elephant, bear, dog, tiger etc. and no birds are left in their dietary items. Fish is regularly relished but due to paucity of supply particularly in the hill areas, fish remains secondary in their menu. But as far as the plain tribes are concerned, fish is very much common and they take fish almost regularly. Fishes are caught in the rivers, beels, ponds and even in the agricultural fields during rainy months and plenty of these are kept dried for consumption in the off season. Next to fish, the aquatic animals which the Nagas are particularly fond of are snails, crabs, and some insects.

It appears that there is a spectacular difference in the food habit between the hill and the plain tribes. Plain tribes normally include plenty of vegetables in their daily dish along with fish, while the hill tribes prefer meat and use little vegetables. The vegetables, which they often use, are mostly tree leaves, roots and fruits. On the contrary, plain tribes and the Karbis have vegetable gardens where they produce, cabbage, brinjal, guard, carrot, radish, ladies finger etc. Besides, they are also traditionally fond of some items found in the jungle in abundance. They are not accustomed with any kind of spicy preparation, instead, the spice which they normally use are all pure jungle products. Imported spices are seldom used by the tribal people of this region.

Being mostly rural, the people irrespective of hills or plain usually take food three times a day. Morning meal is taken before leaving for field. In some families of the hill areas of course, the older members take tiffin (*Jalpan*) instead of heavy food and the youngers only take morning food. Midday meal is taken returning from their work place. During the peak period of cultivation, people working in the field take midday meal in the field. The evening meal is taken after returning from their field, but the time varies from place to place and from tribe-to-tribe. The hill tribes normally complete their evening meal immediately after Sun set while the people of the plain complete it around 9-10 pm. Although tea is a common drink, but all the tribes have their home made traditional drinks. The preparation of the drinks is almost similar but differs in quality and taste. The drinks of different tribes are known differently as *Apang* or *Chai Mod* among the Mishings, *Harlong* among the Karbis and *Jumai* among the Bodos.

2.1.12 Traditional Practices

In a lexical sense, the forest ecology focusing on the relationship between the distribution of human groups with reference to material resources and consequent social and cultural patterns is perhaps more relevant to the traditional practices of the forest tribes. This view point is good enough to succeed in shifting the attention from the much talked about anthropocentrism to the man-nature interdependency. It takes into account ecological infrastructure viz—soil, water, animal, mineral and vegetable bases of society which play a crucial role in deciding the socio-cultural patterns (Sen, 2002). Tribals and forests have been interdependent and interrelated. They have developed their culture and style of life well matched to the forest type since forests have been fulfiling their various needs from time immemorial. The forest has maintained the very existence of the tribals since centuries (Verma, 2002).

The forest, in a rigid sense, is an indispensable part of tribal society which inspires them to believe that the spirit of their ancestral generation has been residing with them in and around the forest. They establish supernatural entities on the bushes, trees, animals, birds and sacred groves and perform worship regularly. Traditionally, these practices are passed over from generation to generation transferring their ancestral knowledge base to the upcoming generation. Such age old practices and belief have immense bearing in solving bearing in solving problems faced by the present-day society. Movement for the revival of tribalism, emerging socio-economic unrests in the tribal societies, movement for liberation and many more sensitive issues need a threadbare analysis. The tribes have suffered from economic devastation due to ecological changes brought about by development measures in the tribal areas making their survival extremely difficult despite their efforts at adaptation under changing circumstances. Ecological degradation of tribal value system and life is seriously affecting their self-respect and blurring their identity. (Singh, 2006). Being a bridge of coexistence between the forests and the tribes, the traditional practices are their heart and soul for survival in the forest ecology. At the same time, it has other broader implications while talking about sustainable practices in the context of fast deteriorating global environmental scenario.

Table 2.13: Medicinal plants associated with traditional practice in Assam-Nagaland Border Region

Local name or trade name	*Botanical name*	*Uses*
Mishmi Teeta	*Coptis vasica*	Debility tonic, stomach disorder
Bahakteeta	*Adhatoda vasica*	Cough and cold
Kordoi	*Averrhoa corambola*	Vegetable, anti-jaundice anti scorbutic and spot remover
Chatiana	*Alstonia scholaris*	Antidote to fertility in woman, cure fever, asthma, and leprosy
Ganja (Bhang)	*Canabis sativa*	Holy offering to lord Siva, Narcotic, cure loose motion of cow, goat etc.
Karbir	*Thavetia peruvitana*	Seeds powder used to ail scars.
Matikathal	*Anana scomosus*	Liver disorder, vomiting, worm infestation
Hilikha	*Terminalia citrina*	Holy fruits, traditional ink, digestion, stomach disorder, diabetic
Bihpatal	*Trichosant hesdioica*	Fever, lowering body temperature
Siju	*Manihote sculanta*	Worshipped as a symbol of God by the Bodos, used to cure cough and tuberculosis.
Pate Gaja	*Bryophylhum pinnatum*	To cure jaundice, diabetes and urinary problem.
Bhomora	*Terminalia belerica*	use for stomach problem and asthma
Arjun	*Terminali aarjuna*	Anti hypertension and anti-jaundice
Bhotera	*Jatropha gossipifolia*	Cure tooth decay and the pain
Chirata	*Sweatia chirata*	As tonic for stomach ache, worm and laxative
Bah gaj (bamboo shoots)	*Bambusa bambos*	As vegetable, protin supplement, prevent tape worm
Dubori	*Cynodon dactylon*	Antiseptic, cure skin ulcer and cut.
Ghila	*Entadas candens*	Hair nutrient and hair wash

(Contd.)

Local name or trade name	*Botanical name*	*Uses*
Amlokhi	*Phyllanthus embica*	Stomach trouble, hair tonic, curing jaundice, dispesia and cough
Tulashi	*Ocinumora tissimum*	To worship, to cure cold and cough, as antiseptic
Lochan	*Mallotus philipinesis*	To cure round worm and used as purgative
Sonaru	*Cassia fistula*	To cure tongue ulcer of babies and act as purgative
Challkuawri	*Agave veracruz*	For burnt injury
Jetuka	*Lasoniain nermis*	Prevent snake bite, hair tonic and decorative item and nail disease
Raktajaba	*Hibiscus chinensis*	To stop bleeding during menstrual cycle or after delivery.
Dimoru	*Ficus nemolis*	Antidote to diabetes, to cure swollen neck of cow
Mahaneem	*Azadira chtaindica*	Antidote to round worm, to cure chicken pox, skin ailment, as pesticide, anti-diabetic
Punnarnava	*Boerha aviarepens*	To cure anemia and edema.
Kolijamu	*Eugenia cumini*	Curing liver, sore throat, diabetes and jaundice.
Bhebelilata	*Paederia foetida*	Good for ailing stomach, anemia used as vegetable
Bih Dhekia	*Dryopteris dentata*	Used in enchanting mantras to cure pain and against evil spirit
Doron ban	*Leucuslavendula efolia*	Used as anti-worm, stomach tonic and anti-sinusitis drug
Manichal	*Pygmaepremna herbacea*	Used as hair tonic and pesticide
Tengechi	*Oxalis conniculata*	Dietary item; good in caring diarrhea and dysentery.
Manimuni	*Hydrocotylerotun difolia*	Good for ailing stomach and nutrient supplement
Nefafu	*Clerodaendron colebrookianum*	As vegetable, as anti-hypertension and anti-diabetic

(*Contd.*)

Local name or trade name	Botanical name	Uses
Rajghanta	*Datura candida*	Used for urinary problem and to prevent bleeding
Sagunilata	*Tinospora crista*	Used to cure pain, bronchitis, Gonorrhea, syphilis, jaundice and skin disease.
Satmul	*Asparagus racemosus*	Oil used to cure rheumatic and intestinal pain. Juice with honey cures indigestion, gastric and also used to cure problems of mothers' milk.
Sukoloti	*Pogostemon benghalensis*	Stomach problem and after delivery problem of woman
Shymalata	*Ichnocarpus frutescens*	To cure diabetic and gall bladder stone
Sarpajiva	*Oldenlandi acorymbosa*	To cure chronic fever, gastric, jaundice, worm and nuro problem.
Siddhilata	*Tinospora cordifolia*	Urinary problem, malaria, chronic fever and gonorrhea is cured
Orkamul	*Aristolochia indica*	Used to cure fever, stomach trouble, insect bite etc.
Bhimkol or Athiyakol	*Musa sapientumvav. Musa balbisiana colla*	Used to cure stomach problem, to prepare local drinks and spice.
Cow	*Bos indicus*	Urine used to cure ailing eye, cow dung for purification of house, and as anti-irritant. Ghee, a byproduct of milk used as health supplement, as a preventive to hydrophobia, as massaging ointment to cure pain and lighten earthen lamp.
Dolphin (Sihu) River Dolphin	*Platanista gangetica*	Dolphin oil used to cure pain, pulp of dolphin conch used to prevent drowsiness of pregnant women.
Sparrow House sparrow	*Passer domesticus*	Used to revitalise sexual potency and to prompt up youth fullness.
Human hair	*Homo sapiens*	Used as antiseptic in cut injury
Bat (Indian flying fox)	*Pteropus giganteus*	Meat used to cure asthma

(Contd.)

Local name or trade name	*Botanical name*	*Uses*
Egg Domestic Chicken Domestic Duck	*Gallus domesticus* *Anaspla tyrhyncha*	Yolk is used to cure unconsciousness caused due to falling from height.
Earthworm	*Lumbricina spp.* *Monili gastrida*	Earthworm soil (kechumata) applied around the naval of child to prevent round worm, infestation and stomach ache.
Cockroach	*Periplaneta americana*	Head of cockroach mixed with specific herbs used to cure dog bite.
Fire fly	*Photuris spp.*	Gives with banana to cure night blindness.
Tiger (Bengal Tiger)	*Panthera tigris*	Meat and milk eat as to make once bold and courageous. Vegetal part of female is given to pregnant woman to prevent drowsiness.

Source: Mazumder and Medhi, 1993.

3

Outline of the Forest Cover and Deforestation

3.1 Extent of Forest Cover

Forests and wildlife are essential ingredients for a balanced ecosystem in an area. As such, forests are regarded as inseparable component of environment as well as economy. Being an important renewable resource, forests have been playing diversified role since time immemorial. With a congenial environment for the growth of diverse plants and animals the Assam-Nagaland Border region in particular and the entire North East India in general represent as one of the very rich forested areas of the country. The history of peopling in the area also indicates its richness in forest cover. Arrangement of settlements during that period had close association with the forests. Forestlands were primarily inhabited by hunter-gatherers and food gatherers while the agriculturist used to live adjacent to but with striking distance from forests, and the urban settlements were located away from the forests (Gadgil and Guha, 1992). W. Shakespeare (1929), a British official, forwarded a lively description on the nature of forest cover in Assam. He wrote—"From the Brahmaputra for 20 or 30 miles when the border is reached, the level country is covered with the thick jungle everywhere and much intersected streams. Near to and beyond the border the forest occurs, enormous trees with dense undergrowth flourishing up to 8000 feet." All the British officers and travellers, who visited this area during the colonial rule, overwhelmingly appreciated the natural beauty and grandeur of the area. British officials like Allen (1905), McCosh (1834), Butler (1841), Hunter (1869) and Mills (1848) mentioned about the unique forest cover that the area manifested all throughout.

It is quite illuminating that the writings of ancient scholars of Assam present memorable romantic portrait of the serene beauty of green forest of the Brahmaputra and the adjacent green hills of the region. Narrations on the nature's blog are found in the writings from *Yoginitantra* to the writings of great *Vaisnavite* scholar Srimanta Sankardeva. Folk tales as well as the folk songs and dances of the region have a reflections of their native forest environment.

Global ecology has significantly been altered by western capitalism, first through trade and later by colonialism. The inherent philosophical spirit of the colonialist is well reflected in the thinking of Marx and Engel (1975). Under capitalism, justice and equality for every person could never be achieved because of the structural constraints built into capital's need to expand its sphere continually, by using nature and human as resources (Horkeimer, *et al.*, 1972). The disenchantment of external nature was achieved by despiritualising a human being's internal nature.

East India Company, a merchandised concern, turned into colonial ruler grabbing the kingdoms one after another. Policies were framed accordingly to persue their motives of property generation. Thus, the congregation of three 'P'-power, policy and property (Fig. 3.1) with a strong back up from capitalist economy and imperialist power devised

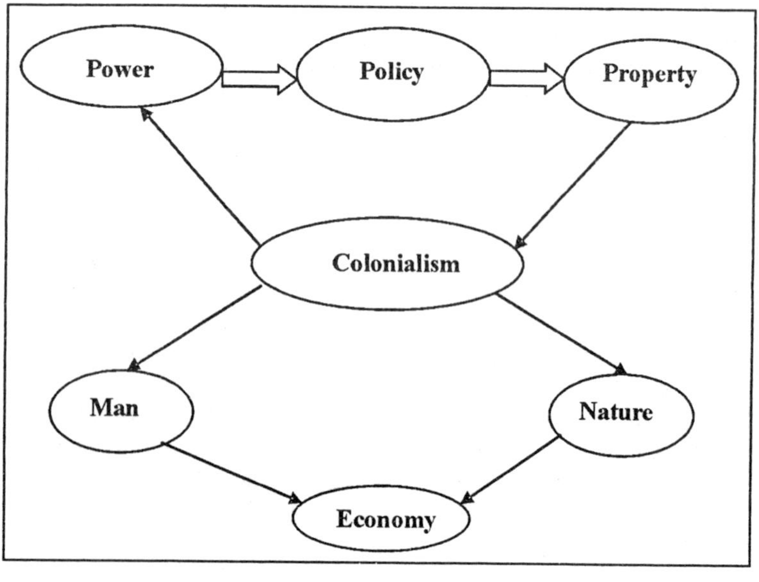

Source: Based on K. Marx's concept on colonialism, 1975.

Fig. 3.1: The Three 'P' Model of Colonialism

the tactical strategy to keep their grip over both man and nature to build a strong colonial economy (Marx, 1975).

During the peak period of colonialism from 1850 to 1945 the entire world had all the bitterness of witnessing the wanton destruction of forest particularly thrusted upon by the world wars. Marked political instability and disrupted economy played a key role in areas of high activity. The adverse effects of political instability continued until the nineteenth and twentieth centuries. In the upheaval that followed the Greek war of Independence in 1821, for example, many forest areas that had previously been protected by their inaccessibility were now destroyed or degraded. In North Africa, the arrival of French Colonialists led to the partial displacement of the native population of the hills, bringing new demands for fuelwood and new intensities of grazing in the forests. Loss of traditional grazing grounds in the plains gave rise to bitterness expressed in the deliberate burning of low land forests (Chauhan, 2007). It happened invariably in the areas of the world where the grip of colonial rule was consolidated to serve their motives of exploitation.

It is noteworthy that the virgin forest of Assam started to have a process of reshaping from the onset of colonial hegemony in 1826. The encounter of the forested landscape of Assam with the imperial rule can be traced back to the period when the East India Company gradually became interested in this region. Once the company administration was secured, the possibilities of integrating the existing complex range of forest-based trade practices with the imperial economy became clear (Borpujari, 1963). And, therefore, the extent of forest cover needs a search from historical perspectives since the core concept of the nature of forest cover lies in a sequential form of change in a significant way from the British period onwards. Map produced on the basis of the description given by Wilhelm Schlich to illustrate the nature of forest cover (Map 3.1) discourses comprehensively the extent of distribution during the period of 1870s. Nowhere except the Brahmaputra floodplain agriculture was practiced intensively. Such a perception is portrayed in the descriptions of W. Schlich.

As per the description of Wilhelm, the entire Assam-Nagaland Border region was covered by dense forest of lofty trees having a thick cover of herbs, creepers, grasses etc. at the bottom. This is quite illative particularly in a forest characterized by virginity all along, as reflected in the historiography of the region. Footpaths are often obliterated by the inseparable jungle which in denseness can be matched by very few places in the world (Viswanath, 1957). Finally, when Assam went into the British

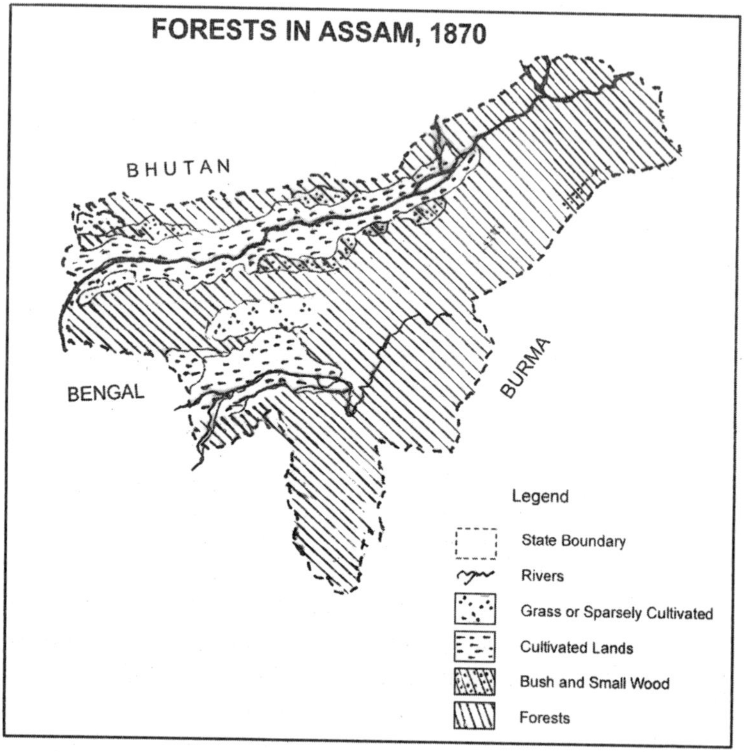

Map 3.1: Forests in Assam, 1870

Source: *Forest and Ecological History of Assam*, 1826-2000.
Map showing distribution of forest in Assam based on H. Schlich's description on Assam during 1870. *Courtesy*–Prasanta Bhattacharya.

imperial control as per the provisions of the Treaty of Yandaboo (February 24, 1826) the province with sparse population still had large forest areas (Ribbentrop, 1889). Indubitably, the assessment of Wilhelm Schilch on the forest cover is compatible and rational.

Joseph Dalton Hooker (1817-1911), a British botanist played a vital role in identifying the forest resources and their economic uses in the British occupied Assam. The survey conducted by Hooker made an estimation of the available tropical and semi-tropical forest of Assam and opened-up a new era for the British colonialist to invest in a rich sector of resources (David, 2002). The East India Company, within a decade of the annexation of Assam prepared a detailed report on the forest resources of the region. Accounts were published describing the mercantile importance of these forest resources (Saikia, 2011). Accumulating all the information and explanation available in the then reports namely "A Note of Inspection on Some Forest of Assam" (Bryant, 1912), Annual Progress Report of Forest Administration of Assam etc., the area of reserved forest was estimated to be 3, 258 sq. km., 3275 sq. km, 4004, 5 sq. km., 546 sq. km. and 5477 sq. km. respectively in 1892, 1902, 1912, 1932 and 1950. The successive increase in the area of the reserved forests was not because of afforestation conducted by colonial government rather it was due to the inclusion of newer and newer unexplored areas into the reserved category. As such, the district Sibsagar shows a very fluctuating figure of reserved forest area. Table 3.1 shows the reserved forest area from 1892 to 1950 in Assam which can be used to assess the actual forest cover as a whole in the state. A gradual rise in the total area under reserved forest is well marked. Against a total area of 4.004 sq. mile under reserved forest, the un-classed open forest in 1910 stood at 15531 sq. mile and the percentage to the total area of the state was 58.44. This account was for only the British occupied territory excluding the unexplored parts. The old Sivsagar district was constituted by three sub-divisions namely Sibsagar, Jorhat, Golaghat and a large part of Karbi plateau lying along the Naga Hills. In fact, the then old Sibsagar district occupied the whole of Assam-Nagaland Border. During the period 1910-11, the total unclassed open state forests was 2889 sq. mile and the area under reserved forest was 1043 sq. mile in the district. Out of the district's total area of 4995 sq. mile, 3882 sq. mile was under forest cover accounting for 77.72 per cent of the total area.

Table 3.1: Area of reserved forest in Assam and Sibsagar (1892-1950)

(Area in sq. km.)

Year	Assam	Sibsagar	% Area of the District
1892	3258	847	16.95
1902	3275	939	18.80
1912	4004	1003	20.88
1932	5546	660	13.21
1950	5497	752	15.06

Source: Compiled from Annual Progress Report of Forest of Assam (area of Sibsagar—4995 sq. km).

The Nagaland part of the border area could never be appreciated for human settlement prior to the country's independence. Except Dimapur

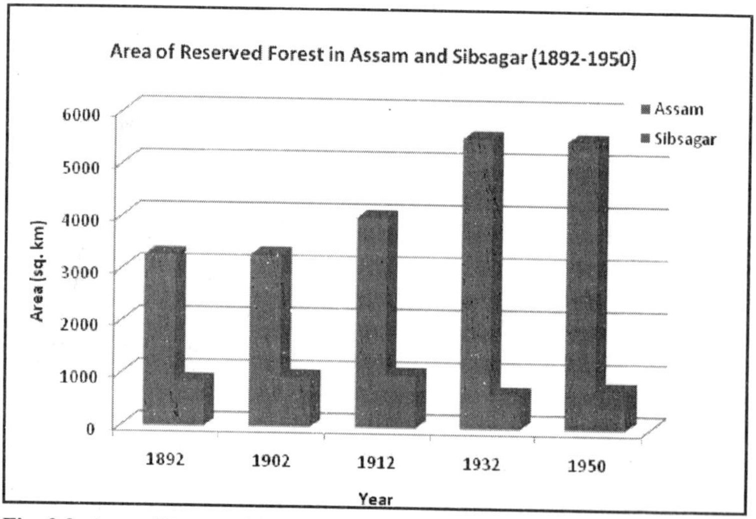

Fig. 3.2: Area of Reserved Forest in Assam and Sibsagar (1892-1950)

plain nowhere along the border region had a sizeable population to have any impact upon the dense forest cover. Travelling through the Rengma hill of Assam-Nagaland Border Butler (1855) described—"The whole route was through a dark, damp, chilly, gloomy forest with small undulating hills, and neither the sky nor sun was seen throughout the day. Our road was a mere footpath and the forest so thick that we could not see ten paces before us". He also mentioned about human habitation as—"not a vestige of any habitation or human being was seen between Mohung, Dehooa and Dhemapoor, a distance of 30 miles". The evidences thus available suggest that the border region was blanketed by dense forest as portrayed in Butler's travel accounts.

The nature of forest cover of the past leaves its imprint and the relics are reflected on the present pattern of forest cover. The number of wildlife sanctuaries and reserved forests along the Assam-Nagaland Border is somewhat a typical representation of the past pattern of forest cover. Moreover, the line of divide between Assam and Nagaland was seen as a *de-facto* no man's land zone till the seventies and was covered with impenetrable jungles. Of course, few scattered hamlets with few residents of Naga communities were there but with no significance. A near-authentic forest cover map can easily be derived on the basis of various historical writings and travelogues of western visitors. The map so prepared (Map 3.2 and Fig. 3.2) displays the nature of forest cover particularly of the period earlier to twentieth century.

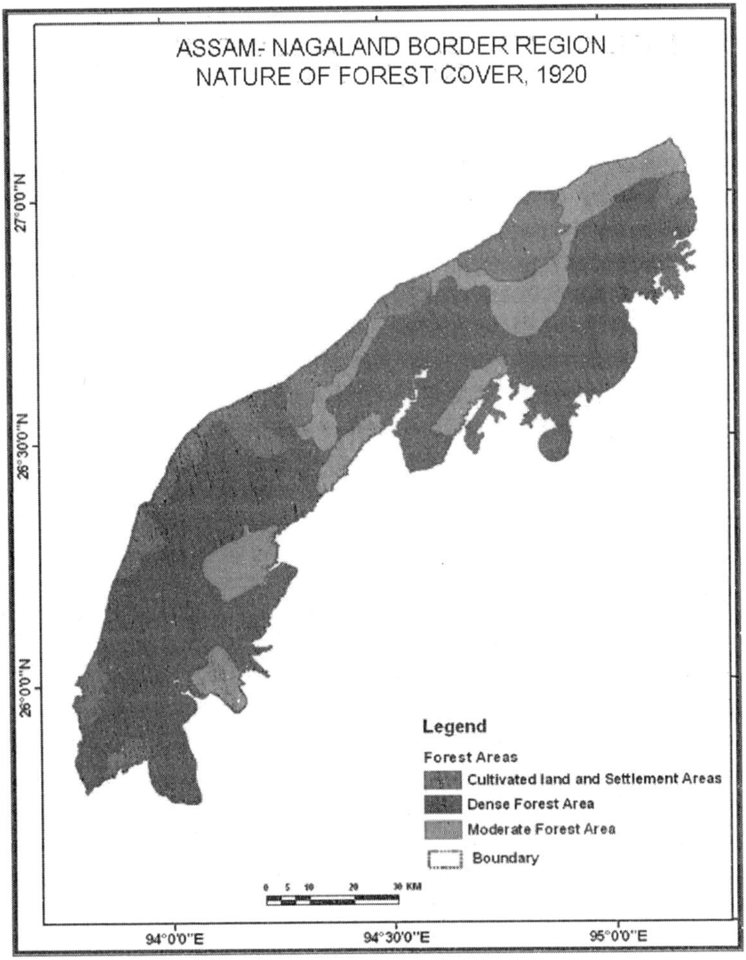

Map 3.2: Assam-Nagaland Border Region: Nature of Forest Cover, 1920

It is obvious that towards the upland part of the Naga hills forest density is found to decrease as human habitation increases towards the high altitude to avoid inter-racial conflicts. Moreover, the climate in the high altitude zone is distinctly different from the foothills and low hill zones. Even the present pattern of forest meaningfully reflects the past pattern in terms of distribution and density. The map prepared on the basis of the historical evidences is somewhat a rational presentation of the forest cover of the period prior to the enactment of British forest policy, 1887.

A conceptual frame on the distribution of forest can be derived incorporating variables like climate, topography, space etc. (Fig. 3.3) to elaborate the nature of forest cover which augments the scope of understanding the process of change with time and space. Considering all these variables, e.g. climate, altitude, space and human interference, three functional zones can be demarcated to specify the nature of forest cover in the Assam-Nagaland Border region: (i) focal zone, (ii) orbital zone and (iii) optical zone. The focal zone is the core forested area with no human interference extending from 105 to 200 meters contour supplemented by tropical monsoon climate. The orbital zone is practically working as a protective envelop of the focal zone with slight human interference and its presence is only felt towards the plain part of the region. The optical zone, on the contrary, is a zone of human intervention

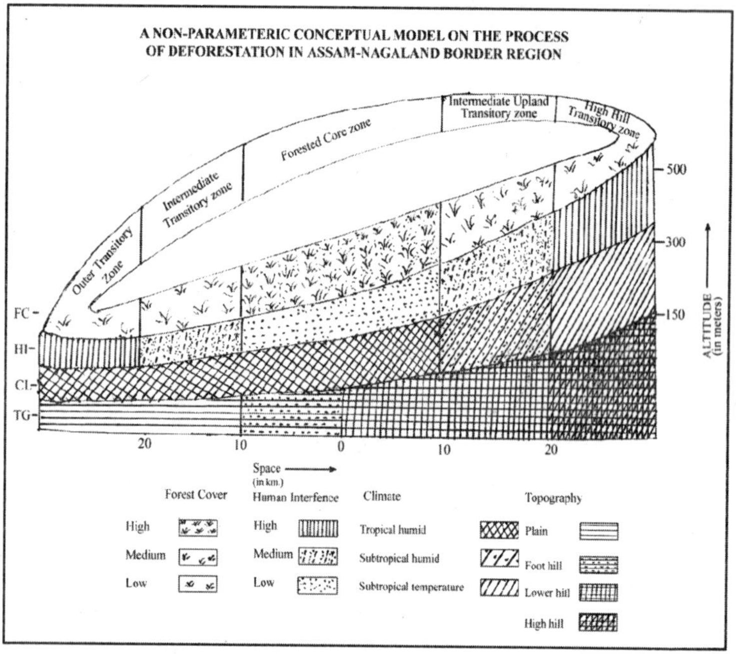

Fig. 3.3: A Non-Parameteric Conceptual Model on the Process of Deforestation in Assam-Nagaland Border Region

Source: Map showing distribution of forest in Assam-Nagaland border region based on the descriptions found in the travelogue of western scholars.

with a moderate type of forest cover. This zone is extensive and profound human activities dominate the forest cover of this zone.

The onset of colonialism was practically an act to emulate extensive tracts of virgin forest of Assam and in no way the colonial outlook on forest dispelled the troubles and sufferings of the ecological society of Assam and the neighbouring areas. The establishment of the Forest Department in Assam began in 1868 with the deputation of Gustav Mann, an assistant conservator of forest, to inspect the forests of Assam (Ribbentrop, 1900). It was the beginning of formal process to rule over the forest of Assam and which continued until the time of Independence with frequent revision and addition of forest laws. Largely following the administrative arrangement of the time, an unorganized supervisory mechanism continued to function until 1873 when Assam became an independent province. As territorial arrangement was carried out in 1874, the province was divided into two divisions—Lower Assam and Upper Assam—and its forested tracts became part of this arrangement. Thus, the forests in Kamrup and Goalpara became part of lower Assam division, while the forests of Lakhimpur, Sibsagar and Naga hills were included in the upper Assam division (Stebbing, 1926). The entire endeavour of the then Government was to establish a total control over the forest wealth of the state. This colonial hegemony over forest of the region gradually turned up to procure maximum benefit which, in fact, introduced a new era of forest depletion by means of deriving newer acts regulations in favour of the purpose. Although the management of forests in Assam started since the 1860s, a well-defined forest policy was promulgated only in 1894. Already the Indian Forest Acts 1865 and 1878 were in force, again another Act was passed in 1927 to make the colonial grip more formidable. These regulations, in fact, tried to legitimize the imperial exploitation of Assam's forest resources (Handique, 2004).

Under this umbrella of colonialism and their enhanced grip over the forest resources, the entire forest cover of North-East India started getting a new shape. In order to overwhelm the forest and forest resources, the Assam Forest Regulation VII of 1891 was approved by the Governor General in Council on 26th December, 1891. This regulation empowered the local Government to constitute any forest land at the disposal of Government a reserved land through public notification.

Thus, a series of acts and regulations were made to serve their interest of revenue collection from forest and the wastelands of the region. Following Indian Forest Act 1878, formation of reserved forest under Assam Forest Regulation, 1891, formation of village forest under section

27 of the Indian Forest Act, 1878; formation of protected forest areas under Assam Forest Regulation, 1891; revision on the formation of village forest in 1931-32 etc. propelled the colonial hegemony over forest of the region and turned up other land available outside those declared either as reserved forests or protected forests for other uses primarily for tea cultivation.

As per records, during the period 1879-1880 the extent of the reserved forests in Sibsagar district and Naga Hills was 857.33 km² (Table 3.2). Noticeably, the area of reserved forests as shown in the table was much lower than the today's reserved forest area since there had been areas left back unexplored due to inaccessibility and inhospitable conditions. Moreover, excluding the areas which had already been declared reserved or protected or village forest, these were areas covered by forest of either low density or degraded nature not taken into account of forested areas.

Table 3.2: Area under reserved forests in Assam-Nagaland Border Region, 1879-80

Name of the reserved forest	*District*	*Total area (sq.km.)*
Abhoypur	Sibsagar	24.15
Hahchorr	Sibsagar	2.42
Kakadonga	Sibsagar	48.30
Nambor	Naga Hills	626.29
Mikir Hills	Naga Hills	130.41
Daigrung	Naga Hills	25.76
Total	**06**	**857.33**

Source: D. Brandis, *Suggestions Regarding Forest Administration in Assam*, 1879.

Establishment of tea estates in large number all along the border districts at the cost of forest land resulted in large scale reduction in forest cover. Following the spirit of imperial wisdom later the remnants of forest came under severe destruction at the sponsorship of outside log businessman and newly established plywood and saw mills. The accountability of forest cover is now left to the existing reserved forest in the border districts of Assam which also experienced human interferences (*see* Table 3.3).

3.2 Reserved Forest

The Forest Department in Assam practically came into existence in 1868

Table 3.3: Altitude-wise forest cover of Assam (2007)

Attitude zone (meter)	*VDF (km^2)*	*MDF(km^2)*	*OF(km^2)*	*Total (km^2)*
0-500	1071	9,132	12,139	22,342
500-1000	313	2096	2,274	4,623
1000-2000	77	330	320	727
Total	**1461**	**11,558**	**14,733**	**27,692**

Source: Forest Survey of India, 2007.
VDF = very dense forest, MDF = medium dense forest and OF= open forest

and in combination with the Bengal the Forest Administration continued its service till 1874. The forest administration, however, was separated from Bengal in 1874 as it was impossible for the administration to serve the whole of Assam and Bengal together. It was the beginning of Assam Forest Department under total control of colonial rule. The Government forests in Assam, which were gazatted under the Act VII of 1865 either as 'reserves' or 'open-forest' were managed under the Bengal Forest Rules, sanctioned by the Supreme Government in PWD notification No. 13F (*Calcutta Gazette*, 1871). Accordingly, subsequent proposals were submitted to enhance the jurisdiction of Forest Department covering all the districts of Assam. Prior to the period 1877-78, Lakhimpur, Sibsagar and Sylhet districts were out of the reach of Forest Department land. The most important regulation that was used to administer the reserved forest of Assam was the Assam Forest Regulation VII of 1891 (Handique 2004). According to the Assam Forest Regulation, 1891, the local Government might constitute any land at the disposal of the Government a reserved land through the publication of a notification in the official gazette (Assam Forest Regulations, 1891).

On the basis of this regulation, initiatives were taken to bring more and more forests under reserved forest area. Although the Governments forest accounted for 17 per cent of the total area during 1877-78, maximum forest land was either under local Government or person concerned or private ownership and thus 17 per cent did not mean that there was paucity of forested areas under government reserved forest. The history of reserved forest at its initial stage during 1874-75 started with the inclusion of just 269 square mile areas under its domain. Within a span of 25 years from 1875 to 1900, it was backed up by a substantial increase to as high as 4,609 square mile. Surprisingly, in the next 30 years the figure stood at more than double measuring 6,147 square miles in the year 1930 (Fig. 3.4). Table 3.4 showing periodical increase of area under reserve forest in Assam bears the real implication of the increasing trend.

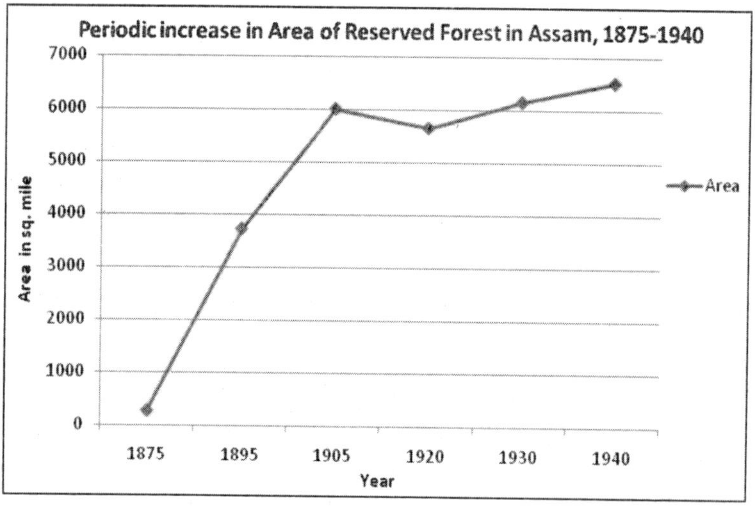

Source: Compiled from Progress Report of Forest Administration, Assam.

Fig. 3.4: Periodic increase in area of reserved forests in Assam, 1875-1940

Table 3.4: Periodic increase in area of reserved forests in Assam

Years	*1875*	*1895*	*1905*	*1920*	*1930*	*1940*
Area (sq. mile)	269	3,716	6,002	5,648	6,147	6,514

Source: Compiled from Progress Report of Forest Administration, Assam.

It was reported that towards the end of British rule Assam possessed a higher percentage of forest-cover which was significantly satisfactory compared to other states except Andaman & Nicobar archipelago. As per the survey, Assam had nearly 41.2 per cent forest cover. The suzerainty although took hold for a long period with the same account but still then a large part of forest cover remained unexplored due to the impenetrability of the jungles and hostile topography of the state. Summarily, it can be said that the state along with other areas of North-east India possessed a higher percentage of forest cover and perhaps the remote areas remained out of the control of the British colonialists of that time (*see* Table 3.5).

The Sibsagar district during British period alone occupied a substantial area including the entire plains countering the Naga hills, part of Naga hills and a section of Karbi plateau even. And therefore, any analysis made to surmise the nature of forest and extent of forest cover

Table 3.5: Name and area of reserved forests in Assam-Nagaland Border, 1879

District	*Name of the reserved forest*	*Area (sq.mile)*
Naga Hills	Nambar	389.0
	Mikir Hills	81.0
	Daigurung	16.0
Sibsagar	Pani Dehing	34.0
	Dirai	19.0
	Obhoypur	15.0
	Solah	1.50
	Hahchora	1.50
	Kakadonga	30.0

Source: D. Brandis: *Suggestions Regarding Forest Administration in Assam*, 1879.

would be predominated by the Sibsagar district. A list of reserved forests occupying the Assam-Nagaland Border region as per the report of D. Brandis, in 1879, is inserted here to have an idea of the then forest cover and the reserved forests of the region. The area covered by the respective reserved forests as shown in the table was exceedingly very low in comparison to the present day extent of those reserve forests. As such, as time passes, new areas were included and number of new reserved forests emerged out in the name of forest conservation. For instance, 1937 witnessed the emergence of few new reserved forests in Sibsagar district which are now in existence. These are Dayang, Kaliani, Holongapar, Desoi etc. Most of the reserved forests of Assam-Nagaland Border are located along the transitory part of hills countering the plains. Supereminence of foothills and lowhills in the distribution of forests does not mean that other areas except these are not congenial for the growth of forest. It was the absolute reflectance of colonial motive on the forest wealth of the region which could better be understood from the text of the circular, from Inspector General of Forests. In Clause-4 of the circular it is stated—"The first class of forests are generally situated on hill slopes, where the preservation of such vegetation as exists, or the encouragement of further growth is essential to the protection from the devastating action of hill torrents on the cultivated plains that lie below them. Here, the interests to be protected are important beyond all comparison with the interests which it was be necessary to restrict; and, so long as there is a reasonable hope of the restrictions being effectual, the lesser, interest must not be allowed to stand in the way". As such Clause-5 dictates the importance of second class forest which is most useful from both economic and commercial points of view. It is said—"The second class of state forests include the great tracts from which our supply of the more valuable timbers—teak, sal, deodar and the like—is obtained. They are for most part (though not always) essentially forests tracts and encumbered by very limited rights of user; and when this is the case, they should be managed mainly on commercial lines as a valuable properties of, and sources of revenues to the state". The location of the reserved forests, therefore, is strictly confined mostly to the areas of culminating hills in one side and plains on the other while the broad forest tracts of the plains are cleared off and randomly left for non-forest use.

After Independence, the declaration for new forest policy was made in 1952 emphasizing primarily on the preservation of national forest. This forest policy of 1952 abolishes the rights of cultivation in the forest land by the tribes. These forests are demarcated by erecting boundary pillars in the possible areas after due notification of the area as the reserved forest and also made provisions for the village forest in order to supply the requirements of the villages. This new policy even stopped grazing in the forest. However, few concessions were declared in the policy by the national government to provide livelihood for the tribals of forested areas. The new policy reaffirmed its trust with the imperial foundation by suggesting that it 'still holds good' (Saikia, 2011). Wildlife Protection Act, 1972 extended to Assam after a gap of five years in 1977. In fact, this was the year to introduce a new conservation strategy, but till then the process of dereservation was continued and its direct effect was seen in the dereservation of Kakadonga, Hanhchora, Daigrung, etc. in the parts of Assam-Nagaland Border. Forest Conservation Act, 1980, which practically came into force in October, 1988 in Assam, was a milestone in blocking the process of dereservation of the reserved forests. Legislation was strictly implemented to protect the existing forest and its expansion in the probable areas. The Forest Policy 1988 as such put little attention to the cause and concerns of people. However, the policy statement does not analyse any cause of deforestation. It only observes the critical situation and the urgent need to find a proper and suitable solution. It further observes that environmental stability should be the priority (Chaudhury, 2007).

In Assam, the Forest Conservation Act, 1980 becomes the *modus operandi* to handle the most sensitive issue of forest conservation which has been experiencing high fluctuation in terms of area and forest density. A series of government notifications converting all possible forest areas to protected forest and the open forest to reserve forest was issued during the post 80s period.

The overall scenario of reserved forest has been changed by both quality and quantity from the British period (prior to the year 1947). As per the record of Forest Survey of India, the recorded forest area of Assam accounts for a total of 26,832 square kilometer in 2006, of which 66.58 per cent is shared by the reserved forests as per legal status while the rest 33.42 per cent is under unclassed forests. FSI again claims—"The forest cover in the state, based on interpretation of satellite data of October 2006 and January 2007, is 27,692 square kms, which is 35.30 per cent of the state's geographical area". As per the record of Department of Forest and Environment, Assam, the total number of reserved forest in 2005 was 312 and the total area under them stood at 13,870 square kilometer; thus the share was 17.68 per cent of the state's total geographical area.

Surprisingly, Nagaland, a hilly state having a congenial environment for the growth of forest is not at the expected level in respect of forest cover as well as the condition of reserved forests. There are just two reserved forests covering a small proportion of the state's forest. Rangapahar of Kohima forest division and the Singphan of the Mon forest division are the two reserved forests existing in Nagaland. Most part of the state, particularly the high altitude areas above 700 metres are covered by "Swidden fallow secondary forest". These are the abandoned shifting cultivation areas undergoing rapid regeneration resulting in the formation of swidden fallow secondary forests (Adhikari and Arunachalam, 2010). Moreover, in parts, post-extraction secondary forests are well exposed. The areas of the two reserved forests, i.e. Rangapahar and Singphan are 62.26 and 23.57 square kilometers respectively. In addition, the state possesses only four wildlife sanctuaries namely Ingtanki, Fakim, Puliebedge and Rangapahar with small area coverage. It is thus clear that the open forests in the form of Swidden fallow and post-extraction secondary forests dominate the forest cover of the state. The most significant aspect is that except Fakim and Puliebedge, all other sanctuaries and the reserved forests are located only along the Assam-Nagaland Border areas.

Apprehensively the high concentration of reserved forests in an interstate boundary belt diffused its overall suzerainty in the socio-economic activities of the region. A total of fourteen reserved forests are found in a linear arrangement along the interstate boundary line (Map 3.3). Table 3.6 gives the picture of the existence of the reserved forests in this belt of Assam-Nagaland Border which measure a total of 2274.29 square kilometer. The share of the reserved forest thus stands at 36.60 per cent of total geographical area.

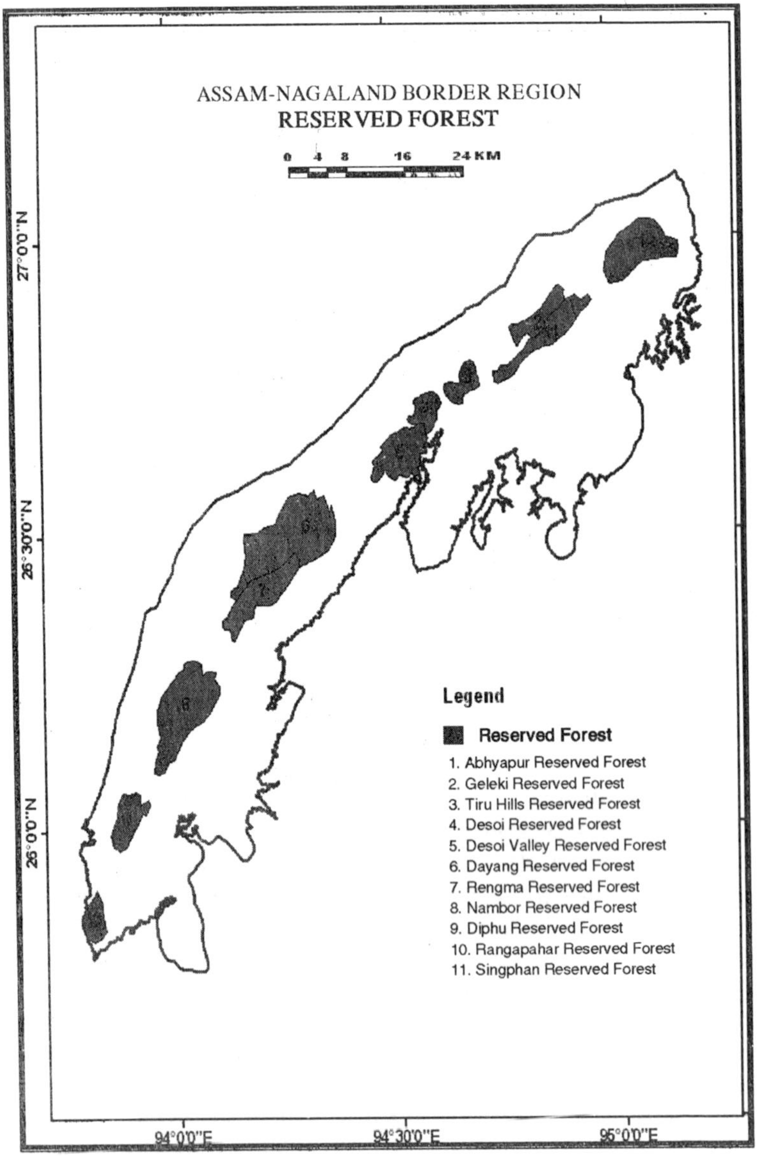

Map. 3.3: Assam-Nagaland Border Region: Reserved Forest

Table 3.6: Reserved forests in Assam-Nagaland Border, 2006-07

State	*District*	*Name of reserved forest*	*Area (sq. km)*
Assam	Golaghat	Dayang	246.36
		Rengma	139.21
		Diphu	183.63
	Jorhat	Dessoi	27.97
		Dessoi valley	163.81
		Tiru hills	58.58
	Sibsagar	Abhaypur	67.38
		Deroi	48.34
		Geleki	59.27
		Sapekhati	7.36
		Panidihing	20.22
	Karbi Anglong	Dhansiri	770.58
		Daldali	123.33
		S. Namabor	272.40
Nagaland	Dimapur	Rangapahar	62.26
	Mon	Singphan	23.57

Source: Office of the Chief Conservator of Forest, Assam, 2006-07.

3.3 Present Status of Forestry

Nobody with minimum conscience can ever be in contradiction with this universal postulate—"Man is the product of nature and natural system". Apparently, man has been playing a decisive role in framing and reframing the nature and the natural set-up. The work of man is such that no other agents or agencies become so capable to alter the nature as man does. It is therefore, apparent that any study on the present status of nature cannot be complete ignoring the human component. Present status of the forestry, in that sense, needs a deep insight and proper investigation to uncover the hidden reality—what, in fact, is going on with the forestry. There is no commonly agreed definition of the forestry sector. Ideally, the sector should be defined to include all economic activities that mostly depend on the production of goods and services from forests (FAO). Activities related to the management of forests and other wooded land for the production and supply of wood and/or other goods and services (Annex-6, FAO: Definition and Basic Principles.). The definitions mentioned above give a broad and inclusive character of the forestry sector, but a narrower and less precise definition of the sector had to be used in this study. This is due to limitations such as non-availability of published statistics.

In all the definitions of forestry mentioned above the involvement of human component is not overlooked. Human component, therefore, either for its positive or negative role, is the most perspicuous and dynamic ingredient of forestry. Forest was there with full practices of forestry since the time immemorial while, in fact, lacked proper and conscious orientation. Hunting, food gathering etc. was simply the means of coping of the primitive people. Thus, forestry needs conscious human endeavour to run over the forests which is considered as the most essential and inseparable precondition and prelude to forestry.

The scientific forestry practices in this part of India is said to have begun with the coming of Sir Dietrich Brandis, a German forest expert, as the first Inspector-General of Forest, in 1864 (Saldanha, 1996). It was the dawn of forestry in India to peep into the tree cladded forest lands for management, administration and conservation. After a rigorous survey, forest areas were demarcated and mapped for a judicious settlement as reserved and protected forests under the guidance of an integrated administration and dynamic management system (Ribbentrop, 1889). As such principles, rules, regulations were framed to sculpture the forests and people of the country and then ramified those as per the needs and the reality. Keeping aside the lucrative colonial imperial motive, it can be said that forests of India for the first time came under scientific forestry with the enactment of the Forest Policy, 1894. Dr. Voelcker, again a German expert, came to India at the invitation of the Government to study the condition of agriculture *vis-à-vis* the role of forests and suggested the need for formulating a concrete forest policy emphasizing agriculture as the priority sector. Thus, a new forest policy came up in 19th October, 1894. The basic principles of this new policy are outlined as follows:

(i) The sole object with which state forests are administered is public benefit. In general the constitution and preservation of a forest involved the regulation of rights and the restrictions of privileges of the user of the forest by the neighbouring population.

(ii) Forest situated on hill slopes should be maintained as protection for forests to preserve the climatic and physical condition of the country and to protect the cultivated plains that lie below them from the devastating action of hill torrents.

(iii) Forests which are the store house of valuable timbers should be managed on commercial lines as a source of revenue to the state.

(iv) Ordinarily, if a demand for agricultural land arises and can be met from a forest alone, it should be conceded without hesitation, subject to the following conditions.
   (a) Honey combing of a valuable forest by patches of cultivation should not be allowed.
   (b) Cultivation must be permanent and must not be allowed to extend so as to encroach upon the minimum area of forest that is needed to meet the reasonable forest requirements, present and prospective.

(v) Forests that yield only inferior timber, fuelwood or fodder, or are used for grazing, should be managed mainly in the interest of the local population, care being taken to see that the users do not annihilate its subjects and the people are protected against their own improvidence (Sagreiya, 2000).

Prompt and sincere implementation of the Forest Policy, 1894, pushed the forestry to enter in a new era of high productivity under strict management system. It was, in fact, the milestone in the long history of the forestry which continued to serve several decades under colonial hegemony as well as in the post-Independent India and has remained as a role model for the subsequent forest policy framed from time-to-time. Following the spirit of Forest Policy, 1894 and as per recommendations the Central Board of Forestry was constituted in 1950 with the Union Minister for Agriculture as Chairman. The fundamental purpose of the Central Board of Forestry was to provide necessary guidance to the State Governments in formulating appropriate measures to develop forestry. At present, the Minister of Forest and Environment is the officiating Chairman of the Board. Necessary revision and addition of rules and regulations of the Board is made as per the demand of time and situation, especially after each major forest act came in force, for instance, the Wildlife Protection Act, 1972, Forest Conservation Act, 1980 etc.

Synchronizing the various forest acts enacted at national level, the State's forest legislation undertook all necessary measures to brand the forest practices at all level of the state forest. Forest areas under the control of the State fall primarily under three broad categories, namely reserved forests, unclassed state forest and forest under the control of autonomous bodies in the hills and plains. The reserved forests are the only one which can be considered for scientific management at present and the other two categories fil the bill rather as free lands than forests (Changkakati, 1986). Foilowing the latest all India classification, the forests of this part can be broadly grouped into six types: (i) the zone of plywood, (ii) the zone of sal, (iii) the potential teak area, (iv) the zone of miscellaneous hardwood, (v) the zone of matchwood, and (vi) the zone of pulpable material. This classification of forest type is justifiably compatible from the spirit of forestry practices as well as from the utility of the forest. Thus, areas, predominated by the kinds of specific trees of use value are authenticated for demarcation to enhance the effectiveness of forestry function (Changkakati, 1986).

Palpably, Assam-Nagaland Border region with all its past reputation as a store house of vast forest, draws attention to open up the third generation intervention into it. A long forested track of 434 km pragmatically presents a wide diversity of forest type and thereby it becomes prone to an intensive forestry practices with the enforcement of new forestry regulations. As per the classification these forested belts harbour a substantial tree cover, with potentiality for plywood, eastern hollock forest for matchwood along with pulpable materials in areas of Karbi Anglong and Nagaland hills. It is noteworthy that the forestry in this part of the region got proper attention towards the end of the nineteenth century as the forests of Goalpara and Kamrup got gradually exhausted and could not supply timbers as per the demand. A departmental report prepared in 1875 provided a picture of the intensity of timber trade. It suggested that the hard trees used for dugouts in Goalpara 'had already been exhausted (Saikia, 2011). The next choice after Sal forest of Goalpara and Kamrup was forspecies like Sam, Hollok, Gamari, Nahar, Titachapa, Jamu, Hilikha etc. which were available in the districts of eastern Assam. Unfortunately, the trade of hardwood did not flourish and remained confined only to the local markets. On the other hand, the chief consumer of hardwood, the tea gardens managed their seeds either from the forested track they owned or from the enclosed state forest. As such, transportation hurdles stood as major constraints. To overcome the hurdles of transportation, a trolley line from Jorhat to Kokilamukh was constructed which in turn spearheaded the easy supply of forest products to load the steamer. It was long before the construction of Assam-Bengal Railway passing through the areas of dense jungle of Assam-Nagaland Border. The entire arrangement was in fact, the *modus operandi* to exploit the plentiful forest wealth of the entire Assam-Nagaland Border including the forest of North Cachar hills. The increasing load of forest products in the successive periods after the construction of railway line can be understood from Table 3.7.

Table 3.7: Growth of forest products in Assam (1899-1924)

Period	Major forest products (million cubic feet)		Minor forest products		
	Timber	Fuel	Bamboo (million nos)	Lac (Quintals)	Others (million ton)
1899-1904	24.8	39.9	132.4	4,457.60	1.58
1904-1909	22.2	34.7	150.1	1,6,126.40	2.17
1909-1914	28.8	38.7	162.6	15538.80	2.26
1914-1919	25.1	41.9	144.6	14,413.60	2.07
1919-1924	34.5	41.1	147.8	18,203.20	2.59

Source: Successive Annual Forest Report, Department of Forest, Assam.

From Table 3.7 it is quite clear that from 1899 onwards the growth of all forest products sets an increasing trend because of the cheap means of transportation and other favourable factors. Indubitably the extension of Assam-Bengal Railway to the easternmost part of the state geared up the process of export of forest product and precisely it continued until the end of British regime in the country. During the period 1944-45, the total products reached the highest amounting to 109.9 million cubic feet and 164.5 million cubic feet respectively for timber and fuelwood products. This trend eventually dropped immediately after the Independence of the country in 1947 and virtually the total accounts of forest product came down to 10.0 and 10.5 million cubic feet respectively for timber and fuel-wood in the year 1950.

To understand and to surmise the metamorphosis of the British forest policy and forestry it is indispensable to examine the nature of goods collected as forest products and the commercial value of those items exported from the areas they intervened. However, major concern of the colonial forestry practices was the poor communication. In areas of high demand, Public Works Department came forward to render necessary communications. On the other hand, tea garden managements took this as opportunity to open new areas for expansion at the cost of transportation development. In association of all these efforts it was still not possible to connect the reserved forest for probable extraction of the forest resources. During the summer months as the rivers remain in spate, the timber traders took the advantage particularly to transship the logs through the rivers. This traditional means of transportation required skilled workers usually hired from the local areas. People competent in local technology of river transportation helped traders to carry logs on the locally made huge bamboo raft called *Meleng*. The rivers of the monsoon period very easily and at a cheap rate carried logs which was risky as well as very challenging (Das, 2005). During the rainy season, as most of the rivers are fetched up by high volume of water, most of the forest products are transshipped from inaccessible forest areas to areas accessible for other sharp means of transport. Today even big bamboo rafts or *Meleng* are found commonly everywhere, especially in the rivers flowing down from the forested hills. Because of the paucity of separate recorded data, forestry practices performed during the pre-Independence period in the Assam-Nagaland Border region could not be properly assessed. But a spectacular fall was seen in the major forest products (MFP) and non-wood forest products (NWFP) after Independence. Though importance in the National Forest Policy, 1952 was laid to make more beneficial for development but it largely failed to achieve the target affixed. However, the return from the forestry practices was satisfactory as it showed a rising trend in the subsequent period. The impact of the policy was extremely penetrative. A substantial portion of the revenue of the State of Assam came from the forest produces. The revenue of Rs. 338.9 lakhs in the first plan period reached Rs. 883.8 lakhs in the Sixth plan period. The yearly average therefore stands at Rs. 1732.74 lakhs during the sixth plan period. There found to be an over increasing trend in the revenue earnings of the Forest Department. In 2007-08 the revenue earned amounted to Rs. 502.70 lakhs while the highest is recorded in the year 2009-10. From timber alone and other forest produce, the earning stands at Rs. 8049.41 lakhs. Table 3.8 showing the year-wise earnings of Forest Department is perhaps a genuine reflection of the forestry practices in the state. The important major forest products were timber, fuelwood, stone, sand, clay and were the major source of revenue earnings (Fig. 3.5).

From 1998 onwards the revenue collection from the forest products shows a steady increasing trend which is quite comprehensive from Table 3.8. During 1998, as per record of Department of Forest, Assam the production of various MFPs were 34,141 cubic metre timber, 1288 stack cubic metre fuelwood, 19,79,815 cubic metric ton stone, 24,70,587 cubic metric ton sand and 17,30,252 cubic metric ton clay.

Amidst a steady rising trend of forest revenue the forestry practice in Assam-Nagaland Border region continued with full efficiency. As most of the forest areas (90%) of the four plain districts of the region are concentrated along the border belt, maximum forestry activities and revenue collection are appreciated from this belt. During 2006-2007, approximately 417,315 cubic metric ton of industrial timber was collected from this forest of the four plain districts of the border region. As such,

Table 3.8: Year-wise revenue earnings of Forest Department, Assam

(*Rs. in lakh*)

Year	*Timber*	*Others*	*Total*
1997-1998	58.13	721.73	779.86
1998-1999	58.01	901.46	959.47
1999-2000	299.85	1172.98	1472.83
2000-2001	286.40	1190.10	1476.50
2001-2002	117.67	1090.10	1207.77
2002-2003	67.37	1786.63	1850.00
2003-2004	158.07	1771.59	1929.66
2004-2005	201.60	2176.24	2197.84
2005-2006	271.01	4067.67	4338.26
2006-2007	126.48	4363.52	4490.00
2007-2008	168.08	4894.62	5062.70
2008-2009	88.24	6178.16	6266.40
2009-2010	68.79	7980.62	8049.41
2010-2011	590.68	5712.21	6302.89

Source: Forest Survey of India, Assam, 2011.

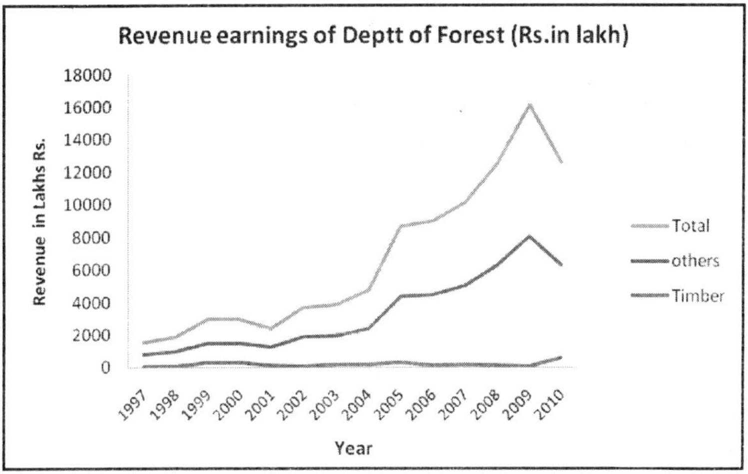

Source: Forest Survey of India, Assam, 2011.

Fig. 3.5: Revenue earnings of Deptt. of Forest (*Rs. in lakh*)

the hilly areas of the border region contribute substantially to the MFPs. In spite of its significant share on the MFPs, the records are not well preserved which creates a shadow over forestry development programme. Moreover, preponderance of community forest and private owned forest also dig a hole in the genuine portrayal of the forestry of the region [(*see* Figs. 3.6(a) and (b)].

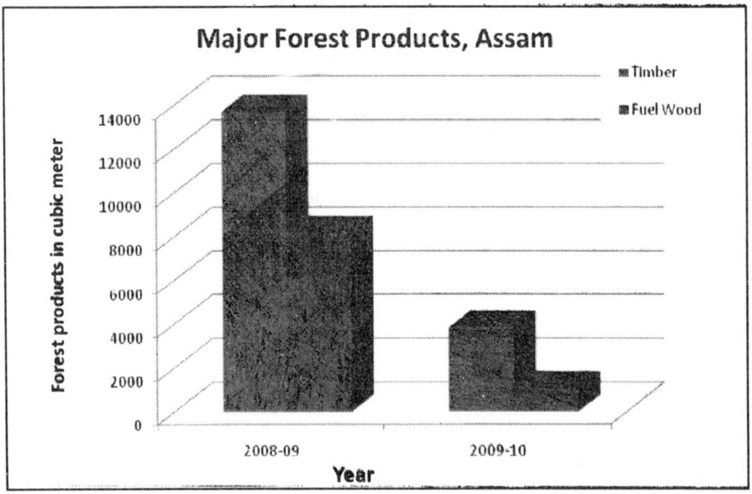

Source: Economic Survey, Assam, 2010-11.

Fig. 3.6(a): Major Forest Products, Assam

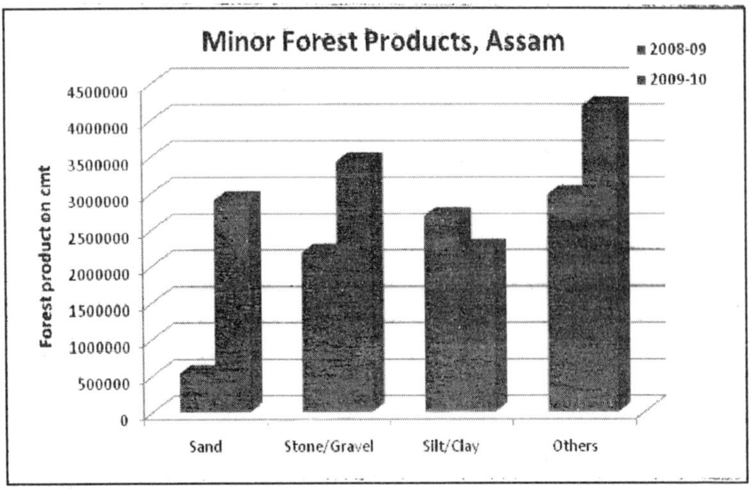

Source: Economic Survey, Assam, 2010-11.

Fig. 3.6(b): Minor Forest Products, Assam

Table 3.9: Major and minor forest products, Assam

Forest Products	2008-09 (in cm)	2009-10 (in cm)
(a) Major Forest Produce		
Timber	13731	3839
Fuel Wood	8169	1063
(b) Minor Forest Produce		
Sand	525198	2905333
Stone/Gravel	2182197	3429919
Silt/Clay	2682504	2243569
Others	2974431	4192455

Source: Economic Survey, Assam, 2010-11; cm-cubic metre, cmt—cubic metric ton.

Table 3.10 however, is not enough to understand the state of forestry in these districts of Assam as the products of both MFP and NWFP are insignificant compared to the total forest area [Fig. 3.6 (a) and (b)]. The 1988 revised National Forest Policy, although extensively infuse new spirit of forestry development, its effectiveness and dimension of application in a sustainable manner could not turn positive. Much of the forest of the region already was obviated partly by the government sponsored rehabilitation programme and partly by the encroachers and illegal log business agencies. Towards the later part of 1990s, the forestry development seldom gained momentum. The assessment made in the successive period on forestry development virtually dictates a deep shadow which instigated the Ministry of Environment and Forests to bring out a circular dated June 1, 1990, setting specific guidelines for the involvement of village communities and voluntary agencies in the protection and development of forests all throughout the country. The concept of Joint Forest Management (JFM) or Participatory Forest Management was the product of this circular.

JFM is, in fact, a concept which is based on the principle of rights of the local communities, also an approach involving the evolution of a very complex property rights required to generate a sustainable interface between the forest department and the local communities. Thus, Forest Development Agencies (FDA) and at further lower level JFMCs are constituted replacing the earlier forest management policy of commercial forestry and revenue generation (MoEF, 1990). Assam Forest Policy, 2004 adopted JFMC agenda to develop community forest management aiming at sustainable approach for forest management. The after initiatives in the forest areas of Assam-Nagaland Border undertaken by Forest Department drew active response from the localities and sizeable activities under JFMCs geared up the status report of Forest Development Agencies as shown in table 3.12.

Table 3.10: Major and minor forest products, plain districts of Assam-Nagaland Border, 2010-11

District	Industrial Timber (cubic metre)	Fuel-wood (stack cubic metre)	Minor			
			Sand (cmt)	Gravel/ Stone (cmt)	Silt/clay (cmt)	Others (cmt)
Golaghat	0.854	0	13532.00	40826.59	0	0
Jorhat	3.218	3.00	5909.50	00	0	59000.00
Sibsagar	10.292	2.00	5050.00	36375.00	2400.00	100860.00
Karbi Anglong	N.A.	N.A.	N.A.	N.A.	N.A.	N.A.
Total	**14.364**	**5.00**	**24491.50**	**77201.59**	**2400.00**	**159,860.00**

Source: Principal Chief Conservator of Forest, Government of Assam; cmt—cubic metric ton.

On the contrary, the districts of Nagaland part namely Dimapur, Wokha, Mokokchung and Mon have witnessed a splendid growth of the new agenda of JFMCs to speed up the protection and developmental process of forestry. It was virtually a difficult task for the government and the Department of Forest in the State where 85.3 per cent of forests is owned by villagers and government have no control over the felling of trees in those areas. Ecological disorder as a result of extensive deforestation in the forested border belt has already set a serious problem to the tribal mode of life. It was necessary and inevitable to undertake a sincere effort to rejuvenate the forest to supplement the forest-based livelihood of the inhabitants of the border tract. This perspective set the Forest Department at taking up afforestation programme for regeneration of the degraded forests with the objectives of converting them into 'productive forests' and as the active participation of the land owners is needed for successful implementation of the programme, the Department concomitantly made campaign to grow a "Resource based economy for the villagers" (Notification no.-FOR-153/80 (Vol. II), Kohima) (*see* Table 3.11).

Under a mandatory planning proposal, State Forests Development Agencies (FDA) has initiated the formation of FDA in all the territorial

Table 3.11: Status of forest development agencies and joint forest management committees in the Border districts of Assam (2006)

(*Rs. in lakh*)

Name of FDA	Project outlay	No. of JFMC	Treatable area	Amount of Fund releamed
Golaghat	45.90	8	400	13.00
Jorhat	40.30	11	330	22.00
Sibsagar	60.68	10	500	17.00
Karbi Anglong East	315.31	41	2100	228.00

Source: Economic Survey, Assam, 2010-11.

forests divisions including the social forestry division. It was a difficult task for both the Government and the Department of Forests to convince the local landowners, who virtually owned nearly 94 per cent of the state forest, to join Joint Forest Management Programme. As a result of relentless effort, many JFMCs are formed in all the FDA's of the state. The total number of JFMC in the Nagaland border areas is 85, of which Wokha and Mokokchung districts have 67 JFMCs (Table 3.13).

Table 3.12: District-wise distribution of JFMC in Nagaland, 2008

Forest District	Mokokchung	Wokha	Dayang	Mon
No. of JFMC	33	34	09	19
Area expected to be covered (ha)	575	728	258	730

Source: Indian Institute of Forest Management, Nagaland, 2008.

However, the Forest Department primarily emphasizes on the intensification of JFMC's activity and attempts to incorporate more areas under this programme. The social forestry programme under direct finance of the Government of India accordingly put stress to achieve success in association with agro-forestry programme in the region.

Social Forestry

Social forestry as a strategy can be made effective to raise the possibility of extensive afforestation in both rural and urban areas. Social forestry, simply means the management and protection of forests along with afforestation on barren or vacant land to subside the loss of forest cover and to enhance environmental and social development of a region. The term 'social forestry' was first used in 1976 by the National Commission on Agriculture, Government of India. From then, the Department embarked upon a social forestry project with the aim of taking the pressure off from the forest by intensive plantation on all unused and fallow land (The National Commission on Agriculture, GoI, 1976).

Social forestry is categorized into from groups: (i) farm forestry, (ii) community/rural forestry, (iii) extension/urban forestry, and (iv) agro-forestry. Social forestry practically aims at raising plantations by the common man so as to meet the growing demand for timber, fuelwood, fodder etc. thereby releasing the pressure on the traditional forest area. With the introduction of this scheme the Government formally recognized the local community's rights on forest resources. The Assam-Nagaland Border region obviously demands for such an effective scheme as the traditional forests of the region have been completely destroyed. Social forestry got proper recommendation by the National Commission on Agriculture in 1981. Subsequently, late Prime Minister Indira Gandhi incorporated this programme in her 20-point programme for poverty alleviation.

As per guideline and the objectives, Social Forestry Programme in Assam has taken up plantations in vacant unclassed state forests, village grazing reserves, roadside, canal bank, embankment quite extensively (Goswami, 2007). Social forestry gradually entered into other allied fields like biomass generation, formation of JFMC, distribution of Jatropha seedling for commercial plantation etc. It is to be noted that the shift of National Forest Policy to conservation oriented in 1988 was a boon to both the people and forest as it primarily aimed at benefit for the people through forest conservation. Social forestry is such a practical measure that ensures people's participation in forest conservation programme (*see* Tables 3.13 and 3.14).

A total of 19 FDAs covering the State of Assam along with the support of 550 JFMCs were constituted to intensify the afforestation measures: The target area was fixed at 26,955 hectares with a fund allocation of Rs. 36.56 crores from the Ministry of Environment and Forest, Government of India. As such, the neighbouring State Nagaland fixed their target area at 25,528 hectares with a fund allocation of Rs. 37.71 crores under the jurisdiction of 16 FDA.

Social forestry programme, on the contrary remains a far dream for Nagaland as it has shortage of open fallow land or unused land. Current *jhum, jhum* regrowth and maximum of land under private proprietorship perhaps stood as constraints in the way of its successful implementation. As such the border belt of the state remains untouched from such forestry programme. Khatowang Kanyak, a retired forest officer of Hahchara Naga

Table 3.13: Social forestry parks in Assam-Nagaland Border Region 1984-2005

Name of Park	*Location*	*Year of creation*
Green Park	Jorhat	1984-85
Rajabari Park	Golaghat	1990-91
Napukuri Park	Sibsagar	1991-92
Bio-diversity Park	Golaghat	2004-05

Source: http://www.assamforest.coin. dated 26th September, 2012.

Table 3.14: Achievement under forestry programme in Assam (1999-2003)

(*area in hectares*)

Sl. No.	*Programme*	*1999-2000*	*2000-01*	*2001-02*	*2002-03*
1.	Regeneration	1295	1794	498	104
2.	RDF	209	278	277	133
3.	FGS	355	396	395	Nil
4.	Plywood	—	—	—	Nil
5.	Teakwood	709	709	788	Nil
6.	Matchwood	404	419	419	40
7.	MFP	—	—	—	Nil

Source: Office of the Chief Conservator of Forests, Government of Assam.
RDF = Rehabilitation of Degraded Forests, FGS = Fast Growing Species.

describes it as—"The shortage of government fallow land and the topographic adverse virtually restricts the implementation of social forestry programme, and instead the Department of Forest, accentuating the importance of afforestation in the highly degraded forest area mostly owned by private owner or by the community, directly recommended the formation of JFMC as an effective measure under such a condition". On the other hand, as most of forestry activities are concentrated in the private or community owned forest, very little has been made under the direct government involvement (*see* Table 3.15).

3.4 Deforestation

Deforestation which refers to thinning, changing and elimination of forest, deforestation, is not a recent phenomenon (Williams, 2006) and therefore, any analysis on deforestation demands strict observation on the sequence of this dynamic process. Earthquake, forest fire, floods, hazards etc., although are brought to the list of the forces of deforestation, their contributions are quite insignificant when compared with the role played

Table 3.15: Achievement under various schemes of social forestry, 2007

District	No. of FDA	No. of forest village	Area targeted (in ha)	Achievement (in ha)	No. of seedling planted (in '000)
Golaghat	200	120	323	323	259500
Jorhat	330	10	340	340	274000
Sibsagar	250	250	508	508	358800
Karbi Anglong	950	50	1000	1000	100000
Total	**1730**	**430**	**2171**	**2171**	**992300**

Source: Directorate of Economics and Statistics, Government of Assam, 2007.

by human forces. Deforestation is the permanent destruction of indigenous forests and woodlands. The term, however, does not include the removal of industrial forests such as plantations of gums or pines. Deforestation has resulted in the reduction of indigenous forests to four-fifths of their pre-used or pre-agricultural area (*Wikipedia Encyclopedia*).

Destruction of forest is not merely an outcome of natural hazards as often referred to the great mass extinction of species as a result of the carboniferous rainforest collapse perhaps 300 million years ago due to climate change (Williams, 2006). The change was, undoubtedly abrupt and repetition is uncommon at a regular interval of time. Man's footprint on the earth's soil, perhaps 10,000 years back, can be tagged as the mark of the fast changing forest cover of the earth. As the human activities made gradual inroads into the arena of nature to have the steps rigid on the soil, the natural environment started receding to reach this present state of almost no return. Changed forest cover provide human to settle and thus intrude into the vegetated land, with remarkable rapidity, doing all those things like—foraging, firing, hunting, selecting their needs and rejecting others. Slowly and silently forests entered into the modern period with new form and style turning its height, density, size, structure, distributing over time and space. The forest transition theory as Perz and Skole (2003) described it—"Posits that over time forest cover exhibits a U-shaped curve, beginning with an initial decline in forest cover due to deforestation. This decline is later reduced, offset and eventually overweighed at some point by new forest expansion, allowing for forest recover". Besides, the natural and climaticallv induced changes of forest cover, the human impact was early, widespread and significant, and the forests of the world changed accordingly (Williams, 2006). All the available literature concerning deforestation points out to the conformity in value, process and manner which varies over time and space. Disregard of intrinsic value, lack of ascribed value, weak forest management and environmental laws are some of the factors that allow deforestation to occur on a large scale. Deforestation ultimately causes extinction of species, loss of habitat, changes in climatic conditions, desertification, displacement of people, imbalances in ecology, changes in livelihoods and many more as observed today as well as in the past. Urbanization, industrialization, commodity production, communication and all other developmental works 'punched the nature to bleed dangerously' (Foster, 2011).

In any consideration of the forest cover change i.e. deforestation, human factor absolutely has total credit and perhaps no confronting elements in the environment are there to influence the vegetation in any impressive way. Following Hamel and Dansereau (1949, cited by Frenkel, 1970) one can recognize five principal degrees of interference:

1. Natural habitats: those that develop in the absence of human activities.
2. Degraded habitats: those produced by sporadic, yet incomplete, disturbances; for example the cutting of forest trees, burning and the non-intensive grazing in the forest land.
3. Ruderal habitats: where disturbance is sustained, but where there is no intentional substitution of vegetation.
4. Cultivated habitats: when constant disturbance is accompanied by the introduction of plants.
5. Artificial habitats: which are developed when humans modify the ambient climate and soil, as in greenhouse cultivation.

Westhof (1983) derives an alternative model to illustrate the human influence on the plant covers as follows:

1. *Natural*: a landscape or an ecosystem not influenced by human activity.
2. *Sub-natural*: a landscape or ecosystem partly influenced by human, but still belonging to the same (structures) formation type as the natural system from which it derives.
3. *Semi-natural*: a landscape or ecosystem in which flora and fauna are largely spontaneous, but the vegetation structure is altered so that it belongs to another formation type.
4. *Cultural*: a landscape or ecosystem in which flora and fauna have been essentially affected by human agency in such a way that the dominant species may have been replaced by other species.

The schemes derived to explain the classification of human interference in the vegetation world reflects the changing steps of forest cover on the earth. And perhaps, as the two schemes advocate, the present-day world has already attained the last stage of transformation. Natural hazards although was the beginners of deforestation but they allow the nature to recover and recapture it. The role of fire is widely confirmed as the most devastating in reducing natural forest cover all over the world. There is certainly a great deal of evidence for the use of wood throughout the Paleolithic Age for building, ladders, fire, pigment (charcoal), drying wood and digging sticks (Goudie, 1981). Tyldesley and Bahn (1983) go as far as to suggest that "The Paleolithic might more accurately be termed the "Palaeoxylic" or "Old Wood Age".

Fires: The Weapon to Dominate Environment

Discovery of fire was a milestone in the evolution of human civilization. It shapes and reshapes the diagnostic role of man all through the ages of human history. People have utilized fire for great variety of reasons: to clear forest for agriculture; to improve grazing land for domestic animals or to attract game; to deprive game of cover, to drive game from cover in hunting; to kill or drive away predatory animals; to repel the attacks of enemies, for cooking; to break up stone for tool making; to protect settlements or encampments from great fires by controlled burning; to make pottery; to smelt ores; to provide warmth; to make charcoal etc. Bartlett (1956) very judiciously and rationally pointed out the importance of fire that man has been using since prehistoric time.

May be natural or anthropogenic, effects of fire are indifferent and pose problems. Anthropogenically induced fire obviously serves purpose when purposefully used. The natural process is basically involved with (i) lightening which on average strikes the land surface of the earth 100,000 times each day (Tuan, 1971), (ii) spontaneous combustion in areas of heavy vegetal accumulation which are compacted, rotted, fermented and thus generating heat, and (iii) fire produced as a result of friction caused by falling boulders or landslides. In 1993, the western United States experienced a total of 12,750 lightening while Belize records a total of 59 lightning in 1975. It is important to note 27.4 per cent of deforested area of South Africa were destroyed by forest fire caused by lightning. The cases of forest fire due to lightening in India are not well recorded. Naredran (2001), a scientist working in the centre for Ecological Sciences, Indian Institute of Science, Bangalore intrigued by the phenomenon of forest fire discloses his experiences as—"Wild land fires" as they are commonly known today occur at varying frequencies in different parts of the globe. Natural causes of forest fires are usually lightening. Strikes or burning coal reams, heat from within the earth could be transferred to the charcoal layers above, from there onto the peat and other vegetation in the soil and finally when it comes in contact with forest litter it would develop into a natural forest fire." Geological Survey of India confirmed that South Rewa Gondowana Basin of Madhya Pradesh experienced forest fire during late Triassic era for unknown reasons. Fires occur on a regular basis in many parts of India. It is seen frequently along the Himalayan foothills and in the deciduous forests elsewhere particularly during the months from February to May. Most of the deciduous forests of India shade leaves during the dry months and the ground below remain usually covered by large amount of liters. The biomass so generated is prone to fire and as it comes in contact of fire generation it creates all devastating forest fire. Obviously, humans are responsible for most of the fires here.

Contrary to the natural fire, man induced fire is the most effective which plays a vital role in removing a substantial forest cover from the earth's surface. Fire was, in the words of Stewart (1956), "The first great force employed by man; and it was crucial in the history of deforestation. Humans very intelligently assimilated fire to frame up a biological heritage which helps them to access the world's biota and in turn it gives birth to a new regimen of fire transformed human society". Wildfire obviously played a decisive role as a great modifier of our ecology. The effects of wildfire are elaborated in the figure (Fig. 3.7) with all ramifications to present both positive and negative footmarks it usually left.

Table 3.16: Some historically significant wildland fires

Time	*Name*	*Location*	*Significance*
Oct, 1804	Recorded by Lewis and Clark	North Dakota	A practice was set on fire
March, 1805	-do-	Undetermined	Common practice of native Americans to benefit the horses and buffaloes
1845	Great fire	Orogen	1,500,000 acres burned
1956	Inaja	California	56000 acres burned
1972	Moccasin Mega	New Mexico	2,680 acres burned

Source: National Interagency Co-ordination Centre, Idaho, USA.

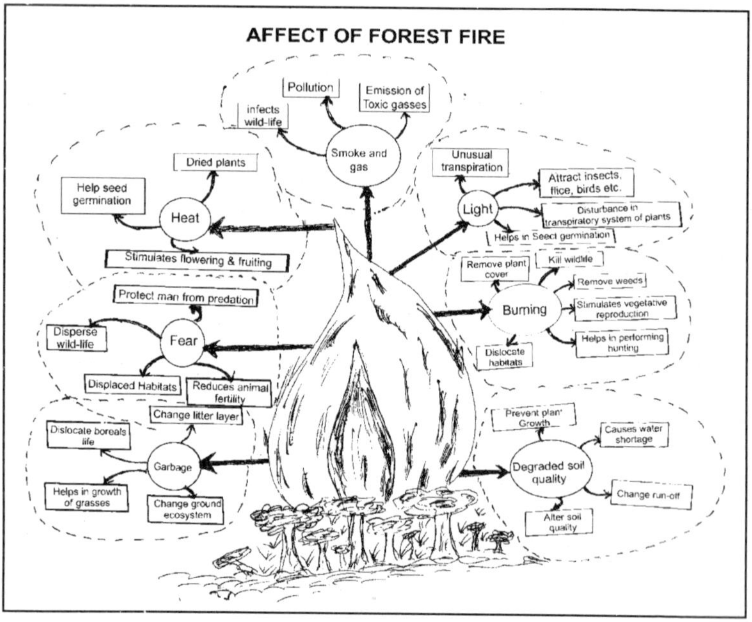

Source: Goudie, A. (1981): *The Human Impact on Natural Environment.*

Fig. 3.7: Affect of Forest Fire

It is important to note that fire was frequently used as an effective tool for deforestation and thus grassland fire or overland fire is more gentle than the crown fire. The effects of fires on the environment depend very much on their size, duration and intensity. Some forest fires are relatively quick and only destroy ground vegetation. Crown fires affect whole forest up to crown level and generate very high temperature. In general, forest fires are hotter than grassland fire (Goudie, 1981).

The Human Factor and Fire

History of forest fire is not a recent phenomenon. Practice of deforestation using fire is a prehistoric activity which is evident in mythological writings including the *Vedas*, *Upanisads*, *Puranas* and other relevant ancient literatures. *Agni* the god of fire occupies a prominent place in the Vedic literature and is described everywhere as one of the most powerful god. *Agni* is the first word of the first hymn of the *Rigveda* (I. 1.1) and is mentioned.

> *agnīmīle purohitaṁ yajñasya devām ṛtījam*
> *hotaraṁ ratnadhātamam.*

(Agni I laud, the high priest, god, minister of sacrifice, the invoker, lavishest of wealth). It is usually apprehensive that the entire India during Vedic periods was luxuriantly covered with rich forest. The region was wetter than what it is today and forests covered what are now vast plains, although some parts of the Punjab were likely to be semi-arid and favourable for cattle rearing. Migration continued into the Ganga Plain as mentioned in the *Brahmanas.* Videgha Madhava led his people along the Himalayan foothills eastwards as far as the Gondaka. The land across the river had to be cleared by fire before it could be settled (Thapar, 2002). Deforestation during the Vedic period was mostly done using fire. The pastoralist Aryans turned into agriculturist, perhaps incorporating knowhow acquired from the local clans. Chalcolithic cultures practiced agriculture, so there would have been a combining of agriculturalists and pastoralists. But for agriculture to be extended, the clearing of land was required. Fire played its part in this process and the burning of forests is described, perhaps initially in imitation of shifting cultivation (Thapar, 2002).

Expansion of agricultural area at the expanse of forest land continued to be a regular phenomenon. Maurya dynasty (321 to 185 BC) was one of the powerful ruling dynasties of ancient India and perhaps, forest for the first time drew attention of the king as a most resourceful wealth. It is clearly mentioned in *Arthashastra* of Kautilya as—"On the border of the forest, he should establish a forest for elephants guarded by foresters. The office of the Chief Elephant Forester should with the help of guard protect the elephants in any terrain. The slaying of an elephant is punishable by death." It is clear that elephant, important from war strategy, probably had been sizeably reducing in number as a result of fast deteriorating forest cover (Sen, 1989). The Mauryas valued certain forest tracts in strategic or economic terms and instituted curbs and control measures over them. They regarded all forest tribes with distrust and controlled them with bribery and political subjugation, Ashoka, the great of the Maurya dynasty, who embraced Buddhism, changed the style of governance, which included providing protection to fauna and even relinquished the royal hunt. He was, perhaps the first ruler in the history of India to advocate conservation measures for wildlife. Following his appeal, many kings of later period gave up slaughtering of animals. The legal restrictions conflicted with the practices freely exercised by the common people in hunting, fishing and setting fires in forests (Rangarajan, 2001).

In Assam-Nagaland Border region, slash and burn agriculture *(Jhum)* became dominant in the hill areas. Shifting agriculture, using the *jhum* system, is a major economic activity of this humid climatic region. *Jhum* is in harmony with the environment as long as the *jhum* cycle is long enough for the forest to recover. It is however observed that no major causalities to the forest is occurred due to the practice of shifting agriculture. This human induced forest fire since is a controlled one therefore damages to the forest is not significant in comparison to wild land fire. On the other hand the long rainy months (from April to October) against the shorter dry season (from November to February) keeps the forest wet which ultimately prevents the occurrence of forest fire.

The genesis of deforestation, however, needs a thorough and in-depth analysis in order to have an appreciation of present-day forest cover. Social, cultural, political and economic activities of historic past bear ample evidences of the close relationship between human and forest. Assuming the Vedic period as zero point or the starting point of deforestation, it could easily be concluded that we are in the last lap of the great run of deforestation.

Forest under Imperialist Hegemony

The advent of the British colonialists in the Indian territory brought a total change in the system of man-nature co-existence which Indian society acquired by virtue of socio-cultural ethics. Prior to the establishment of colonial rule social ethics in no way was against the ecology and the carrying capacity of nature. People within Indian society, particularly the pastoralists and nomads, who directly depended on natural floral and faunal resources, developed specific ways of utilizing these resources. They were aware that the resource had supported them for generations in the past and will have to continue to support the generations to come (Gadgil and Malhotra, 1994). Instances of traditional eco-friendly practices are ample all throughout the country. Worshipping of tree, snake, cow, elephant, etc. is such religious tradition usually seen particularly among the tribes. Hunters never killed a pregnant deer or the immature cabs and often the females are freed so that the balance in resource base remains intact for their future security.

The British found a resourceful land in India and imposed much higher levels of demands on natural resources to enrich their own economy. It is now an established fact that the history of modern Indian forestry was a process by which the British gradually appropriated forests resources for revenue generation only. With a total capitalistic aggression, the colonialist established control first over the territory and then shifted it to the resource base. Under capitalism, the economic system is the basic organizer of space (Castells, 1977) and the most obvious and the apparent steps the colonial ruler put were on its strong forest resource base. Political system organizes space through its two essential functions of domination/ regulation and integration/repression (Castells, 1977). All throughout the colonies they faced same fate of forced integration, otherwise repression. The firepower of European vanguard and the complex of weeds, animals and diseases it brought, devastated the flora and fauna and human societies of the new world (Gadgil and Guha, 1992). Guha and Gadgil (1994) also stated—"World ecology has been profoundly altered by western capitalism, in whose dynamic expansion other ecosystems were disrupted, first through trade and later by colonialism."

To pursue the colonial interest, a commissioner was appointed to look into the availability of teak in the Malabar forests. In 1806, the Madras Government appointed Capt. Watson as the Commissioner of Forests for organizing the production of teak and other timber suitable for ship-building. The attempt of the colonial ruler was to exploit the resources which they found available at their close hands. In 1855, Lord Dalhousie framed regulations for conservation of forests of the country. Following this policy, Gibson passed order prohibiting shifting cultivation and plantation of teak forests. From 1865 onwards, forest reserves were established to secure material for imperial needs and to ensure the continuity of supply of forest products. By around 1860, Britain had emerged as the world leader in deforestation, devastating its own woods and the forests of other countries to draw timber for ship-building, iron-smelting and farming (Gadgil and Guha, 1992). Timber suitable for ship-building got the priority to withstand the world situation where a high degree of competition among the European countries was in force. This within contradiction of homocentrist led these colonial groups to acquire more and more wealth from the areas of availability. Since, capital formation is their chief motive therefore economic system becomes the dominant factor for spatial organization (Peet and Thrift, 2002). The British imperialist attempted to organize the space, i.e. forest area by bringing the concept of reserved forest where state's intervention is permissible and people's intervention rejected. Declaring rich forest areas as reserved ultimately ensures the total intervention of the state only.

The year 1865, hence is credited for the introduction of a new episode of deforestation in the name of forest conservation in India. It practically opened-up two ways of exploitation: (i) forest areas other than reserved forest came under waste land category and remained as open access land; and (ii) conversion of these waste lands to farm land following. Wanton tree felling became the policy priority to accumulate more revenue from the farm lands. During the first half of the nineteenth century, British land use policy and its emphasis on agricultural expansion were far more important factors (Haeuber, 1993). Stebbing (1926), an early Indian Forest Historian, said—"in many localities forests were an obstruction to agriculture and therefore a limiting factor to the prosperity of the country."

Table 3.17: Few important events in the process of scientific forestry in British India

Year	*Events*
1856	Dietrich Brandis introduces scientific forestry in India
1864	Creation of the Indian forestry services
1867	First forestry students from India are sent to Germany and France
1872	Hugh Cleghorn elected as the president of Scottish arboricultural society
1878	Forestry school established at Dehra Dun for the training of Indian foresters
1881	William Schlich takes over the charge as Inspector General of Forests from D. Brandis
1885	Schlich is succeeded by Berthold Rebentrop and established the Royal Engineering College to train the foresters for the Indian forestry services

Source: Scientific Forestry in India, 1900.

The whole policy was to extend agriculture and watchword of the time was to destroy the forests with this end in view. "The political economy of British India is crucial in formulating the forest policy and their philosophy is reflected in their entire policy making." Sinha (online) vehemently criticizes the opinions of Guha, Gadgil and others. Advocating the British favour Sinha writes—"Dr. Ramchandra Guha, Dr. Madhav Gadgil and others have painted a picture which depicts our colonial rulers as the worst exploiters of our natural forest under the support of draconian forest policy and law enacted by them. This line of argument has been espoused by political thinkers figuring out to the left of the centre. But unfortunately this is not true. Sufficient injustice has been caused to the founding fathers of British India's Forestry." Sinha's statement is contradictory and quite baseless. One of the eminent early conservators of forest in India expressed his views regarding the attitude of Britishers towards forest as—"the English have been most regardless of the value of the forests" (Cleghorn, 1860). Crosby comments—"population densities, resistance to disease, agricultural technology and sophisticated socio-political organizations—all made these areas more resistant to the ecological imperialism of Europe. Thus, the rule (not the law) that although Europeans may conquer the tropics, they do not Europeanized the tropics, not even country sides with European temperatures" (Crosby, 1986). Citing examples of Hausa Peasantry Watts writes—"for large section of Hausa peasantry, the margin of subsistence security was progressively undermined by a retarded capitalism; the bases of the moral economy were eroded in a significant way. Colonialism dissolved many of the response system that served to buffer households from the vagaries of a harsh and variable semiarid environment... The patterns of change ... not only altered the extent of hunger in a statistical sense but changed its very etiology" (Watts, 1983). These instances are enough to nullify Sing's appreciation of the British policy. Again, he came forward with self-contradictory explanation when he put his hold on the colonial policy on resource use. Circumspecting the attitude and the policy frame of resource-utilization, he screamed—"They had realized that state has to intervene in the matters of general welfare in India if the British Raj was to be sustained. Creation of vast network of roads, rails and other physical infrastructure were reflection of this conviction." Anybody investigating the nature and pattern of transport network developed by the British will certainly ascertain that all these were developed only to intensify the exploitation of resources and obviously the network was only to link up the areas of rich resource base. Interestingly his all benevolent appreciation of British policy is crashed by his own words ... "allowed private parties to exploit resources for immediate gain without regard for the future" (Sinha, online, 2011).

In the early nineteenth century, trade in forest products in general and timber in particular, was confined to the Terai-Bhabar region and the outer hills. Statistics in terms of the volume of trade are not available, but the collection of duty on the export of forest products is indicative of the trend. The collection (excluding pasture dues) increased from Rs. 6,302 in 1822-23 to Rs. 6,958 in 1833 (Batten, 1878a) and Rs. 13,668 in 1846-47 (Batten, 1878b). The inconvenience of communication was largely felt where acute hurdles in transportation of forest products were grievously faced. The government attempted to build roads to ease the dispatch of the forest products. This brought a large number of traders to the submontane tracts. So, intense was the tree-felling activity that large number of trees could not be transported out and were left to rot or to be burnt in the forest (Atkinson, 1982). Expounding all the essence of the colonial attitude of the British, Dangawal (2005) illustrated the material cause of deforestation in a lucid manner. He pin-pointedly mentioned that an English businessman Wilson had secured the lease of the forests of the Tehri Kingdom and was floating timber down the Bhagirathi to railway deports as well as to markets in the plains.

The colonial rulers, simultaneously put interest in extracting the teak of South Indian forests to meet the increasing demand of quality wood for ship-building since overseas competition among the European countries geared up the clash to claim their occupation in countries of Asia, Africa and America. Quality timber was their utter cry which played a prominent role in the arrangement of appointing an official to take care of the Indian forest. The company appointed a conservator of forests in 1807, to preserve and improve the protection of teak tree and other timber suitable for shipbuilding (Stebbing, 1922). Their entire attempt and initiatives in the early part of the company's rule was to galore up the valuable forest of India primarily to fulfil the demand of the shipbuilding industry in England (Saravanan, 2006).

Table 3.18: Teak wood export from India (1840-1848)

Year	*1840*	*1841*	*1842*	*1843*	*1844*	*1845*	*1846*	*1847*	*1848*
Total Export in M. tons	4952	6399	11487	10528	14245	13360	16798	11250	18000

Source: Report of the 21st Procedures of the British Association for the Advancement of Science, 1851.

In the nineteenth century particularly tribal movements became endemic events in many parts of British India. At the lower strata of the society, the tribals substituted agricultural labourers, wage labour in plantations, mines and factories. The colonial rulers overwhelmed the forested belts to reap maximum gain through revenue and therefore banned shifting cultivation. Adivasi revolt of Chotanagpur in 1855 by the Santhal community against British forest policy is a historic one. As such, the revolt of Gudem-Rampa in Tamil Nadu in 1879-80 was formidable against the British imperialist. The rebellion rose against the lordship attitude of the colonialist for imposition of undue taxes on timber and grazing, police exactions, excise regulations restricting production of domestic liquor of toddy, exploitation of moneylenders and traders etc. This revolt also ends in a brutal suppression. A series of unrest particularly among the forest tribes of India took place against of the British forest policy which attempted to deprive the tribals from their ancestral livelihood practices related to the forest ecology. A series of tribal movements opposing the British forest policy took place in several parts of forested tracts of India.

Mention may be made of (i) the Kol and Bhumij revolt of the early nineteenth century; (ii) the Birsa-Munda led agitation during 1890s; (iii) the uprising of Jgadalpur of Bastar in 1911; (iv) the protest in Gudem-Rampa in 1929; (v) Sitarama Raju led movement in the Godavari hills in Andhra; and (vi) Warli revolt of 1945-46.

The tribal communities who were once in harmony with the forests became uprooted. Their age-old traditional practices were dismantled and dislodged and which caused a total deploration of forest based livelihood and thus cracked down the symbiotic relationship between forest and forest tribes. The entire episode of these tribal unrests was politically induced leading to a distorted ecological scenario in the areas of their hegemony. In fact, it is an integral part of political ecology without which proper intervention into the problem cannot be accomplished. Political ecological studies are chiefly concerned with the effects of human activities on the physical environment.

The advent of British colonialism in the Indian forest land was in fact, a severe blow particularly to the rights of the ecosystem people. All the commercial instinct and exploitative attitude of the Britishers fabricated a domain of distrust and intolerance within the ecological societies. And therefore, resistance movements during the colonial period were widespread and to some extent characterized by aggressiveness. Some important impacts of colonial forest policy on the ecological societies can be summarized as: (i) it effectively either destroyed or crippled the social and cultural institutions which existed during pre-colonial period; (ii) people lost control over the use of natural resources, such as forests, minerals, land etc.; and (iii) it forcibly pushed people to certain crisis in the form of hunger, inter-group clash, disbelief and discontent to their moral and social ethics.

For most of the tribes of India forest was their habitat, livelihood and security against diseases, and the fear psychosis of dislocation for their forest homeland made them aggressive which eventually united them to strive relentlessly against all the adverses of the imposed forest.

Deforestation and Community Culture

The morphogenesis of the forest has close association with soil, climate, topography, and the attitude of the inhabitants therein. The age of exploration during sixteenth and seventeenth century opened-up ways to reach the areas that remained unexplored particularly by the Europeans. The curiosity to explore the unknown synchronising with the target of the expedition for valuable metals like gold, diamond, silver, copper etc. to enrich the kings who sponsored took a turn into competition among the European powerful states. The year 1775, which was the ceremonious year of industrial revolution initially in England and then the competition to being more and more areas under their hegemony created great demand for wood and fuel (Hussain, 2004). This gave birth to the extensive deforestation first at their own soil and then the forest of their colonies. The ship-building, locomotives and other industries, the railway communication, the plantation farming etc. over loaded the demand for woods and fuel. Then came the two World Wars, which also enforced large scale forest destruction in the war headed countries and their colonies (Williams, 2006). Abolishing all the feudal remnants from the socio-political frame, a new set of economy prevailed where production value, use value, sale value etc. were measured by the market value and the profit therefrom. This changing scenario of the entire world is presented by Dowd (2009) quoting K. Marx:

> "The discovery of gold and silver in America, the extirpation, enslavement and entombment in mines of the aboriginal population, the beginning of the conquest and looting of the East Indies, the turning of Africa into a warren for the hunting of black skins, signalized the rosy dawn of the era of capitalist production" (Douglas Dowd, 2009).

Forest in India primarily was under community control. Not only the forest tribes and forest dwellers depended largely on the forest produce, but also almost all the communities of ancient India were more or less dependent on forest. Long before the British arrived, India's inhabitants relied upon forest resources as an essential component of their life styles (Haeuber, 1993). Although forest suffered a lot resulting from large-scale expansion of agricultural field, the practices they performed in the forest were not much effective to put imprint of devastation. Circumstantially, it can be concluded that practically two vital social systems were prevalent during this period for a formidable resource use. The first one is characteristically primitive and profound in the areas of tribal dominance and forested hilly tracts. Hunting, food gathering and shifting cultivation are the three prime means of resource use. Although they were fully dependent on the forest resources, their practices were ecofriendly. Seldom they had brought severe irrecoverable damages to the forest. Apart from these, the forest-based produces like honey, wax, ivory etc. had all limitations as these were occasionally used as market commodity. The flow of materials was largely within the territory. This meant that the tribal population had a real stake in the security of resource base of their territory (Gadgil, 1990). It is however, noteworthy that the shifting cultivation is more often blamed for deforestation. But the practices shifting cultivation of long cycles by the tribes provide time for regeneration and they usually do not go for felling big trees. Still today it remains as a common practice among the tribes.

The second system of resource use is largely seen to concentrate in the alluvial plains of India. Settlements were found in high concentration in the river plains in comparison to other remote areas which is well reflected in the location of most of the holy places and the antiques of that time. Fuelwood and the housing materials for the plain dwellers were gathered from the nearest forest. Although, use of forest produces were mandatory, they were conscious about the continuity of resource supply. Forest, for all the people was not merely a tree cover to meet their requirement but at the same time forests hold a very important place in the life and philosophy of the people of the country (Chaudhuri, 2007). Amidst urban expansion prior to the colonial period, the forest resource bases were well maintained and managed. Kings like Ashoka, Harshavardhana, Sher Shah and Akbar took sufficient care of nature and natural wealth. King Ashoka had reputation for planting herbs, medicinal plants and shade trees along the roadside. Reduction in Cheetah population was a concern for King Akbar. He imported Cheetah from outside and released them in the Indian jungles. Not only this, the people of the country strictly observed all the sustainable approaches while performing hunting or lumbering. Few instances related to such practices may be cited here as reported by the *Gaonbuhra* (village headman) of Pathar Shyam village located along the Assam-Nagaland Border. Irrespective of caste, community and tribe, people living in the close proximity of the forests of Assam-Nagaland Border observed same norms particularly with regard to the forest related activities. Table 3.19 shows the pattern of ethics strictly maintained by the people.

Agriculture is the mainstay of the economy and the people intend to produce more to feed the growing population and to enrich the economy. Even in ancient India, expansion of agricultural land was nearly a product of extensive clearance of dense forest. Forest land is normally converted into agricultural land only after partial or complete removal of the big trees and this practice still persists in India particularly among the agricultural society. Thus, the subsistence agriculture practiced by the

Table 3.19: Forest related ethical practices of the Turungs

Practice	*Ethical values followed*	
	Dos	*Don'ts*
Hunting	(1) Kill only the matured, preferably male (2) Practice twice or thrice in a year (3) Practice with due permission from the village chiefs	(1) Never kill the pregnant mother (2) Avoid killing a mother with young cabs (3) Stops hunting during matting period
Tree felling	(1) Cut only the matured trees (2) Cut a sacred big tree, they usually arrange a pre-cut worship (3) Prefer branches of matured trees or dead trees for fuel wood (4) Consider big trees as sacred	(1) Never cut banyan, mango and other fruit trees (2) Never cut big trees (3) Never cut big trees (4) Never uproot herbs, creepers and plants
Food collection	(1) Only collect the matured seeds and plants (2) Leave seed of plants during harvest for regeneration (3) Leave ample seeds for germination	(1) Over harvest is considered as a crime (2) Never destroy the field (3) Leave mother seeds un-plucked

Source: Interview with the Gaoburha, Pathar Shyam village, 8-11-2011.

ancient society was seldom responsible for destruction of forest. People enjoyed full right to use forest resources and protected the forest land under their occupation.

Grazing is more often made responsible for sizeable deforestation in the areas of intensive animal husbandry. The farmers grazed their animals on village common lands subject to community control; the nomadic herds too had their own understanding as to the areas to be grazed by different groups and the relationships to be maintained with settled cultivators (Whyte, 1968). The overall impact of grazing on forest is, therefore, negligible. Thus, grazing was not a major cause of deforestation.

Penetration of Colonial Rule

The East India Company arrived in India in 1608 during the rule of Mughal

Emperor Jahangir and took permission to establish a factory at Surat. Gradually, the company eclipsed the Portuguese and within few years they achieved massive expansion of their trading presidency, i.e. Madras, Bombay and Calcutta by the year 1717. Following the battle of Plassey in 1757, the East India Company built their stronghold almost all over the country and brought it under the rule of a governor appointed by the British Government in England. In fact, it was the dawn of well-planned forestry practices under the sponsorship of colonial government that led to massive deforestation. When the British came to power, they realized the commercial value of the forests and tried to impose a number of restrictions on the use of forests and exploitation of forest resources (Chaudhuri, 2007).

Interfering over the rights of forest dwellers and users of forest resources, restriction was imposed upon in 1855 to conserve the forest. The declaration was—"The sole objects with which states forest administered is the public benefit. In some cases the public is the whole body of the tax payers, in others the people on the tract within which the forest is situated, but in almost all cases the constitution and preservation of a forest involve, in greater or lesser degrees, the regulation of rights and restrictions of privileges of uses in the forest area which may have previously been enjoyed by the inhabitants of its immediate neighbourhood" (Patty, 2007).

Forest Act, 1865

In 1865, the Forest Act of India was first introduced in a legal form. This act was so formulated that it handed over the supreme power to the Government to administer the forest directly. The overall impacts of this act are: (i) it enables the government to declare any forest land as government forest; (ii) it empowered the government to punish anyone found violating the act; and (iii) it helps the government to rigid its grip over the vast forest-wealth of India and thus confirmed state monopoly over the forest (Gadgil and Guha, 1992). This act was the virtual outcome of a report submitted by Dr. McClelland who travelled in the forests of India and proposed for curtailment to the exploitation by private parties (Ribbentrop, 1900).

The Forest Act, 1865 was considered insufficient because of its incompetency in distinctly demarcating the line between private and government forest. With a view to amend the Act 1865, a conference on forest was held in Allahabad where Baden Powell presented a paper entitled "Forest Legislation and the Defects of the Existing Law". He outright criticized the act of 1865 and recommended to surface a new forest policy. Accordingly, D. Brandis submitted a memorandum on the forest legislation. In 1878, the Indian Forest Act VII was passed, extending to all provinces of British India, except Madras, Burma, the Hazra district of Punjab, Ajmer, Coorg, Berar and Beluchistan (Ribbentrap, 1900).

Forest Act, 1878 was recommended with planned scrutinization which in fact was brought to tighten the grip of Imperialist power over the forest resources following strict curtailment of people's right over the forest. The act was a comprehensive piece of legislation which by one stroke of the executive pen, attempted to obliterate centuries of customary use by rural population all over India (Gadgil and Guha, 1992). It enabled the Government to convert protected land to reserved land as they consolidated full control over the forests. As a result, within a decade the total area of state forest increased from 14,000 to 81,400 square miles (Stebbing, 1922).

The Act 1878, indeed was thought to be inefficient to fulfil the imperialist interest. At the same time a series of peasant unrests over the forest policy opened-up way for a more rigid forest policy. The forest policy, 1894 was the outcome of the problems they faced with the question of rights over forest resources. The principle of state monopoly also formed the cornerstone of the important forest policy statement of 1894 (Gadgil and Guha, 1992).

The spirit of this policy is well conspicuous and the intention of the colonial ruler to consolidate their hold on the forest was also exposed. A critical review of the first forest policy of the British Government in India provides few clues to understand the colonial motives of exploitation. The policy allowed the forest dwellers to enjoy the rights with limitations and interestingly restricted the ownership. The policy stated:

(1) The sole object to which the management of forest is to be dedicated is to promote the general well-being of the country.

(2) The maintenance of adequate forests is dictated primarily for the preservation of the climatic and physical conditions of the country, and secondly, to fulfil the needs of the people but there were the following conditions:

   (a) Permanent cultivation should come before forestry.

   (b) The satisfaction of the needs of the local population at non-competitive rates, if not free overriding all considerations of revenue.

(c) After the fulfilment of the above conditions the realizations of maximum revenue should be the guiding factor.

A review of the revenue accumulation of the Forest Department of the country from 1869 to 1920 probably reflects the nature of colonial policy and tells about the growth pattern of revenue. During the period from 1870 to 1880, the yearly average of the revenue collection was 6.15 million rupees with a yearly surplus of 1.9 million rupees which within a span of 50 years rose to 37.1 million rupees and the surplus reached a maximum of 16.0 million rupees. The rate of gross increase was approximately 450 times over the period 1870-1880 (Table 3.20):

Table 3.20: Revenue and Surplus of Forest Department in India (1870-1920)

Period	*Average yearly revenue (Rs. million)*	*Yearly surplus (Rs. in million)*	*Cumulative p.c. of revenue growth*
1870-1880	6.10	1.90	—
1880-1890	10.25	3.70	63.03
1890-1900	16.80	7.60	175.41
1900-1910	22.70	10.00	272.13
1910-1920	33.35	14.60	446.72

Source: Compiled from Annual Progress Report on Forest Administration in India, file no. 69/80.

Capitalist Penetration: Through "The Passage to India, 1750-1850", Michal William (2006) tried to unfold the history of forest destruction in India. He wrote—"A distinctive aspect of the story of India deforestation was the activity and 'networking' of some 800-odd influential and botanically well versed surgeons of the EIC. Edward Belfour, Hugh Cleghorn, Alexander Gibson, John McClelland, William Roxburgh and John Stocks were the intellectual offspring of Scottish scientific, medical and philosophical enlightenment and usually men of a radical social and political persuasion. ... Hugh Cleghorn did just that and reported to the British Association meeting in Ipswich about 'the probable effects in an economical and physical point of view of the destruction of tropical forests." Cleghorn (1852) described that indiscriminate *havoc*, shortage and impending deficiency and timber famine became the basis for most subsequent colonial responses to problems of environmental degradation in India. On the basis of this report it can clearly be assessed that despite the advices from the appointed experts of forestry, the colonial government pursued everything as per their economic and political interest and policies were also framed accordingly. The various policies they formulated aimed particularly at revenue collection. Table 3.20 showing revenue and surplus of Forest Department is just one example of such exploitative motive of the colonial rulers.

In order to pursue all the policies concerning forests of India several amendments and acts were brought. A series of acts were passed following the 1894 forest policies. These amendments and acts were, in fact, brought to the surface to make the forest policies clueless. In 1901 Indian forest (Amendment) Act, the Repealing and Amending Act, 1920, the Devolution Amendment Act, 1927, the Indian Forest (Amendment) Act were the outcome of such attempts.

Forest and the Colonial Economy

The Suez Canal was excavated in 1869 and the fortune for the British colonialist in South East Asia got an inspiration to work with more coverage. It was a crucial stepping stone on the passage of India. Until the Cepoy Mutiny of 1857, the entire India was governed by East India Company. The great event of 1857 was the turning point which changed the fate of India as the whole control was taken over by the British Government. Britain undoubtedly gained much economically from the control of this vast empire, but immense sums of capital had to be invested (William, 2006) in the development of infrastructure such as railways, roads and other communications to enhance their persuasion of colonial policy. In fact, the development that they made was not virtually for the overall development of the country. Like "all roads lead to Rome"—their developmental policy was triggered to make the resource rich areas more accessible and exploitable. Their prime target was chiefly three resources—(i) land, (ii) forests, and (iii) mines. The very progress that ensured the prosperity, territorial control and power of the developed western world also increased resource exploitation. Timber and land were the greatest concerns particularly to match up the competition among those advanced colonial countries (Marx, 1844). For ship-building, railway communication, smelting of iron, steam engines and construction works had high demand for timber as raw materials. Reviewing the entire world political and economic situation Woeikof (1901) commented that world civilization had led to the growing disassociation of man and the earth. German philosopher, Ernst Friedrich (1904) remarked—"European global expansion and resource gathering was based on an exploitative and destructive economy (Raubwirtschaft) that had already destroyed the flora, fauna and soils over vast areas".

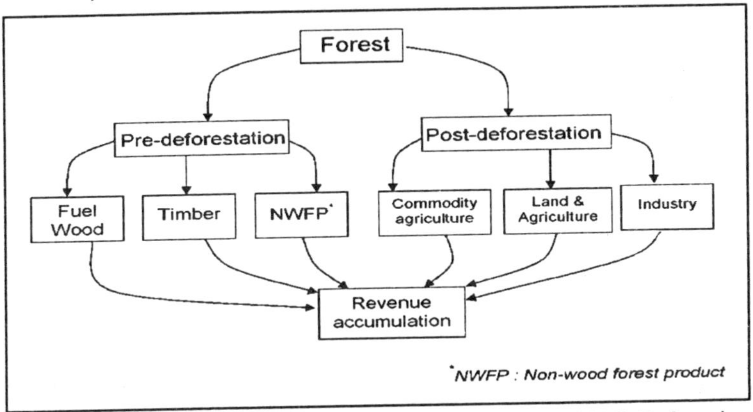

Source: Concept of the model developed from M. Williams (2006): Deforesting the Earth from Prehistory to Global Crisis, An Abridgement.

Fig. 3.8: A Capitalistic View on Forest Resources

Using teak forests from the whole of North and South India to feed their ship-building industry and to compensate the fresh demand for quality wood in England, the colonial empire tried to explore new areas for timber extraction. The forest was their chief target since it had the ability to generate more and more revenue in both pre and post deforestation stage. The process of deforestation and associated benefit as viewed by the capitalist can be put diagrammatically (Fig. 3.8).

To satisfy the imperialist demand, the colonial government attempted to remove the inaccessibility hurdles from the country by undertaking construction of railway lines. Construction of railway lines began in 1852 from Bombay to the foothills of the ghats and from Calcutta to Raniganj coalfields at a distance of 195 km. Within a span of just 15 years, i.e. from 1852 to 1867, 19 of then India's largest city were linked and surprisingly by 1900 the construction of railway line touched a mark of 65,037.56 km. During 1860-1870 forests were destroyed at the rate of 28,611 hectares and that amount immediately stepped up to 52,631.58 hectares in 1900. Again, the loss of forest for railway ties (which need replacement at a certain time interval because of either rotting or eaten up by termites) estimated to be 286,118 hectares and the increase of cultivated land at the cost of forest area of 6.0 million hectares over the same period.

Table 3.21: Estimates of sleepers used and acres of forest cleared in India, 1850-1940.

Year	Miles of track	Ties used in new construction (in million)	Ties renewed annually (in million)	Total ties (in million)	Forests cleared ('000 ha)
1850	0	—	—	—	—
1860	1,542	2.8	0.3	3.1	6.28
1870	8,637	12.8	1.3	14.1	28.54
1880	15,764	12.8	1.3	14.1	28.54
1890	27,227	20.6	2.1	22.7	45.95
1900	40,396	23.7	2.4	26.1	52.83
1910	52,767	22.3	2.3	24.6	49.80
1920	61,957	16.5	1.7	18.2	36.84
1930	70,565	15.5	1.6	17.1	34.62
1940	72,144	2.8	0.3	3.1	6.32

Source: M.D. Morirs and C.D. Dudley, "*Selected Railway Statistics for the Indian Sub-continent*, 1853-1946".

Table 3.21 reflects the severity of forest destruction, the total area deforested being 2,89,716.60 hectares within a period of nearly 90 years. As such, forest clearance for construction of railway line amounted to approximately 16,259.39 sq.km. Thus, the total area suffered from deforestation was 30,933.16 sq.km during the period 1850-1940. It was a very complex and tragic picture which more often is overlooked and ignored as if the colonial rulers contemplated everything for the sake of a total welfare of India.

3.5 A Discourse on the Political-Ecology of Deforestation in Assam-Nagaland Border

Endowed with plenty of natural resources, including dense and impenetrable forest and a hostile topography with a congenial climatic condition the Assam-Nagaland Border region has been experiencing all adversity resulting from ruthless removal and extirpation of all nature's gift by profit making agencies within a span of just 100 years (1870-1970). The capitalist intervention was started with the annexation of the Ahom kingdom by the British colonialist *vide* Yandabu Pact, 1826 signed between the East India Company and the Burmese rulers (Barpujari, 1992). Prior to the advent of the British, forestry practices were extremely limited and reference could be made in this regard about the three officials namely Habiyal Baruah, Kathkotiya Baruah, Hati Baruah (Barbarua) appointed by the Ahom kings in the later part of their reign. They were entrusted to take care of the forest products, forest timbers and the abundant elephant population which eventually occupied an important place in the market of that time (Gogoi, 1983). Mackenzie (1989) wrote—"From the lips or pens of them and many others—Dalton, Hopkinson, Agnew, Haughton, Graham and Power—to say nothing of the untiring officers of the survey, for whom no peak is inaccessible, no jungle impenetrable and no tribe to rude to be faced, I had stores of gathered material which cannot now be used. I had, indeed, hoped at one time to have had the aid of some of them in putting the wild story of this frontier into complete and fitting dress." Prior to the time of Mackenzie's expedition, the whole region was under the domain chiefly of the Ahom kings. It is therefore, quite comprehensive and surmising that accept few settlements and agricultural fields the entire patch was formidably a land of jungle characterized by all hostility. Although in quantity it was insignificant, substantial forest products were exported to the neighbouring kingdom by the Ahom rulers. Moreover, royalties were realized on timber and elephants. Elephants played a vital role both in trade and war. Wild elephants were plentiful and more in large herds (McCosh, 1837). A sizeable number of elephants were caught during those periods by way of Khedah Chikar and Melah Chikar. Place names linking elephant catching operation, such as *Hati Pati* (elephant corridor), *Hatighuli* (resting place of elephants), *Hatigarh* (place for elephant captivity), *Hatisal* (training camp for domestication of elephants) etc. are still portraying the ancient heritage. The British traveller J. M'Cosh (1837) wrote—"From 700 to 1000 elephants are exported from Assam every year. Their average value is 300 rupees. A duty of 10 rupees was formerly levied at Goalpara on every elephant exported. Great numbers are killed every year merely for their Ivory".

Timbers, during those periods used especially as housing materials, to make boats, and to prepare wooden furniture and seldom people needed to enter into deep jungles to procure woods. The *Bastiland*—a land of plantations along with the residence, hold by each family, or specific wooded area under their occupations efficiently supplied all their timber requirements and fuelwood. Shihabuddin Talish, an eminent chronicler of Mughal period in India mentioned in his book "*Fathiya-i-ibriyah*"—"Many kinds of odorous fruits and herbs of Bengal and Hindustan grow in Assam. We saw here certain varieties of flowers and fruits, both wild and cultivated, which are not to be met with elsewhere in the whole of India." Talish's description confirms the traditional practices of planting fruits, and herbs in the *bastiland* of the then society (Barpujari, 1992). Lac had an important place in trade with outside countries. Apart from these, as the Muslims are traditionally perfume lover, there was a high demand for Assam's Agoru (*Aquilaria agallocha*) among the Mughal kings.

A substantial portion of Assam-Nagaland Border region since was under the dominance of Ahom kingdom besides parts towards south was ruled by the Kacharis in the earlier periods, the socio-economic and political dominance of the Ahoms naturally had some impact over resource utilization. Being the centre for most of the economic and political caricature of the rulers, few urban centres with a potential population size were developed in this region. Prominence of war politics to dominate neighbouring kingdom gave birth to number of Army Camps, around which settlements had grown to supply the needs of the army and turned into an urban agglomeration. Desoi, Morongi, Kaliabor, Gargaon, Dimapur etc. are such urban agglomerations. No doubt, in the absence of sufficient open space these were erected at the cost of considerable deforestations. Agriculture was subsistence in nature which in no measure could be accorded as an active factor of deforestation supported by a low population growth.

Table 3.22: Population of Sibsagar, 1871

Religion	*Total*	*Male*	*Female*	*% of Total*
Hindu	2,82,969	1,47,479	1,35,490	95.4
Muhammadan	12,619	6,873	5,746	4.3
Christian	283	180	103	0.1
Buddhist	153	94	59	—
Others	565	34	251	0.2
Total	**2,96,589**	**154660**	**1,41,649**	**100**

Source: W.W. Hunter: *A Statistical Account of Assam*, 1975.

W.W. Hunter (1871), John M'Cosh (1837), M. Mills (1854) etc. conducted surveys and recorded their findings. As presented in the book *Topography of Assam* of John M'Cosh, the total population of the area under Assam Rajah was 2,20,000 and the total population of whole of Assam region was 7,99,519. It is obvious that though population had decreased due to (i) Moamoriah Revolt and (ii) Massacre by Mann during the Pre-British period, the total population certainly was not more than that estimated by John M'Cosh.

Table 3.23: Population of Assam (1833-1834)

Districts	Total Population	Percentage of Total
Assam Rajah**	2,20,000	27.52
Darrung	89,519	11.20
Nowgong	90,000	11.27
Kamrup	3,00,000	37.52
Goalpara	1,00,000	12.51
Total	**7,99,519**	

Source: J.M'Cosh, 1837: *Topography of Assam.*

* Assam Rajah meant the Ahom kingdom

The genocide of Assam by the Mann Army not only reduced the population of Ahom kingdom but also disrupted the settlements and depopulated villages after villages. The long three years barbaric repression pushed the inhabitants to take shelter mostly in the inaccessible hills and jungles which subsequently became large settlement zone particularly in the jungle areas of the Nagaland foothills. Among the three Burmese invasions into Assam, the third one was extremely devastating which uprooted thousands of people. They took shelter in the forest subsequently. No written records or any documents left to estimate the amount of area deforested for settling in the forest.

Survey conducted in the villages of Assam-Nagaland Border area very clearly complement the tentative time period of the growth of settlement in this once dense forested track. Twenty villages from various districts were surveyed with the help of a schedule. As many as 62 per cent households of Sibsagar District disclosed that their forefathers came here around 250 years ago. Table 3.22 shows the time of settlements to assess and analyse the inherent causes of the growth of settlement in different districts of the region which except few pockets were attached to the Ahom kingdom (*see* Table 3.24).

Human activities are in most cases responsible for deforestations. The fact of diminishing nature and of human ubiquity is now obvious (Tuan, 1971). Gregory (1985) observed the human activities and the changing pattern of nature and wrote: "On the one hand the effect of human activity upon earth environment has been very apparent and increasing, and yet on the other hand until 1950s and 1960s the significance of human activity did not attract much attention of physical geographers, who instead often chose to study environmental change before man, to seek processes largely modified by man, or at best to

Table 3.24: Percentage of respondents regarding time of their settlements in the districts of Assam-Nagaland Border Region

Districts	*No. of surveyed villages*	*% of respondent stating time of settlements*		
		<250 years	*250-100 years*	*< 100years*
Sibsagar	3	52.41	30.24	17.35
Jorhat	3	37.00	43.42	19.58
Golaghat	3	18.45	27.15	54.40
Karbi Anglong	2	Nil	20.59	79.41
Dimapur	2	21.68	18.32	60.00
Wokha	1	10.57	31.92	57.51
Mokokchung	3	18.21	11.87	69.92
Mon	2	9.45	35.19	55.36
Region		20.97	27.34	51.36

Source: Survey conducted in the villages of Assam-Nagaland Border in 2011.

include man as an afterthought or an appendage." Deforestation is apparently a planned manifestation of human activity where politics on one side and the economy, a product of the system, on the other, pushed people to the forest for shelter and livelihood. The whole episode of the peopling in Assam-Nagaland Border region is the same except for areas in the plains of the Brahmaputra Valley. The process of peopling can be summarized as:

(a) Little traces or no traces of early human settlement during prehistoric periods can be observed in this thick forested zone of the border area.

(b) One-fifth of the settlements came up during the period of Kachari and Ahom regime and these were characteristically the forced settlement at the initiatives of the then administration.

(c) More than one-fourth of the settlements grew as a result of a number of factors:

  (i) The third Burmese invasion in 1822 forced people to take shelter in the inaccessible dense forest of the Nagaland foothills.

  (ii) Opening of tea gardens in large number along this border region particularly during the later part of the 19th and the early part of the 20th century under British hegemony attracted human settlement.

  (iii) Intense logging to procure valuable timber from the forest to fulfil the demand of the British imperialist opened a huge space to ensure further intervention of the landless peasantry either for settlements or for extension of farmland.

(iv) Nearly half of the settlements grew as a result of establishment of several tea gardens during British rule.

(v) Encroachment by the Naga tribes seeking more farmland and the rehabilitation measure taken by the Government of Assam to settle the people affected by flood and river bank erosion.

(vi) Immigrants from Bangladesh and Nepal encroached forest areas for settlement and agriculture.

The onset of the major ecological catastrophe in this border belt was brought about by imperial forestry practices during the middle of the nineteenth century. The most apparent evidence of the thick dense forest cover of this border region can be found in the writings of Butler (1978)—"The whole route was through a dark, damp, chilly, gloomy forest with small undulating hills, and neither the sky nor sun was seen throughout the day. Our road was a mere footpath, and the forest so thick that we could not see ten paces before us". It was a travelling account of John Butler who was entrusted to conduct a survey into the province of Assam in 1841. The time of Butler's travel was very much close to the last part of Ahom dynasty and therefore it is comprehensive to surmise the attributes of the then forest cover.

The Era of Imperial Forestry

Capitalism under British lordship penetrated into all the resources of the world to generate more profit and to establish their suzerainty all over the globe. Otherwise, a region of thick forest with a group of people having just traditional life style would never attract a dozen of soldiers with one Cornel to take over the region to their subjugation. Moamoria revolt of 1786 and the brutal Burmese invasion in 1824 ensured a mandatory intervention of the British, i.e. East India Company, which most possibly provided a preconceived idea to the colonial representatives about the rich natural resources of Assam in particular and of the whole North East in general. East India Company already set their trading with Assam in the later part of seventeenth century. At the earlier stage, the British were content to play in Assam the modest role of shopkeepers (Borpujari; 1992). Political power, or to get control of the region was not their destination since the East India Company heavily engaged with the problems of South India until 1792, the end of the Mysore war. As trade was their real interest in Assam, Captain Welsh, with a good trading concern reported in February 1794 that since the enforcement of the commercial agreement concluded Gaurinath Sinha in February 1793, Arcot rupees 12,012-2-9 had been received as part of the collections at the Kandahar Chokey. As regards exports, he mentioned about sugarcane, pepper, vine, poppy, indigo, mustard seeds, tobacco, betel nut, ginger, rice, minerals products and animal products (lac, *muga* silk, elephant tusk, rhinoceros's horn, buffalo's hide and deer's skin). A large number of navigable streams provided great facilities for commercial intercourse (FPC)). The Burmese intervention within the British territory also worked as another immediate cause for British dissatisfaction. The entire situation opened-up the way for the British colonialist to take hold over the entire province of Assam. The Yandaboo Treaty of 24th February, 1826 therefore, more often regarded as the gate pass to establish imperialist hegemony in Assam. The year 1838 witnessed the total occupation by the British imperialist capturing all political, economic and social staff of the state (Mackenzie, 1937). Till then Assam-Nagaland Border in large was under the Ahom regime and had experienced very little forestry practices in the form of collection of lac, timber, elephant's tusk, rhinoceros's horns, buffalo's hide, resin etc. to meet their minimum requirement. A substantial amount of forest produces were exported to neighbouring kingdoms and rests were released to trade in the localities particularly in the Duars, the entrance into the Ahom kingdom. Numerous such Duars around the region acted as focal centres exchanging goods with the hill people as per their needs and demands. Disturbances and prevailing unrest all throughout the region provided a sound back up to the imperial power to establish imperial suzerainty and to upset the entire existing traditional system of social, cultural and economic fabric of North East India. The diplomacy of colonialist thus worked positively in their favour and in due course it gave them a freehand to expand all policies of exploitation over all the resources both living and non-living of the region. The history of forest policy of British India is inseparable from the history of forest policy of North East India in general and of Assam in particular.

Except few scattered areas including Assam, most of the provinces of India have already seized under the jurisdiction of Forest Department. The Forest Department for Assam was first opened in 1868 (Ribbentrop, 1900). In the meantime, the government took all necessary initiatives to promote agriculture, a genuine and fast profit making economy and attempted to widen the horizon of revenue collection which in turn would augment the transfer of fallow deforested land into farmland or other non-forest use. Dr. Voelker, a German expert was entrusted to conduct a survey on the status of Indian agriculture with a view to improve it in 1893. Voelker thoroughly discussed and analysed the role of forests *vis-à-vis* agriculture and stressed the need for formulating a forest policy with definite bias for serving agriculture more directly than before (Sagreiya, 2009). On the basis of this report and recommendations therein, the Government of India issued Resolution No. 22F dated 19th October, 1894 declaring its forest policy which was indeed a landmark in the ecological history of Assam (Darlong, 2002).

Prior to the enactment of the 1894 forest policy, the forests in Assam were managed under the Bengal Forest Rules (Notification No. 13F dated the 16th February, 1871). The Chief Commissioner, perhaps with dissatisfaction on the forest rules, submitted a revised forest rules for the province of Assam in 1875 requesting a prompt sanction thereupon. Table 3.25 presents the focal events of the colonial forestry practices in Assam under British rule.

The forests of the entire state were thoroughly surveyed by the British prior to their occupation. This indicates their eagerness to intervene into the ecological and political system of the state. The second important aspect portrayed in the framework of colonial forestry is that the forest rights of local people, which they had been enjoying for generations, were brought under their control and imposed all regulations to procure more profit. The total revenue collection of the Forest Department during the period 1881-1904 gives a good illustration on the revenue oriented forestry practices of the British Government.

Within a span of just 24 years the forest revenue increased from Rs. 2,33,487 to Rs. 6,76,944, a growth of 189.93 per cent, which indicates the inherent attitude of the colonial forestry. Notably, the forest policy of 1894 made provisions to classify all government forests into four broad categories. The first category forests, those resting on hill slopes, were to be preserved for protection of farmland of plains from hill torrents (Darlong, 2002), the second category forests of valuable timbers were to be managed commercially for earning revenue after meeting the local needs subject to some terms and conditions. The third and fourth categories of forests were to be managed as per convenience of the local people. The vital concern of this policy, however, was to achieve advantages in agricultural sector which in their sense is a milking cow to earn more revenue even at the cost of forests. Therefore, the priority sector of the policy was permanent cultivation (*see* Table 3.26).

Table 3.25: A framework of the events of colonial forestry practice in Assam (1750-1890)

Sl. No.	Period	Concerned authority	Particulars of events
1.	1750	Jean Baptise Chavodier	Reported the presence of gold sand at the river beds and about the forests of Assam
2.	1804	Charles Hatchet	Put interest in the analysis of industrial quality of lac of Assam
3.	1825	Lieutenant Wilcox	In an expedition discovered petroleum deposits in eastern Assam districts
4.	1834	William Grifith and Nathanial Wallich	Conducted a thorough survey of Assam under East India Company
5.	1835	Francis Jenkins	Prepared an account of trees of Assam
	1835	R. Bruce	Discovered wild tea plants in Assam
6.	1841	William Robinson	Studied Botany of Assam and published "Descriptive Accounts of Assam Forests"
7.	1845	Captain S.F. Hannay	Identified exotic forests land of valuable timbers
8.	1849	Forest Department	Forest survey conducted to complete cataloguing and mapping of forested tracts. 2000 Indian rubber trees were identified by the surveyor
9.	1850	Forest Department	Tax levied on timber felling by the private woodcutter at the rate of Rs. 15/100 logs
10.	1952	Forest Department	(i) Abolition of prevailing tax collection (ii) New rule introduced to allot forest land farming to the highest bidder (iii) Created Forest Mahal for the private contractors
11.	1856	Geological Survey of India	Formally constituted the Geological Survey of India Invested to discover more mineral fields
12.	1868	Gustav Mann	Appointed as Assistant Conservator: surveyed the forests of Assam from 1808 to 1871

(Contd.)

Sl. No.	*Period*	*Concerned authority*	*Particulars of events*
13.	1870	Gustav Mann	Completed inspection of forests and selection of forest reserves, timber and plantation work started (*teak, sal* etc.) Demarcation of area of reserve forests started Complete transfer of several thousand square miles of area to the Forest Department
14.	1874	Gustav Mann	Gustav Mann was appointed as Deputy Conservator of Forests Provincial Forest Department was established

Source: Stracey, P.D., 1949.

Table 3.26: Growth of revenue of Forest Department, Assam, 1881-1904

Period	*Average accumulation of revenue (Rs.)*	*Cumulative growth (P.C.)*
1881-1890	2,33,487	—
1891-1900	4,27,610	83.14
1900-1901	5,63,400	141.30
1903-1904	6,76,944	189.93

Source: Prepared from Gazetteer of Bengal and North East, 2008.

The principles for the grant of privileges to local people in minor forests were enunciated because it was found that the local people had acquired maximum usage rights there. Forest areas were to be relinquished if there was an effective demand for cultivation, provided (i) the cultivation was permanent and not shifting, (ii) forests were not being honey combed with patches of cultivated land and (iii) cultivation was not encroaching on the minimum forest requirements. However, after 1894, forest administration continued to reduce the customary rights of the local people because (i) forest regulations were extended over ever-widening areas of forests; (ii) there was a bias in favour of conservation and against the interests of local population; and (iii) compulsions were imposed by the imperial government for the maximization of revenue.

Prior to the enactment of a forest law special to Assam forest, the general law for India and the forest law for Bengal which was sanctioned in 1871 were the chief guidelines for forest administration in Assam. The Bengal laws were revised during the year 1876-77 with special reference to Assam, and received the approval of the Government of India (*The Assam Forest Manual*, Vol. I, p. 65). To improve the service quality and management system it became essential to the Government of India to devise a law special to Assam after procuring a total picture of the forest of the region. On the other hand, because of the exhaustion of forest in North and South India, Assam's forest got priority. To feed the demands and to bring the forest of Assam under strict management of Assam Forest Regulation VII of 1891 came into force. However, the most important regulation that was used to administer the forest resources of Assam was the Assam Forest Regulation VII of 1891 (Handique, 2004). It enables the administration to constitute any land a reserved forest through publication of a notification in the official Gazette [Assam Forest Regulation, U/S 5(i) 1891]. However, in no way it differs from Indian Forest Act 1865 or India Forest Act VI of 1878. The colonial attitude is quite distinct while the references are brought under scrutiny. In section 27, of the Act it is mentioned that "The local Government may from time-to-time assign to any village community the rights of Government to or over any land which has been constituted a reserve forest and may cancel such assignments." It practically kept open the way to do anything as per their needs and demands. The regulation of 1891 kept scope for deforestation and accordingly, under the provision of section 28 of the Assam Forest Regulation 1891, deforestation was permitted with the sanction of the Government of India (Saikia, 2011). By Gazette notification No. 25D/ the 25th April, 1887, Diphu reserved forest was recognized with a total area of 42,080 hectares. After the enactment of Assam Forest Regulation 1891, the Civil District of Territory and Sub-division issued a notice (No. 904R D/22, March, 1895) to exclude a substantial portion of the reserved forest for other non-forest use. As such, a total area of 135,08 acres of Nambor South reserved forests was notified on 15th September, 1905 to disforest along with 16.70 acres of Diphu reserved forests (*A Handbook of Government Notification on Reserved Forests* and protected areas of Assam, 2011). A series of disforestation activities subsequently after 1891 took place at the direct intervention of the then Forest Department. Surprisingly, the trend continued even to the post-Independence period of India. The aim was to maximize the revenue potential of the Government. Initially, lands lying fallow or without any commercially productive timber were deforested or disposed to meet the requirement of the tea companies (Saikia, 2011). The basis of deforestation in many cases was shown to be the expansion of cultivation, which practically benefitted railway companies, tea planters and few individual landholders. Conservation of forest in the name of reserved forest or other forms deliberately took into consideration the future supply of timber and other forest products.

It is, however, noticed that as per Indian Forest Act 1878 and the Assam Forest Regulation, 1891, a number of village forests were constituted in Assam under the direct supervision of State Forest Department. The Regulation further provided the local government necessary power to make rules for regulating forest management of the village forests and major burden of management was imposed on the village community (Handique, 2004). Normally, the villagers were allowed to take-up land along the fire lines as the Forest Department believed that cultivation in these tracts would minimize the spread of fire (A.I. Home; Conservator of Forest in Assam to the secretary to the Chief Commissioner of Assam; No. 109A, Shillong, 4 September, 1897). The formation of forest village not only helped in protecting the forests from fire and the trespassers and illegal practices of individuals but also rendered an indirect service to generate more revenue from the forest. It also helped in procuring labour for the works to be done in the forest. The Government took initiative to increase the number of village forests as it became more productive from the view point of forest management. Accordingly, in 1920, the Government began the process of declaring certain tracts in Sibsagar as village forests (ASF nos. 41-62, Forest-A, June 1920; Financial Department (ASA). Reserved forest like Dirai, Abhayapur, Galeki, Tiru Hills, Desai, Desai Valley, Dayang, Rengma, Diphu of the Assam-Nagaland Border tracts were brought under provision to constitute village forests. Though the Panchayats and Mouzadars were entrusted to look after the matters of village forests the response was too poor to extract benefit from them and as such the entire idea of establishing of village forest became doubtful. The attempt to constitute village forest in the reserved forests although was practical and productive from the view point of people—forest relations, but imposition of several restrictions and levies worked adversely to their interest. Little or no enthusiasm was noticed among the inhabitants of village forests. Only a few numbering 11 forest village were established up to the period of 1937 in the long forested tract of Assam-Nagaland Border (*see* Table 3.27).

Another significant aspect of colonial policies to extract more revenue from forest was the tax levied at the rate of Rs. 4.40 per axe used for felling trees. Thus, axe users and the timber contractors put more emphasis to harvest more trees with their axes within the given time and space. Moreover, taxes were imposed on timber, reeds and grazing of domestic animals in the forest (Goswami, 1987) (*see* Table 3.28).

Table 3.27: Number of village forests in Assam-Nagaland Border, 1937

Name of Divisions	*Name of Sub-divisions*	*Name of reserved forests*	*No. of forest village*
Sibsagar	Karbi-Anglong	Upper Daigrung Kaliani Mikir Hills	1 1 1
	Golaghat	Nambor Dayang	2 4
	Jorhat	Holongapar Dsoi	1 1
		Total	11

Source: Assam Legislative Assembly Debate, 8-9 December, Vol. III, pp. 2050-52.

Table 3.28: Pattern of tax imposed by the British administration

Type	*Forest articles*	*Rate of taxes*
Gorkhati	Timber (cutting)	Rs. 4.4/Axe
Khasury	Grazing	2 anna/cow 4 anna/buffalo
Bunkur	Reeds (cutting)	8 annas/Dao 4 annas/sickle

Source: Goswami, S.D., *Aspects of Revenue Administration in Assam*, 1987.

It is more often told that the dawn of scientific forestry in India was launched with the appointment of Dietrich Brandis on 1st April, 1854 (Ribentrop, 1989). He was, in fact, a successor of Dr. McClelland who submitted a report to the Government of India demanding a curtailment of the right of exploitation by private parties. The then Governor General, Lord Dalhousie, according to their need perhaps issued the "Charter of the Indian Forests" outlining conservancy for the whole of India (Ribentrop, 1989). Brandis was the person who introduced from the very outset principles of enumeration and organization of the working of forests. Introducing the 'Linear valuation method' of survey, Brandis took initiative to survey the whole of Indian forests. The trees were classified according to their girth and age. Table 3.29 compiled from Ribentrop's 'Forestry in British India' represents Brandis' classification especially made on a commercial view.

Table 3.29: Classification of forest trees of Indian forest

Category	*Girth (in feet)*	*Age in years*
Category-I	6 feet and above	62 and above
Category-II	4.6 feet-6 feet	39-62
Category-III	3 feet-4.6 feet	18-39
Category-IV	Below 3 feet	Below 18

Source: Ribentrop, *Forestry in British India*, 1989.

Brandis also emphasized on the line that twenty-fourth of the first class trees in each forest might annually be felled (Ribentrop, 1989). Assam under the British forestry policy was no exception to this principle. In the subsequent period, Gustav Mann had submitted two reports with details of forest of Assam (Mann, 1873). As per Mann reports the forests of Nagaland are rich in timber quality and other forest resources. *Jhuming* practices in Nagaland had been working adversely to this valuable forest resource disposition. Visiting Assam in 1873, Schlich, the Conservator of Forests in Bengal, estimated that of 92 per cent of uncultivated land, mostly under forest, gave the country an "extremely jungle aspect" (Memorandum on Forest Operations in Assam, 1873). As per Schlich's estimation a total of 4,565 square miles area in Assam was under the forest cover. Again, Brandis visited Assam in 1879 and conducted a detailed survey on the forest of Assam in collaboration of Gustav Mann and local forest officials. The report of Brandis was a milestone in the history of forestry of Assam. The growing interest of British colonialist aimed at procuring maximum revenue and accordingly the classification was made.

From all these forest related activities it is clear that the imperialist British Government emphasized more on revenue generation and formulated measures to augment profits from forestry practices. Conversion of forest land to cultivated land was such a measure which ensured continuous flow of revenue to their deposits. Brandi's suggestion on forestry development was to back up the colonial policy of exploitation of forest wealth. The eminent scholar of political history Doglas Dowd, (2009) very skillfully offers a view on the nature of capitalism. 'Capitalism', as per his elaboration, is and must be not only an economic but also a political and social system whose processes go well beyond production and trade for profit. From the seventeenth century on, Britain was first to seek and achieve the necessary depth and breadth of the processes systematic to capitalism: (1) expansion, (2) exploitation and

(3) oligarchic rule. In turn, those essentials of capitalist 'health' could only be met within the larger processes that characterize "the modern world". This nature of capitalism worked with full enthusiasm to appreciate the colonial policies in India as well as in Assam.

Wasteland Management Policy under Colonial Environment

The Ministry of Rural Development, Government of India, screening all the practical aspects defines wasteland as—"Degraded land which can be brought under vegetative cover with reasonable efforts and which is currently underutilized and land which is deteriorating for lack of appropriate water and soil management or on account of natural causes." Thus, the government identified the wasteland on the basis of three attributes: (i) degraded land, (ii) underutilized land, and (iii) poorly managed land. But for the colonial government, the concept of wasteland was quite different. For them wasteland appears to denote those tracts of land which are uncultivated, and unsettled. Extensive such tracts in Assam were lying unutilized and unsettled as many of the people left their own settlements as a result of the barbarous atrocities for a period of about five years launched by the Burmese soldiers (Borpujari, 1992). Agriculture was reported to be in a very backward state throughout Sibsagar. Two causes are assigned for this by the Survey Officer: first, the scantiness of population, and secondly, that the rent demanded for wasteland approaches too closely that for cultivated fields, the difference being only 4 *annas* per acre.

Discussing Locke's theory on wasteland Arneil (1996) commented—"However, the entire episode of wasteland politics no longer be judged in isolation from the policies adopted to govern and to manage the wasteland by the British colonialist all throughout the world". John Lock focused on the early English settlement in America and the subsequent conquest of the 'New World'. A discursive examination of Locke's category of 'wasteland' and the way it was applied in India between 1893 and 1878 shows the Locke's theory of property which remained a major influence on the South Asian landscape throughout much of the colonial period. On the other hand, forest legislation is not often applied for land settlement on par with the *zamindari* and *ryotari* revenue systems due to the disjuncture between 'the field' and the 'forest' that has characterized recent environmental history (Menon, 2004). Capitalists measure everything in term of a value. A wasteland, therefore, became a hidden opposition to the category of value in the sense that it is a land that lacked value because it had not been enclosed, privatized and modified (Whitehead, 2010). British in India found everywhere extensive tracts lying unutilized with no permanent property rights of any individual. Having all potentials to make a source of their revenue profit, the British introduced the category of wasteland into Indian law and revenue politics from the permanent settlement of Bengal in 1793 (Guha, 1984). In the eyes of colonial government wasteland was not a natural category applied to infertile, barren lands rather it was a social category that applied both to the supposedly unproductive uses and to land left idle (Menon, 2004).

Assam possessed a glaring uncultivated forest land at the time of British annexation. The colonialist aptly concentrated their interest to ramify and investigate the sources of revenue earnings. Attempts to make generous grants of wastelands were made from the time of David Scot, who in September 1827 proposed to grant wasteland to anyone who would initiate to bring such land under cultivation (Barooah, 1970). Under the condition that the total land allocated to the grantee would successfully bring into cultivation stepwise within nine years and after which he would be entitled to hold the land subject to the payment of revenue as per prevailing rates. Towards the end of the nineteenth century, the colonial administration began to relinquish its view that forested woodlands were merely a barrier to the extension of cultivation (Gadgil and Guha, 1988). To promote the magnitude of revenue collection clearance of the woodlands of no property rights became essential (Guha, 2005). Assam, particularly the Upper Brahmaputra valley, with little cultivation and scanty of population, possessing vast areas of forest drew attention of the colonial government. Efforts continued to make the wastelands profitable to the company. Beginning of tea cultivation marked an epoch in the management of wastelands in Assam (Hindique, 2004). In order to bring the wasteland under meaningful utilization subject to the revenue orientation attributes, the Wasteland Grant Rules of 1838 (also known as 99 years' Lease Rules), Fee Simple Rules of 1826, Revised Fee Simple Rules of 1874 and the New Lease Rules of 1876 were framed (Borpujari, 1992). The prime criteria of these wasteland rules were: (i) productivity, and (ii) the land revenue. With productivity and the revenue as the ordering criteria, it was now possible to view 'wasteland' as a synonym for 'idle land', that is, land untapped for its commercial potential. The *zamindars* although opposed the wasteland rule but the permanent settlement was made in *zamindar's* favour for reasons of political expediency and stability (Whitehead, 2010).

The wasteland rules as formulated were aimed chiefly at the vast forest areas of no property rights either of the government or of any individual. For a smooth execution of the rules, the government took initiatives by few amendments to the older version of wasteland lease rules. Earlier, the ceiling of wasteland grants was 500 acres, which was subsequently decreased to 100 acres in 1856 (Borpujari, 2004). The grantees, therefore, were offered to take-up more land as per their requirement so that maximum of wasteland could be brought under settlement. It primarily favoured the tea growers and applications were rushed in seeking large blocks of land in lease. There were no inducements for applications to limit their urge of the area actually required by them, and hence large areas of forest land were alienated by the government for tea plantations (Brandis, 1879). The forest department had to face a big challenge from the planter community as there was a growing competition between them over the control of the wastelands in Assam. The total grants of 115 in 1861-62 rose to 418 in 1867-68 (Borpujari, 2004). By the end of 1874, the total area under tea cultivation in Sibsagar district was 22,573 acres; the total out-turn was 4,528,329 lbs. Table 3.30 showing tea statistics of Sibsagar districts for 1872 is quite important from the view point of wasteland management policy of the colonial government.

Surprisingly against a total grant of 55,548 acres only 12,708 acres of land were brought in use during the year 1872 and hence an area accounting for 77.12 per cent of the total grants were kept fellow.

Table 3.30: Wasteland allotment and its uses for tea cultivation in Sibsagar district, 1872

Name of sub-division	*Total allotment (acres)*	*Area under tea cultivation (acres)*	*Total unused land (acre)*
Sibsagar	25,175	5,727	19,448
Jorhat	9,843	3,537	6,306
Golaghat	20,530	3,444	17086
Total	**55,548**	**12,708**	**42,840**

Source: Compiled from W.W. Hunter's (1975) *Statistical Account of Assam.*

The allotment of land for tea cultivation in the three sub-divisions of Assam-Nagaland Border depicts how a vast dense forested track was leased out to open up the area for the capitalist mode of production. The Imperial Government with all backup from capitalist system of economy pursued the programmes of resource utilization as per their profit maximization attitude. Wasteland in their eyes was unused resource needing proper policy to make them more profitable and therefore, policies were formulated and amended from time-to-time to fulfil their interest. Instances of extreme liberal approach of the government are found on several cases: (i) Governor General in Council allowed Assam company or any other concern to commence operations and occupy such lands as might be required under Wasteland Grants Rules, 1838; (ii) wasteland rules were amended following Lord Canning's guideline on 30th August, 1862 to reduce the purchase value of wasteland to Rs. 2-8 per acre which inspired the speculators to purchase wastelands at a very low rate; (iii) provisions were made to ease the revenue payment and, in cases, made revenue-free on promise of a revenue to be paid hereafter and on condition of production; and (iv) on the representation of planters and commercial interest, the government had to withdraw the restrictions by permitting the grantees leasehold tenures to commute the grants into Fee Simple tenures without reference to clearance conditions. All these conditions ended up in getting large estates without any payment or a little payment. In 1880, as a result of all these, the area under tea was 153,657 acres and it rose to 337,327 acres in 1900 (*Report on the Cultivation of Tea in Assam*, 1901, pp. 2-3). In fact, all the latter amendments on wasteland rule were made to extract maximum revenue and to enlarge the profit making capacity of the system as a whole. The suzerainty of capitalist system is well apprehensive from all these acts and the later perspectives of resource accumulation. The wasteland, which once was considered as a rich natural abode, turned into a vital spot for capital intensive mode of production, Capitalism, however, does not thereby socialize nature but capitalizes it, converting it into the 'inorganic body' of profit rather than of man. This system inevitably takes hold of nature as a means of multiplying capital and not man's essential forces and creative capabilities (Smirnov, 1983). A logical link between the wasteland rules and the capitalist system of economy up held the later developmental phase of exploitation everywhere in the country.

Wasteland and Commodity Agriculture

David Scott was not aware of the high futuristic possibilities of wasteland of Assam at the time when he proposed that wastelands be granted to anyone who could bring such a land under cultivation. The intention behind such a proposal of the company was to make the wastelands profitable. The accidental discovery of tea in the jungles of Jaipur, Upper

Assam by Mr. C.A. Bruce was a momentous event in the history of East India Company and also to the vast areas of wasteland lying particularly in Upper Assam. A Tea Committee was formed in 1834 as per the directives of William Bentinck (Baruah, 2008) to make necessary study on the possibility of commercial cultivation of tea. The discovery of indigenous tea was acknowledged by the Government and immediately after a scientific panel was constituted in 1835 with Dr. N. Wallich, Dr. J. McClelland and Dr. Griffith primarily to advice on the most congenial location for tea plantation. Against Dr. Wallich's choice of the Himalayan region, the other two preferred Upper Assam region as the most favourable site for tea cultivation (Baruah, 2008). Accordingly Bruce, who was promoted to the post of Superintendent, identified 80 tea tracts in Matak country, 12 in the Singphos and 28 in the west of Buridihing, Tipam, Jaipur, and in Rangpur (now Sibsagar) and Gabru (Harler, 1933). The tracts identified by Bruce were cultivable waste covered with thick forest. McCosh (1837), in his book *Topography of Assam* states—"Assam, with all its waste and jungles, however, much neglected and abused by man, has not been altogether forgotten by nature in her distribution of the good things of this life." Having all congeniality to grow tea in the soils of Assam, the Governor of East India Company decided to invite private enterprise to undertake tea cultivation (Baruah, 1989). Direct entry of monopoly capitalist into the tea industry thus got red carpets to invest in full in this high profit oriented labour intensive extravaganza of economy. As a result, the tea industry witnessed a heavy rush of corporates who felt comfortable to accomplish their interest under government substitutions. In the early stage of the tea cultivation, the corporates came forward as a quick response to the call of the colonial government (Table 3.31).

Table 3.31: Corporates of the early period of tea cultivation in Assam

Sl. No.	*Name of the corporate*	*Year of establishment (as tea Co.)*	*Headquarters*
1.	Bengal Tea Association	1839	Calcutta
2.	Assam Company	1839	Nazira
3.	Williamson, Magor and Co.	1853	Sibsagar
4.	Jorheaut Tea Company	1859	Jorhat (Chinamra)
5.	Brahmaputra Company	1902	Negheriting

Source: G.P. Baruah, '*Asomot Chah Silpar Adikatha*', 1989.

Table 3.32 shows the trend of handing over of huge wasteland to the private enterprise in the name of quick promotion of tea cultivation.

Invitation of the private sector to enter into the commodity agriculture on the one hand and incentives given by the government for the tea merchants on the other, brought tremendous transformation to the so-called vast wasteland of Upper Assam covered with dense forest. Hunter (1975) in describing the configuration and general aspect of Sibsagar districts writes—"It is furrowed by numerous ravines and water courses; and presents in some parts so broken an appearance that the cultivable lands are divided in a similar manner into innumerable small sunken patches termed '*holas*'. In the inner part of the district toward the hills, the country is clothed in dense forest with an underwood of thorny creepers, which swarm with leeches when the rains begin to set in. This later region is generally preferred for tea cultivation, as high forest glades are considered more suitable for the tea plant than grassland." Within a span of 140 years from 1850 to 1990, the annual growth of area under tea was as high as 504 per cent. Except for the year 1950 the overall trend of growth was high all throughout.

Table 3.32: Growth of area under tea cultivation in Assam, 1850-1965

Year	*Area (thousand hectares)*	*Average annual percentage of growth*	*Percentage of increase or decrease*
1850	0.75	—	—
1890	152.00	504.00	201.67
1918	275.00	2.90	80.92
1939	337.00	1.10	22.55
1950	316.00	–0.56	–6.23
1955	321.00	0.30	1.26
1960	331.00	0.62	3.12
1965	345.00	0.80	4.20

Source: P. Baruah, (2008). *The Tea Industry of Assam: Origin and Development.*

The district Sibsagar consisting of three sub-divisions namely Sibsagar, Jorhat and Golaghat had been a favourable area for tea cultivation. Sibsagar has long been a great centre of the tea industry. By 1852, the Assam Company had opened 15 factories with 2,500 acres under cultivation. In 1904 there were 159 tea estates in the district with 79,251 acres under cultivation (Allen *et al.*, 1904). Hunter (1975) provided a comprehensive statistics on the status of agriculture of Sibsagar district for the period 1871-72 and 1875-76 which helps in understanding the growth of tea industry in the district.

Table 3.33 reveals that cultivable wasteland recorded the highest among the three categories of land accounting for 76.39 per cent of the

Table 3.33: Pattern of land distribution in Sibsagar District (1875-76)

Category of land	*Total area (sq.mile)*	*Percentage of area*
Cultivated	482	16.88
Cultivable wasteland	2181	76.39
Uncultivable wasteland	192	6.73
Total	**2855**	**100.00**

Source: W.W. Hunter, 1975. *Statistical Account of Assam.*

total reported geographical area of the district. On the other hand the cultivated and uncultivable wasteland measure only 16.88 per cent and 6.73 per cent respectively. The cultivable wasteland practically became the epicentre of tea cultivation for the colonial government. As per the record of Wasteland Survey of India, NRSA (2003) the amount of wasteland in the border districts of Assam came down to only 16.35 per cent of total geographical area. As per records of Gazetteer of Bengal and North East India compiled by B.C. Allen, E. Gait, H.F. Howard and C.G.H. Allen, the total area under reserved forests in Sibsagar district was 876 sq. mile or 1,410.36 sq. kilometer in 1903-04 and nearly nine-tenths of it were confined within Mikir Hills and the valley of the Dhansiri. The Nambor reserved forests covering over 994.98 sq. kilometer in 1903-04 reduced to only 366.72 square kilometer in 2007. Nambor and the adjacent forested track of the southern part of Sibsagar district along the Assam-Nagaland Border was rich in valuable timbers which could be used as substitutes for teak. The most valued trees are Nahor (*Masua ferrea*), Ajhar (*Lagerstroemia flos reginae*), Sam (*Artocarpus chaplasha*), Tita sapa (*Michelia champaca*), Urium (*Bischofia javanica*) etc. Interestingly, part of the Nambor reserved forests was de-reserved on a number of occasions in the past to provide land for other non-forest use. A seriesof deforestation activities were carried out over the Nambor reserved forest (Table 3.34).

A substantial area of the reserved forests situated along the Assam-Nagaland Border region was deforested on a number of occasions. Mention may be made of dereservation of 3418.78 hectares, 66.88 hectares and 2145.54 hectares by Government notification No. 2807 R of 17.8.1928, GER 92/47/81 of 3.11.1949 and FOR/Sept/570/68/131 respectively of Panidihing reserved forests. Likewise Desoi, Desoi valley, Tiru hills, Galeki, Abayapur, Diphu, Rengma etc. reserved forests also witnessed deforestation of extensive areas during pre and post-British period. It is surprising to note that by the end of 1874, the total area

Table 3.34: Government notification, occasion and area deforested from Nambor reserved forest

Notification No.	*Date of notification*	*Area deforested (acre)*	*Reason shown in notification*
No. 64/dt. Shillong	27-09-1891	872.80	Required for Assam-Bengal Railway
No. 1214/dt. Shillong	09-04-1896	8.26	Construction of brick field
No. 3010 R/Dt. Shillong	01-11-1926	2016.00	Extension of cultivation (tea)
FOR /Sept/351/60/158	15-09-1965	1361.86	Settlement
FOR/Sept/351/60/159	15-09-1965	135.01	Railway extension

Source: *A Handbook of Government Notification*, Forest Department, Assam, Vol. II.

under tea cultivation in the plain part of Assam-Nagaland Border was 22,573 acres, which quickly reached 108,050 acres at the end of the same year by virtue of Assam Wasteland Rules (Ray, 2011). Apart from this, the tea garden owners particularly the private enterprises occupied a huge amount of land which was yet to be brought under cultivation. As per the record of *Tea Area Handbook* published in 1991 the total area under the disposal of the tea garden owners having tea gardens within Assam-Nagaland Border region measured a total of 72,012.48 hectares, out of which only 28,492 hectares were actually under tea cultivation. Again, this fertile forested track, which is most favourable for tea cultivation, contained a total of 159 tea estates, almost 60 per cent of the total number of tea estates of the entire old Sibsagar district.

Table 3.35 illustrates the number and area of the tea estates in Assam-Nagaland Border where the actual cultivated area is much lower than the area leased out to the tea garden owners. The imperial government insisted to bring more and more wasteland, i.e. unutilized open forest land, under proprietary scheme to augment the revenue collection and to open-up the path for capitalist mode of production. By mapping the wasteland of the districts of the border region of Assam-Nagaland, it can be concluded that capitalism by virtue compelled to intervene in all sorts of resources to keep their profit dynamic. The vast wasteland for the British colonialist, therefore, stands as golden egg to invest to uphold the profit extraction for future. Table 3.36 would speak in support of the statement.

By 1830's, when the British annexed Assam, seven-eighth of the total area of Upper Assam was covered by moderate to dense forest including the vast wasteland (McCosh, 1975). The wasteland was perhaps

Table 3.35: Distribution of tea estates in Assam-Nagaland Border, 1991

Districts	*No. of tea estates*	*Area allotted to tea estates (hectare)*	*Percentage of total*	*Percentage of area*
Sibsagar	63	28761.35	39.62	39.94
Jorhat	47	24047.00	29.56	33.39
Golaghat	44	17808.41	27.67	24.73
Karbi Anglong	05	1395.72	3.14	1.94
Assam-Nagaland Border Region	159	72,012.48		

Source: *Tea Area Handbook*, 1991.

Table 3.36: Wastelands in the Districts of Border Region, 2003

District	*Total geographical area (km²)*	*Total area under Wasteland (km²)*	*Percentage of TGA*
Sibsagar	2888	228.16	8.48
Jorhat	2861	128.37	4.43
Golaghat	3502	880.17	26.13
Karbi Anglong	10434	3882.86	37.21

Source: *Wasteland Atlas of India*, NRSA, 2003.

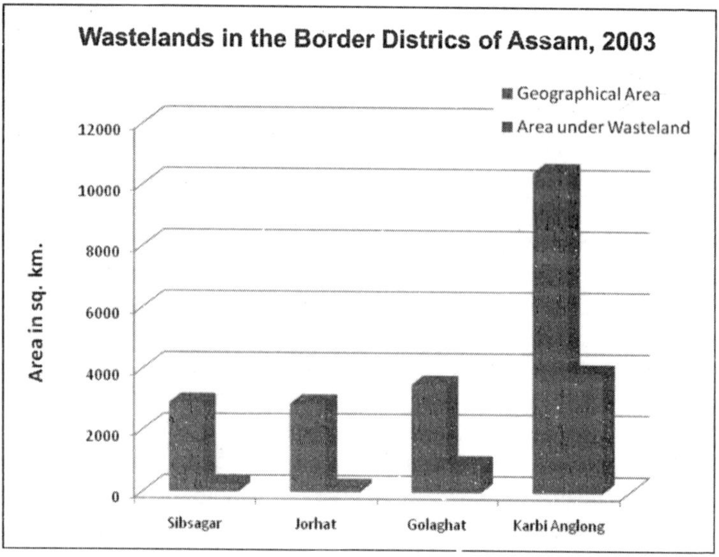

Source: *Wasteland Atlas of India*, NRSA, 2003.

Fig. 3.9: Wastelands in the Border Districts of Assam, 2003

constituted by no other than the waterlogged areas, lakes, rivers, beels, swamps, marshy lands etc. The existence of a large number of tea gardens on the one hand and the continuous cross border encroachment both by Naga and Assamese peasantry on the other made indiscriminate inroads into the wasteland of the region. The data represented in the above tables are enough to substantiate the role of the British colonialist in the elimination of huge forest land for the monopoly tea cultivation in this part of Assam-Nagaland Border.

Imperialist Initiatives and In-migration to Wasteland

The dawn of population migration into Assam was started with total and deliberate initiatives of the colonial government to meet-up the shortage of labour in the tea plantations of the state. The paucity of local labour and unwillingness of the indigenous people to work in the tea gardens compelled to recruit workers from outside the state. In the mid-nineteenth century, the British colonialist tapped other socially marginalized groups for tea estate works. As the tea industry was a well-organized system, labour recruitment from various parts like Jharkhand, Chotanagpur, Singbhum etc. took place that resulted in the migration of thousands of lower caste Hindus (Xaxa, 1985). It was not a spontaneous one rather it was characteristically a forced migration. The British official observed that even with a sizeable settlement in the Brahmaputra Valley, over four-fifths of land remained untouched by plough. Amidst vast wasteland, endeavour had been made by the authorities to encourage migration into the valley (Borpujari, 1992). As early as 1832, letters were issued inviting settlers to Cachar through respective collectors to populous districts of Bengal offering wastelands rent free under certain but accessible terms and conditions. Moreover, the Nepalese were encouraged to migrate with all incentives to reach particularly the Upper Assam area. A section of the Nepali immigrants were engaged in rubber cutting, buffalo rearing and many of them got engaged in large scale sugarcane cultivation and dairy farming clearing jungles (Borpujari, 1992). A sizeable area, particularly of the Golaghat sub-division faced large scale elimination of forest cover resulting from introduction of sugarcane cultivation.

Rice lands, which are fit for wet cultivation, are not suitable for tea cultivation. Although both tea and rice need humid and hot tropical climate, tea does not tolerate submergence of its root under water. It is therefore true that all the tea gardens of Assam were developed at the cost of forested highland which the British considered as wastelands.

From reclamation to plantation since it needs a large man-day's work, large number of migrant workers were brought to the area of plantation, particularly in Upper Assam. It was the first big wave of migration that Assam witnessed during the British regime. This group of migrants was brought to open-up tea cultivation by reclaiming the forest land suitable for tea cultivation. As per the Tea Board Statistics, 2002, the area under tea was 2,70,163 hectares and it can easily be surmised that these were originally forest land, which was identified by the imperial government as culturable wastelands.

The growth of population in the Census decade of 1891-1901 showed 30.92 per cent in Sibsagar district and this was chiefly due to the in-migration of workers into the tea gardens. Although a large part of cultivable wastelands was brought under tillage but out of the total cultivable wastelands only 1,685,078 acres were under cultivation (Borpujari, 2004). Since, 1866 revenue on land was increased four times but the increase in the amount of land under cultivation remained very low. Chief Commissioner, S.H. Cotton (1911) was serious about the vast areas of uncultivated wastelands in Assam. In a letter to the Secretary, Government of India, he wrote—"The millions of acres of uncultivable wastelands now lying wastes represent millions of rupees which might be dug out of the soil". He emphasized that cultivable wasteland had already been brought under tea cultivation, but it was a call of the time to cover the areas with food crops. He also urged the Government to establish the rail communication between Assam and Bengal so that labourers needed here could be brought easily. The second wave of migration after the teagarden labourers was primarily constituted by two categories of people: one solely constituted by the cultivators who took up the wastelands for cultivation and the other group was constituted by people from Bihar, U.P., Rajasthan and Punjab. Most of the migrants came from presidency of Bengal, particularly the Muslim migrants settled down in the wastelands of Lower Assam along the banks of the river Brahmaputra. Colonial Government saw everything from profit making perspectives and hence the areas suitable for tea cultivation were already settled and leased out preferably to the European planters. Flood-prone areas of western and central Assam were provided to the Muslim cultivators from Bengal province. The Muslim immigrants, today seen in some pockets of Upper Assam are the product of post-Independence migration, who were mostly hired by the big holders to work in their fields. All along the Assam-Bengal Railway stoppage or station, the Bengali Hindu immigrants who came in search of living means, developed clusters of settlements which are still quite prevalent all over the state. Migrants from Rajasthan, often called Marwari, engaged themselves as traders, moneylenders, agents of tea garden managers etc. During that time trade was under their control even in the remote areas.

Table 3.37 reveals a very important picture of immigrant population pattern of the state during the early part of the British period where the total influx into the state in a period of just 30 years (1881-1911) recorded an increase of 166.80 per cent.

Table 3.37: Total number of migrated population from different parts of India (1881-1911)

Year	*Bengal*	*Madras*	*Central province*	*North-western province*	*Total migrants*
1880-81	2,21,256	753	825	48,802	2,80,609
1890-91	4,18,360	10,654	3,844	57,851	5,10,672
1900-01	4,53,876	21,308	84,170	108,875	6,68,229
1910-11	—	—	—	—	7,48,650

Source: Compiled from Census, 1891 and H.K. Borpujari's, *The Comprehensive History of Assam*, Vol. V, 1992.

In course of time this trend of influx of population became a strong determinant of demographic structure of the state. Mention may be made here that except the tea garden workers, the entire Assam-Nagaland Border did not witness any other accountable flow of immigrants into the region. Settlers from Bengal belonging to Hindu community usually occupied the areas mostly around the railway station.

Ecosystem People, Immigration and Colonial Agenda

The dominance of British over Indian economy and society had affected the ecosystem people since the policies of the colonial Government gradually disturbed the age old traditional livelihood practices particularly of the tribal people and the backward communities. Forests had to face intense penetration of the capitalist forces. The people engaged in food gathering or growing crops in their fields following traditional means, maintained symbiotic relationship with the biotic and abiotic resources. They built shelters collecting materials from the forests and depended mostly on environment for their material needs. Such people are regarded as ecosystem people, a term used by Dasmann (1988). Perhaps four-fifths of India's rural people belong to this category (Gadgil and Guha,

1995). As the natural wealth recedes, so as the natural wealth recedes, the capabilities of local ecosystems to support the life of these people start shrinking. Dasmann (1988) identified three categories of society: omnivores or biosphere people, ecosystem people and ecological refugees. However, in Indian context and also in the context of immigration into Assam, the first two category people perhaps were in confrontation and in consequence thousands of people migrated to Assam. These immigrants in no way can be regarded as ecological refugees since their migration is not the sole product of ecological inducement. The push factors, when analysed, would reflect that they are not ecological refugees. The people, on the other hand, who have acquired the right and might to enjoy the produce of the entire biosphere are called biosphere people (Dasmann, 1988). The British colonialists, in this sense and spirit may be put in this category of people.

Table 3.38: Push and pull factors of migration into Assam

Sl. No.	*Push factors*	*Pull factors*
1.	Increasing scarcity of resources in the source region	1. Colonial hegemony, power and conspiracy
2.	Growing density of population	2. Availability of resources
3.	Elimination of forest based livelihood by deforestation	3. Easy means for livelihood practice
4.	Loss of support base for sustenance	4. Incitement from the swindlers
5.	Prevailing famine	5. Continuous provocation from local recruiting agents
6.	Hard life	6. Inter-group conflicts and competition to acquire more resources
7.	High aspirations	7. Hope of high achievements

Source: Personal field-based observation, 2011.

The European planters were in great confusion wherefrom they would pick up workers to work in the harsh environment of Assam. Synchronizing all sorts of situation of the environment of Assam, they could find some similarities with that of the forested zones of Central India and also they could observe there people's aspiration for livelihood alternatives. The Forest Act of 1865 was not enough to fulfil the requirements of the tea planters which, therefore was amended in 1870 and it was reinforced under the Inland Emigration Act of 1882 and the same statutory wages continued in practice up to 1901 (Guha, 1977). The perspectives under which lakhs of tea garden workers migrated to Assam were not much convincing to regard them as ecological refugees. On the other hand, the biosphere people—the British bourgeois were so organized that anybody found opposing them were immediately punished. The Assam Labour and Emigration Bill, for instance, were enacted on 8 March, 1901 by fifteen votes—all British—to four, including the lone British vote of Cotton. After this showdown, Cotton had to finally go into retirement from service under pressure (Cotton, 1911). The planters under bourgeois shelter did everything possible to execute their intension even at the expense of all inhumane approach. Thus, the conclusion that can be drawn that the ecosystem people in their homeland were uprooted as a result of (i) continuous and planned invasion of colonial power into the areas of their habitat; (ii) disruption of symbiotic life system of people and nature; (iii) wanton destruction of forest and forest-based livelihood of the tribal of Central India; and (iv) both push and pull factors have simultaneous effect on mass migration tribals into Assam.

These uprooted ecosystem people, virtually pushed by the imperialist for a forced migration into new land again to disrupt the prevailing ecosystem of another region. Assam-Nagaland Border with its virgin identity as pristine forest with all symbiotic character to support the balance in ecological settings was thus brought under a new capitalistic vista in the form of monoculture. The plain parts of Assam-Nagaland Border measures approximately 3289 sq.km. and out of these, the cultivable wastelands accounted for 76.39 per cent.

It is apprehensive that the tribes living in the forested track of Assam-Nagaland Border have suffered from economic devastation due to ecological changes brought about by the colonial intervention. It resulted in shifting from traditional practices, social unrest, unemployment pauperization etc. as well as complete dislocation and rupture to socio-cultural life and value system of the tribal people (Singh, 2006). Forested hilly tracts of Karbi Anglong and Nagaland section of Assam-Nagaland Border experienced shifting cultivation which is, in fact a typical form of agriculture practiced by the hill tribes. The relationship between the time the land is cultivated and the time it is left fallow is critical to the stability of shifting cultivation. The shifting cultivation is a time-tested system of agricultural practice, most often evolved indigenously and is strongly based on traditional knowledge (Tripathi *et al.*, 2003). However, this traditional knowledge based shifting cultivation practiced extensively in the forested areas of the region had to face hurdles as the colonial forestry advanced.

In the early period of British rule, foresters engaged in forest management did not have any idea about shifting cultivation and its impact on forest (Saikia, 2011). To protect the forest from shifting cultivation, the Chief Commissioner of the province issued a circular in 1875. Although restrictions were imposed to the areas which were left out from reserved category of forest, it could not effectively stop the practice of shifting cultivation. Baden-Powell's view expressed at a forest conference in Allahabad in 1874 bear significance in this regard—"The fact is that the system is so wasteful that somehow or the other it must but a stop to, just like 'Suttee' or any other great evil. It consists in destroying a large and valuable capital to produce a miserable and temporary return. To put a stop to it, is only to anticipate by a few years, the natural determination of the system which will happen if the system continues long enough, because there will be no more forest to cut down and burn. The wayout to reserve large areas and prohibit *jhum*". Baden-Powell's anxiety was only with the valuable timbers of the forest and not virtually with the poor economy of the hill tribes. Valuable forests easy for transshipment were removed and other valuable forests were declared reserved or brought under reserved category. No doubt, shifting cultivation on the steep hill sides is responsible for damage on the downhill areas. Apart from forest destruction, shifting cultivation may cause landslips, silting up and drying up of springs and rivers.

Assam-Nagaland Border, being a transitional belt in between hills and plains, has been experiencing great pressure of shifting cultivation particularly in the hilly parts. Areas adjoining the foothills and the plains, which were already marked under the category of reserved forests and the low hill areas covered with impenetrable jungle were not favourable for shifting cultivation. Beyond this zone, the uphill areas were conspicuous with extensive patch of secondary fallow forest. Moreover, the prevailing practice of head hunting among the Naga tribes prevented them to settle in the low hill areas and as a result expansion of shifting cultivation to the downhill part was limited. The Karbi Plateau, apart of the Assam-Nagaland Border along the N.F. Railway, was appropriated for *jhum* cultivation. From Bokajan to the interface of the Barail range, large tracts were found covered with swiden fallow secondary forest. As most of the eastern margin of the Karbi Plateau consisted of many reserved forests, shifting cultivation was limited compared to the Nagaland part. As per record of Forest Survey of India (FSI), the total area under swiden fallow secondary forests in Nagaland was 1011 sq.km. in 2003. Of course, some areas also are there which are the products of clear-felling or selective felling or other extractive activities (Adhikari and Arunachalam, 2010).

Accordingly, the secondary regrowth, those found all along the hilly tracts of Assam-Nagaland Border are characteristically a representation of secondary forests resulting from long years *jhum* cycle of 8-10 years. Nearly 80 per cent of the swiden fallow secondary forests are *jhum*-induced forests dominated by bushy trees, tall grasses and bamboo (Fig. 3.6 (a), (b). After completion of total suzerainty over Nagaland by the British colonialist, there happened to be a tremendous change in social and cultural life of the Naga tribes. Practice of head hunting was almost eliminated. People got relief to come down and settle in the low hill areas and to acquire more land under shifting cultivation. Thus, downhill areas suffered from clearance for shifting cultivation. Although specific regulations on the restriction of shifting cultivation were in force, it was quite inactive toward checking the practice of shifting cultivation. At the same time the government officials somehow showed discontentment to execute the regulations on shifting cultivation as the need for timber grew to meet the requirement for railway construction along with increasing outside demand.

Experiment with Taungya Cultivation

Taungya cultivation was introduced perhaps with a hidden agenda to resist the spread of shifting cultivation to new areas and to bring a total haultage to the *jhum* cycle. The practice, in practical sense, was a complex combination of both artificial regeneration of forest and shifting cultivation (Saikia, 2011) where cultivators are allowed to clear the land to sow crops and simultaneously the cleared land was put to uniform forest crops. The whole programme was developed solely in the interest of the government and in no way it could be judged as an endeavour for conservation of forests. The model of Taungya cultivation provided a sound response in Burma where large-scale teak plantation was practiced to meet up the requirement of quality wood supply. To keep forest and shifting cultivation as one parallel practice in the forested tracks of Assam, Brandis introduced Taungya method in parts of Upper Brahmaputra valley. The plantation of *Simul* trees in the Dibru reserved forests in an estimated area of 51 acres is a part of this method (Saikia, 2011). At the same time, the Forest Department enforced regulations so that general peasants could plant saplings of *Simul* tree. Abundance of *Simul* tree once seen in the River island Majuli was perhaps the result of Taungya practice introduced by the colonial forestry.

The Department of Forests primarily emphasized on the plantation of hard wood like *teak, sal, nahar* etc. and *simul* particularly to meet the demand of tea industry and match factory. On the contrary, the peasants were not eager to abide by the guidance of the Forest Department particularly in selecting tree species to be planted as Taungya practice. For instance, cocoons have higher local demand in comparison to other tree crops and the peasants' first choice usually was in favour of cocoons which was practically *e*-contra to the empirical forestry policy. Taungya practice, therefore, failed to bear fruit due to this duality of the peasants on the one hand and department of forest on the other. On the other hand, the peasants involved in the scheme were more often deprived of the benefits of developmental scheme as they were left to reside inside the forest. They also felt insecured as land rights were not provided to them. All these factors caused a general disregard to the Taungya method of forest regeneration introduced by the government.

It is notable that the peasants, who were basically ecosystem people, depended more on a strong ecosystem based mechanism rather than other vices of livelihood practices. Since, the Taungya practice was attached to overall elimination of natural forest base in exchange of selected tree crops plantation and confirmed termination of ecosystem based livelihood practice, the peasants became uninterested to pursue it. Another important factor was the lack of sufficient knowledge and the disinclination of the subordinate forest employees to enhance the Taungya practice (Stebbing, 1926). The Tribal economy by virtue is a product of the combination of agrarian and forest based economies. Although Brandis had dreamt a beautiful regeneration of forests through Taungaya practice, his idea was totally contrary to the motives of imperial forestry. Analyzing all the imperial activities on world forests, Williams (2006) commented—"the forests were barely touched before the coming of the exploitative European invaders because the native people were ecologically noble savages who lived in harmony and balance with their surroundings."

A number of measures were adopted to inspire the peasants for Taungya practice but it could not attract response from the tribes. The tribes, who are highly sensitive to their tradition, were in no way ready to change their lifestyle practices. The Assam-Nagaland Border perhaps was out of any such scheme of Taungya as it was least affected by shifting cultivation since the long hilly forested track possessed only few hamlets in isolation with traditional practices. Inhabited mostly by Angami, Lotha and Rengma tribes the southern margin of the Assam-Nagaland Border tract was very close to dense forest except few scattered *jhum* fields. There were many more mouths than usual to be fed and much land, especially in the neighbourhood of Kohima, was uncultivated (MacKenjie, 1979). After total annexation of Naga Hills by the British, head hunting, the most barbaric practice among the Naga tribes, came to an end which in fact, opened-up the way for the highlanders to migrate down to the low hill areas. Since, shifting cultivation in the western margin was a later development, Taungya cultivation could not make any impact. On the other hand, the concept of Taungya was a later development following Brandis experiment in Burma and since annexation of Naga Hills also took few years to complete, the Taungya cultivation did not reach the Assam-Nagaland Border Region.

Assam Forest Regulation, 1891 described the agenda on the formation of forest village as—"Forest villages are designed for the purpose of supplying a source of suitable local labour or in the case of temporary cultivation with a view to restocking the areas so cleared and cultivated with valuable species of trees on the Taungya method". The regulations strictly mentioned that only those would be allowed who are habituated, compatible and interested to work in the forest under certain terms and conditions framed for plantations and Taungyas (*The Assam Forest Manual,* 1930). With a clear observation on the condition of Taungya plan, Brandis felt that in framing the plan, the important reality is that Assam is situated outside the range of the natural growth area of teak and that its climate is widely different from that of Burma and other countries in which the teak tree has its home, was not taken into account (Brandis, 1879). He further disclosed his dissatisfaction—"the hope of converting the Assam forests into teak forests should be entirely abandoned. Nor is this measure in any way necessary." The history of Taungya cultivation in Assam thus framed its closed chapter.

It is needed to be mentioned here that a group of imperial ecologists tried to interpret the Taungya practice as an effective measure of forest conservation and saw all the possibilities of sustenance with no clash with the tribal mode of living. But the case in reality is opposite. Nowhere in the world, has forest of mono-crop formed comfortable habitat for ecosystem people liked the forest tribes. Sufficient supply of forest produce ensured a supportive means of living for the tribals, otherwise survival became impossible. This backdrop of tribal philosophy never worked together with Taungya like practice. Plantations never can be forests, they do not fulfil the functions of maintaining biodiversity, soils, water, and regulating climate. They also influence negatively the local ecosystems and livelihood of the people.

Calibrating the issues of plantations over and above the whole ecological spectrum of the Assam-Nagaland Border region it can be concluded that whether it is Taungya, or the tea cultivation, monoculture does not fulfil the needs of the ecosystem people. A natural forest usually contains a support base for varieties of life forms or in other word harbours a strong biodiversity base which is totally absent in the areas of monoculture. Specific flora against selective fauna may be sustainable to a small extent but the destruction it caused to the ecology of the area remained irrecoverable. Regeneration of forest in this sense, through Taungya or through any kind of monoculture, is quite misleading. The forest cover, therefore, as we see today on Lands at imagery or aerial photograph is happened to be illusive, since vast areas of this border tract is occupied by tea plantations (Map 3.4).

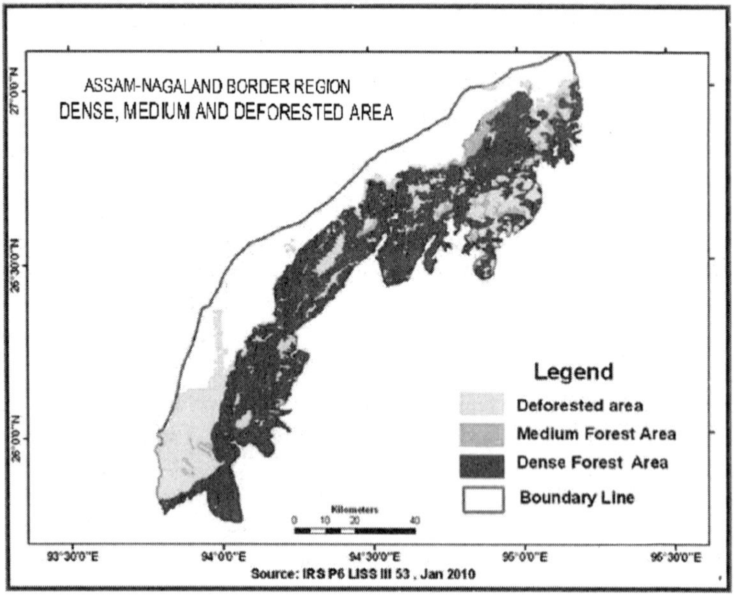

Source: IRS P6 LISS III 53, Jan, 2010.

Map 3.4: Assam-Nagaland Border Region: Dense, Medium and Deforested Area

3.6 Railways and the Forest Ecology

The construction of railways was as an integral part of British colonial military and commercial policy (Williams, 2006). Lord Dalhousie, the administrator of East India Company, felt that the establishment of railway line in India would change the whole socio-economic set-up and make all the areas of possible resource base accessible. Accordingly construction of railway lines began in 1852 from Bombay inland to the foot of the Ghats and from Calcutta to the Raniganj coalfields. By 1900 the railway length became 40,396 miles and it reached 61,957 miles marks in 1920. Assam brought into the map of railway in 1882 by constructing a railway line connecting Dibrugarh ghat with Makum. The construction of Assam-Bengal Railway traversing the state was completed in 1903. The extension of Assam-Bengal Railway line through Lumding to Tinisukia occupied a track of 600 feet width crossing over through the forested belt which, as a result, destroyed the forest measuring a total area of 160.21 sq. mile. The Government notification dated 22nd March, 1895 specified the land to be deforested in Dayang and Diphu reserved forests. It states—"from where the railway crosses the Dhansiri river to where it crossed the Bokajan, 300 feet wide and about one mile long; from Bokajan to northern boundary of the Nambor forest the Railway crosses the Doing river, 300 feet in width and about 26 miles in length, and on the station sites at Bokajan, Naojan and Barapajan near the bank of the Doing river varying in width from 300 to 2000 feet" (*A Handbook of Government Notifications*, Vol. II). During the construction stage a total of 3604.87 acres were deforested within the southern part of Sibsagar district. Nambor reserved forest had a deforested area of approximately 1234.63 acres, while it was 1220.00 and 150.24 acres for Borpathar and Diphu reserved forests respectively. Areas deforested for railway construction as shown in Table 3.37 are only representatives of the deforested area *vide* Government notification.

The plan of the imperial government to establish railway line connecting the tea gardens of the plains on one side and the vast forests land and coal mines on the other was apprehensive and clear cut. To ease the way of transshipment of timber, tea produce, coal etc. from all the inaccessible hostile areas, establishment of the railway line through this part was inevitable. Leaving MFP (minor forest produce) for the livelihood practice of ecosystem people of the area, the colonialist attempted to ease the transshipment of MFP (major forest produce) having high need abroad. The traditional means of transportation was expensive and time consuming. Bryant (1912) expressed his dismay on the condition of roads and communication. The boats namely Meleng, Panshis, Bajras etc. had a limited carrying capacity and required more labour until its arrival at the destination. Moreover, the numerous tributaries created difficulties in harvesting the MFPs during the rainy months. After all, the transsshipment of forest produces was both risky and challenging. Assam-Nagaland Border area was too hostile topographically, and from the perspectives of accessibility and prospect for growing tea estates, it had high demand for a good transport network. The tramway constructed in 1885 connecting Mariani, a traditional inter-state trading centre, with Kakilamukh and Nimatighat at the bank of the Brahmaputra through Jorhat was assertive to pursue the trade of MFP (Sharma, 1998). The advantage of using tramways was not restricted to the saving in transport charges, but rendered feasible the working of valuable sal and other wood products in waterless forests which otherwise could not be utilized (Monro, 1912).

Table 3.39: Area deforested for railway construction along Assam-Nagaland Border

Name of area	*Total area deforested (acres)*	*Government Notification No.*
Borpathar	1220.00	904/R
Diphu	150.24	361/60/159
Nambor, South	1361.86	361/60/159
Nambor	872.77	No. 54

Source: *A Handbook of Government Notification*, Forest Department, Assam, 2010.

The network of resource mobilization by colonial Government attained a favourable position as soon as railway connection came up in many parts of their interest. At the beginning railway sleepers were supplied mostly from the teak forest of South India. The Assam forests were endowed with Sal and Nahar, which were subsequently used for manufacturing railway sleepers (Annual Forest Report, 1902-03).

Most of the forests of Sibsagar district were eliminated either by cutting trees for manufacturing railway sleeper and fuel for rail engines or by aligning the railway line through the heart of the forest. In addition, Assam forests had to take the burden of supplying required wood for manufacturing tea boxes. Earlier tea boxes were imported from outside. Sibsagar district, being the area of tea industry had great demand for a continuous supply of locally made tea boxes.

Thus, tremendous pressure on forest resources was created. The brokers concerned with the import of tea boxes from outside sometimes created problems so that local production gets declined. Eventually, the government completely withdrew the royalty on tea boxes (Annual Forest Report, 1912-13). Number of saw mills started coming-up to meet the demand of tea boxes in various parts of Upper Assam. Sibsagar districts alone had a dozen of sawmills in the first half of the twentieth century. Thus, the railway on one hand and the tea-industries on the other, encouraged the growth of sawmills as a lucrative enterprise solely to thrive on exploitation of the forest resources (Saikia, 2011).

Merciless Administration on Fauna

In ancient India, there were rules and religious ethics on flora and fauna. The gathering activities performed by the ecosystem people were also governed by certain mandatory rules and ethics which they strictly maintained in their life. Anthropological studies have identified religious beliefs and rituals intimately related to the management of ecosystem (Vidyarthy, 1963). Traditions in our society asserts that the ecosystem people has its root in anthropological orientation under which nature is not treated as alien, but is respected as an entity from where everything we need for our survival and existence is derived (Joshi and Srivastava, 1990).

The tribes, accustomed to *jhum* cultivation had seldom done any illogical act to the ecology. Big trees are left untouched and religious functions are performed prior to the onset of *jhuming* process. The purpose and spirit of these rituals is to take oath not to do any harm to the nature and seek excuse from the almighty for their unknown and unwanted doings. Moreover, in hunting also social and religious ethics are followed. For instance, they never kill any pregnant wild animals. Over killing or over harvesting is also considered as a crime. Big trees, for them are the habitats and shelter for the gods and demi gods and hence they worship them. The way of life of the tribes and the indigenous people is closely linked with flora and fauna. One of the most interesting traditional customs among the Karbis of Assam is that they prohibit felling trees like mango, jackfruit and pearl trees locally known as *Thabit Arot, Jhongplong* and *Air Arot* respectively. These trees cannot be felled without the recommendation of the village councils. The Karbis refer to these trees as *Thengpi Asar*, meaning old man and old woman. The violator of the norm is punished heavily by the *Sarthe* (village head man) (Athparia, 2002). Tiger is highly honoured by the Karbis and attack of tiger on any person is considered as a sign of great sin. Kanyak Naga, a sub-tribe of Naga, perform hunting once in a year particularly during the month of April. The Tai-shyam of the foothills of Assam-Nagaland Border still adhere to their traditional customs where hunting, fishing, tree felling etc. are done following some fixed rituals.

The traditional concept of management of forest resources was jeopardized as the colonial forestry policy proceeded to cover more and more forest areas under their hegemony. The British considered Indian forests as inexhaustible sources of timber and carried out thoughtless exploitation of the flora and fauna. The multiplicity of fauna in this part of the country undoubtedly was eye-catching which is expressed many a time by the elderly people on different occasions.

British administration at the initial stage of their rule hardly felt the need of a specific policy for fauna. The entire region was endowed with a variety of wild animals ranging from microbial to gigantic mammals like elephants, and rhinoceros. While clearing the wasteland for opening tea gardens, the workers had to face frequent confrontation with the wild beasts. It is reported that in 1868, a total of 129 persons lost their lives either because of snake bites or attack from wild animals (Handique, 2004). Thousands of tea workers flee away from their work place and also from the captive of tea garden owner to avoid certain hazard of life. Not for the safety of common man, the urge to formulate measures to sake the attack of wildlife on tea garden workers, the government passed necessary orders on destruction of wild animals. In 1859, 18 pounds 4 shillings was paid in rewards for the destruction of wild animals (Hunter, 1975). In 1865, it increased to 67.18 pounds. Depredation of wild animals into the crop field was frequent and as a result, in cases, villagers had to abandon the area. In 1869, the number of deaths from attack of wild bears was reported to be 9. In 1904, 6 persons and 990 cattle were killed by wild animals and rewards were paid for killing of 27 tigers and leopards. Again a small amount of 10 shillings was paid as reward for snake killing. Wild animal killing was highly inspired by not only the Government, but by the European tea planters and the ivory merchants also. Since there was no trade of animal skin, people of high status used the skin of animals like tiger, leopard, spotted deer for decoration. Also beautiful horns of big deer used as decorative items. As penetration of tea gardens into the jungle became more extensive and removal of forest came up depredation of wild animals also became more frequent. Thus, loss of habitat and scarcity of food caused fast decline of biodiversity in the region.

Gorman's True Island Biogeography and the Assam-Nagaland Border

It was a horrible situation in this region of rich biodiversity created by the British colonialist who had done irrecoverable damage to the innumerable flora and fauna. Establishment of tea gardens, construction of railway lines, large-scale tree felling to meet the domestic and outside demand, providing land and shelter to the immigrants, opening-up of reserved forests for various purposes, coal mining in the forest areas etc. changed the ecological settings of the region, which are possibly the most fundamental ways by which human activities are causing extinction or decline of species (Goudie, 1981). It is established through the classic studies in true island biogeography that the number of species living at a particular location is related to the area. Islands support fewer species than do similar areas of mainland, and small islands have fewer species than the larger ones. Thus, it may well follow that if humans destroy the greater part of a vast belt of natural forests, leaving just a small reserve, no doubt the number of species would be found more there at the initial stage. But with the decrease in support area the number of species tends to decrease to reach the equilibrium (Gorman, 1979). With the decrease of population size of species living in the forests, the possibility of extinction rate will increase. For this reason, it may be advisable to make reserves as large as possible.

The principle of true island biogeography of Gorman may be taken as the basis for analysing the changing ecological scenario of the Assam-Nagaland Border region. Before the advent of the British, the entire region was said to be 'super saturated' with species of both flora and fauna. The growing interferences like tea cultivation, construction of railway lines, clearing jungles, wastelands, intensive coal mining etc. had reduced the area under forest. The incentives and reward provided by the colonialists to destroy wildlife caused ecological imbalance disturbing the food web among the flora and fauna. The herbivores were the first victim as they lost both food and habitat. The forest area became smaller and smaller and thus lost the support base for the variety of life forms. Reduction in area of the forest leads to reduction in number of flora and fauna, and this in turn can lead to genetic impoverishment through inbreeding (Frankel, 1984). Gorman also emphasized on the performance of reproduction process. He claimed that inbreeding is not only the effect of small population size, but also for a longer period may be responsible for the depletion of genetic diversity. It practically reduces the capacity for adaptive change. Space, in his analysis is an important consideration, especially for those animals that require large expenses of territory. An adult elephant requires about 20 km^2 of area for its comfortable survival. Therefore, a herd of elephants numbering 50-60 needs a total area of 1200 km^2. But such a larger forest area is rearly found anywhere in the world. The great bulk of extinction of species therefore will take place because of the removal of humid tropical forests and the extinction may even extend to the insect order (Fig. 3.10). Myers' calculation showed that the demise of one species every four years is due to the human factor alone and in the coming periods we could be losing one species every hour.

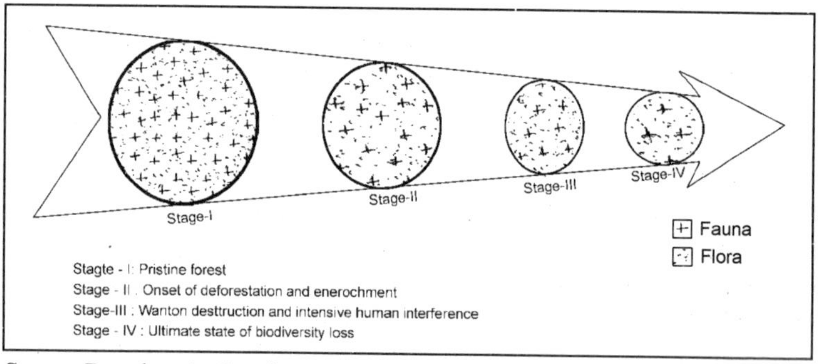

Source: Based on A. Goudie, 1981.

Fig. 3.10: A Model showing Space-Species Relationship

The principle of "true island biogeography" proved to be a reality which contains all assertions to substantiate the dramatic change in the ecology of Assam-Nagaland Border region. Being a zone of topographic diversity constituted by plains, hills and plateaus, this border tract was over saturated with species prior to the colonial rule. Indiscriminate tree felling, removal of jungles, growth of settlements, commercial agriculture, etc. came up to affect the symbiosis between human and nature. Decline of population size of various species, destruction of habitats, scarcity of food and inter and intra species competition for survival ultimately lead to chaos in ecological settings of the region. Along with the species, the ecosystem people, particularly the tribals of the region, were pushed to a crisis in their livelihood practices. Forest based livelihoods of the tribes were jeopardized as most of the support bases were eliminated by the new version of colonial intervention.

The tribal groups namely Mishing, Sonowal Kachari, Thengal Kachari, Tai-Turung, Tai-Khamiyang, Bodo, Karbi, Naga, etc. in the course of colonial management of forestry became the worst sufferer as their forest based livelihood practices gradually got eliminated. Some of the important common herbal dietary items used by the tribes include *mechaki, majenga, chengmra, mamai, dimarupat, nefafu, kalmou, meteka, bhedailata, naltenga, suklati, kaldil, madhusoleng, taragaj, barpaleng, manimuni, machandari, matikaduri, narasingha, banjaluk, hatikerala, jam-lakhuti* etc. Moreover, the tribes of the region are also accustomed with the use of some insects and aquatic life found in the forests. Some of these are *kodo baral*, honey, *amarali, chakson, lingkai, jhejhaima, jupijang, hetalaliya, kekora, wechiringa, faring, amfutani* etc. As these forests based life forms disappear due to removal of forest cover, the native tribes have to search for alternatives. Thus, establishment of tea gardens and the construction of railway line pushed back the tribes to the interior of the forests where they found themselves comfortable. The concentration of tribal settlements in the border region is thus the result of the push factors like deforestation and development.

3.7 Post-Independence Venture

Except some occasional revision of the forest policy, 1894 there was no any second forest policy until the end of the colonial rule. After Independence, a revised forest policy to accommodate new aspirations and issues in India was inevitable. Government of India, therefore introduced a revised forest policy *vide* resolution No. 13.1/52-Fdated May 12, 1952 (GoI-1952). This revised policy was a guideline for the state to derive their own policies and legislation for conservation and management of their own forests. This policy also abolished all the provisions of preferential claim of agriculture on forest land (Darlong, 2002). It also proposed the classification of forests on a functional basis and accordingly classified as protection forests, national forests and village forests. The policy considered it necessary to establish tree lands wherever possible for improving the physical and the climatic condition and the general well-being of people. Since, this was a revised policy, the recommendations of the forest policy 1894, remained unchanged except few changes and revisions.

The policy repeatedly emphasized that the national forests were to be managed to meet the growing requirements of defense, communication and industry. Apart from this the national policy also contrived against the indiscriminate extension of agriculture at the cost of forests and stressed on diverting the tribes from the practice of shifting cultivation (Sagreiya, 1967). Development, a fully human-induced process, is pushed against the ecological sustainability and the government's attempt to meet the growing requirement by extracting forest resources is equivalent to commit an ecological suicide. The Government of Independent India although framed a revised forest policy, its spirit and attitude was tuned to the colonial forestry practices. The relationship between the forest and the industries became much intensive even after Independence (Saikia, 2011). Stracey, for instance, categorized the forest type according to the industrial use (Stracey, 1949). More importantly, during the first five year plan (1951-56) a number of development projects were implemented such as major river valley projects, development of industries and communications and other allied projects leaned heavily on the utilization of the forests and forest areas (Sagreiya, 1967). Assam also witnessed the growth of forest-based industries namely sawmills, plywood, vanier mill, match factory and paper mills during the post-plan period. The timber treatment plant at Naharkatiya was an effective aid to the forestry management and the concerned industries. Forest Research Institute, Dehradun provided the necessary technical help to all the forest-based activities. With such technical and scientific support Assam's forest resources were promoted to be more commercial which consequently brought about a drastic change in the ecological system of the area.

Assam-Nagaland Border region as a focal area of forestry activities and having cheap transportation link like railway and bounded by dense forests on the hills and plains became central to the timber products and other MFPs. Wood crafts, Assam, a Birala industrial concern and the largest plywood factory in Asia came up at the heart of Mariani, a border town with good railway connectivity, in 1957. It was reported that the Department of Forest issued a letter sanctioning permission to cut 100,000 cubic feet trees to the wood-craft, Assam in 1959. The area of timber operation prescribed by the Forest Department was Desoi R.F., Desoi Valley R.F., Tiru Hill R.F. and Kakadonga R.F. Timber collection continued up to 1995. Investigation confirmed that the authority of the plywood industry did not have a second sectioning letter received or procured from the Department of Forest. Surprisingly, within a span of 35 years the entire reserved forests were totally wiped out leaving only the imprints of large-scale tree felling in the area.

Octogenarian freedom fighter Moni Basak of Bahani, a village at the foot of the Naga Hills, comments that the entire Desoi Valley reserved forest and the Desoi reserved forest got deforested as a result of exclusive felling of trees for the Jayshree Plywood Factory at Mariani. It was alleged that forest officials at Sonowal Check Gate, NSTC Check Gate and Nagadhuli Check Gate regularly collected huge amount of ransom from each of the truck load timber ranging from Rs. 300.00 to Rs. 700.00 at that time. Basak also reports that as the large trees were removed by the timber merchants the area had only small trees, bushes and shrubs which were then cleared by the people, mostly the ex-tea garden workers, to create a cluster of settlements (Interview with Basak held on 8th January, 2011).

Mr. Bhaben Saikia, the *Gaonburha* of Bachagao reported that the whole forest at the valley of Desoi (Bhogdoi) was characteristically a rain forest. Trees of unimaginable girth were plenty. Sky high trees were felled which destroyed all the small trees lying below. A tree with girth ranging from 8 feet to 12 feet can smash 200-400 square feet of area under forest. Lopping, piecing, and transshipment using elephants also destroyed the undergrowth. Thus, nearly 1000 square feet of undergrowth get destroyed in the process from cutting to transshipment. As he was well-experienced particularly with the situation of Desoi and Desoi valley reserved forest, he reported that he himself saw many trees of 10 feet to 12 feet girths. And now nowhere in the two reserved forests one can find a tree even of a girth of 2 feet. Jayshree Plywood was not the sole user of the timbers of these reserved forests, saw mills of Langthu, Changki, Plywood and Vanier mill at Lerumen, Naginijan also used a substantial portion of timber products of these forests (Interview with Saikia held on 19th January, 2011).

Mr. Chandi Gogoi of Mograi village near Tiru hills reserved forest narrated that a few families of Nepali community were residing at the edge of the reserved forests. A combined labour force of Nepali and tea community was engaged in tree felling and encroachment of the reserved forests. Chayan Singh, a timber merchant from Jorhat took a forest *mahal* on contract from the Department of Forest in 1960. Tree felling operation continued there upto 1962. During these two years along with the marked trees (marked for cutting by the Forest Department) many unmarked trees were also felled under a secret understanding with the forester. In spite of strong protest from the villagers and even after a '*Gherao*' programme organized by the villagers against illegal tree felling there had been no change in the attitude of the foresters. The Ranger of the Mariani Forest Range, at that time was from Muslim community. Trespassing of trees was intensive and the villagers were engaged by paying them well. A group of timber merchants established saw mills and vainer mills at Naginijan and Lerumen of Nagaland. Forests of Tiru Hills were their main source of raw materials and the products were transshipped with full support from the forest officials. Destruction of Tiru Hills reserved forests was completed before 1990. According to Mr. Gogoi any elderly people of the area would say all these without hesitation. We are the people residing here facing at present a variety of problems in the absence of forest (Interview with Gogoi held on 24th April, 2011).

The growth of plywood factory in Assam has a close relation with the forest policy as well as the nature of forests. Soft tree species with long fibre are preferable for manufacturing plywood and hence presence of trees like holong, makai, etc. in the forests provides good ground for establishment of plywood, ply board and Veneer mills. The first plywood industry came up in the Tinsukia division of Upper Brahmaputra valley in 1881 to meet the railway requirements. Thus, based on the supply of raw-materials from the forests of Upper Assam, Assam valley plywood, National plywood and Himalayan plywood factories grew up. By the end of 1975, the total number of plywood factories in Assam stood at 36 and of which 28 per cent were in the Upper Brahmaputra Valley region.

Table 3.40: Growth of plywood factories in Assam (1881-1975)

Period	*No. of mills*
1881-1944	02
1952-1957	08
1958-1963	07
1964-1969	08
1970-1975	11
Total	**36**

Source: Report on the Employment Review Committee on Plywood Industry in Assam, 1979.

Among all the plywood factories of Assam, M/s. Woodcrafts, Assam, Mariani was the largest one and also regarded as the largest unit in Asia. Located at the close proximity of dense forests of Assam-Nagaland Border, this has been the pioneer plywood industry in Assam for manufacturing of tea chests, commercial plywood, black board, teak and champ plywood, marine plywood, etc. The factory, of course, in the later period stopped producing tea chests. After the establishment of this factory in 1955-57 and its progress, many similar units came up in Assam at different locations bringing the state prominently in the plywood industrial map of India (Sharmah, 1994). The production of this factory was also splendid which can be understood from Table 3.40.

Most of the industries grew up all along the Assam-Nagaland Border and got boosted from the ample supply of raw materials from the forests of the region. During this period the region witnessed the growth of approximately 175 units of forest-based industries including the saw mills. Along with 4 plywood factories, 13 plyboard factories and 51 venire mills were also established in the region. An investigation was made in the region to have an idea of the growth and distribution of factories with the help of Mr. Bijayendra Chakravarty, a timber contractor of the seventies, Mr. Longerlita Ao, and Mr. Imujungba. We observed that the Assam-Nagaland Border region witnessed substantial growth of forest-based industries. The important areas in this regard are Tizit, Tuli of Mon district, Lerumen, Chanki, Longthu valley of Mokokchung district, Dimapur of Kohima district, Naginimara, Safrai, Amguri of Sibsagar district, Mariani, Naginijan, Titabor of Jorhat district, Bokajan, Merapani, Uriamghat of Golaghat district and Diphu of Karbi Anglong (Map. 3.5). Most of these wood-based factories exclusively grew up during 60s and 70s of the twentieth century.

Table 3.41: Growth of production of M/s. Woodcrafts, Assam

Year	*Nature of products (Sq. ft)*		*Total amount (Sq.ft)*
	Commercial plywood	*Tea chests*	
1957	925645	1671109	2596754
1958	4505069	1361693	5866762
1959	8166535	2264575	10431110
1960	11595084	2824527	14419611

Source: Department of Agriculture and Co-operation Forestry Division, July, 1981.

A total of 175 units of wood-based industries operating in the region do not require much time to eat up the entire forests. For instance, M/s. Woodcrafts, Assam, Mariani everyday required 8 trucks load of timber (each truck with a capacity of 7.0 metric tons) plus 6 trucks load of firewood for the boiler operation. Thus, if 98 tons of timber are consumed everyday by one unit of plywood then the total annual consumption will be 35,280 tons. Such a plywood unit is capable of destroying a forest of several square kilometers within a short period. The most negative clause of the 1952 Forest Policy was that the national forests were to be managed on the principle of progressively increasing and eventually the highest sustained yield to meet the requirements of defense, industries and communication and accordingly, the state forest departments interpret with full appreciation of the forest resources to gear up all the developmental perspectives of the region. The Forest Department was

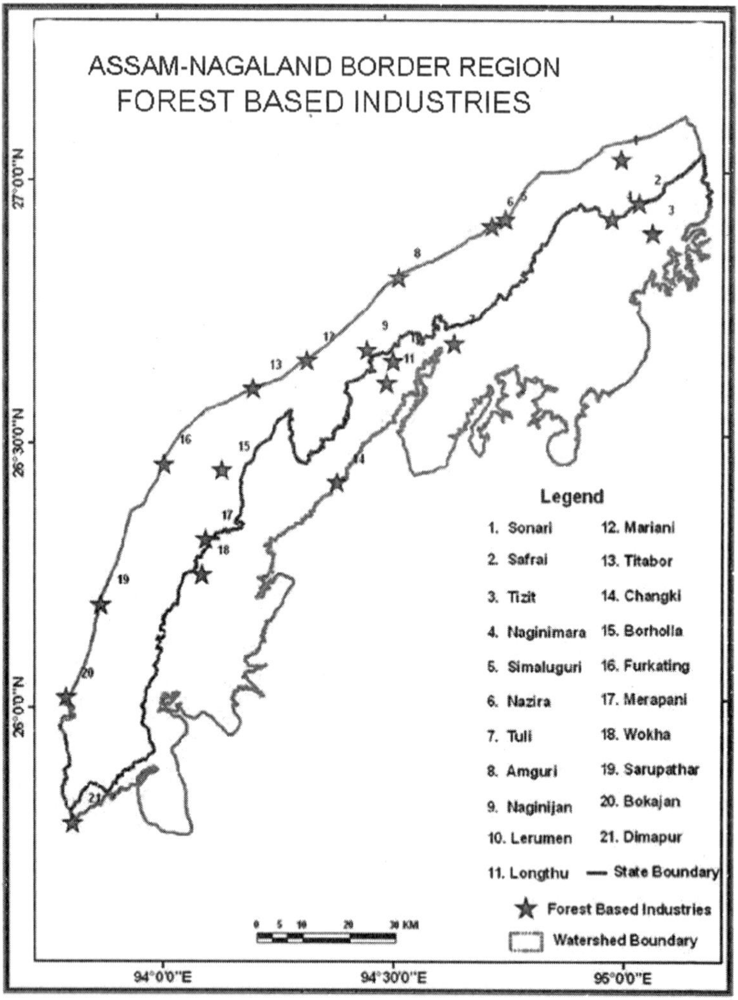

Map 3.5: Assam-Nagaland Border Region: Forest-Based Industries

totally unaware of the consequences of the changing ecological condition following the large-scale intervention in the forests of the region. Along with these intense forestry activities a nexus between the timber traders and forest officials developed. It was often disclosed by a number of local people that with one TP (transshipment pass) a timber trader transshipped hundreds of truck load timber by paying ransom to the forest officials. Forest check gates attached to the reserved forests and sanctuaries had active role in the process of all trespassing works. The sample survey conducted to justify this preconceived notion also affirmed the negative attitudes of some forest officials. When asked who is responsible for deforestation majority of the respondents nodded against (i) outside log businessman; and (ii) government agencies and a few nodded against poaching of trees.

Table 3.42 clearly shows the causes of wanton deforestation in the zone of Assam-Nagaland Border in terms of two major factors—(i) malpractices of government officials; and (ii) timber traders. It is found that maximum of the respondents pointed to the factors of timber traders and government agencies.

General people are often regarded as the silent observer of all the misdeeds. They are kept dumb by the powerful illegitimate trade lobbies. As they have been suffering badly from the problems, they did not hesitate to open their mouths. No doubt, a friendly approach during investigation worked positively in arriving at the truth. It is a difficult task to unearth the hidden facts since there is paucity of recorded data to establish "who are responsible for deforestation?" Apart from all these, the eye witness of the entire history of deforestation, who are now residing with all deprivation from their forest-based livelihood, open-mindedly expressed that within a span of 45 years starting from 1950 to 1995 (the year in which honourable Supreme Court of India banned tree felling in North East India) the forests of Assam-Nagaland Border were eliminated.

Table 3.42: Factors responsible for deforestation in Assam-Nagaland Border

(in %)

Factors responsible for deforestation	*Preferences from the respondent*				*Total*
	1st	*2nd*	*3rd*	*4th*	
Local people	10	12	25	53	100
Government agencies	36	34	20	10	100
Timber traders	40	38	14	8	100
Encroachment by peasants	14	16	41	29	100
Total	**100**	**100**	**100**	**100**	

Source: Personal Survey, 2010.

The people who are responsible for deforestation are not necessarily the poor peasants who like to live with nature and who are partly dependent on nature for livelihood. The poor peasants in the world history were neither given the right of proprietorship of high-tech machineries to cut the big trees of 8-12 feet girth nor to build their homesteads with valuable timbers. Socio-economic systems never made them capital baron to invest and hire labourers to work in the jungles. They never owned trucks to transship millions of square feet of processed and unprocessed timber. The first national forest policy of post-Independence period laid down in 1952, brought a tremendous change in the environmental and social set-up of the country. Environmental crisis gradually was galloping up and the government was in a compulsion to derive a new forest policy for the purpose of wildlife conservation. The Government of India introduced a new forest policy in December 1988. The salient features of the policy in brief are (Ministry of Environment and Forest, GoI):

- Maintenance of environmental stability through preservation and, where necessary, restoration of ecological balance that has been adversely disturbed by serious depletion of the forests of the country.
- Conserving the natural heritage of the country by preserving the remaining natural forests with the vast variety of flora and fauna, which represent the remarkable biological diversity and genetic resources of the country.
- Checking soil erosion and denudation in the interest of soil and water conservation for mitigating floods and droughts and for the retardation of siltation of reservoirs.
- Increasing substantially the forest and tree cover in the country through massive afforestation and social forestry programmes specially on all denuded, degraded and unproductive lands.
- Encouraging efficient utilization of forest produce and maximizing substitution of wood.
- Creating a massive people's movement with the involvement of women, for achieving these objectives and to minimize pressure on existing forests.

As such a working plan to guide management and the strategic perspectives was also attached where priority was given to the protection of existing forests, elimination of the process of diversion of productive agricultural land to forestry, assurance to supply fuel, fodder and MFPs to the tribal people within sustainable limit. Three major national Acts governing forestry have been promulgated over the past 127 years, the Indian Forest Act of 1878, the Indian Forest Act of 1927 and the Forest Conservation Act of 1980. As such three prominent forest policies have been announced in Independent India: the Forest Policy of 1952, the National Commission on Agriculture of 1976, the 1988 Forest Policy and the Indian Wildlife (Protection) Act, 1972. Again the Ministry of Environment and Forests issued a policy circular in June 1990 encouraging the state forest departments to involve communities directly in forest management (JFM). However, the 1988 policy has been criticized for promoting a mechanical type of forest conservation.

The National Forest Policy of 1988 states: "The life of tribals and others living within and near forests revolves around forests. The right and concessions enjoyed by them should be fully protected. Their domestic requirements of fuelwood, fodder, minor forest produce and construction of timber should be the first charge on forest produce" (GoI, Resolution No. 3-1/86-FP dated 7th December, 1988). Earlier, the Forest Conservation Act, 1980, although was brought into enactment, failed to check deforestation all throughout the country. For instance, in 1995, T.N. Gadavarman filed a writ petition with the Supreme Court of India to protect the Nilgiri forest from illegal timber felling (*Down to Earth*, 2002). In its first major order in December 12,1996, the court *inter-alia* redefined the scope of the Forest Conservation Act, 1980, suspended tree felling across the entire country, and sougth to radically re-orient the licensing and functioning of forest-based industries (Rosenerans and Lele, 2008). Not only the writ petition of Gadavarman alone, subsequently more than 2000 interlocutory applications have been admitted (*Political and Economic Weekly*, February 2, 2008). The Supreme Court put sincere consideration on this case and began its judgement by reinterpreting the meaning of 'Forest' in the Forest Conservation Act of 1980 (FCA). Till 1996, the FCA was assumed to apply only to reserved forests. The Ministry of Environment and Forests, at the same time, also tried to roll back the court's interpretation by redefining the term 'forest' as a concern of FCA. It tried to establish 'forests' as 'legally notified forests'. On the other hand, the FCA essentially required proper approval from Central Government for conversion of forest land to non-forest uses. To remove all these confusion the Supreme Court ordered all non-forestry activities anywhere in the country to cease immediately which had not received approval from the Central Government. It completely banned tree felling totally in three states and partially in four other states of the north-east. Finally, it banned all transportation of timber out of the north-eastern states (*Economic and Political Weekly*, Vol. XLIII, No. 5, 2008).

The Supreme Court ordered banning all kinds of forestry activities in the states of North-East which bear some significance particularly for a region like Assam-Nagaland Border. Most of the unclassed state forests and the reserved forests have already been destroyed and finally it results in ecological disorder. The entire episode of deforestation, exclusively a process of transformation from forest land into settlement, had witnessed three distinct stages of forest destruction. The stages are: (i) extensive *jhuming* in the hilly parts of the region; (ii) growth of tea estates in large number in the highland forested areas of the plain; and (iii) the process of rehabilitation in the reserved forests of the region.

The hilly border belt has been experiencing *jhum* cultivation sporadically in the past and extensively in the recent time as demand for more food crops is mounting due to increasing population pressure. In the early part, prior to twentieth century, the length of a *jhum* cycle ranged from 15 to 18 years. Reduction in *jhum* cycle in the later part of the twentieth century to about 8 years caused heavy damage to the forest cover in the low hill zone of the border area. Ao (1987) states—"there is only one region which is accessible and promising from developmental aspects and therefore people tend to migrate westwards from the unproductive, inaccessible and topographically extreme region of eastern part of Naga Hills." As a result, *jhuming* became intensive which caused extensive depletion of forests. Moreover, the Government of Nagaland with no specific regulations on *jhum* cultivation did not like to interfere in the customary rights of the people. Table 3.41 illustrating the forest land distribution in Nagaland reflects the critical position of the Government where legislation only can directly be executed on 6.06 per cent forest area of the state.

Table 3.43: Type and distribution of forests in Nagaland, 1986-87

Particular	*Area (in hectare)*	*% of total geographical area of the state*
1. Forest under Government control	100,420	6.06
2. Forest under private control		
A. Village forests	187,832	11.33
(i) Virgin accessible forests	290,000	17.50
(ii) Virgin non-accessible forests	284,280	17.14
(iii) Degraded forests		
3. *Jhum* Land		
(i) Current *Jhum*	1,01,400	6.12
(ii) *Jhum* regrowth	5,31,600	32.06
Total	**14,95,532.00**	**90.21**

Source: Draft Annual Plan, 1986-87, Nagaland Planning and Co-ordination Department, Kohima, pp. 21-22.

Surprisingly, the Nagaland Government lately started a process of purchasing the forest land from private ownership in order to recover the lost ecological balance. Against a total of just 100,420 hectares of Government forests, the private concerned has owned 13,95,112 hectares of forest land of the state. To enhance the Government forest land, the Government of Nagaland has already completed purchasing of a total of 19,246.73 hectares forests by the year 2009. Out of the total purchase, 13,399.54 hectares are purchased from the forested tract of Assam-Nagaland Border which accounts for 69.61 per cent of the total purchase.

Table 3.44: Purchase of forest land in border districts of Nagaland 2009

Districts	*Area purchased (hectare)*	*P.C. of total purchase*
Dimapur	812.38	4.22
Wokha	693.12	3.60
Mokokchung	4548.79	23.63
Mon	7345.05	38.16

Source: Directorate of Information and Public Relations, Kohima, Nagaland, 2009.

However, the status of state forests still remains in a poor state, where degraded forests, *jhum* regrowth and current *jhum* altogether constitutes 61.33 per cent of the total forest cover of the state. The survey conducted in this border tract also confirmed the fast deteriorating condition of the forests. Amidst extensive *jhum* field and *jhum* regrowth, dense forest cover could not be spotted all along the hill slope of Nagaland. Except few areas of Mon and Wokha districts nowhere one can find an area of virgin forest under either private or community occupation or under Government ownership. The condition of the two reserved forests (Singphan and Rangapahar) on the other hand, has not been found congenial to provide food and shelter to the fauna still available there.

Nagaland Forest Act, 1968 measurably failed to protect the forest which, in fact, put more emphasis on the regulation of harvesting forest resources to augment the state economy since options for revenue collection except forest land were limited (AAR, 2008-09). As such, Nagaland *jhum* land Act very positively aimed at the steady conversion of *jhum* land areas into economically and ecologically sustainable woodlands but mounting pressure on land for cultivation and uprising of extremist activities stood as great impediment in the path of achievements. Debarring the past forest Acts proposed by the Government of Nagaland, Acts like Nagaland Tree Felling Regulation, 2002, The Biodiversity Act,

2002 with sound support from positive and timely programmes like Joint Forest Management (JFM), Integrated Forest Protection Scheme (IFPS), Standardized Agro-Forestry practices in *jhum* areas, Village Forest Committees Implement Afforestation Scheme etc. appropriated a base for rejuvenation of forest cover in the state as a whole (Directorate of Information and Public Relations, Kohima). Apart from these, the Government took initiatives by prompt implementation of various working plans such as—(i) conservation and sustainable use of medicinal plants and augmentation of resources including development of marketing network in Nagaland; (ii) establishment of medicinal plants conservation area (MPCA); and (iii) establishment of nursery and distribution centre under "Year of Farmer". This endeavour of the Government evoked a warm response particularly from the agro-forestry sector. People started planting economically beneficial timber along with *jhum* cultivation which seems to be a bit similar to the Taungya cultivation introduced by the colonialist in the later part of the twentieth century.

Peasant Struggle for Land

The hon'ble Supreme Court in an order dated 19.2.2002 issued a notice to the Chief Secretaries of Assam and eight other states to file affidavits within four weeks in relation to the steps required to be taken by them to restrict further encroachment of forest land and also to mention the steps so far taken to clear encroachment of forests. The Union Minister of Environment and Forest also *vide* letter No. 716/2002-FC dated 3.5.2002 asked the Governments to summarily evict all encroachers in a time bound manner within 30th September, 2002.

Accordingly an eviction drive was conducted in first week of May, 2002 using elephant to raze down hutmen and homesteads as per the land record of the Forest Department. Eventually and surprisingly the drive came to a stop owing to the rainy season and most interestingly may be for the coming election in several states of the country. Almost after a gap of nearly ten years the encroachment in forest land in Assam hits the newspaper headlines. *The Hindu, Seven Sister's Post, The Assam Tribune* published news simultaneously reflecting the grave situation of Assam forests. *The Hindu* (10 March, 2010) focused news as—"Assam has topped the list of states in terms of encroachment in forest land, with about 4,85,674 hectares of area being occupied. The Government told Lok Sabha on Wednesday." *Seven Sister's Post* displayed news in same tune with headlines "Assam tops forest encroachment in country" on Saturday, 22 December, 2012. The summary text was—"Assam has earned the dubious distinction of being worst state in terms of illegal encroachment of forest areas. In Assam, 2,59,700 hectares of forest areas are under encroachment." These few instances point to the crisis climbing situation of the forest of Assam. No doubt, the political dilemma is no less important as one searches the legitimate cause of this unprecedented intervention in the forest of Assam. Initially, it was the political economy of the colonial government who by late nineteenth century took up the process of settling the immigrant peasants from East Bengal in the wasteland and *char* areas of Assam. In 1898, the Assistant Director in the Department of Land Records and Agriculture of Assam, in a report mentioned that immigrant peasants could be placed as an alternative to the indigenous peasants to take-up jute cultivation in the vast wasteland (Monahan, 1898). The ultimate result was large scale influx of immigrant peasants to settle and to cultivate lands remained unused. The growing migration of immigrant peasants induced by colonial interest of the British in the early part of the twentieth century influenced the whole set of peasant economy of the state. In the meantime the tea planters requested the government to preserve the congenial land for further expansion of tea plantation in the Brahmaputra Valley (Behal, 1983). This move of planters, however, worked positively and penetration of immigrant peasants remained confined to the districts of lower and central Assam. Guha (1977) in this regard writes—"Landless immigrants from overpopulated East Bengal of whom some 85 per cent were Muslims—found land in Assam's water-logged, jungle-infested, riverine belt, used to an amphibians mode of living and industrious, they came by rail, steamers and boats up the Brahmaputra to reclaim these malarial areas. All they want was land. From their riverine base, they further pressed forward in all directions in search of more leaving space, to areas held by autochthones". Seeing the growing unrest and increasing conflict between the indigenous and the immigrants the colonial government introduced the "Line system". The inherent purpose of this system, which was introduced in 1920, was to empower the land rights of the immigrants and to continue the influx of the immigrants to Assam. As per census report, the number of settlers including born children after their arrival, increased from an estimated three lakhs in 1921 to over a half million in 1931. The Upper Assam belt, congenial ground for tea cultivation, however, remained untouched from immigrant settlements as the European tea planters appealed the government to leave land for tea cultivations. Sibsagar district, the plain part of Assam-Nagaland Border possessed a sizeable waste land accounting for 14,82,573 acres as per report of Munawal Ali on 14th August, 1937 in Assam Legislative Assembly (ALAP, 1937). During the same period, the amount of net area sown was almost half of the wasteland, which accounted for 7,54,856 acres. The hilly areas of Nagaland and Karbi Anglong were almost virgin except few interceptions by shifting cultivation and few scattered hamlets.

The migration of large-scale peasant settlers mainly from East Bengal had significant impact on the ecological setting primarily in certain areas of Goalpara, Kamrup, Nagaon and Darrang districts. Tribal life system was pushed to disharmony. Ketera Boro, a resident of Golakpur village of Dayang R.F. area, in an interview, said—"We did not have much land and other amenities needed to run our life. Someone, high profile Officer of the Department of Forest, reported that plenty of lands with thick jungles were lying unused; if you have problem here with the shortage of amenities you might come and settled there. Accordingly, not only myself hundreds of our people joined us and we arrived here." Bher Doimari, aged 58 years, described that they arrived in a place full of jungle. Few big trees were there, but most of the big trees were removed before their arrival. Creepers, climbers, grasses, shrubs etc. have built a thick cover which they cleared first to settle and to cultivate the land. They were guided by one forest official in 1969 to migrate into the Dayang region (Bher Doimari, Golakpur). Thousands of tribal, especially of the Bodo community, were compelled to migrate to Sibsagar, Karbi Anglong etc. as their forest-based livelihood system faced problem in their place of origin. Earlier by 1940, the provincial government opened-up few reserved forests to deforest so that pressure on land from landless peasants could be minimized. Thus, intensity of deforestation got a quick response from all corner irrespective of landless or big holders. The post-Independence period witnessed long peasant movement throughout the state demanding land to the landless and "Land to the Tiller." These peasants up rise were mostly organized under leadership of RCPI and CPI. They chiefly targeted grazing reserves, waste lands, forest lands, and sometimes land of the big landholders (Saikia, 2011). The movement of landless peasantry reached climax in Sibsagar district demanding land for the people who were evicted by river bank erosion and flood. Although it was a part of forest land encroachment, but in scale it was less significant compared to the forest land encroached by new settlers mostly of tribal origin.

Politics of Rehabilitation and Encroachment

Land occupation movement through deforestation of reserved forests by the landless peasants reached climax during 1950s and 1960s in Golaghat district. However, majority of the encroachers were people from tribal communities. High concentration of tribal settlements along the border belt in the reserved forests reflects the onset of ecological disaster. The factors of such disaster can be briefed as: (i) destruction of forest-based livelihood by the waves of new settlers; (ii) leasing out of waste land/ unclassed state forest for tea plantation to the European planters; (iii) large scale trade of forest products; (iv) establishing political supremacy through the movement of peasantry; and (v) frequent natural hazards like flood and river bank erosion. Mention may be made of the Mishing and the fishing community who are traditionally riverine dwellers. These riverine dwellers in the absence of secured alternatives came to settle in the forested areas. The causes mentioned above together forced the tribals to evacuate their homeland and to settle down in the areas where they could adapt. No doubt, the available forest land within their easy reach was their first choice for a comfortable settlement.

Table 3.45 presents the causes of migration of the tribal people from their ancestral origin. As high as 75.24 per cent of the respondents migrated seeking better livelihood and only 14.53 per cent migrated as a result of frequent occurrence of natural hazards. Other causes like, famine, eviction by government or other such agencies and occurrence of animal depredation are quite insignificant.

Table 3.45: Causes of migration from ancestral village to the villages of Assam-Nagaland Border Region

(%)

Sl. No.	*Sample Village*	*Better livelihood*	*Eviction by Govt./ others*	*Animal depredation*	*Natural hazards*	*Famine/ others*
1.	Aochongum	89.40	—	—	11.60	—
2.	Akatitto	92.22	—	—	4.80	2.98
3.	Than Pathar	63.44	—	—	30.50	6.06
4.	Naganadi	54.92	10.66	—	24.20	10.22
5.	Golokpur	95.81	—	—	—	4.19
6.	Gamariguri	82.67	7.44	—	—	9.89
7.	Betbari	48.19	—	4.41	30.62	16.78
	Average	**75.24**	**2.59**	**0.63**	**14.53**	**7.16**

Source: Field Survey, 2010.

Officially described as peasant colonization scheme (Saikia, 2008), some parts of the reserved forests, which were considered to be not commercially viable, were made available for cultivation under the supervision of the Forest Department. The history of greater Tengani area of Golaghat is associated with such deforestation scheme of Nambor reserved forests in 1890. A.H.W. Bentinck, Chief Secretary to the Government of Assam by a notification, dated 1st November, 1926 opened-up an area of 2016 acres of Nambor reserved forests for cultivation. This South block again suffered badly under deforestation scheme with the notification No. 64 dated 27th September, 1894 where an area of 872.73 acres of dense evergreen forest brought under deforestation to pro*vide* land for extension of Assam-Bengal Railway (Forest Department, Assam).* The notification no. 3392 R issued on 27th July, 1894 had already confirmed deforestation of 3418.779 hectares of forest land of Nambor reserve. Such notifications were issued from time-to-time as per the need and demand of the colonial government. Same act of deforestation was also continued by the government of post-Independent period (Table 3.46).

Table 3.46: Instances of Government notifications for deforestation of Reserved Forests in Assam-Nagaland Border

(*in ha*)

Sl. No.	*Notification No./Date*	*Reserved Forest*	*Total Area Deforested*	*Reasons*
1.	No. 64 R 27th Sept., 1894	Nambor	353.33	Land to Assam-Bengal Railway
2.	3392 R 27th July, 1894	Panidihing	3418.779	For cultivation
3.	(A.H.W. Bentinck) 1st November, 1926	Nambor	816.19	Extension of cultivation
4.	FR/5/50/67 6th March, 1952	Nambor (West Block)	1548.42	To settle the Hill Mikirs
5.	FOR/Sctt/351/60/158 15th Sept., 1965	Diphu	765.24	For planned settlement with a view to protect the railway line against Naga hostilities
6.	FOR/Sctt/351/60/159 15th Sept., 1965	-do-	54.58	-do-
7.	9th February, 1977	Nambor South	2145.54	For settlement and rice cultivation

Source: *A Handbook of Government Notifications*, Forest Department, Assam, 2010.

Hunter mentioned that during the early twentieth century much of the highland in the central and south Sibsagar district was originally covered with tree forest but much of it had been taken up by the tea planters (Hunter, 1908). Understanding the utility of land a section of rich peasantry also claimed forest land for agricultural expansion along with the landless peasantry seeking rehabilitation and land for cultivation (Saikia, 2008). The colonial government immediately took up various schemes of deforestation and also encouraged the forest land reclamation activity of the peasantry. To meet the recurring shortage of labour to work in the forest, four forest villages were established in 1905. And almost at the same time three Taungya villages namely Gomariguri, Tarani and Jamuguri were established in Dayang reserve forest. Thus, 14 forest villages in Diroi, 3 in Abhaypur, 2 in Geleki, 1 in Tiruhills, 4 in Desoi and Desoi Valley and 2 in Kakadonga came up to serve the interest of the Forest Department. This endeavour, however, had provided relief to the problem of labour shortage. It was the initial stage of peopling the reserved forest areas during the colonial regime.

The 1940s witnessed a strong peasant up-rise under the leadership of Communist Party of India (CPI), Revolutionary Communist Party of India (RCPI), and Congress Socialist Party (CSP). The movement earned popularity as slogans like "land to the tillers" and "land to the landless peasant" were added. More and more peasants were united under the banner of the peasant organisations. As such, movement of sharecroppers cropped up in parts of the region against the absentee landowners which took a serious turn all throughout the state. The provincial Government of Assam led by the Congress Party had to face a stiff challenge from the growing peasant movement and thought to formulate a way out from this debacle of peasant unrest. Congress Socialist Party (CSP) organized a movement which was popularly known as "Ghiladhari Satyagraha" (Hussain, 2004) demanding land from the tea grants of the area. The agitationist came out even to forcibly occupy land of Ghiladhari tea estate. As per report of Newspaper, near about 35 acres of land of the tea estate was occupied by nearly 350 landless peasants of the areas nearby the tea estate (*Sadiniya Assamiya*, 1950). The movement grew stronger as the people who lost their land and property due to flood and river bank erosion joined the movement of land occupation. Under growing pressure from all corners right from the press to the people and politicians, the Congress Government was pushed to grave crisis. The then president of Assam Pradesh Congress Committee, Bimala Prasad Chaliha (1954), at this critical political juncture requested the government's concerned department to provide forest lands to the landless peasants of the state by dereserving the reserved forest of Sibsagar district (Assam State Archive). Under such growing pressure, the government opened-up patches of land from grazing reserves for expansion of cultivation. In 1950, the government distributed 9,839 *bighas* of village grazing land and 29,174 *bighas* from professional grazing reserves to the landless peasants and flood-affected people. Again, the government distributed about 37,290 *bighas* of forest land among the landless peasants (Das, 1951). Subsequently R.V. Subramaniam, Secretary to the Government of Assam, Tribal Areas and Development Department, issued an order *vide* notification No.TAD/FR/5/50/67 dated 6th March, 1952 to deforest 3824.6 acres (1548.42 hectares) of Nambor West Block to provide land to the Karbi people to cultivate in the plains and to settle therein. As such, Joint Secretary of Forest Department, Government of Assam issued two consecutive notices No. FOR/Sctt/351/60/158 and 159 to deforest 765.24 hectares and 54.84 hectares respectively from Diphu and Nambor South reserved forests in 1965. As news on land to landless and tillers spread, peasants in thousands from the surrounding areas started rushing into the forest land of Assam-Nagaland Border. The tribal people were the major constituent of the land occupants as they somehow lost their traditional means of livelihood. Sonowal Kachari, Thengal Kachari, Bodo, Mishing, Karbi etc. all came out seeking new areas to settle amidst all hostilities of the border areas.

The scrolling of deforestation measures of the Government, the Deputy Conservator of Forests of Sibsagar opposed and tried to convince that this kind of deforestation measure would seriously affect the edaphic, climatic and flood conditions of the country (Confidential Memo, 1954). The Forest Department, however, kept its effort to ensure plantation programme simultaneously with the cultivation practice and introduced Taungya cultivation in the low hill areas of Dayang-Tengani region. The Department established several Taungya villages particularly in Tengani area (BTUSS, 2004). But it failed to cover larger tract as financial constraints of the Department posed restrictions to expand it to other areas.

Meanwhile, Soneswar Borah, an eminent political leader and ex-Minister of Government of Assam led the peasant movement of Dayang from the forefront. Elected to the Assembly in 1978 he was given the portfolio of Agriculture. As Agriculture Minister of the Government, Borah favoured the cause of settlers of the Dayang region and agreed to recommend their demands for rights over forest land. It naturally brought a great relief to the encroachers and other settlers of the region. They celebrated the judgement by organizing "Dayang Bijoy Utshav" in 1978 which was attended by the then Chief Minister Golap Borbora as Chief Guest (Borah, 1978). This act was spearheaded by the creation of Nagaland state in 1963. After declaration of State, Nagaland created dispute over the boundary line between the two states. Pressure to fix the boundary was mounting as Nagaland Government became more aggressive to the problem. The politicians and the administration of Assam immediately took step to keep control over the border areas by settling more and more Assamese peasants in the forested border areas. The Government in the meantime decided to distribute 10 bighas of land per peasant. In a diplomatic move, the Government of Assam introduced a system, officially known as "half-a-mile settlement". The *modus operandi* of this system was that the settlers of Assam could settle within a distance of half-a-mile from the boundary line between the two states. Thus, opening of Dayang reserved forests for the peasant came into a reality. Chief Minister Golap Borbora did not even hesitate to spell out that peasantisation had already been taken place in part of these forests (ALAP, 1978).

The debate and conflict however continued to be more strenuous as Naga extremist outfit geared up their activities in and around the border areas. A violent turn took place in 1979 in which a few Assamese peasants were killed and houses of villagers were burnt. Under all hostility the trans-border conflict grew violent in 1985 and many lives of both sides were lost. To ease the situation security forces were deployed in most of the vulnerable areas of the border. The Forest Department, in the meantime took initiative to evict the illegal encroachers from the reserved forest area but all their endeavour was in vain. The struggle of the peasantry against eviction in support of various political and non-political groups came out to rescue the evicted families and rehabilitate them. It is apparent that the forerunners of this decade long peasant movement were Brihattar Tengani Unnayan Sangram Samittee (BTUSS), Dayang Mukti Sangram Sammittee (DMSS) and Krishak Mukti Sangram Samittee (KMSS). These three organisations mainly guided the struggle for acquiring rights over forest land. Notice was issued to the Department of Forest and concerned Minister of States in 2002 by the hon'ble Supreme Court of India to appraise the status of the implementation of forest policy. Therefore, the Department renewed the eviction drive in the reserved forests of Assam. Nambor-Tengani again came under eviction. Peasants of Dayang-Tengani again got united opposing the eviction (Saikia, 2008). The resistance to the eviction was unique which ultimately paralysed the eviction drive. BTUSS, in the meantime handed over a proposal—"*Gache Manuhe Jiyai Thakar Sankalpa*" to the then Forest Minister Pradyut Bardoloi on 29th January, 2003 (Gogoi, 2011). Increasing pressure from the peasantry induced the government to take steps in favour of the agitationist. Meanwhile, the Forest Minister declared in the Assam Assembly that Government was willing to grant land title to the peasants who settled in the forest before 1980 (ALAP, 2005). The Chief Minister of Assam also wrote letter to the Ministry of Environment and Forest, New Delhi requesting permission to convert forest villages into revenue villages.

The game of rehabilitation of the flood and river bank erosion affected people was mounting high in many parts of Sibsagar district under the leadership of Kamala Saikia, a journalist who was later killed by extremist outfit at his home district. The movement was supported by several left organizations. Realizing the rationality of the struggle for rehabilitation and also to widen the support base, the Congress-led Government arranged forest areas to settle the flood and river bank erosion affected people. On 7th February, 1977, the government issued a notification No. FOR/Sett/570/65/31 and deforested an area of 2145-54 hectares of Sibsagar district (PCCF, 2007). The period of 70s and 80s witnessed a massive instability among a section of people belonging to higher middle class to grab more and more land. Some influential political leader of the rulling class acquired land around Desoi and Desoi valley reserved forests (Assam State Archive).

Trans-Border Encroachment

"While the total area of Assam is 78,550 sq.km, over 86,886.12 hectares have been encroached by as many as five neighbouring states. Nagaland alone has been accused of encroaching 66,241 hectares" (*Indian Express*, August 13, 2007). Nagaland encroached areas mostly belonging to reserved forests like Diphu R.F., Nambor R.F., Dayang R.F., Desoi Valley R.F., Tiru hills R.F. and Abhaypur R.F. Latest report from the Department of Forest, Government of Assam confirmed that 17,500 hectares of Diphu R.F., 10,000 hectares of Nambor South R.F., 11,800 hectares of Rengma R.F. are solely encroached by Nagaland. In the E-sector of the border, 14 villages have been already established by Nagaland (*Dainik Janambhumi*, 13 August, 2011 and "*Aphal Loi Gol Nagai*" (one part picked-up by Nagas), a staff reporter news item in *Dainik Janambhumi*, (May 26, 2009).

Table 3.47: Encroachment of land by Nagaland

(*in ha*)

Forest Sector	*Total Area Encroached*	*Establishment*
A (Diphu R.F.)	17,500	Sub-division-2 Village-38
B (South Nambor R.F.)	10,000	Village-51
C (Rengma R.F.)	7,000	Village-4
E (Desoi, Desoi Valley and Tiru Hills R.F.)	3,513	Police point-2 Village-4

Source: *Dainik Janambhumi*, May 26, 2009.

The border dispute between Assam and Nagaland is undoubtedly a product of the competition between the contending peasants for agricultural land. Ao (1987) made an analysis on the developmental aspects of Nagaland where he showed that the western low hill zone facing the broad plain is the most accessible area from economic point of view since the interior eastern part of Nagaland is not productive and highly inaccessible (Lannusosang, 1987). For an overall development of Nagaland this western part is projected as the core zone and hence maximum activities concerning the economy concentrates in this part. The Government as such put necessary interest to expand arable land grabbing from the plains. Citing reference of an interview with Nobal Hongrai, a Nepali-speaking settler from Borhollah village, Dolly Kikon claimed that this village has been paying taxes to the Nagaland Government since 1969. On the foothill border areas, residents settled around 1980s faced a compulsion to pay taxes to the Naga. Most of the settlers confessed that the Government of Assam permitted them to settle in these border areas. Contrary to this, Naga authority claims land of the foothill zone and pursued a regular practice for building up a strong infrastructure to facilitate their people. Tsurmen basti, a Naga village in Tiru hills reserved forest has acquired all facilities including schooling, electricity, water supply etc. from the Nagaland Government which inspire Naga people to settle in new areas of the plain land. "It is really astonishing as to how inside a sovereign country like India, NSCN rebels, could built bunkers near the Assam-Nagaland Border of Merapani, Golaghat district—that too, with an intention to forcefully occupy lands of Assam" (*Times of Assam*, 2013). Dr. H. Sarmah, the spokesman and Minister, Government of Assam told Zee news in an interview—"There are no Naga areas in Assam and only some Zeme Nagas are there in the North

Cachar Hills District. The few Nagas who stay in other parts of the state are 'encroachers' and not inhabitants" (Zee news. com, November 18, 2011; 19.07 pm). The opposite views are also from its counterpart, the Nagaland Government. "Nagaland Border Affair Minister T.C.K. Lotha refuted Assam's delegation that Nagaland had encroached border areas and charged the Assam Government with rampantly encroaching into Nagaland, citing the instance of Merapani under Wokha district where Nagas' land was forcibly allotted to Assam soldiers a few month ago" (Oriental Times, 1999). Amidst all these tug of war, there took place several deadly gun battles between the two states where involvement of extremist out fit to the government's security personal and people was reported (*Statesman*, January 31, 2011). The first clash stemming from the border dispute with Nagaland took place in 1968 when Nagaland police allegedly attacked Assamese villages inside Doyang forest reserve. A similar incident was reported in January, 1979 in Rengma forest reserve. The worst violence, however, took place in June 1985, when over 100 people, most of them on the Assam side, was killed as police forces of the two states clashed in Golaghat district (*Indian Express*, 13 August, 2007).

These caricatures of border dispute create a widespread unrest and insecurity all along the Assam-Nagaland Border. "Border landscape, as seen by the social scientist, is a set of cultural, economic and political interaction and process occurring in space" (Rumley and Minghi, 1991). The failure to integrate land alienation and conflicts leaves much ambiguity, which often results in conflicts. The borders have either not been marked properly or the border landmarks have somehow disappeared. The people inhabiting these areas have interacted with each other for over a century (Farnandes and Borbora, 2008). But their knowledge is not recognized or get due importance from colonial periods onward and no formal alternative is worked out. The conflict has, therefore, continued for a longer time.

3.8 Empirical Analysis on Deforestation

Research has been increasingly focused on automated information extraction methods. Use of satellite remote sensing today becomes instrumental for research since it provides information accurately over a large area. Furthermore, remotely sensed data may cover scales from a few meters to some kilometers. It is useful for ecological studies. Remote sensing data sources are usually used to develop information on landscape pattern. Observed spatial variability is dependent on spatial resolution of the imaging system. Low resolution sensor is effective to study the type and pattern of forest cover. Accordingly, to study the nature and extent of forest cover of the study area imageries of IRS P6 LISS-III, 53, January, 2010 with 23.5 meter resolution are exclusively used. To acquire a total coverage, imagery sheets are selected from row 52 and 53 and path 112,113,114 and 115 imaged by the sensor LISS-III in 2010. These imageries are converted into geocoded form to identify the area. The spectral character of the sensor gives a detailed image of the overall forest cover of the Assam-Nagaland Border region. However, with few limitations such as (i) higher reflection co-efficient of plant cover during rainy summer months creates problem in identification of exact nature of forest cover. It requires imageries of winter months which may usually help in differentiating actual character of the forest cover over the region; (ii) existence of plantation crops and *basti* land depicts a misleading image of forest cover; and (iii) the *jhum* regrowth cannot be separated from other forests as leaf area expands to maximum during rainy months.

As such topographic sheets of Survey of India, 1974 representing the whole of Assam-Nagaland Border region are consulted. The topographic sheets corresponding to the study area are: 83 J/13, J/3.J/9, J/2, J/7, J/6, J/5, G/9, N/1, I/16, F/15 and M/18.

Maps are prepared accordingly representing the study area with special emphasis on forest cover and topographic characteristics from both Landsat imageries (2010) (Fig. 3.16) and respective topographic sheets (1974) (Fig. 3.17). Forest areas are then delineated according to the density. Forest areas on the topographic sheets are classified as: (i) dense forest, (ii) moderate forest, and (iii) low or degraded forest (Map. 3.6). As such forest areas are also identified as per density from the map prepared from Landsat imageries. The two maps are superimposed and areas deforested are identified and measured ARC-GIS software is used in the entire process of identification, classification and to develop necessary data base. Analysis of the two maps gives the following results on nature and extent of forest cover of the Assam-Nagaland Border region. The results are presented in Tables 3.48 and 3.49.

Table 3.49 reveals that in 1974, the total area under forest was 4682.54 km² which was 75.36 per cent of the total geographical area (6213.35 km²). The area under dense forest was 2741.15 km² (58.54% of total forest area), and 468.78 sq. km. of medium forest accounted only for 10.02 per cent of the total forest area. Area under degraded or low forest was 1472.61 km². The comparison made with the RS data, 2010 shows

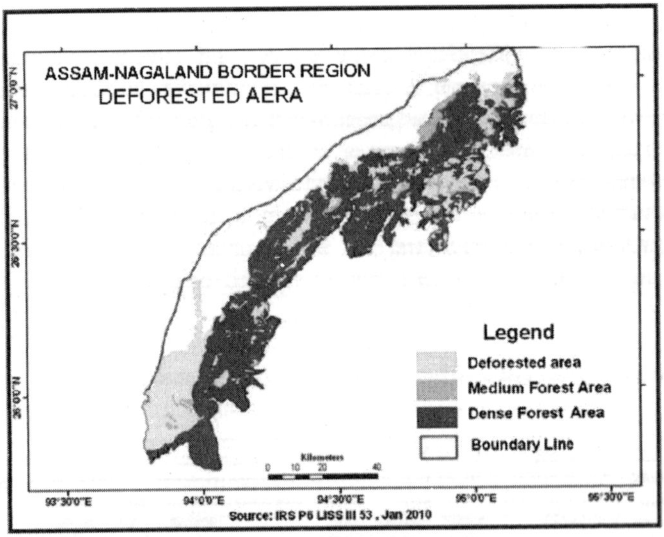

Source: IRS P6 LISS III 53, January, 2010.

Map 3.6: Assam-Nagaland Border Region: Deforested Area

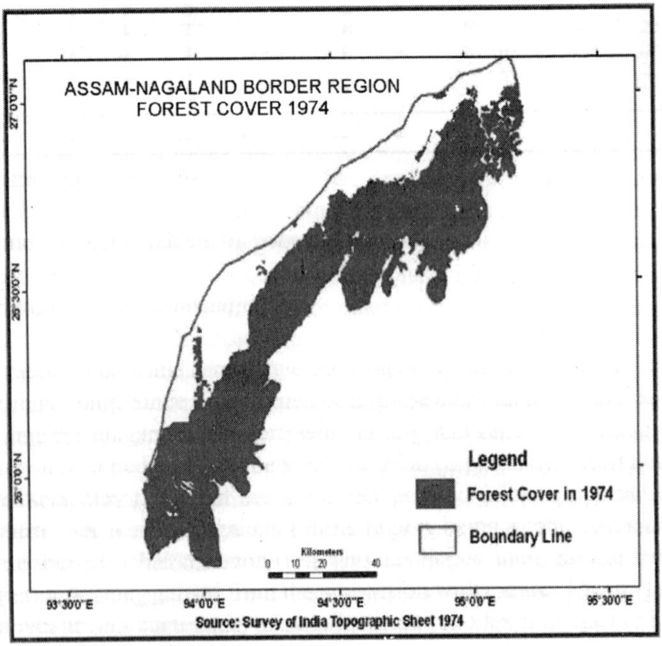

Source: Survey of India Topographic Sheet, 1974.

Map 3.7: Assam-Nagaland Border Region: Forest Cover, 1974

Table 3.48: Area and percentage of forest cover of Assam-Nagaland Border Region, 1974

Types of forest	*Area (km²)*	*% of forest area*
Dense forest	2741.15	58.54
Medium forest	468.78	10.02
Low forest	1472.61	31.44
Total forest area	4632.54	75.36
Total geographical area	6213.35	—

Source: Topographical Sheets, Survey of India, 1974.

Table 3.49: Analytical charts on change of forest cover Assam-Nagaland Border Region (1974-2010)

Year of assessment	*Total forest area (km²)*	*% of total area*
1974	4682.54	75.36
2010	2741.15	44.12
Total loss of forest	**1941.39**	**31.24**

Source: Survey of India, Topographical Sheets, 1974; Landsat-LISS-III Imagery, 2010.

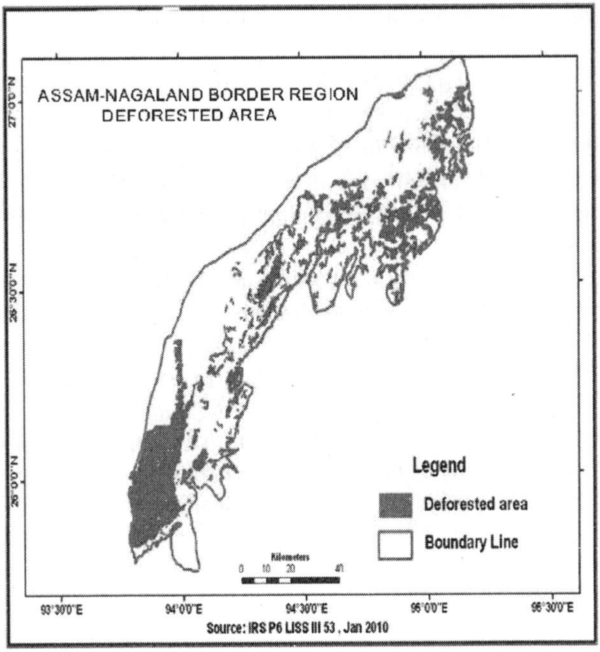

Source: IRS P6 LISS III 53, January, 2010.

Map 3.8: Assam-Nagaland Border Region: Deforested Area

that the total area under forest came down to 2741.15 km^2, which confirmed a loss of 1941.39 km^2 of forest area. At present the area under forest measures only 2741.15 km^2 including all types of forest and plantation areas (Table 3.47).

On the basis of the above analysis and data, the annual loss of forest can be computed. Ecologist usually prefers the formulae of compound interest to compute the annual loss of forest. Accordingly, the formulae (Puyravaud, 2002) is—

$$P = \frac{100}{t_2 - t_1} \times \frac{a_1}{a_2}$$

Where, P is the annual loss of forest, t_1 is the time of base year and t_2 is the time of current year, a_1 is the total forest area during t_1 and a_2 is the forest area during t_2 time.

Computation shows that the rate of annual loss of forest for the Assam-Nagaland Border is 4.745 km^2 area per year. On the other hand, on an average the annual loss of forest is 53.93 km^2. The overall scenario of forest loss approves that deforestation process has still been continuing at an accelerating pace in this part of Assam-Nagaland Border.

The chief causes of deforestation so far identified are: (i) incapability of the Department of Forest and Environment to implement the Forest Conservation Act, 1988; (ii) increasing encroachment of forest land by the peasantry of both the states; (iii) lack of co-ordination between the Department of Land Revenue and the Department of Forest and Environment; (iv) poor and incompetent planning and management system; (v) unresolved issues like border dispute between the two concerned states; (vi) absence of effective state forest policy; (vii) illegal timber felling and timber trade; (viii) illegal coal mining and quarrying; (ix) increasing population; and (x) expansion of *jhum* land and reduction in *jhum* cycle.

It, however, needs a systematic and well planned approach in order to mitigate the rising ecological crisis of the region. The two State Governments in consultation with the concerned department of Central Government should formulate a very practical, effective and eco-friendly forest policy to repair and recover the damages caused to ecological settings of the region.

4
Forest Tribes of the Border Region and Ecological Relation

4.1 Racial Composition of Assam-Nagaland Border Region

The tribes of this region may be primarily grouped into two categories—(i) Plain tribes, and (ii) Hill tribes. The tribals of the plain are, to some extent, different from those living in the hills. Changes brought by sharp fall in forest resource base, developmental policies of Government and quick rise of a consumerist market to the tribal life style have already made a slow invasion which creates chaos in tribal ethics—particularly in the areas attached to the urban centres (Gadgil and Guha, 1995). This change is observed especially among the Sonowal Kachari and Thengal Kachari of plain tribes and Ao and Angami of the Hill tribes.

The border region is virtually dominated by several tribal groups mostly belonging to Burmese Mongoloid stream. Ao, Angami, Rengma, Lotha, Sema and Chakhesang are the major tribes living in parts of Nagaland border, while the Assam part is occupied by tribal groups like Sonowal Kachari, Thengal Kachari, Tai Khamayang, Mishing, Bodo and Karbis along with the tea tribes in the areas dominated by tea gardens.

Inter-border conflict, especially between the agricultural communities of Assam and Nagaland arising out of the occupation of fertile land has in the meantime, brought some significant change in the demography of the region (*see* Table 4.1).

The clusters of tribal groups consistently reflect the multi-tribe dominance amidst differences in their ethnic identity. Excluding tea tribes, the percentage share of the tribal population in the Assam border part accounts is approximately 54.84 per cent and with the addition of tea tribes its share becomes 68.38 per cent of the total population. Similarly, in the Nagaland part, the tribes constitute 89.05 per cent of the total

Table 4.1: Major tribal groups in Assam-Nagaland Border Area

Plain tribes	*Located in*	*Hill tribe*	*Located in*
Sonowal Kachari	Assam	Ao	Nagaland
Thengal Kachari	Assam	Lotha	Nagaland
Tai Khamayang	Assam	Karbi	Assam
Bodo	Assam	Rengama	Nagaland
Mishing	Assam	Konyak	Nagaland
Turung	Assam	Angami	Nagaland
Kanyak	Assam	Sema	Nagaland

Source: Personal Survey, 2010.

population of the region. The Ao community is the largest constituent comprising 22.14 per cent of the tribal population. Table 4.2 given below, presents the pattern of tribal dominance in the region.

It appears that the influx of tradesman, workers, agricultural labour and people engaged in developmental works like PWD, forests, agriculture etc. caused a gradual change in the demographic and social structure of the region. And palpably, the prevailing Bioregionalism is kicked back to open-up a way for a new kind of anthropocentrism to settle in this traditional tribal belt. The intrinsic value of tribalism is therefore in a doldrums or on the verge of jeopardy.

Table 4.2: Population of various tribal groups of Assam-Nagaland Border Region, 2001

Racial groups	*Population*	*P.C. share of tribal group to the total population*
A. Plain Tribes		
Sonowal Kachari	4,09,313	18.50
Tai Khamayang	22,346	1.01
Thengal Kachari	4,32,544	19.55
Mishing	50,223	2.27
Bodo Kachari	2,85,191	12.89
Tai Turung	13,717	0.62
B. Hill Tribes		
Angami	1,57,383	18.50
Sema	56,998	6.70
Rengma	34,369	4.04
Lotha	67,122	7.39
Ao	1,88,350	22.14
Phoms	42,280	4.97
Kanyak	1,31,011	15.40
Karbi	80,053	9.41

Source: Census of India, Series 14 and 15 and *Statistical Handbook, Nagaland*, 2006.

4.2 Tradition and Sociology of the Forest Tribes

Marriam Webster dictionary defines the word tradition as—

1. (a) An inherited, established, or customary pattern of right, action or behaviour (as a religious practice of social customs).
   (b) A belief or story or body of beliefs or stories relating to the part that are commonly accepted as historical though not verifiable.
2. The handing down of information, beliefs and customs by word of mouth or by example from one generation to another without written instruction.
3. Cultural continuity in social attitudes, customs and institutions.
4. Characteristic manner, method or style < in the best liberal tradition >(www. marriam-webster.com).

The definitions of tradition of Webster dictionary by and large represent the traditional societies, characteristically primitive in nature, manner, form and style. Traditions are not written documents. These are inherited from one generation to another and the elderly people of the society, as the most experienced with the traditional practices, play an important role in imparting the knowledge and experience attached to the traditional practices. Most of the primitive societies are tradition bound and strictly maintain the norms with all honesty and devotion. Most of the traditional societies are analogous to a biological community made-up of a number of cultural traits. Guha (2004) placed these communities in the strata of lowest trophic level. The lowest one, according to Guha, is made-up by cultivators, pastorals and hunter—gatherers who merely depend upon land and biological resources. This trophic organization is apparent and distinctive feature in a region like Assam-Nagaland Border mostly inhabited by tribal population. It is a specific region located at the meeting zone of two distinct ecological regions—the hills and plains. Amidst some anthropogenic similarities in structure and behaviour, the ecological distinction keep them separate from each other and as such their traditions also found to differ. The attributes of a tribal society are associated with their political structure, kinship and ritual organization. They display this system as a set of rules and the mutual interdependence of the rules that fit between the society and its ecological frame (Fortes, 1949, Evans-Pitchard 1951, and Forde, 1934). Kinship is a distinctive attribute of all tribal societies. A kinship system is not simply a collection of apparent and mutually exclusive terms, each recognize a different kind of genealogical and social relationship. In most of the tribal societies, kinship is used to establish and define their corporate social units.

Table 4.3: Kinship and kinship usages among the tribes of Assam-Nagaland Border

Tribe	*Kinship usages*
Angami	Prejudice against cross-cousin marriage with MBD, though allowed.
Sonowal	No cross cousin-marriage with FSD, FBD, MB, MBS, MSS etc. Relationship of avoidance within relatives strictly observed.
Karbi	Kinship terms denote seniority and juniority in age. Cross cousin-marriage with MSD is most favoured.
Ao	No cross cousin-marriage; kinship terms—classificatory and descriptive.
Lotha	Cross cousin-marriage—allowed with MBD and not favoured with FSD, SD, MSD etc.
Bodo	Restriction imposed on marriage with maternal or paternal lineage.
Mishing	No marriage among phraity (friendly Gumun/Clan) Two Apun (Clan) : 1. Pegu, Kardong, Megu, Taid, Pait, Patar, Chungkrang, Bori, Lagachu, Medok, etc. 2. Kutum, Kuli, Kaman, Doley, Taye, Char, Kumbang, Paw, Daw etc.
Thengal	No cross cousin-marriage; kinship denotes blood relation and close association.
Khamyang	Prevalence of teknonymy. Marriage with MBD favoured but with FSD forbidden.

Abbreviations

MBD : Mother's brother's daughter
FS : Father's sister's daughter
MB : Mother's brother
FBD : Father's brother's daughter
MSS : Mother's sister's son
MBS : Mother's brother's son

Sources: Kumar, B.B.: *The Tribal Societies of India*, 2009.
Pegu, N.: *Mishing Sakalor Itibritta Aru Sanskriti*, 2000.
Narzi, B.: *Bodo-Kacharir Samaj Aru Sanskriti*, 2009.
Terang, R.: *Karbi Sanskritir Ruprekha and Own Investigation*, 2010.

The Naga tribes, overwhelming in the Hilly parts of Assam-Nagaland Border, provide typical example of strong kinship, which has still been maintained among their respective clans. Prior to the entrance of

Christianity in their lives in 1851, they believed the doctrine that attributes spirits to surrounding inmate objects and to natural phenomena. Not only among the Naga tribes, this kind of belief system is found prevalent among the plain tribes including Mishing, Bodo Kachari, Thengal Kachari, Sonowal Kachari, Karbi, and tea tribes also. The Sema Naga had an inmate belief on unseen super power that regulated human destiny and as such entitled to worship. They also believe that a kind of spirit inhabits the earth among human beings.

Practice of head hunting among some Naga tribes was associated with variety of social and cultural activities. Carving of wooden head and wearing of it they consider as a symbol of heroism. Dancing, drinking, merry making etc. are such practices related to head hunting. Head hunting, in their belief, is to acquire blessings for human and animal fertility. Head of a woman with long hair is precious since it would stimulate crop productivity. The practice of head hunting is not found among any other tribes than the Nagas.

Totemism

Totemism is an integral component of tribal tradition. It is closely associated with their socio-cultural and religious practices. A totem is maintained hierarchically either from maternal or from paternal side and is symbolic to the racial character and blood relation among groups (Frazer, 1910). A totem may be of an animal species or plants which are always holy for the tribes. Many tribal clans are named after animals, plants, insects, etc. Some of the clans have totem of non-living objects such as stone, soil, river, mountains etc. Some of the clan names of the Ao Nagas are Lungchari (stone clan), Amri (gourd clan), Alingri (tying bamboo clan), etc. The Changkiri clan is believed to be descended from the plantation tree (Mills, 1973). The Karbis have numerous totems. Every clan has its own totem following some specific plants and animals. For instance, Terang clan is the offshoot of wa-terang (Hornbill), Croe clan descended from wa-thekal (Cuckoo) etc. Tiger is honoured and worshiped as their prime God. Exogamy is prevalent and widespread among all the tribes of North East India. Sonowal Kachari tribe has still been maintaining the clan system in which they divide themselves in seven clans. These are: (i) Ujani Kuchia, (ii) Namani Kuchia, (iii) Amara Bamiya, (iv) Tipamiya, (v) Dhulial, (vi) Chiripuria, and (vii) Balikhitari. Although the origin of their family is yet to be explored, most of the scholars believe that these are related to a lineage. This clan system among the Sonowal is perhaps based on geographical and social conditions like location and migration.

Many tribes and clans claim their origin from their totems. Of course, some clans believe in myths relating to specific plants, animals or the non-living object and accordingly they worship and give due regards. Lycanthropy, the belief that humans can metamorphose into an animal such as a tiger or a Methun. This belief is prevalent among the Nagas. They believe that the five claws of each foot of a tiger enable them to receive a human soul. The human soul usually enters the tiger during sleep and return to the human body at day break. Also they believe that the soul can stay in the tiger for several days, during which the man shows unnatural behaviour. It is a common belief among certain Naga clans that their ancestor was certain animals and such totem animals are worshipped as guardian spirit and clan members are identified with the attribute of totem animals. Most of the Naga tribes seem to regard the ancestry of man and tiger. Methun is regarded by the Nagas as a symbol of power and massive size. They believe that the sacrifice of this prestigious animal enables one to acquire spiritual power as the methuen is massive appearance, large and long horns.

At times, totem is considered as one of the most inevitable component of tribal tradition. The interference of modern religion and the changing life style have gradually been distorting the traditional belief system of the tribes. Only in the remote places of the tribal land, the practice of traditional culture still persists in some way. The tribes of Assam-Nagaland Border Region, especially the hill tribes, are much more sensitive to their tradition and customs and, therefore, the practice of totemism occupies an important position in their traditional practices.

Supereminence of Taboo

Taboo is a Polynesian word and is similar in meaning to 'Sacer', a word of the Romak community. The word taboo usually varies in meaning and spirit and in times antonyms in itself. The meaning of the word in its workable usage can be considered as prohibition, objectionable or intolerable. Encyclopedia Britannica defines taboo as: (i) ritual isolation of person or thing as sacred or accursed; (ii) prohibition; and (iii) exclude or prohibit especially by social custom. Taboo is regarded as the most ancient unwritten law of the society and it is of course older than the advent of gods and demons i.e. the period prior to the age of religion.

Froyed (1953) qualifies the purpose of the use of taboo as: (a) to protect the priest or such dignified persons or things from insecurity; (b) to render shelter and help to the poor and destitute; (c) to protect from the impending danger; (d) to secured the birth, marriage, sex etc. from turmoil or illegitimacy; (e) to save human life from the attack of evil elements like devil, ghost, demigod etc.; and (f) for welfare of the infants. Taboo, as it is thought to be an ancient practice, perhaps came into existence in the primitive society as a product of some absurd and abrupt experience gained by the primitive people. Prohibition to eat certain items, prohibition to pronounce certain words or sound, prohibition to touch certain things etc. are the basic of a taboo which are traditionally inherited through generations.

Taboo is characteristically a representation of tribalism and primitiveness. Predominantly inhabited by many tribal groups, Assam-Nagaland Border presents a unique situation so far on the practices of taboo are concerned. Prohibition in taking meat of animal like tiger, leopard, nightjar etc. is followed by the Rengma tribes. Prohibition is imposed on the hunters when he goes for hunting. For instance, they should not keep coins or money with them. It is meaningless to ask about imposition of prohibition as these are unwritten and unsubstantiated tradition.

A long list of such practices of taboo can be narrated from the existing numerous tribal groups residing all along the Assam-Nagaland Border. A comprehensive and illative chart on taboo is attached to make the pervasiveness of taboo in this tribal dominated belt of North East India clear (Table 4.4).

Almost all the tribes have their traditionally inherited taboos and accordingly these are parts of their way of life. The presentation on taboo made in the chart is selective and include only a few from the uncountable list of such practices. It can be said that the tribal societies derived all these from their experiences and the taboos are imposed to keep the society under control and to maintain social discipline. The interference of modernity, however, has brought a remarkable change in the life style of the tribes which has gradually moulded the social settings. Interestingly these taboos help them in maintaining ecological ethics which contribute towards conservation of the ecosystems in their surroundings.

Role of Morung in Tribal Tradition

Every tribe has dormitories where youths of the society gather, play, work for social welfare and sleep. There are separate dormitories for girls where

Table 4.4: Taboos among the tribes of Assam-Nagaland Border

Tribe	*Kind of taboo*	*Detail of practices*
Ao	Food	Meats of tiger, leopard, gibbon, wild dog, civet, squirrel, mole, slow loris, hawks, owls, nightjar, bat, spotted dove, snake, bull frog etc. are tabooed. Beef and pork is tabooed for the Sanglicher clan. Flesh of hornbill is tabooed for Wozukamr clan.
	Social and others	A bull sacrifice and his household could not take bull or mithun. It was taboo to have intercourse with members of a hostile village, to use wood of the tree struck by lightning, to make pots except by the women of the Chanki village. To take bear's flesh in certain villages. To eat with a person with whom one has blood feud. To repaint the mooring carvings by the husband of a pregnant women, and many more taboos and gennas related to birth, marriage, death, sowing, harvesting etc.
Rengma	Food	Flesh of tiger, leopard, animals killed by pig and fire. Other than old man no young men eat flesh of gibbon, parrot and goat. No meat is taken during harvest by Nsenyu stock of this tribe. Taboos imposed on the givers of a feast of merit, the first reaper, the first sower, the first man to spear a tiger during tiger hunt etc. The person giving feast of merit (Kekhe Khamesho) and his wife used to drink only rice-bear (*pitamadhu*) for five days and prohibited to take chilies for ten days. A giver of 'Akhezu Kesa' feast and his wife are denied buffalo flesh for life. Eating of the chilies was not allowed to the platform maker on the day and during 'Tso Kulo' ceremony.

(*Contd.*)

Tribe	*Kind of taboo*	*Detail of practices*
	Social and Others	Pot making was taboo for men. No women catch pig or fowl before pot making. Women were debarred from sleeping on bed and have to sleep apart from husband during menstruation period. Nobody is allowed to pronounce the name of person having unnatural death (*Apotia*). The name of gibbon after dark, possibility of the burning of village, mention of killing the tiger is prohibited. Violation of certain taboos was supposed to cause the clan or family to die out. Snake love is prohibited as it cause the clan die out.
Angami	Food	Children's are prohibited from taking kite, white headed fork tail, brains of cows, pigs, dog etc. The flesh of monkey and tree dwelling animals, the animal killed by wild beasts are taboos for the women of Khonoma. The flesh of the animal killed at the funeral of persons having unnatural death is prohibited from taking by the children.
	Social and Others	Important social taboos are sex contact from outsiders during various *gennas* (function). Absent from work during social function, performer of '*satse genna*' is not allowed to take meat of monkey, crow etc. Performers of "*Lishu genna*" do not take chicken meat during the time of *genna*.
	Food	A large number of birds, animals, and insects are tabooed as food by the Lotha tribe. Tiger, leopard, wild dog, flying squirrel, minuet, sun birds, hawks, hornbill etc. are prohibited as dietary item. Young and middle aged women do not take meat of elephant and snake.

(*Contd.*)

Tribe	*Kind of taboo*	*Detail of practices*
Lotha	Social and others	To watch shaping or firing of pots. Never spread clothes on a granary. Taboo imposed on the sale of tiger's kill and also on joining "Liritang" ceremony after its commencement.
Bodo Kachari	Food	Eating of white guard during the month of July and August. Brinjal and water guard is prohibited in the month of April-May. Meat of tiger is tabooed for Muchahari clan and even they do not take part in tiger hunting. Taking bitter vegetable and on taking rice husk made food during harvesting of paddy. Nobody is allowed to take meat of cow, cat, frog, dog, crow etc.
	Social and others	Restriction is imposed on the woman from visiting the paddy field. Begging and selling fishes for livelihood. No item of the household is sold or carry out from the granary or plucked from the trees during Baichagu festival. Cutting or clearing of trees and plucking or harvesting of crops are strictly prohibited during the observance of Amthichuwa function.
Karbi	Food	Meat of tiger, crow, goat, pig, chicken, cat, cow and various small birds, white guard, purai, bamboo shoots are prohibited. Crab, pangolin, snails are tabooed in Karbi society. Society heads never drink water from Karbi woman.
	Social and others	No woman can talk directly with her husband's elder brother. Ecept "Chamangkon", no Karbi girls particularly of Diphu could take part in dance.

(Contd.)

Tribe	*Kind of taboo*	*Detail of practices*
		Entrance or participation in works on 'Dengza Rongker' is prohibited for others except Teron clan. The use of daily used household accessories in funeral ceremony. Cremation of a dead in cremation ground of other clan is prohibited.
Sonowal Kachari	Food	Meat of cow, cat, tiger, bear, elephant, dog, crow, etc. is prohibited. Curd and bitter items keeps out from dinner. Taking of immature battle nut before October (*Katimah*) is prohibited.
	Social and others	Cremation or religious funeral of the unnatural death is not done. People who accompany cremation ceremony cannot enter into their own home for three days. Unloading of paddy from granary before January-February (*Maghmah*) is prohibited.

Source: (1) Own investigation, 2011.
(2) B.B. Kumar, *Tribal Societies of North-East India*, 2009.

they stay until their marriage. These institutions are differently named by different tribes. However, this is vital to the tribes as it helps to shape and reshape the upcoming generations who would hold the future key of the tribal society. This institution is commonly known as Morung among the tribes of the region. Morung is a word originated from Tai language. This word is used by the Naga tribes for their bachelor's dormitories, although different words are used by different Naga tribes for the same. Under many forms and names, this singular social institution extends from the Himalayas and Formosa on the North to Australia and New Zealand on the south. Taken by the tribes, these barracks for the unmarried are sufficiently suggestive—first as evidence of former racial affinity and second, as an important component of social evolution of the respective tribes (Peal, 1982).

In the Assam-Nagaland Border region, the institution of bachelor's dormitory is found among all the tribes such as 'Arichu' of Ao Naga, 'Morung' of Konyak Naga, 'Deka Chang' or 'Gabharu Chang' of Mishing and so on. Morung institution functions as a dormitory for bachelors where the youths of certain age sleep at night for a definite period or till they get married (Mills, 1980). In the Morungs, they are taught the duties of their lives towards their clan and the society. It is an elaborated system embracing several aspects of their social, cultural and religious profile (Mills, 1980). The Angamis are, however, disagreed to use the term Morung as it belongs to the Konyak tribe and instead they use a common house on the occasion of the ceremonies and gennas where young men of the clan gather to execute the duties allotted to them. Sema tribe, although has no Morung, similar function for the youth is provided by house of the village chief. Chang tribe use the term Haki for the same and perform there similar function.

The Morung plays a vital role in making the younger generation capable to take part in the village council. In broader sense, Morung for the younger generations is a club, a public school, a military training camp, a lodging for boys and meeting place for the village elders. It acts like a centre for all social, political, cultural and religious activities. By entering the Morungs, a boy gains admission to the society of men. Morung, however, does not play uniform role in all the communities and tribes. As the situation differs between hills and plains, the Morung or such institutions have some functional difference. Against using the Morung as a protective cover in the hills, Morung in the plains perform social and cultural activities. Deka Chang of the Mishings is an open long dormitory where both young boys and girls stay during *pahrag* erecting wall to separate them. Deka Chang, however, is commonly used by both boys and girls on different occasions and at times they work together in the Chang as per the demand of the society. *Pahrag* is a festival observed by the Mishing society only to enhance the role of the young girls and boys for the sake of social wellbeing. Both boys and girls collectively work for each of the family as per need to relieve them from work pressure particularly during cultivation, construction of houses, social and cultural functions and some other works of the village or of the clan. A brief chart is prepared to brief up activities of youth dormitories of selected tribal societies (Table 4.5).

Apart from these, all the tribes residing in the Assam-Nagaland Border including the Sonowal, Thengal, Khamayang, Turung, Bodo have their own Morungs representing own style and functions. The dormitories virtually are the creative cultural centre for the tribal youths and an integral part of the tribal society. These dormitories act like a diffusion centre of their tradition and culture. Certainly elimination of such institutions will

Table 4.5: Morung and its functional aspects among different tribes

Tribes	*Kind of dormitory*	*Important aspects*
Karbi	Maro or Terang	It is a bachelor's house build along with the house of village head. There young boys are the vaneguard of the village. They take part in all activities including agriculture, development, cultural functions etc. Nobody remain aloof in the Terang. The chief of the Maro and Terang is called klengcharpawe.
Mishing	Mi′mb′r ya: me Bi′gi′-^{gi}/nam	A common platform for Mishing youth. All youth irrespective of gender are the genuine member of this institution. Construction of Chang Ghar (house), plantation and harvesting of crops, development works are done with the co-operation of the youth members of Mi′mb′r ya: me′. P:rog, s celebrated every after four of five years by these youth as mark of their collectivism. Bi′Kb Gi′nam, Dagdi′k-Aliig etc. are relevant functions where the youths render free labour as per the need of the family of the village.
Tribes	Kind of dormitory	Important aspects.
Angami	Kichuki	It is a dormitory solely for boys and is used as a casual resort. On certain occasions like "Thezukepu' genna boys do not sleep in the Kichuki. Function of Kichuki is limited.
Konyak	Morung	A large bachelor's dormitory. Big posts carved with figures of men, tigers, monkeys, snake etc. and an upright pole projected through the roof are attached with the Morung. It is the centre of learning for the youth of the Konyak tribe.
Ao	Arichu	Arichu has multiple roles-defensive (usually situated near village gate), social, educational and religious. Women are not allowed to enter. Front design differs between the eastern and western Ao villages. Age groups are named as Chongli, Yingar, Mongsen, and Yemgar. At break of three years new batches enter into the Arichu. Junior batch the senior boys. The first batch, called 'nozabarihori', i.e. unripe batch become 'tupakbahori', i.e. ripe batch after three years and then allowed to marry. Fresh entry is done during October after every three years. Strict discipline is maintained. Boys are fined for irrational gossiping. Human skull, human effigies, sculls of sacrificial victims are hung in the Morung.

(*Contd.*)

Note: Words are of missing dialect and accordingly written in the text.

Tribes	Kind of dormitory	Important aspects
Rengma	Resi/Azughu: Eastern Rengma-Awikhu	Entrance of women is prohibited. Each Khel (group) has their own Morung. It is an important centre to perform activities relating to society, culture, education, religion etc. Anybody taking shelter in the Morung is never killed or caused injuries.
Lotha	Champo	It is a young men's sleeping place and women are not allowed to enter. It is built as best Lotha architectural design. War and raid are planned in the courtier of champo. Prisoners of war, skull of dead, horn of Mithun and enemy's head are brought to the champo. These are built in the corner of the village with beautifully carved posts.

Source: (1) Own investigation, 2011.
(2) B.B. Kumar, *Tribal Societies of North-East India*, 2009.
Note: Words are belonging to Rengma district..

mean elimination of tribal nature and spirit. Social system of the tribes as exposed gradually to the scrutiny of modernity and consumerism faces degeneration and finally extinction in course of time. The scenario of such social dynamics is found to be similar all throughout the Assam-Nagaland Border.

Social Administration

"There is a balance between the natural and the vegetal and the animal environment, including human, in which nature delights. It is maintained by chains of actions and reactions, which link man with the rest of his living realm, reaching up and down and all around his invisible biological and social destiny. Such a balance assumes great significance in old countries like India and China," (Mukherjee, 2004). Indubitably the balance between the nature and human activity is preserved amidst high population pressure and increasing intervention of human activities within the nature. It is more pronounced and distinct in the areas dominated by tribal people. North East India, popularly known as the "land of tribes and land of jungle" bears immense significance in this regard. The long forested track harbours many tribal groups, most of which were pushed to the remote margin by factors of modern development and also by the colonial lucrative policies implemented to earn cheap revenue (Gadgil and Guha, 1994).

The daily life of most of the tribes is governed by old tradition of customary codes of law which, although unwritten, are universally understood and pursued. The differences with the plain tribes in system of governance lie in the fact that most of the hill tribes are extremely loyal to the chieftains or the village headman. The chief of the tribal group is the highly honoured and respected man and his decision is the final decision which everybody observes and pursues with all honesty and discipline. The nature of chieftainship, however, varies from tribe-to-tribe. The chief of many tribes enjoys absolute political and economic power, while in some others the chief is regarded as top political and religious functionary. In many cases, the chieftainship is democratically controlled. On the basis of these criteria the societies with chieftainship may be divided into a few categories as given below:

(a) Chieftainship where chiefs are the political and religious head of the community. For example, the Konyak Angs (Headman) are the chiefs and the priests of the Konyak Nagas.
(b) Chieftainship with political and economic power under supereminence of the Community Chief. For example, the Chief of Sema Naga and some Bodo communities enjoys supreme power in this two aspects.
(c) Democratically controlled chieftainship: for example, few Karbi tribes elect their Chief democratically by the elders of the clan. Most of the Naga tribes and Karbis duly elect village council.

The system of Angami Naga is an exception from others. They have neither the chieftainship nor the duly elected village council. All the members of the society gather to settle any dispute and the discussion among them continues until certain consensus is attained. The Angami villages are found to have internal cohesion and they never lack internal discipline. Another most significant character of the Karbi society in respect of council is that any person can be removed from the council if he marries more than one woman or on his conversion to the Christianity. In many cases, eating beef forms sufficient ground for the expulsion not only from the council post, but also from the clan or community.

Other Sociological Attributes

Social structure refers to a network of relationship. Social structure of kinship, family, community, totem, taboo, marriage etc. of the primitive people has close association with nature and natural elements around their habitats. It is pertinent that social structure is one of the key characteristics of understanding social relations in real sense. Social structure, in a sense, is an offshoot of the interaction between culture and environment. In this interaction, the culture of societies get changed from simple to complex. The complexity comes up in the process of modification and control over the environment by human beings. Anthropologists acknowledge the theory of needs: basic needs and derived needs (Malinowski, 1944). The basic needs primarily are food, shelter and mating and the derived needs primarily are those which emerge in the way to satisfy the basic needs (Pundir, 2006). In the course of satisfaction of needs, human beings in group, have always tried to make use of the natural resources of environment and also tried to alter it. In this process of co-operation and adjustment among human beings realize the need of collective functioning and mutual interaction. The process of use and reuse, more and more use and alteration has further opened-up the processes of innovation, invention and production by way of human habit and for satisfaction of their growing needs. Thus, the society goes on transforming their culture while interacting with nature.

The very first functional prerequisite of social system refers to the adjustment of human beings with the environment (Parsons, 1972). Villages are in these sense functional systems within which society, culture and the environment interact with each other. Villages, therefore, are basic functional unit of a group of people of similar mind set and behaviour. Tribal villages can be cited as one such model that still surviving in places as the basic functional unit. Tribal villages in Assam-Nagaland Border differ from area to area and also from tribe-to-tribe. Communities of different areas create different ways of 'imaging nature' including dreams and visions of those forms of social and individual practice. In this process the communities evolve "liberation ecologies" which see nature, environment and place as sources of thinking, reasoning and imagining the social aspects (Peet and Watts, 1996). Scope for livelihood, sources of water supply, security from all adverses etc. are the main considerations in selecting a village site. Tribes preferring fishing usually settle near the rivers and wetlands, for example the Mishings, head hunting Nagas preferred hill tops for their defense, for example the Angamis. Tribes preferring settled cultivation usually settle in the fertile plain and so on. Thus, a significant variation exists among the villages of the tribes inhabiting this border belt.

The size of the villages also varies from tribe-to-tribe. The villages of Angami Naga, Lotha Naga, Sonowal Kachari, Bodo, Thengal Kachari are big in size, while Karbi, Mishing, Khamayang, Turung villages are found to be smaller. However, the size of the villages in most cases is conditioned by the terrain structure. As the entire border region is predominantly a succession of plains, hills and forests, the size of the village has all the restrictions to facilitate the settlement to expand except the areas lying over the vast plain of the Brahmaputra Valley. In parts of the rugged hill areas, the size of the villages is smaller in comparison to open flat hilly areas. At the same time, groups preferring shifting cultivation require a sizeable *jhum* land and therefore availability of *jhum* land also works as an effective factor in determining the village size, particularly in the hill areas. From the latest report of Census of India, 2011, the average size of a village in the broad alluvial plains of Assam-Nagaland Border is 1.25-1.50 sq.km. On the other hand, that a sizeable area attached to the residential sites used for plantation crops and other allied uses is a common feature in the village of plain tribes, it is non-existent in the villages of the hill tribes. Forest under private ownership renders a big support for the livelihood of most of the Naga tribes. Angamis, accustomed to terrace cultivation, usually build big size village (Table 4.6).

In the hills and also in the plains, seldom any village is there where more than one tribe lives together. The tribes of the entire region can easily be identified by the villages they live. Most of the Naga and Karbi villages are separated by some areas in between. Few newly settled villages are found in the plain areas where different tribal communities live together. This character is conspicuous in the areas of encroachment which are primarily concentrated in the reserved forests of the plain districts.

4.3 Eco-Friendly Practices

In this spirit of the meaning of ecology, it refers to a family of all living organisms each in close proximity to the other sharing the same physical space with conflicting nature or complementary needs (Arnold and Guha, 1995). Donald Worster (1998) realizes that in the contemporary context the ecology has tended to focus more narrowly upon the study of nature, the non-human world and looks man as an irrelevant or extraneous factor in shaping the natural environment. Keeping human factor aside will certainly disrupt the integrated study or observation on ecology. As the natural environment not only provides the natural habitat to human beings, but also shapes their socio-economic activities, their belief system and culture as a whole, is quite inseparable to make the study integrated and scientific. From time immemorial, human beings have been on this globe

Table 4.6: Location, size and arrangement of tribal villages in Assam-Nagaland Border Region

Tribe	*Location of village*	*Size*	*Arrangement*
Karbi	Moderately elevated flat land	Size varies from small to medium	No fixed pattern of terrain structure dominates
Angami	On hill top or on the spurs	Usually big	Built on two sides of the roads, not very congested
Sema	On hill tops or at the flat part of hill side	Mostly small	Compact and built on the roadside
Ao	On the spurs or hill tops	Usually big	Built on two sides of the roads, not very congested
Lotha	On the spurs or hill tops	Usually big	Built on two sides of the roads, not very congested
Plain tribes (including Sonowal, Thengal, Mishing etc.)	On flat plains or river valley plains	Usually big, Mishing villages vary in size	Built along road side, not congested Mishing tribe build houses with fields or on the river bank
Khamayang	Flat plain	Size varies from medium to small	Built along road side, not congested
Turung	Flat plain	Size varies from medium to small	Built along road side, not congested

Source: Personal Survey, 2010.

keeping a close relation with nature which taught them how to survive, what to do for survival, what not to do for the sake of survival, which one should be preserved, how much should be consumed etc. It was, perhaps, the first lesson of human being to develop an eco-friendly practice and thereby fabricated a strong base of symbiosis which they have been maintaining traditionally.

Almost all the tribal people in North-East India live in and around the forests. Forefathers of these tribes settled themselves within the forests and had been surviving on forests and other natural resources available in the forests. In consequence, their economic, social and cultural practices closely revolve round the forest life cycle and thus became the foster children of the forest (Basu, 1987). Forest is the basis of their social, economic and cultural life; it is a pivot of their emotions, ethos and aspirations and there has been an in-built concern about nature and its importance in the tribal customs and traditions (Deogaonkar, 2004). The forest has been providing almost all sorts of need of the forest tribe for centuries and as such they consider forest as their sacred property. In this way, there has been a symbiotic relation between forest and tribals (Srivastava, 2007) which has been maintained since historic past. So, long forest was under the domain of the tribes, there was no damage to the forest cover and their practices in the forest were always co-friendly in nature.

It is however, seen that ignorance still exists in evaluation of eco-friendly practices of the tribals. Negligence or ignorance to these age-old practices on the part of many leads to some unscientific idea on the issue. Three important aspects are of great concern in evaluating these age-old practices—(i) eco-friendly practices are not imaginary cognitive formulations, they emerge out of interaction with nature and the experiences gained by the people; (ii) these practices are mostly collective and shared among the concerned people; and (iii) eco-friendly practices are not abrupt and upshot of indiscipline usage, these are adaptive responses subject to certain functional value. The strategies they formulate in response to the ecology ensure their survival as well as the livelihood. Anthropological approach under the shade of cultural ecology is indubitably holistic. The existence of numerous tribes in the topographically heterogeneous, dense forested track of Assam-Nagaland Border symbolise their harmonious relationship with nature and natural processes.

Genesis of the Practices

Eco-friendly practices are not an abrupt product generated by most of the primitive people; these are inherited through generations and traditionally maintained to preserve their forest-based livelihoods with the determination of ensuring future course of comfortable survival. Being a local need-based knowledge, indigenous knowledge system is based on available local resources without any input from outside.

Eco-friendly manipulation of immediate environment, judicious application of plant and animal products, management of soil and water are some of the important components of indigenous knowledge system.

The tribes living in the Assam-Nagaland Border region have well ramified practices performed keeping in view their local environmental condition. Two major groups can be identified on the basis of their livelihood related practices: (1) the hill tribes consisting of Nagas and Karbis who are mostly dependent on *jhum* cultivation, (2) the plain tribes consisting of Thengal Kachari, Sonowal Kachari, Mishing, Turung, Khamayang, Bodo etc. performing settled cultivation. Certain aspects of eco-friendly practices (EFP) followed by various tribes of this region are given below in brief to enunciate the traditional idea of the tribes which may provide a way out from the deteriorating environment (Table 4.7).

The entire information presented in Table 4.7 is gathered through the interviews with the elderlies of the villages during field study. It can be concluded that indigenous crop protection devices and practices are simple, cheap, and eco-friendly. No damages to the wildlife or other farm raiders are caused by such practices. Apart from domestic cattle, various wild animals and birds are destructive to crops. The important ones that have been recorded to inflict crop loses include: Rose ringed parakeet (*Psittacula krameri*), Spotted dove (*Streptopelia chinensis*), Spotbilled duck (*Anas poecilor Hyncha*), Ruddy shelduck (*Tadorna ferruginea*), Adjutant stork (*Leptotilos javanicus*), Common *myna* (*Acridotheres tristis*), Eurasian tree sparrow (*Passer montanus*), House sparrow (*Passer domasticus*), House crow (*Corvus splendens*), Jackal (*Conis aureus*), Porcupine (*Hystrix indica*), Rats, Mices and various species of ungulates, insects etc.

EFP Relating to Hunting, Fishing and Food Gathering

The tribal communities have acquired over the centuries the know-how to use the forest resources in a sustainable manner. Forests constitute the resource base for the tribal to pursue their livelihood. Most part of their life style is associated with the forest and obviously forests are integral part of their life. It reveals that the tribe of Assam-Nagaland Border has many unwritten systems of biodiversity management. Wildlife forms part of the ecosystem in the tribal dominated areas in combination with the tribes of the locality (Behura, 1999). The tribes started inhabiting the region and as stakeholder of biological resources tried their best to maintain equilibrium in the ecological settings. The need for social control and distribution of the forest products leads to adaptive changes in the cultural pattern (Malik, 2004). Rules for using and protecting bio-resources are formulated by the community itself and are backed by threat of religious sanction and social ostracism. Anybody intended to perform hunting or to accomplish a food gathering ceremony in the local area, has to take prior approval from the concerned community head.

Table 4.7: Eco-friendly practices among different tribes in the Assam-Nagaland Border Region

Sl. No.	*Kind of practice*	*Details of EFP*	*Concerned tribes*
1.	Land preparation for cultivation Tools: Plough, Bullock etc.	• Boreal insects remain safe which are often called farmers' friend • No scope for pollution or chemical contamination • Moisture holding capacity remain intact • Crop roots can spread to the deep soil zone	All tribes practiced settled cultivation
2.	Harvesting of crops Tools: Sickle, knife, Spade, Basket etc.	• Only the seeds are collected, stems are left in the field to decompose • The remnant stems get decom-posed and thus enriched the soil fertility	All tribes of the region
3.	Storage of paddy in granary and paddy seeds	• Harvested seeds are kept open in the field and also brought open so that birds, insects etc. can share a little of it and survive • Seeds of some crops are not harvested totally, few of them left for germination for the next harvest.	
4.	Storing of other seeds	• Specially prepared granaries plastered with mixture of cow-dung and mustard oil cake and leaves of Neem, Pachetiya, Bihdhekia are spread at the top of the granary to prevent pest and pathogen. No chemical is used in storing the crops.	Plain tribes including, Thengal, Mishing, Bodo, Sonowal Khamayang etc.
		• The seeds of paddy are kept packed with paddy grasses to inhibit the entry of pests and pathogens. No toxic chemical or any kind of	All tribes

(Contd.)

Sl. No.	*Kind of practice*	*Details of EFP*	*Concerned tribes*
		hormonic chemicals are ever used. Smokes are often released to keep safe the seeds from attack of pests and pathogens.	
		• Seeds of maize and legumenous crops are often kept in-touch along with their outer husk and hang over the kitchens and cowsheds.	Naga, Karbi and Mishing
		• Collection of healthy seeds before general harvest. No HYV is used except some specific variety of rice. Seeds are preserved mixing with ashes or similar matters.	All tribes
		• Few specific seeds susceptible to quick attack of pests are: rice, maize, pumpkin, alum, chilli etc.	
		• Preserved mixing them with neem leaf powder or aromatic plants like citronella grass, lemon grass, peels of pomelo etc.	All tribes
4	Treatment of pest and disease of plants and crops	Following methods are employed for treatment of disease in plants and pests in crops:	
		• Foliar application of wood ashes, and grass cure diseases of plants and prevent attack from aphids pod borers (mostly vegetables).	Naga, Karbi and other plain tribes
		• Hokah water and fine dust of tobacco leaves control pest and diseases of major and minor crops such as blast of rice, pod borers, sucking bugs of vegetables etc.	Sonowal, Thengal and Bodo tribes

(Contd.)

Sl. No.	*Kind of practice*	*Details of EFP*	*Concerned tribes*
5	Control of blast and Chara problem in terrace cultivation	Paddy husk spreaded over the field before 4/5 months to control the blast diseases of rice. The husk also helps soil by making it clay/loamy which enhance the aeration of plants. The field is dried up first by draining out the water and then husk is applied to get rid of the attack of chara, a green algae. Under the cover of husk the chara algae get decomposed and fertilize the soil. Chara do not come up again and thus enrich the soil quality.	Angami, Zeliang and few tribes practicing terrace-cultivation
6	Control of pest and pathogen in *jhum* system	• Instead of using weedicides mulching through the removal of unwanted weeds immediately after sowing paddy controls the pathogens effectively. The decomposed mulch inhibits the pathogens and also enriches soil fertility. It also protects the *jhum* field from erosion. • Mixed cultivation of rice with maize legume crops, job's tear, shorghum and vegetables protects rice from diseases and pests. These crops not only provide food but also act as perch for birds to feed on insects and pest of paddy in the *jhum* fields. Job's tear, a medicinal plant, inhibits the root pathogens of soil.	Ao, Kanyak, Lotha, Sema, Karbi etc.
7	Pest control of sedentary wetland by erecting perch and conserving sacred groves	• Insectivore birds such as Egrets, Sparrow, Dove etc. prey on leaf folder larvae leaf insects, stem borer, grass hoppers etc. of rice in the sedentary	Sonowal, Thengal, Mishing, Turung, Bodo, Khamayang etc.

(*Contd.*)

Sl. No.	Kind of practice	Details of EFP	Concerned tribes
		wet land rice are provided shelter by erecting perches in sufficient numbers. In the large fields, sacred groves are conserved by community which also provide shelter to a large variety of birds. Further, the excreta of these birds act as fumigant to the growth of pathogens in the wet land.	
8	Eco-technology in controlling diseases	• To avoid irrigation by contaminated water most of the tribes in the hills adapt bamboo drip method of irrigation. As such bench terracing for soil conservation and nutrient loss, cultivation of potato in the highland areas and cultivation of tuberous crops in shorter *jhum* cycle as compared to cereals under longer *jhum* cycles are some need-based eco-friendly techniques adapted by the farmers of the region.	Ao, Kanyak, Lotha, Sema, Karbi etc.
9	Crop protection from wildlife pests and predators	• Machan, Flogged bamboos, Effigy of straw etc. are used to drive away the farm raider. Machans are erected amidst the field when it is large enough to manage from ground. Oral sounds, drum beating, warning signals to the villagers etc. are performed through erection of Machan. Long bamboo flag and dreadful effigy is placed in the farm field which also works effectively in driving out the farm raiders. Fire crackers are also used to protect crops from wildlife.	Sonowal, Thengal, Bodo, Karbi, Mishings etc.

Source: Field Observation, 2011 and D.K. Medhi, 1993.

Hunting has been a part of life for the tribal societies. As such fishing, food gathering etc. have been playing a vital role in their survival strategies. Even today, when legislation on wildlife protection is in force, hunting remains a common affair and observed as a customary ritual at a specific day of the year. The plain tribes of the region (Bodo, Mishing etc.) observe the month of April (during Baisagoo or Bohag Bihu) as most congenial period and observed a day by performing identical hunting. Due to fast depletion of prey animals in the forest the Konyak Naga also observed a day in the month of April for traditional hunting. The adults of the community enter into the forest and exercise a symbolic hunting, a practice which they inherited from their progenitor.

It is however, observed that hunting, fishing or food gathering practices, which are now in a diminishing trend due to paucity of bio-resources, have been still regulating their age-old tradition and belief system. The ethics maintained by the tribes can be summarized as:

(i) Hunt animals as per the requirement of the community as a whole. Over hunting is punishable and condemnable in the societies.

(ii) The hunt is equally shared and every household of the community must have a share of it. Among some tribes, an additional share is kept for the persons taking part in performing hunting.

(iii) Killing of tabooed animals is considered as a great sin and the person who kills the tabooed has to face community judiciaries where the kind of punishment to be made is finalized and, in cases the whole family of the person is declared criminal and ousted from the area.

(iv) The Bodo tribes affix the total number of animals to be hunt in the year in the worship held before going out for hunting. The number of hunt, therefore, never exceeds and any misdeed in this regard is condemnable.

(v) Pregnant, immature and cubs are never hunt. A mother with immature cubs is not targeted for hunting. If anybody does so, he is immediately asked for rectification through some rituals.

(vi) No animals are killed at the time of their matting. In the belief of the tribes, such activity may cause sorrow in their family relationship and therefore not admissible.

Apart from these few aspects of their ethics related to hunting, there are, of course, inter-and intra-tribe variations in the practice of hunting. Survey conducted in few selected villages of the study area of different tribes in order to know some aspects of traditional practices reveal that most of the respondents preferred hunting during winter season. Although most of the tribal people now-a-days are not-interested in hunting with the depletion of forests, but most of them prefer winter season as their first choice for hunting, which accounts nearly 59.09 per cent. Out of the total respondents only 21.82 per cent preferred spring season, 10.00 per cent preferred autumn season and 6.36 per cent remained in the category of no response (Table 4.8). Similarly, the quarry on the maintenance of traditional ethics during hunting got verified response from the people of different tribes. Out of a total of 110 respondents, 54.54 per cent favour the traditional ethics on hunting, 20.91 per cent favour partially, while 12.73 per cent of the total has no link at all with the traditions and remaining 11.82 per cent shows no response (Table 4.9).

Table 4.8: EFP practice: choice for hunting season among tribe of Assam-Nagaland Border

Name of village	*Dominant tribe*	*No. of person preferring season for hunting*					
		Summer	*Winter*	*Spring*	*Autumn*	*None*	*Total*
Aochongum	Naga (Ao)	—	8	2	—	2	12
Akatitto	Naga (mixed)	—	7	3	2	—	12
Than Pathar	Mixed	—	12	5	—	3	20
Naganadi	Mixed	2	7	3	2	—	14
Golakpur	Bodo	—	14	5	3	2	24
Gamariguri	Sonowal	1	9	2	3	—	15
Betabari	Khamayang	—	8	4	1	—	13
	Total	**3**	**65**	**24**	**11**	**7**	**110**
	% of Total	**2.73**	**59.09**	**21.82**	**10.00**	**6.36**	**100.00**

Source: Personal Survey, 2011.

Among all the tribal villages surveyed for the purpose of understanding the level of traditional ecological knowledge (TEK), the Bodo tribes are found much more sensitive and responsive to their tradition. More importantly, the villages inhabited by tribes of different sect are poor in maintaining traditions. During the field survey it was found that the affluent families section is not responsive at all to their tradition

It is noteworthy that the tribes have a very close association with the forest and part of their livelihood is forest based. Food gathering in that sense is a day-to-day routine work for most of the families. On the occasion of festivals or functions, they organized a community feast to collect specific

Table 4.9: EFP practice: traditional ethics of hunting maintained by the tribes

Name of villages	*Dominant tribes*	*No. of respondents to traditional ethics of hunting*				
		Fully favoured	*Partially favoured*	*No link*	*No response*	*Total*
Aochongum	Naga (Ao)	6 (50.00)	3 (25.00)	2 (16.67)	1 (8.33)	12
Akatitto	Naga (mixed)	5 (41.67)	2 (16.67)	—	5 (41.67)	12
Than Pathar	Mixed	10 (50.00)	5 (25.00	4 (20.00)	1 (5.00)	20
Naganadi	Mixed	6 (46.15)	2 (15.38)	4 (30.76)	1 (7.69)	13 (7.14)
Golakpur	Bodo	18 (75.00)	5 (20.83)	1 (4.17)	—	24
Gamariguri	Sonowal	7 (46.67)	4 (26.67)	3 (20.00)	1 (6.67)	15
Betabari	Khamayang	8 (61.53)	2 (15.38)	—	3 (23.08)	13
	Total	**60**	**23**	**14**	**12**	**109**
	% of Total	**55.05**	**21.10**	**12.84**	**11.01**	**100.00**

Source: Personal Survey, 2011.
% respondents is shown in parenthesis.

items from the forest and pertaining rituals are performed accordingly in the presence of the village head or elderly people of the community. Apart from community participation in construction of houses, sowing of crops, harvesting etc. the members of the community has to co-operate in the functions of any individual of the community. The items they collect chiefly from the forests are plant leaf, roots, fruits, honey, wax, etc. They have a very good knowledge of edible roots, fruits and plant leaf to use as vegetables. The minor forests produces, collected by the tribes include—(i) medicinal plants and herbs; (ii) gums and resins; (iii) honey and wax; (iv) bamboo and cane; (v) fodder and grasses; (vi) fuelwood; (vii) plants with edible roots, fruits, shoots, flower, seeds etc. (Table 4.10).

In order to have a comprehensive idea relating to the eco-friendly practices (EFP) of food gathering some relevant questions were asked. These are: (i) Whether foods are collected in groups or individually? (ii) Whether food items are collected from the forest as per requirement or more than what is required? (iii) Whether the respondent himself collects food items from the forest?

Table 4.10: Choice for collection of minor forest products

Village name	*Tribe*	*Collection in group (% person)*		*Collection individually (% person)*		*Collecting more than require-ment (in %)*	*As per require-ment (in %)*	*Left for future (in %)*
Aochongum	Naga (Ao)	30.45	71.49	69.55	28.51	20.45	79.55	63.72
Akatitto	Naga (mixed)	22.70	54.91	78.30	45.09	42.65	57.35	40.79
Than Pathar	Mixed	12.41	30.59	87.59	69.41	56.99	43.01	66.70
Naganadi	Mixed	29.22	40.38	70.78	59.62	49.79	50.21	48.37
Golakpur	Bodo	37.48	61.66	62.52	38.34	23.10	76.90	30.63
Gomariguri	Sonowal	20.26	56.89	79.74	43.11	47.71	52.29	42.56
Betbari	Khamayang	39.77	74.79	61.23	25.31	21.20	78.80	31.22

Source: Personal Survey, 2011.

Importantly, villages of mixed tribal population are not much interested to follow their tradition. On the contrary, single community tribal villages are more attached to their traditional practices. Akatitto, Than Pathar and Naganadi are the villages of mixed tribes, while Aochongum, Golokpur, Goraimari and Betbari are inhabited by single tribe namely Ao Naga, Bodo, Sonowal and Khamayang respectively.

Trees and vegetables are of great importance to all the tribes. Trees, sacred groves etc. are subject matter to indolate and hence mandatory for conservation. "Garja Sali" of the Bodo community are places of worship established amidst substantial tree cover. Sonowal, Thengal, Turung, Khamayang tribes have similar customs where tree or the sacred groves are placed as high priority as divine objects. Ambubachi is sincerely observed by almost all the plain tribes and during this festival cutting of trees, plucking of fruits, leaf, collection of roots are prohibited. During Baisagu festival (or Bihu) cows are worshipped on the very first day.

Sonowal, Thengal, Mishing, Turung, Khamayang also observe this first day of Bohag (13th April) like the Bodo tribe. Before felling a big tree rituals are observed in common as they regard all the big trees as the abode of divine life. The Bodo tribe believe that eating a curry of Khungkha, a bitter tested herbs, total debouchment with the close relatives can be completed (Narzi, 2009). Biholongani, Agra, paddy grass, etc. are burnt to spread smoke in the residential campus to drive away harmful insects from the campus. Most of the tribes organize forest worshiping every year which have different meaning for different tribes. Even to start reclamation of a new forest patch rituals are performed. Often big and fruit-bearing trees, sacred groves are left untouched and provision for their conservation is made with a belief that those would protect them from any untoward incidents. Ample instances pertaining to eco-friendly practices (EFP) can be cited in relation to the forest and trees which, in fact, fabricate the base of the tribal livelihood and practices of their daily life.

5
The Impact of Deforestation

5.1 Depletion of Forest and Forest Resources

From prehistoric time the forests are regarded as no-man's land and every household closed to forest exercise their community right over them as per their customary law. Kalidasa mentioned that Kamrupa (means ancient Assam) was covered with valuable trees. Among these, the '*Vata*' (*Ficus indica*) and the '*Asvattha*' (*Ficus religiosa*) were used for religious purposes. Bamboo and cane also were largely found in the forest of Kamrupa. Periplus gave a detail account on trade of forest products of Kamrupa. Aromatic product like resin, *agaru* or aloe wood, *tejpat* (unique in Asia for its scented leaf), black peeper etc. were exported to other countries. Agriculture was not extensive and confined to the periphery of the small racial kingdoms like Barahi, Kachari, Moran, Koch, Chutiya, etc. Reclamation of forest for agricultural expansion although was there, it came up as a result of frequent change of boundary of their kingdom caused by inter-kingdom conflict (Borpujari, 1992). As demographic transition was in its initial stage, population pressure was stagnant and did not have any remarkable effect on the general forest cover.

Long before the occupation of Assam by British, the East India Company had started its intervention in the area. Captain Thomas Welsh was deputed to Assam to help Raja Gaurinath Singha. He furnished a lot of information on the social, economic and commercial aspects of Assam. David Scott (1829), an agent to the Governor General, North-East Frontier, forwarded an account on Assam from 1603 to 1822 AD. He elaborated his experience in the dense forest of Assam in his accounts. John Mc'Cosh arrived at Assam in 1834 to collect statistical information for colonial government and submitted his report in 1837. Mc'Cosh, in his book *Topography of Assam*, furnished data on trade items of Assam which were stated in Captain Pemberton's "Report on the Eastern Frontier" in 1809. Most of the trade items [about 90% were forest-based (Table 5.1)].

Table 5.1: Export items from Assam procured from forest, 1809 and 1855

Item	*1809*		*1855*	
	Amount (mounds)	*Value (Rs.)*	*Amount (mounds)*	*Value (Rs.)*
Stick lac	10,000	35,000	3,292	36,104
Moonga silk	65	11,350	224	53,889
Moonga cloth	75	17,500	—	—
Munjeet (India Madder)	—	500	2,244	13,636
Black pepper	50	500	504	2,846
Ivory	—	6,00	145	14,153
Thaikol fruit	50	150	—	—

Source: J.M.'Cosh, *Topography of Assam*, 1975 (one mound = 40 kg).

A look into the attributes in the table and the notes furnished provides the picture of a region blanketed heavily by forest. Prior to the establishment of colonial rule in the region, the entire North-East India had a rich stock of forest. Assam-Nagaland Border region was also a rich forest zone which can be substantiated from the existence of a series of reserved forests covering the whole border belt. The reserved forests extending from the south-west to north-east of the border are: (i) Nambor, (ii) Diphu, (iii) Rengma, (iv) Doyang, (v) Kakadonga (dereserved), (vi) Desoi valley, (vii) Desoi, (viii) Janjhi (dereserved), (ix) Galeki, (x) Abhaypur, (xi) Rangapahar, and (xii) Singphan. A study of the topographic sheets prepared by Survey of India (1974) also confirmed the existence of extensive forests all along the border region. As per the topographic sheets, the total forest area of the region measured 4862.54 sq.km., which is 75.36 per cent of the total geographical area.

Survey conducted among the inhabitants of the forest belt of the region with a schedule (Appendix A) where inhabitants of this forested belt were asked, (i) wherefrom have they migrated, (ii) was the area a dense forest at the time of their arrival, and (iii) when did they arrive to settle here, etc. On the basis of their response to the quarries, a picture of the nature of forest cover as they experienced at the time of migration is derived. Table 5.2 shows that 94.62 per cent of the people who migrated before 1950 found the area densely forested and only 5.38 per cent saw moderate forest in the areas of their arrival. As high as 62.67 per cent people migrating during 1960-70 witnessed dense forests in the areas of their new settlement and 30.23 per cent experienced moderate forest at the time of their arrival. Table 5.2 also reveals that the dense forest cover is decreasing in course of time as more and more people started migrating to the region. People, accounting for only 20.33 per cent, coming after 1980, responded positively in favour of dense forest. However, the percentage of people witnessing moderate and degraded forests are increasing as time passes which accounts for 27.47 per cent and 40.19 per cent respectively for the period after 1980. Another contrasting picture is seen between the inhabitants of foothill and plain areas where their views regarding forest cover show significant difference. Before 1950, the entire foothill zone was covered by dense forest as per 98.01 per cent of inhabitants who came there earlier to 1950 but it was 88.87 per cent for the plain part of the region. Again, 22.69 per cent inhabitants saw dense forest in the foothill areas, while the same for the plain is only 8.08 per cent for those who settled after 1980. Except the undergrowth of *jhum* land found near the settlement areas of foothills most parts contain crown cover of trees (measuring 70% canopy) during the period of 1960-70 (Tables 5.2 and 5.3).

Table 5.2: Changing forest cover as viewed by the settlers in different periods

(*in* %)

Period of settlement	*Dense forest*	*Moderate forest*	*Degraded forest*	*Open patch*
Before 1950	94.62	5.38	—	—
1950-1960	70.12	20.48	9.32	—
1960-1970	62.67	30.23	7.12	—
1970-1980	31.40	49.22	15.01	9.37
After 1980	20.33	27.42	40.19	12.01

Source: Personal Survey, 2011.

Table 5.3: Periodical change of dense forest cover as viewed by the settlers of hills and plains

(*in* %)

Zone of settlers	*Before 1950*	*1950-60*	*1960-70*	*1970-80*	*After 1980*
Foothill zone	98.01	92.45	92.45	40.51	22.69
Plain zone	88.87	69.92	48.93	12.29	8.08

Source: Personal Survey, 2011.

Tables 5.2 and 5.3 depict the extent of forest depletion. The changing scenario of forest cover of the region is dramatic, where the number of viewers of dense forest came down from 94.62 per cent to only 20.33 per cent within a span of approximately 30 years. Maps prepared from satellite imagery (IRS-LISS-III) also confirmed this sharp depletion of forest in this border belt. Superimposition of forest cover maps from satellite imagery (2010) over topographic sheets (RF 1:50,000) of Survey of India, 1974 shows a marked variation of forest areas of the region (*See* Map 3.8).

Forest resources are often regarded as mainstay of the tribal people (Goel and Sharma, 1998). Tribes living in the forest and forest fringe areas depend on forest products for their livelihood. Any dislocation of forests would cause substantial damage to their traditional mode of living. The national forest policy of 1988 directs protection and enhancement of production of non-wood forest products which provide sustenance to the tribal people and other communities residing in and around the forests. People residing permanently in the areas of Assam-Nagaland Border, since historic past recall a time when everything of their basic needs came from the forest. They used forest land for agriculture, grazed their livestock in the forest, collected fire-wood, housing materials, etc. But during the colonial period most of the forestland favourable for agricultural extension was appropriated for European tea planters and people inhabiting the neighbouring areas were pushed to remote border areas (Ghimire and Pimbert, 2006). Plain tribes accustomed with permanent cultivation rather than shifting engaged themselves in clearing the forest of the border land. By joining hands with the inhabitants of the forest and Taungya villages, migrants also removed the forest to settle and perform their agricultural pursuits and thus brought a sharp reduction in the forest based resources. Naturally, it jeopardized the forest-based livelihood of the people living in and around the forest. In the hilly areas, the Government of Nagaland concentrated maximum developmental activities and built new settlement areas. Encroachment from hills and plains, intensive logging in the forests of border areas, opening of tea gardens in large number and rehabilitation of the flood and erosion effected people and the intervention of the rich peasantry to grab more lands finally resulted in large scale destruction of forest resources.

The paucity of recorded data on the extent and intensity of depletion of forest resources is a constraint for proper analysis of the dependency of forest dwellers on the forest resources. Depletion of forest resources is a direct result of deforestation and hence deforestation of any kind implies a reduction of intact forest resources. The Assam-Nagaland

Border, once known as rich harbour of wilderness, was converted into open patch of scattered and spotted forest areas within a span of not more than 50 years. A chronological discourse on the forest cover indicates the facts behind deforestation in the area. During 1910-11, Sibasagar districts (Sibsagar, Jorhat, Golaghat districts and parts of Nagaland) had a forest cover of 56.83 per cent to the total geographical area of 4,995 sq. mile, while Karbi Anglong had 95.97 per cent to the total geographical area (Bryant, 1912). However, the forest cover of the whole district including Jorhat and Golaghat came down to 20.80 per cent in 2007. Karbi Anglong, showed a decline in forest cover by about 20.00 per cent during the period. Table 5.4 shows the distribution of forests and the state of forest cover in the districts attached to the Assam-Nagaland Border. Moreover, in 1952, the Techno-Economic Survey, Assam observed that approximately 39 per cent of the state's total area was covered with forest. In the next 38 years, the forest covers of the state came down to 30.20 per cent (FSI-2003). Forest cover of Nagaland, however, remained static with 52.45 per cent for the same period. Surprisingly, the border districts measure far less than the state's average forest cover. Mon, Mokokchung, Wokha and Dimapur districts show 23.32 per cent, 17.93 per cent, 15.58 per cent and 22.24 per cent respectively (Chief Conservator of Forest, Nagaland, 2001). Under these circumstances, the stock of forest resource decreased sharply which finally left adverse impact on the inhabitants who depend on forest resources for their livelihood partly or fully.

Table 5.4: Type of forest cover in districts attached to the Assam-Nagaland Border

District	*Geographical area (km^2)*	*VDF (km^2)*	*MDF (km^2)*	*Open forest (km^2)*	*Total (km^2)*	*P.C. of Geographical area (%)*
Golaghat	3,502	6	123	392	521	14.88
Jorhat	2,851	2	114	494	610	21.40
Sibsagar	2,668	8	144	541	693	25.97
Karbi Anglong	10,434	578	3,887	3,493	7,958	76.27

Source: Forest Survey of India, 2007.
VDF = Very dense forest MDF = Moderate dense forest.

The forest dependent communities of the north-east may have considerable legal authority over the natural resources of the region, based on the legislation passed during the colonial era, as well the post-Independence period. At present, community based indigenous systems of forest conservation are under threat due to absence of proper mapping, boundary registration and titling. The trends towards privatization, sedentarization of agriculture and commercialization of resources have driven activities that lead to depletion of forest resources (Poffenberger, 2006). Shifting cultivation has also been held responsible for increasing area under "open forest". In Nagaland and Karbi Anglong, much of the lands designated as unclassified forest are part of the *jhum* lands.

Jhum lands are cleared and burnt for cultivation every 5 to 10 years and thus regeneration of forest is greatly hindered. Degraded secondary forests, bamboo thickets and weeds or simply barren land dominate today's *jhumscapes*. In earlier period, say prior to 1950, *jhum* cycle was as long as 15 to 20 years since population pressure was quite low. However, negative effects on the ecology surfaced as population pressure started increasing. Two types of negative effect are seen: (i) shifting of *jhumland* demands clearing of fresh forest land with the reduction of *jhum cycle* to 3-5 years. Thus, abandoned plots do not get enough time for regeneration; and (ii) the secondary growth in the abandoned plots is much poorer in terms of crown density and species diversity and richness in relation to the original forest type (Saikia, http.// www.ibcperu…). The *jhum* practice in the hills with short cycles under increasing population pressure is no longer ecologically viable and hence unsustainable. Comparison of forest cover of 2007 with the previous assessment (satellite data of December 2006-January 2007 and January-February 2005) shows a loss of 201 km^2 of forest cover in Nagaland (Forest Survey of India). This loss of forest cover in Nagaland occurred as a result of further expansion of *jhum* land which means ultimately the depletion of forest resources.

Gradual elimination of community forest management system gives way to both the governmental and non-governmental agencies free intervention in the forest land which, in turn, causes pressure on the forest resource base (Fig. 5.1). From the period of British colonial rule onwards uninterrupted intervention in forest by way of enacting of forest laws, establishing forest based industries, introducing commercial crops, expanding forest area under government jurisdiction, privatizing community forest area etc. caused gross damage to the forest resource base in the Assam-Nagaland Border. Community forest management has failed to have a strong back up as the private sector forces and government backed forces overwhelmed the forest management system of the region. The principal kinds of uses of forest resource in the region are showed in Table 5.5.

It is observed that the endeavours to protect forest under governmental and non-governmental initiatives, however, could not suppress the

PRESSURE ON COMMUNITY FOREST MANAGEMENT SYSTEM

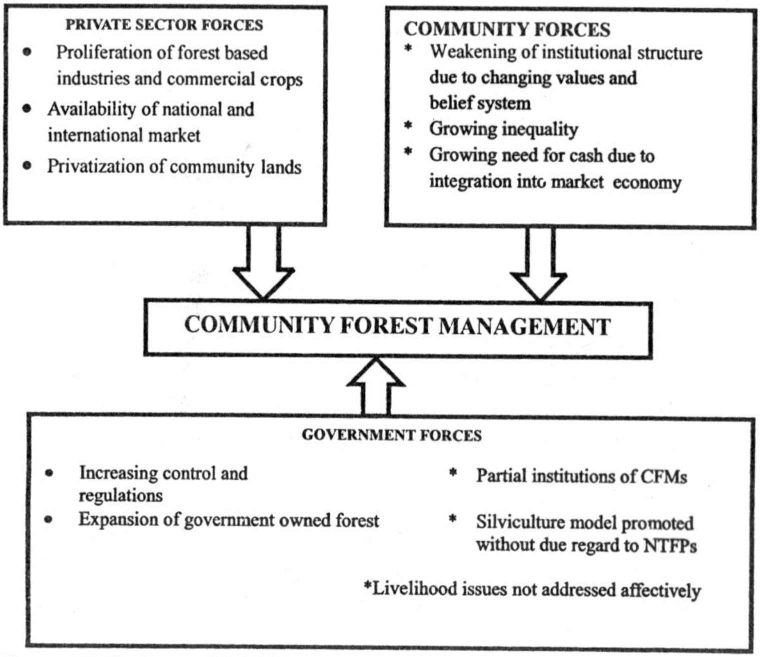

Source: Poffenberger, M. 2006.

Fig. 5.1: Pressure on Community Forest Management System

dominance of firm sector and household sector activity on the forest resources. Increasing pressure of population and tendency to reap economic benefit from forest resources negatively affected the cause of forest protection. On the other hand, 88 per cent of the forests in Nagaland are owned and managed privately or by the village councils and communities themselves, while the government has control over only 11.7 per cent of the forests (FSI, 2011). In terms of forest quality, the state has only 9.7 per cent of total forest cover as very dense forest, while 37 per cent of the total forest cover is moderately dense and 53.3 per cent is classed as open forest. Indian Institute of Science (IISc), Bangalore in an assessment confirmed that 99,850 hectares of green forest of the state has been eroded during 2007-2009 period (www.indiaenvironment portal.org. in, p. 5). A sharp contrast in the forest cover change can be observed from the records of Forest Survey India. The assessment of forest survey of India presented a disastrous scenario of dense forest

Table 5.5: Use and Management of Forest Resources

Household Sector	*Firm Sector*	*Environmental Protection*
• House building materials	• Industrial raw materials	• Conservation of soil, water and animal life
• Firewood • Charcoal • Food • Fodder for domestic animals • Shifting cultivation • Grazing	• Fuel • Construction materials for industrial housing, public works, railway works, defence needs etc.	• In situ preservation of genetic diversity of plants and crops (gene pool)

Source: Ganguly, J. B., 1986.

which came down from 27.82 per cent to 0.70 per cent within a period of two years from 2009 to 2011.

It is seen that the whole of Assam-Nagaland Border, which was once rich in forest, is now transformed into a region of degraded forest. It now experiences intensive human activity in the areas where extensive forested patch once dominated. Depletion of forest resource base pushed the forest dwellers to adopt alternative livelihood practices and in the absence of required incentives and protection measures for the forest dwellers, who were once in a symbiotic relationship with forest, cornered their traditional ethics and engaged themselves in encroachment of forest land for a better livelihood. The paucity of recorded data on depletion of forest resources restricts a detailed analysis on this aspect. However, a simple comparison is made with all limitations to depict the state of forest resources of the plain districts of the border region (Table 5.7).

Table 5.6: Change of forest cover in the border districts of Nagaland, 2009-2011

District	*Geographical area (km^2)*	*Percentage of forest cover*				*% of change*
		2009		*2011*		
		Dense forest	*Open forest*	*Dense forest*	*Open forest*	
Dimapur	758	16.62	33.91	—	51.72	+1.19
Mokokchung	1615	33.31	53.07	0.86	83.52	–2.86
Mon	1786	29.89	42.55	1.85	69.37	–3.07
Wokha	1628	31.45	55.41	0.08	84.64	–2.22

Source: Forest Survey of India, 2011.

Table 5.7: Production of MFP and volume of change in the border districts of Assam

Districts	Production of MFP					
	2007-08		2010-11		Volume of Change	
	Industrial timber (Cubic meter)	Fuel-wood stack (Cubic meter)	Industrial timber (Cubic meter)	Fuel-wood stack (Cubic meter)	Industrial timber (Cubic meter)	Fuel-wood stack (Cubic meter)
Golaghat	2342.645	10.00	0.854	0	–2341.791	–10.00
Jorhat	1751.912	19.00	3.218	3.00	–1748.694	–16.00
Sibsagar	28.670	8.00	10.292	2.00	–18.378	–6.00
Karbi Anglong	N.A.	N.A.	N.A.	N.A.	N.A.	N.A.
Total	**4123.227**	**37.00**	**14.364**	**5.00**	**–4108.863**	**–32.00**

Source: Economic Survey, Assam, 2010-11; *Statistical Handbook of Assam*, 2008-09.

Data on non-wood forest product pertaining to the area are not available. Hence, comparison is confined to the major forest products like industrial timber and fuelwood. Table 5.7 reveals that a substantial difference exists in between the MFP product of the period 2007-08 and 2010-11. Production of industrial timber in 2007-08 was 4123.227 cubic meter which came down to 14.364 cubic meter by 2010-11. Again, the fate of fuelwood production is also same which has decreased from 37.00 stack cubic meter to 5.00 stack cubic meter during the same period.

The field data have also shown the similar trend. Involvement of people in the collection of NWFP is decreasing as depletion of forest and forest resources are increasing. Throughout the region, large tracts of forestlands have been reduced to degraded forest and as such forest resources have been dwindling steadily. NWFP collection obviously experienced a sharp decline. Table 5.8 shows that there exists a contrast among the villages where economy and life style play determining role in the choice of NWFP collection. For instance, 8 and 11 persons respectively of sample Naga villages—Aochangum and Akatitto-located in the Desoi and Desoi valley reserved forests are involved in log business, while the involvement of people in plain areas in log business is much lesser. On the other hand, the people, particularly of the plain areas, engaged in fuelwood business are from the low income group. The number of people involved is found to be 18, 15, 12 and 14 respectively for Thanpathar, Naganadi, Golakpur and Napam villages.

Table 5.8 shows that there is significant change in the livelihood practices mainly from forest-based to non-forest-based activities. The involvement of very few people in the business of forest product indicates the decreasing trend of availability of forest resources in the area.

NWFP like honey, resin, medicinal plants and herbs, animal flash, roots and fruits etc. also shows a steady decline in production which, however, is well reflected in table 5.8. Inhabitants of the area unanimously confessed that the continuous destruction of habitats results in depletion of NWFP in their locality. It is seen that the tribal communities residing in this belt have a land-based strategy of livelihood. The people belonging to tribal communities having settled or shifting agriculture are drawing necessary economic support from the forest resources.

Table 5.8: Number of people involved in selling forest products, 2011

Sample Villages	*Log*	*Fuel-wood*	*Honey*	*Resin*	*Medicinal products*	*Animal flash*	*Roots and fruits*
Aochongum	0	—	02	—	02	06	12
Akatitto	11	—	01	—	01	03	07
Thanpathar	02	18	04	02	03	—	16
Naganadi	03	15	02	01	04	—	10
Golokpur	04	12	—	—	02	02	04
Napam	05	14	01	01	03	—	06
Betbari	01	03	—	—	01	—	02
Total	**26**	**62**	**10**	**04**	**16**	**11**	**57**

Source: Personal Survey, 2011.

Changes in the existing livelihood practices of the tribals are brought about by factors like close contact with modern know-how of agriculture, benefit of commercial crops, efforts and incentives provided by governmental and non-governmental agencies, fast depletion of forest resources, competition among cultivators to occupy more fertile forested land and the inter-state boundary conflict. Moreover, in the context of cultural changes, it is notable that the belief system, traditional practices and values, social relations etc. in a community do not develop all of a sudden. Therefore, the acceptance of change by the community becomes easier when it is to some extent compatible with the ethos of tribal culture. These basic relations of tribal way of life play a decisive role in the process of modification of their livelihood strategies.

Table 5.9: People's response on the issue of depletion of forest resources, 2011

Sample village	*Shortage of food stuff (%)*	*Shortage of herbs (%)*	*Insecurity of dwellers (%)*	*Occurr-ence of hazards (%)*	*Change of climate (%)*	*Others (%)*	*Total house-hold respon-dents*
Aochongum	20(71.42)	15(53.57)	3(10.71)	2(7.14)	8(28.57)	2(7.14)	28
Akatitto	24(96.00)	19(76.00)	7(28.00)	3(12.0)	5(20.0)	3(12.0)	25
Thanpathar	18(60.00)	12(40.00)	5(16.67)	7(23.33)	8(26.67)	1(3.33)	30
Naganadi	18(72.00)	10(40.00)	8(32.00)	—	10(40.0)	2(8.0)	25
Golokpur	21(91.30)	9(39.13)	12(52.17)	4(17.39)	6(26.08)	2(8.69)	23
Namati	20(66.67)	9(30.00)	10(33.33)	—	7(23.33)	—	30
Betbari	8(44.44)	4(22.22)	6(33.33)	1(556)	15(83.33)	3(16.67)	18

Source: Personal Survey, 2011.

(i) Others primarily include Non-Timber Forest Product (NTFP).
(ii) Figures within bracket indicate percentage to the total.

Forests for them are the backbone and in the absence of sufficient forests as support base to their livelihood they become vulnerable to various problems. When asked—how does depletion of forest resources affect their life and society?—the villagers responded sharply in negative. Table 5.9 presents the opinion of the villagers about the problem faced by them as a result of exhausted forest resources.

Shortage of food stuff is the prime concern of most of the respondents living in the close proximity of the forested foothills. They are also deeply worried about the non-availability of herbs and edible plants. Out of 336 respondents, 61.60 per cent are of the opinion that depletion of forest is responsible for shortage of foodstuff and edible herbs, while 14.16 per cent felt that depletion of forest resources caused insecurity to the dwellers. The matter of climate change, albeit they are not aware of global warming kind of phenomenon, positively responded about the onset of phenomena like change of rainfall pattern, rising temperature, unusual wind movement etc.

It is unfortunate that the forest resources in this region are facing degeneration just because of—(i) unplanned deforestation; (ii) poor socio-economic conditions; (iii) absence of alternatives to face excessive population pressure; (iv) over exploitation and poaching of wild plants and animal resources; (v) unscientific approach towards conservation of forest and forest resources; and (vi) negligence to address livelihood issues of tribals. Extensive and indiscriminate poaching of wildlife has remained common and usual practice from long past in the forest of this region. In most cases the laws of games are not observed strictly and seldom take any appropriate measure for their conservation and protection (Sharma, 1999). The villagers of Assam-Nagaland Border invariably acknowledge the causes behind non-availability of wildlife for hunting. The general view of the respondents affirms three major causes responsible for decreasing number of animals for hunting. These are—(i) over hunting by locals; (ii) increasing poaching; and (iii) declining forest cover or loss of habitat. Out of the total respondents 58.63 per cent pointed to the above mentioned causes (Table 5.10). Golakpur, a Bodo tribe dominated village was established during 1960s to rehabilitate people from Goalpara district. Bher Doimari narrates his experience how they did settle in this forested patch (interview, dated 17th September, 2012). They built small huts using bamboo posts and roof of *takau* (Ashoka) leafs clearing a dense forested plot. He witnessed a *Bheleu* tree having a canopy cover of 1440 sq. feet nearby his residence. They initially earned livelihood by selling cane and bamboo, most of which were purchased by a contractor of Sangkhati. Plenty of wild animals, primarily deer, elephant, leopard, tiger, bear, monkey, python, king cobra and other snakes were there. Brischik (Scorpion) and red crab were also numerous. Most of the red crabs were eaten up by their people and at present no trace of red crab is found in this locality. Now most of these are non-existent.

Table 5.10: Causes behind insufficient number of animals for hunting as perceived by the respondents

Sample villages	*Over hunting by locals*	*Intense poaching*	*Declining forests*	*Natural calamity*	*Others*
Aochongum	20	5	4	2	—
Akatitto	17	7	3	1	—
Thanpathar	9	12	8	—	1
Naganadi	11	14	8	—	2
Golokpur	14	8	12	1	—
Namati	8	7	10	—	—
Betbari	3	7	10	—	2
Total	**82**	**60**	**55**	**4**	**5**

Source: Personal Survey, 2011.
Note: The numbers represent the no. of respondents.

Nirmal Bora of Chaodang Pathar describes here what he listened from his grandfather. It was tormenting when they were forced to settle in the reserved forest. Thick forest on all sides enriched with plenty of wildlife made the life hard and all the doors had to be kept close till the end of the day (16th September, 2012). Khehto Achumi of Mitche (a village of Lotha tribe in the Assam and Nagaland border) village says "here in this village we are all new settlers. One part of the village administration is under the jurisdiction of Assam government and the other part is administered by the Nagaland government. We practice both shifting and settled cultivation to meet our requirement and people collect their housing materials and wild vegetables from the forest, but these are gradually decreasing as a result of reducing forest cover". The importance of forest for ecological security, supply of materials to fulfil people's need and industrial raw materials is inextricable and hence immense. It is an intelligible notion that the economy of forest dwellers and the tribals are built around the forest resources and, therefore, access to these resources has been a matter of great concern. No smooth development of forestry can be planned in isolation and it should be an integrated part of plans formulated for the cause of tribal development. Depletion of forest resources is inimical to tribal culture and economy. Therefore, for the sake of tribal development it is essential to keep the forest enriched with resources and to raise its accessibility to the tribals.

5.2 Behavioural Change of Forest Tribes

Behavioural approach is based on rigorous, extensively developed and logically coherent conceptual framework, which has links both to the biologically-based human sciences and social sciences (Mcguine, 2000). It is a process-driven search of spatial existence. The process is behavioural and includes learning, thinking, forming attitudes, perceiving, giving value and meaning, representing etc. (Golledge and Stimson, 1990). Behavioural change or modification, on the other hand, is usual and common in the social space as a number of reinforcement agents variably pursue activities at different places and different times. Changes in the contingencies of reinforcement modify the pattern of behaviour (Sundel and Sundel, 1993).

The range of methods of behaviour modification is very wide. D'Zurilla and Goldfried (1971) discussed the modification of behaviour depending on the nature and availability of resources. The major type of behaviour modifications are: (i) positive reinforcement, (ii) negative reinforcement, (iii) fading, (iv) punishment, (v) overcorrection, (vi) backward chaining, (vii) successive approximation, and (viii) behavioural assignment. Positive reinforcement is the presentation of reinforcement on a response system to increase the frequency of that response while the negative reinforcement decreases the frequency of response. On the other hand, fading is associated with the transfer of a conditional response from one stimulus to another in progressive step.

It is obvious that a region with plenty of forest resources when converted into a degraded condition, the dwellers living there have to change their response from one stimulus to another. Behaviour modification thus becomes inevitable to adjust with the changing situation and supply of resources. The Assam-Nagaland Border region, as it experienced reinforcement through wanton deforestation, has more or less lost the response that existed earlier. Change in the behaviour of dwellers is certainly intelligible. Change in the response process at time keeps the dwellers accustomed with the changing situation at the cost of modification in behaviour. As Wolpart (1965) has stated—"man is limited to a finite ability to perceive, calculate and predict and to an otherwise imperfect knowledge of the environment," but "he will differentiate between alternative courses of action to their relative utility or expected utility".

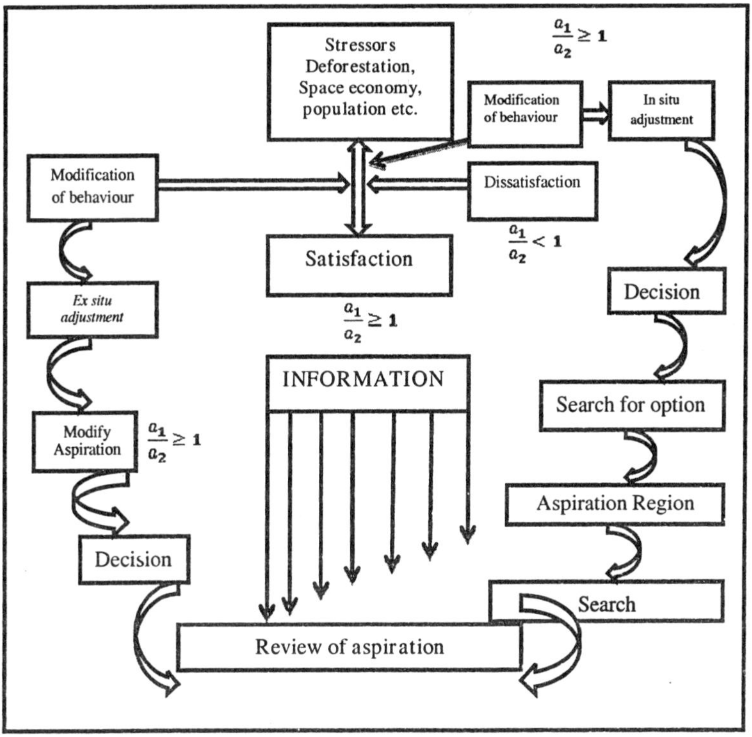

Source: Brown and Moore, 1970.

Fig. 5.2: A Behavioural Model: Modification of Behaviour

Behavioural change, at this backdrop is a compulsion and man with their higher adaptability in a changing environment intended to change some of the behaviour (Brown and Moore, 1970). Brown and Moore (1970) developed a behavoural model to illustrate residential location of decision process. The Stressor component, which dictates a behavioural change, may be either internal or external environment which interferes with the satisfaction of basic needs and disrupt or threatens to disrupt the stability (Wolpart, 1966). Disruption reinforces either adjustment or replacement and brings modification of behaviour to survive under new situation. For instance, animism, the widely practiced religious ethics of the tribal is replaced by modern world religion like—Christianity, Hinduism, Islam etc. Age old traditional ethics of tribal religious belief was uprooted and thus behaviour relating to religion came under modification. The changing face of behaviour of the tribes of Assam-Nagaland Border is a case of adjustment, readjustment and replacement of their ethics and traditions. The behavioural model illustrating the modification of behaviour of the tribes of Assam-Nagaland Border is derived following the behavioural model of Brown and Moore (1970).

Extensive deforestation is considered as a major stress factor. The forest dwellers and the tribes practicing forest-based livelihood came under severe stress. With this impending stress some other stress factors like migration of new settlers, conflict over border issue between the State of Assam and Nagaland, penetration of big landholders, growth of urban centres etc. heralded upon the region the dismantling process of tribal life and livelihood. Achievement level (a_1) came down and as the aspiration (a_2) started shrinking. The resultant dissatisfaction pushed them to decide for alternatives. The entire changing situation, however, compelled them to modify aspiration level to make it a generic satisfaction by order of *in situ* adjustment, i.e.

$$\frac{a_1}{a_2} \geq 1$$

(ratio between achievement level and aspiration level is either more than one or equal to one). Threat caused on traditional tribal behaviour compelled them for certain modification to raise their satisfaction level, i.e. A modified form of behavioural model developed by Brown and Moore (1970) is attached to make the approach comprehensive (Fig. 5.2).

Re-arrangement of Settlement (in-situ adjustment)

The Nagaland border area is characterized by racial homogeneity, common dialects and linear arrangement of homesteads along roadside or river, and hamlet type of settlements in the hilly parts. It is a kind of rearrangement over the earlier settlement when road communication was virtually non-existent. At the beginning, settlements consisted of five to six families and were quite apart from each other. These small settlements had common cultural features and the people followed their age-old traditional practices and habits. They had been living in the forest struggling against tough and hazardous condition.

Continuous intervention of outsiders into the forest resources disestablished the ecological settings with which the forest dwellers are historically accustomed. In this part of Assam-Nagaland Border, the dwellers instead of going for search option, tried their best to adjust in their place by modifying their aspirations. This *in-situ* adjustment leads to a decision to stay in the place of their origin (Golledge and Stimson, 1987). Reduction in forest resources led to relocation of the settlers and the traditionally maintained ecological balance between the dwellers and their environment was disrupted. People were compelled to remain confined to small and unfavourable land areas, traditional social institutions and land management. Thus, short-term problem-solving behaviour replaces long-term planning. The net result is environmental degradation (Colchester, 1987). Such *in-situ* adjustment is conspicuous in their settlement pattern. The forest villages established in the forest areas by the colonial administration to meet the labour shortage and for smooth management were very few in number. Depending upon the extent of the forest, forest villages were established ranging from one to five. For instance, the Tiru Hills reserve forest being smaller in size possessed one forest village (Mogroi in Tiru Hills R F.), while the Dayang forest being larger in size accommodated four forest villages (Chaodung Pathar, Kachamari, Merapani and Amguri) These were established in total isolation from one to the other. People, who came to settle there developed road communications. Dayang, Nambor, Tiru Hill reserved forests witnessed a splendid growth of settlement during the 1960s and 1970s. Gradual extension of road communication, enlargement of settlement area, expansion of farm land etc. resulted in the shrinkage of forest area and resources. The tribes already living there sorted out rearrangement of their settlement giving way to the new settlers and instead of searching other options to raise aspiration level preferred *in-situ* adjustment by modifying behaviours pertaining to livelihood and traditional practices. *In situ* adjustment of settlement behaviour (Fig. 5.4) is apparently penetrative and pervasive in parts of Assam-Nagaland Border where the two state authorities got engaged in the game of border occupation by deploying people to settle there. The hamlet type of settlement at the initial stage thus turned into linear settlement by virtue of *in situ* adjustment (*see* Fig. 5.3).

Another most inextricable behavioural change is spectacularly reflected in their dietary habit and mode of collection of other household needs. Traditional tribal society manages maximum of their household requirements from the forest or from other natural sources. From medicine to primary food items and from cloths to shelter, most of the things they collect from forests. Usually, villages situated in and around the forests procure their daily needs including housing materials either from the forest and the *basti* land attached to their homesteads or from their farm land. Increasing dependence on market is certainly an indication of changing behaviour of the inhabitants of forest and forest fringe areas. To understand the nature of changing behaviour, few meaningful queries were included in the schedule. The response so found from the survey is shown in

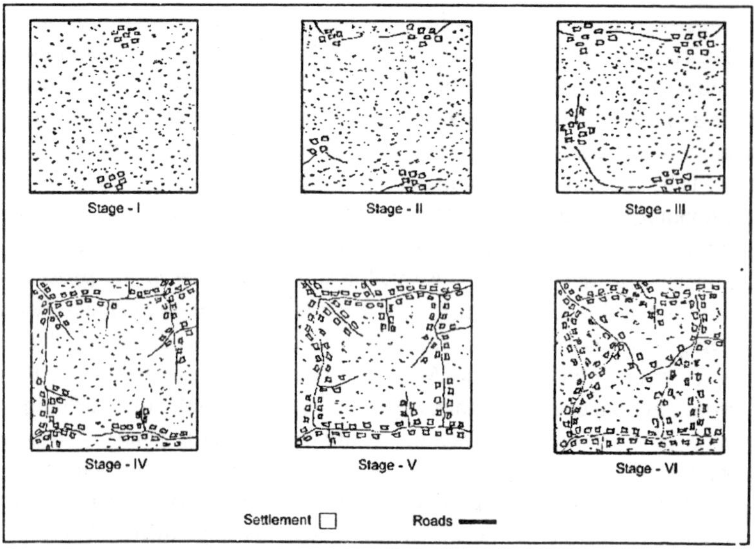

Source: Field Observation.

Fig. 5.3: A Model on *In situ* Adjustment of Settlement Pattern (Conversion from Isolated Hamlet to Liner)

Table 5.11. Intelligibly, Table 5.11 disapproves the longstanding concept of a forest based livelihood of the tribals. They have become more and more market dependent. Except rice, vegetables and few items of housing materials, most of the needs are procured from market. Traditional means of health care practice, which was once practiced extensively in the tribal societies, is now decreasing sharply. Out of the total 110, only 19.17 per cent households, belonging to economically backward section, are still using traditional health care practices. On the other hand, 80.83 per cent households are opting for modern practices. The basic cause, for this is the extinction of medicinal plants and animals needed for traditional treatment of diseases. The new generation is not interested in these practices. However, the knowledge they acquired traditionally to treat the diseases still remain with the elderlies of the family. Table 5.12 which shows aspects of traditional practices is more or less common for all the families of the border area. Plant species used to cure diseases grow abundantly in different areas and most of the inhabitants know the utilities of different bird, animal and insect species available locally. It is reported that more than 5000 species of medicinal plants are found in the hills and plains of Assam (Medhi, 1993). A few aspects of traditional medicine used to cure disease are cited in Table 5.12. It is important to note that the fast depletion of forest resources results in the depletion of wildlife which in turn caused irreparable damage to such traditional health care system which persists for long in the region. The invasion of consumerism at a quicker pace among the local dwellers becomes inimical to this tradition and accordingly a change in behaviour is observed in the society.

The above mentioned means and method of traditional disease treatment was extensively practiced in most of the villages of Assam-Nagaland Border until 1980s of the last century. It is reported that Merapani, a township at the foot of Naga hills possessed a small pharmacy in the early 1980s and the same increased to 12 in 2010. Increasing dependence and faith on allopathic medicine has gradually reduced the importance of ethno-medicine. The advancement of Christianity largely among the Nagas also interdicted the traditional means of health care practice in the hills and the plains as well. No pharmacy was there in and around Galeki market up to 1981. Presently, Galeki has as many as 8 pharmacies which draw sizeable number of consumers from Naga community. Modern methods of treatment and quick relief from sufferings have virtually cornered the practice of ethno-medicine in the area.

A generic diagnosis on the change of behaviour of the tribes living in the areas of Assam-Nagaland Border confirmed that the tendency to

Table 5.11: Sources of collection of major household items of the sample villages of Assam-Nagaland Border

Name of sample villages	*Rice*		*Pulses*		*Masiered Oil*		*Meat and Fish*		*Clothes*		*Herbs and Medicine*		*Housing materials Purchased*			
	Own Produced	*Purchased*	*Own Produced*	*Purchased*	*Own Produced*	*Purchased*	*Own Produced*	*Purchased*	*Home Made*	*Purchased*	*Tradi-tional*	*Pharma-cutical*	*Bamboo*	*Thatch Leaf*	*Cane*	*Timber*
Aochandung	22.40	77.60	5.14	94.86	—	100.00	48.71	51.29	42.06	57.94	27.67	72.33	—	—	—	21.23
Akatito	45.51	54.49	2.04	97.96	2.00	98.00	61.10	38.90	30.72	69.28	25.00	75.00	—	—	—	10.44
Thanpathar	–71.80	28.20	6.99	93.01	12.49	87.51	39.41	60.59	38.91	61.09	18.57	81.43	10.81	5.98	2.79	39.78
Naganadi	84.12	15.88	—	100.00	7.63	92.37	35.78	64.22	18.68	81.32	28.89	71.11	7.68	3.45	—	17.79
Golakpur	82.89	82.89	12.71	87.29	14.27	85.73	41.29	58.71	13.94	86.06	19.51	80.49	21.62	8.38	—	29.68
Napam	100.00	17.11	10.02	89.98	—	100.00	58.61	41.39	19.79	80.21	9.91	90.09	—	—	—	38.29
Betbari	64.75	—	—	100.00	2.78	96.22	70.41	29.59	28.42	71.58	4.62	95.38	2.49	—	4.21	79.81

Source: Personal Survey, 2011.

Note: The figure indicate the P.C. of respondents.

Table 5.12: Animal-based traditional means of treatment of diseases

Animal species	*Scientific name*	*Used part*	*Used to cure*	*Observation*
(1) Tortoise	*Batogus kadhuga*	Shell, Meat	Meat is used to cure pox, shell is kept in cowshed to drive away infectious diseases.	It is now an endangered species, population decreasing at a faster rate. Hunting, killing pollution and habitat loss are the causes of decrease in number.
(2) Inguana	*Veranus begalensis*	Fats, Skin, Meat	To remove the burned spot, Ashes of skin used to cure burning. Meat is believed to be good for dysentery.	It is also endangered. Population decreases due to loss of habitat.
(3) Fox	*Vulpes bengalensis*	Meat	Used to cure Rheumatic pain.	Population decreases due to deforestation and other antithesis works against their reproduction.
(4) Porcupine	*Hystrix indica*	Gaul bladder	Used to cure black fever.	Not easy to capture. Endangered species.
(5) Bat (small) Bat (big)	*Pteropus giganteus* *Cynopterus brachgotis*	Meat	Meat is used to cure asthmatic trouble. A good antidote.	Decreases in number. Used by Sonowal, Thengal and Bodo tribes.
(6) Man	*Homosepious sepians*	Hair	Hair of woman is tied around leg or hand of the person having scar or cut injury to prevent infection.	This practice is prevalent among tribes of plain.
(7) Cockroach	*Periplaneta americana*	Head	Heads with certain herbs is given for curing dog bites.	Found available but the practice is confined in few rural pockets of the region.
(8) Earth worm	*(i) Eutiphosus spp.* *(ii) Pheretima spp*	Body exude Liquids Body with flash	Used to cure piles. Used to cure pox related illness.	Found available in pollutant free damp soil. Found available in banana (*Mulbhog*) trees. This earthworm is white in colour.
(9) Pigeon	*Columbia livia*	Whole body for meat	(i) Pigeon meat prepared with black peeper is used t o cure common cold (ii) Pigeon meat prepared with banana flower is used to raise strength and to cure low blood pressure.	It is a domesticated species, usually found in rural houses. Increasing population pressure and changing house type restricts its growth.
1(0) Green Pigeon	*Treron phoenicoptera*	-do-	-do-	Not available, reduction in forest cover and shortage of food stuffs cause damages to the growth.

(Contd.)

Animal species	*Scientific name*	*Used part*	*Used to cure*	*Observation*
(11) Cat fish	*Clarius batracus*	Whole body	(i) Feed the person after suffering illness to get strength prepared with medicinal herb like Mani-muni (*Hydrocotyl*), Bhedailata (*Rubioceae*) Narasingh (*Currypatty*) (ii) Cat fish prepared with preserved dried leaves of jute (*sukta*) is used to cure pox.	Large scale earth filling works and intensive human intervention in the beels and marshes reduced the population.
(12) Kuchiya	*Angullia angullia*	Whole body	(i) Meat used to cure anemia, leukemia etc. (ii) To enhance strength of an ill person.	Lives in marshy land, beels and swampy areas population is decreasing as a result of human interference in their habitat.
(13) Pig	*Sces scrofa*	Fats	(i) Fats of pig used to cure rheumatic pain and other muscle pain.	Domestic variety found available. Wild varieties are rarely found in the jungle.
(14) Fire fly or fire ant	*Photuris spp.*	Whole body	Put inside a banana and is given for eating to a person having night blindness.	Available everywhere but the practice is confined only in few villages of the border region
(15) Spider	*Tegenario spp.*	Dead spider	Dead and dried spider mixed with coconut oil and is applied to cure scans of outer part of ear .	Found available
(16) Tiger	*Panthera tigris*	Sex organ of the female	The sex organ of a female tiger in small amount is given to the pregnant suffering from dizziness and drowsiness .	Species is endangered. Not found available and is practiced by Misshings and Tarungs
(17) Dolphin	*Platanista gangetica*	Fats, pulp and meat	(i) Oil extracted from dolphin is used to cure pain. (ii) Pulp of dolphin conch is used to cure drowsiness of pregnant woman.	Endangered species. Reducing in number at a faster rate. Sowansiri, *Brahmamaputra* and Dihong are the habitats so far remains. Mishing and Bodo tribes are accustomed with this practice.
(18) Sparrow	*Passer domesticus*	Whole body	Meat is eaten to revitalize the sexual potency.	Number is fast reducing. People alleged that after erection of mobile tower, TV. antena and increasing use of electronic accessories, population of sparrow is decreasing.
(19) Palla's Fish Eagle	*Pandianhaliaetus*	Body for meat	Curry of Eagle meat prepared with black basil (*Tuloshi*) is eaten to the ill to regain energy.	Common only among Mishing tribes. Endengered species. Not locally available.

Source: Medhi: Man and Environment in North East India, 1993.

shift from traditional means of livelihood and other practices is seen to develop among the dwellers as the base of the forest resources is shrinking along with the decreasing forest cover. No endeavour has ever been undertaken either by government or by any non-governmental agency to maintain and conserve their age-old traditions and culture. The adjustment made by the inhabitants is basically an outcome of the fast changing ecological set-up of the region.

5.3 Life and Economy: The Extent of Change

The human civilization has completed a cycle from culture generating from nature to a culture overlording the nature itself. Therefore, ecology that deals with the relations between living organisms focusing on the relationship between the distributions of human groups with reference to material resources and consequent social and cultural patterns is perhaps more relevant in today's context (Webster, 1979). It naturally shifts the attention from anthropocentrism to egocentrism to view human activities as an important product of physical environment under which they exist (Sen, 2007). All empirical evidences, however, now indicate that the fast degradation of ecological pursuits cause irrecoverable damages to the food security and livelihoods of people living in and around the nature's hub, i.e. the forested belt, throughout the world (West and Brachin, 1991) and on occasions, forest communities have been expelled from their settlements as well as from their traditional livelihood practices. Depletion of forest resources acts adversely and uproots the traditional life support system particularly of the tribals living close to the forests. Traditional knowledge base relating to treatment of diseases using medicinal plants, traditional forest conservation methods, food gathering ethics, ecological management system etc., which evolved through generations also disappear (Wood, 1995).

Economy and livelihood systems are diverse in the forested rural landscape, while inhabitants commonly rely on a mixture of wild foods, agricultural produce, remittances and trading. Household decision-making continually adjusts to the changing nature of the environment and economy. Shifting cultivation, hunting and food gathering were practiced by the tribes because of ecological compulsions. It is not because they are tribals. The depth and robustness of the indigenous knowledge base of a community is virtually a reflection of the degree of dependency on their immediate environment and their association with the natural resources (Chaudhury, 2008). The tribal societies of Assam-Nagaland

Border display a strong appreciation of their immediate environment. Their livelihood linkages with the surrounding forests and forest-related activities, acknowledge a rational understanding and a good adjustment with the given set of environmental condition (Ramakrishnan, 1992). The indigenous knowledge system of the tribals is not alone confined to *jhum* fields, hunting, food gathering etc., but extends to a vast field of their entire livelihood practices.

Rampant deforestation, as heralded upon the tribal life of Assam-Nagaland Border has gradually been uprooting the forest-based practices of the tribes. Under the changing ecological condition the forest tribes have adapted to the changes for their survival. The traditional livelihood system of the tribal people has developed on shifting/settled cultivation and collection of forest products. As shifting cultivation began to decline from about the second decade of twentieth century as a result of Regulations and Act formulated by the colonial government, a section of the hill tribes even took to settled agriculture. The Angam are accustomed with terrace cultivation of permanent nature. Likewise, the Aos of Mokokchung and Konyak of Mon districts adopted settled agriculture with the enforcement of certain regulations on shifting cultivation by the Government of Nagaland. Karbi's of the border region also were provided land in the south Nambor reserved forest to practice settled agriculture. It is a common social notion that traditional livelihood system is based on customary rights of the tribal communities over land and forests. It is an extensive system of production. The 'common pool' nature of resources supported customary rights and prevented the intensification of production. It is obviously in the interest of raising the sustainability of land resources which is firmly rooted in a system of 'property rights' over land and forest (Padhi, *et al.*, 2011). Tribals are extremely sensitive to their customs, traditions and racial heritage.

The vast forest areas of Assam-Nagaland Border region and the tribal traditional livelihood practices came under pressure with the advent of British colonial administration. In their eyes, forests were lucrative resource and the eco-friendly tribal livelihood practices were wasteful. Thus, the tribes living in and around the forests of Assam-Nagaland Border had to confront with the policies, firstly framed by the British colonial administration, and secondly by the Indian administrators during post-Independence period as successor of the policies framed earlier.

Forests were cleared to accommodate tea plantations, to meet the demand of timber in and outside the country and to expand agriculture to set the land as permanent source of revenue accumulation. Increasing population pressure and rising aspirations for more agricultural land negatively affected the remaining forests of the border region. Under this adverse backdrop, the tribals of the region came under compulsion to change their traditional practices and behaviour. Apart from these, adoption of Christianity in parts of the Nagaland border by most of the Naga tribes also brought changes in attitude and perception towards forest. The extent of change in one word is vast. The entire border, predominantly inhabited by several tribal groups, witnessed a spectacular change in attitude, behaviour and mode of life. Some aspects of such changes are discussed to make the matter comprehensive and compareable to the earlier status.

Change in the Economy

Forest tribes, with plenty of forest resources around their habitats are fervently accustomed with diet, of which a sizeable part is forest-based. Rice, the staple food for most of the tribal people is supplemented by vegetables and non-vegetable items which were directly collected from forests during the period before the onset of large scale deforestation. Continuous removal of forest cover from the area had gradually jeopardized the life and economy of the ecological community which in turn brought changes to the socio-economic profile of the region. Table 5.12 illustrates the changing nature of life style as well as the economy of the tribes living in this border belt. The people, once regarded as ecosystem people, now have changed their status to become more market dependent. It is, as such, indicative that a trend of consumerism has gradually started capturing the whole society. Increasing number of markets and expanding urban horizon in the border belt subside the traditional values of the tribes which in consequence dismantle tribal mode of living attached to the forests. Food gathering and agriculture being the principal sources of living of the tribal of this region supported the people by providing the basic needs till the time prior to the onset of deforestation. The ecocentric tribals of Assam-Nagaland Border had tried their best to cope with the changing ecological scenario. Intensive activity of timber traders and the upcoming of numerous tea estates in the region opened-up the way to develop market centres. The weekly markets of tea gardens and the entry of Marowari traders from Rajasthan started supplementing the deficit of the subsistence economy of the tribals of the border belt. The period subsequent to the establishment of tea estates and the continuous encroachment of government forest land by people witnessed the growth of several markets and urban agglomerations. Sonari, Naginimara, Lerumen, Amguri, Geleki, Tuli, Chungthiya, Mariani, Titabor, Sarupathar, Bokajan, Wokha, Dimapur, Merapani, etc. are the townships which have been serving as important functional centres in the Assam-Nagaland Border region. Apart from the tea garden markets, there developed sizeable number of important rural periodic markets in the region. The impact of these townships and market centres on the ecology of the region are far reaching.

Table 5.12 showing the sources of major household items reflects the change of life and economy of the tribal of this border belt. A most spectacular turn is observed in the health care aspects of the tribes. A substantial number of households accounting for 80 per cent depend on pharmaceutical medicine instead of the age-old traditional practices. Most of them expressed that the village-medicine men are decreasing in number and the traditional knowledge is almost lost. Moreover, herbs and medicinal plants used to treat diseases cannot be found today easily. The village women weavers, who prepared required clothes and dresses in their handlooms, are now discouraged by the cheaper outside supply. Most of the village weavers are now chiefly engaged in preparing their traditional dresses only. Another significant impact of deforestation on the economy of the tribes is that the subsistence agricultural practice is no longer able to fulfil the requirement of the increasing population and thus dependence on market for their required food staff is increasing. Shortening of *jhum* cycles to 5 to 6 years reduces the crop productivity which in turn forced the tribes, particularly the Nagas, to procure maximum of their needs from the market. Survey conducted in few Naga villages shows that nearly 60 per cent people of the Naga tribes collect their food items from market. On the contrary, the same is low among the plain tribe villages where market dependency accounts for only 19.20 per cent. The existence of vast fertile agricultural land in the plains became possible due to deforestation which helped settled cultivation to flourish.

Replacement of Traditional House-building Materials

Mode of living is an active expression of the adaptations of the human groups to their natural settings (Sorre, 1962). Being a product of culture—environment interaction, house type reflects the cultural heritage, changing fashion, functional needs and consequent positive and negative aspects of non-cultural elements (Kniffen, 1965). The Assam-Nagaland Border region, originally a forested patch with sizeable tribal inhabitants, has experienced a significant change in the form, function and structure of house type during the post-deforestation period. It is a vital question to enquire that what kind of changes have taken place in the house type and to what extent the socio-economic and ecological conditions in the area are experiencing change.

The house types in the Assam-Nagaland Border region can be distinguished on the basis of the building materials used. In all rural landscapes, the tendency in making houses is to use materials available in the locality and to maintain the cultural attributes evolved through generations. Before the onset of large scale deforestation the inhabitants of the region collected all their building materials from the nearby forests. Thatch, bamboo, *ashoka* leaves (*takau pat*), wood, cane, etc. were plenty in the forests which were used as primary building materials by the forest dwellers of this region. The highland forest dwellers mostly used *ashoka* leaves as roofing materials against the extensive use of thatch by the plain dwellers of as thatches were found extensively in the river valleys. However, *ashoka* leaves, bamboo, wood and cane continued to remain as main building materials until 1960. Big thatch houses were the status symbols of the people and were mostly owned by the well-to-do families. Assam type cottage with *ashoka* leaf roofs are found still in many parts of the foothill areas of the border region.

Removal of maximum of the forest cover, establishment of tea estates and expansion of settlements encroaching forest land brought significant change in the house type of the region. The process of large scale forest destruction also reduced the availability of building materials like timber, cane, *ashoka* leaves, reeds and bamboo. Settlers of the plain districts of the border region, however, replaced their *ashoka* leaf roofs by thatches which they used to cultivate in the highlands to supplement the growing demand for roofing materials. On the other hand, houses in the foothill areas as well as the hilly parts remained almost unchanged as plenty of *ashoka* trees were still there to meet the requirement. Two types of Assam type cottage in the rural-scape of the border belt can be identified—(i) *ashoka* leaf roofed cottage of foothills and hill areas, and (ii) thatch roofed cottage of plain areas beyond the hills. During this period the region perhaps for the first time witnessed the growth of Assam type semi-*pucca* and *pucca* houses. The British and the European tea planters introduced this type of building in the administrative centres and in the tea estates of the region.

The second phase of impact of deforestation on house type of the region started during 1970s of twentieth century as most of the forests, especially of the plain part, were wiped out. Scarcity of local building materials was mounting resulting from continuous deforestation and encroachment by the land hungry peasants of the surrounding areas. Conversion of vast grassland and the grazing reserves into productive crop land caused shortage of thatch, reeds, cane, bamboo etc. It is reported that cost of one bundle of thatch (containing 100 fistful thatches) was Rs. 400/- during 1980s in parts of South Nambor area (Tengani area) which was quite high for any lower middle class peasant. A well stitched thatched house usually lasted for 8 to 9 years depending upon the quality of thatch (Borah, 2011). As an alternative the middle class peasants started using corrugated iron sheets and asbestos sheets for roofing. Durability and effectiveness of these materials against all mateorological hazards attracted more and more people to use it and thus a new wave of using iron sheets (tin) and asbestos sheets which brought about a significant change in the house type. Within a period 15 years, from 1990 to 2005, C.I. sheets and asbestos got top priority as roofing materials in the villages of plain tribes and then among the hill tribe villages.

Apart from these, the implementation of "Pradhan Mantri Gram Sadak Yojana" (PMGSY) to connect rural areas by easy means of transport and communication also enhanced the pace of accessibility which contributed towards improving the marketing facilities in the remote rural areas. The third phase of change saw the growth of Assam type semi-*pucca* and Assam type *pucca* house. Change in the house type associated with the process of deforestation can be put in chronological order on the basis of building materials used. Table 5.13 is derived on the basis of intensive field work done and interview carried with the experienced elderly people of the study area.

Contrary to the dominance of Assam type houses in the plain part of the region, the hill tribes of Nagaland and Karbi Anglong have their traditional house types. Raised platform house or *changghar* type was most common among the hill tribes like Karbi, Angami, Lotha, Ao, Kanyak etc. Penetration of Christianity and increasing scarcity of locally available building materials encouraged them to construct low cost Assam type houses replacing the traditional ones. Traditionally, accustomed to *changghar* culture, plain tribes like Mishing, Turung and Khamayang also have developed the habit of living in the flat floored Assam type houses. The survey conducted in the Napam, a Sonowal dominated village of Merapani area and Mithche, a Lotha village of Wokha district reveals that most of the houses are of C.I. sheet roofed Assam type and very few *ashoka* leaf roofed houses are there. Taking help from Dambarudhar Sonowal of Napam and Auchumi Sumi of Mitche village an account of the house type was made (Table 5.14).

Table 5.13: Chronological order of change in house type in Assam-Nagaland Border Region, 1826-2005

Phase	*Period*	*Changing house type*	*Predominant building materials*	*Status of ecology*
Phase-I	Before 1826	Assam Type Cottage	Cane, bamboo, ashoka leaves, wood, reeds etc.	Scanty of population, dense forest cover, high biodiversity
Phase-II	1826-1970	Assam Type Cottage	Cane, bamboo, thatch grasses, ashoka leaves, wood, reeds etc.	Population pressure rising, deforestation engraved the ecology. Heavy loss of biodiversity.
Phase-III	1970-2005	Assam Type Cottage and Semi-*Pucca* house	Bamboo, wood, C.I. Sheets, asbestos, cement etc.	Population pressure high, few isolated forest patch remain.
Phase-IV	2005 and above	Assam Type Cottage and Semi-*Pucca* and *Pucca* house	Bamboo, wood, iron rod, Cement, bricks C.I. sheets, asbestos etc.	Man-land ratio increasing, secondary re-growth dominates forest area, poor in bio-diversity.

Source: Personal Field Survey, 2010.

Table 5.14: Number of households and house type in Napam and Mitche villages

Name of village	*Number of Assam type cottage*			*Assam type semi-pucca*	*Assam type pucca*	*Traditional dwelling*	*Total house-holds*
	Palm leaves roofed	*Thatch roofed*	*C.I. sheet roofed*				
Napam	11	5	23	13	4	2	58
Mitche	3	—	15	2	—	4	24

Source: Personal Survey, 2010 with kind co-operation of locals namely Dambarudhar Sonowal and Achumi Sumi.

Table 5.14 depicts the present status of house types in the two villages which can be logically appreciated for a generic analysis the whole region in general. C.I. sheet, wood and bamboo are the chief building materials of a tin roofed house. Bamboo is locally available since it is grown in the *Basti* land of every household and also in the forest of secondary growth. C.I. sheets and timbers are collected from nearby markets. The whole scenario associated with the changing house type is typically a product of ecological disorder which can be conceived from the building materials they use to construct houses. In the past, most of their needs for housing materials were fulfiled by the forests, because the environment was bounteous and there was no restriction on the use of forest resources. While enquiring about the sources of housing materials, the requirements of respondents vary greatly as they have owned more than one house of different type. Table 5.15 gives an idea of the variety of housing materials collected from different sources.

Table 5.15: Sources of raw-materials used for construction of houses

Materials used	*Number of respondents*				*Total*
	Collected from forest	*Purchased from market*	*From own plantation*	*Government supply*	
Bamboo	52	20	58	—	130 (19.37%)
Wood	18	49	31	26	124 (18.48%)
Thatch	13	10	15	—	38 (5.66%)
Cane	22	09	21	—	52 (7.75%)
Reeds	18	12	08	—	38 (5.66%)
C.I. sheets	—	—	—	26	104 (15.50%)
Nuts	—	38	—	24	62 (9.24%)
Stone	10	17	—	—	27 (4.02%)
Sand	18	15	—	12	45 (6.71%)
Bricks	—	29	—	22	51 (7.60%)
Total	**151 (25.46%)**	**199 (33.56%)**	**133 (22.43%)**	**110 (18.55%)**	**593**

Source: Personal Field Survey, 2010.

Note: Figures in parenthesis are the percentage of total respondents.

Table 5.15 presents the overall pattern of sources of housing materials used by the tribes of the region to construct their houses. Growing dependence on market (percentage of respondents 41.28) is indicative of the aggravating situation of forest-based resources. Out of a total of 671 respondents, only 22.50 per cent collect materials from the forest for construction of houses. However, dependence on market is increasing substantially, while the forests including the plantation plots of the individual family have still been playing a significant role in supplying raw materials for construction of houses. The tribes of Assam-Nagaland Border region have got a heterogeneous cultural pattern largely depending on ecological settings and ethnic environment. Different scholars have suggested a three to eight-fold classification of tribal economy. Broadly the basic economic activities of the tribal people may be classified as follows:

(1) Food gathering including hunting and fishing,
(2) Pastoral practice,
(3) *Jhum* or shifting cultivation,
(4) Settled cultivation,
(5) Handicrafts, and
(6) Wage labour—agricultural and industrial.

Broadly speaking, various tribal groups of this border region follow shifting cultivation in the hills, while the plain tribes pursue settled or permanent cultivation. Apart from these two primary economic activities they simultaneously afford time for food gathering activities also. The most interesting aspect of tribal economy is that they rarely follow one single occupation exclusively. Among subsidiary occupations, handicrafts, gathering, animal rearing, selling of forest products, wage labour etc. are primarily practiced by many of them. A generic analysis on the economy clearly demonstrates the dependence of the tribal on forest resources and forest land. The forest tribes depend largely on the minor forest products for their subsistence. They collect edible items from forest, use the timber, bamboo, grass and cane to construct their houses and to make implements and collect fuelwood for cooking and many other materials as per their household requirement.

The mainstay of both the plain and hill tribes chiefly is cultivation. Shifting and terrace cultivation is typical to the Hill tribes of Nagaland and Karbi Anglong, while the plain tribes are usually accustomed to permanent cultivation. However, in addition to increasing population pressure in the low hills and foothill areas at the western margin of Nagaland, the positive initiatives taken to negate *jhum* cultivation by the Government of Nagaland evoke good response. As a result, there is a substantial fall in the acreage of *jhum* land. Out of the total area of 90,00 hectares under paddy, *jhum* paddy occupies 57.12 per cent, while 42.8 per cent is under terraced paddy in the hilly parts of the Assam-Nagaland Border region. Earlier, terraced cultivation was confined within the Angami areas alone. Terraced cultivation is extended to all low hill districts of the state and all possible areas are brought under this practice. Moreover, *jhum* land is extensively used for agro-forestry and rubber plantation under various forest development agencies (FDAs) of the state. As most of the land of the state is under community ownership, the implementation of the government policies acts as a trouble shooter to boost up the agrarian economy of the region. Table 5.16 presents a profile of the economic pursuits undertaken by the people of the area.

Table 5.16 showing the category-wise distribution of workers indicates the state of economic development in the region. Dimapur, a relatively developed district of the region registers the lowest percentage of cultivators (28.35%), while the percentage share of other works is as high as 64.36 per cent. On the contrary, Mon district has 83.94 per cent cultivators and other works absorb only 10.30 per cent. The percentage of cultivators in the two districts gives a very conclusive idea about the variations in developmental aspects. A comparison between the attributes like cultivator and forest cover of the region also indicates the change of economic pursuits in the two districts. The livelihood practices associated with the primary occupation like cultivation, mining, fishing, hunting etc. have a straight and positive correlation with the forest cover of the region. The correlation analysis made between the percentage of cultivators and the percentage of forest cover in the four districts of border belt shows a positive correlation (r = + 0.711). It means that there exists a strong positive correlation between the percentage of cultivators and percentage of forest covers. The conclusion therefore, can be drawn that higher the forest cover lower is the number of workers engaged in sectors other than primary. Thus, it can be said that the extent of forest cover is a strong determinant of the economic activities performed by the people in the region.

Table 5.16: Category-wise distribution of workers in the border districts of Nagaland, 2004

District	Total workers	Cultivators (%)	Agricultural labour (%)	Workers in household industries (%)	Others (%)
Dimapur	102,260	18.35	4.8	2.71	6435
Wokha	56,53	64.88	1.18	2.54	31.3
Mokokchung	108,779	60.09	6.34	3.73	29.84
Mon	12,915	83.94	4.458	1.18	10.30

Source: Compiled from *Statistical Handbook of Nagaland*, 2004.

In the plain districts, on the other hand, the condition of life and economy is dominated by land-based livelihood practices. Agriculture has been the dominant livelihood practice of the people of the plain districts where cultivators constitute 63.91 per cent of the total workers (Table 5.17). The share of workers in other sectors is found to be higher in the relatively developed districts like Jorhat and Sibsagar with 25.14 per cent and 24.63 per cent workers respectively.

Table 5.17: Category-wise percentage distribution of workers in the Plain districts of Assam-Nagaland Border Region, 2009

District	Cultivators (%)	Agricultural labour (%)	Workers in household industries (%)	Other sectors
Golaghat	73.76	5.32	2.81	1.57
Jorhat	57.80	12.81	4.25	25.14
Sibsagar	55.40	16.92	3.04	24.63
Karbi Anglong	68.66	16.77	3.71	10.86

Source: Compiled from *Statistical Handbook of Assam*, 2009.

The results of the sample survey conducted in some villages of the border districts depict a similarity in the occupational pattern of the households with that of the official figures (Table 5.17). As most of the sample villages are located at close proximity of the forested belt, there exists a slight variation in occupational structure. Workers under primary sector overwhelm other sector as there are limited alternatives for livelihood. Table 5.18 presents the overall occupational structure of the sample villages of Assam-Nagaland Border region.

Table 5.18: Occupational structure in the villages of Assam-Nagaland Border Region, 2011

Name of sample village	No. of households surveyed	Total population of the households	Persons engaged in occupations		
			Primary	Secondary	Tertiary
Aochandang	12	67	18	6	7
Akatito	10	53	2	3	5
Thanpathar	18	84	28	5	12
Naganadi	5	71	17	—	8
Napam	20	108	31	—	14
Golokpur	20	116	29	7	6
Betbari	2	2	12	1	10
Total	**87**	**501**	**137**	**22**	**62**

Source: Personal Survey, 2011.

Depletion of forest is jeopardizing the practice like hunting, fishing and collection of other resources all throughout the border region. Fishing grounds like river, ponds, *beels,* swamps etc. although are there, have scanty aquatic fauna and flora. Today, nobody goes regularly for hunting to the forests. Hunting, however, is occasionally performed by the hill tribes as there is no restrictions except for the totemic animals. Some tribes, such as Kanyak, Bodo and Lotha perform symbolic hunting to mark certain rituals once in a year. Due to non-availability of prey animals the age old tradition of hunting is now virtually non-existent. Table 5.19 shows the means of hunting, i.e. the weapons both traditional and modern used by the tribes of the border region. As reported by them, the weapons they possess are seldom used for hunting. Some of the families keep the traditional weapons as status symbol of the family and to memorize forefather's bravery in hunting. The life and economy of the tribes, therefore, have remarkable differences from their forest based livelihood practice.

Table 5.19: Means of hunting of the tribes of Assam-Nagaland-Border Region, 2011

Name of village	*Traditional weapons*						*Modern weapons*			*No. of household surveyed*
	Bow-arrow	*Trapping*	*Spear/ trident*	*Knife/axe*	*Shooting stone*	*Herbal poisoning*	*Hand made gun*	*Rifle*	*Chemical poisoning*	
Aochandang	5	2	4	2	8	2	5	1	5	28
Akatito	7	1	5	2	10	1	3	—	3	25
Thanpathar	2	3	8	—	6	—	2	—	—	30
Naganadi	3	4	7	—	4	—	1	—	—	25
Napam	5	5	3	—	4	—	1	—	1	23
Golokpur	5	2	4	—	2	1	—	—	—	30
Betbari	1	—	2	—	2	—	—	—	—	18
Total	**28**	**17**	**33**	**4**	**36**	**4**	**12**	**1**	**9**	**179**

Source: Personal Survey, 2011.

5.4 Some Adverse Effects of Forest Depletion

Lost Forest—Lost Knowledge

Tribal rights on land and forest have been the highly talked about subject-matter since long. Since time immemorial these communities have been exploiting the elegance of nature without any hindrance. In course of time there developed a relation between the tribal communities and nature. The cultures they practiced are the direct product of their interaction with nature. The Assam-Nagaland Border region, being a congenial niche for a number of tribal communities, who developed their culture from the experiences they gained from the interaction with nature. The jungles in their eyes are not community of trees but sacred abodes of divine deities. In their belief nobody should disturb forests, cut trees and kill wild animals unless they have prior permission from those divine deities. This kind of belief system spontaneously contributed toward developing certain environmental ethics among the tribal people.

The belief systems and practices relating to forest and wildlife as parts of tradition were there much before the forest and wildlife acts came into force. All the tribal belief systems and practices are outcome of continuous interaction between the tribes and the environment. All the tribes of Assam-Nagaland Border, from hills to plain, have their own tradition and culture to guide their simple livelihood practices within the specific settings of nature. The processes of land alienation through series of Government Acts and policies and deforestation alienated the forest-based tribal people from their age-old tradition and customary rights over the forest land. Under compulsion they have to change their attitude and behaviour and the cultural pursuits which they have been traditionally maintaining. The friendly relation they maintain with forests, the culture they developed to keep the forest and themselves living and the knowledge and experience they gained from their forest-based life style are getting jeopardized. Under new situation the bewildered forest tribes have come under total obliviousness to their tradition and culture. As time passes, the environmental knowledge base of the tribes is losing its strength. Now very little attention has been paid to this aspect by the agencies engaged in modern conservation practices in the area.

The situation of insufficient forests for the tribes of Assam-Nagaland Border has already given rise to a new trend which can be seen in their changing mode of living. During the survey conducted in some selected villages of the border area, it was found that most of the youths expressed their helplessness when asked about the continuity of their age-old tradition, customs, rituals and knowledge about their immediate environment. This phenomenon is well reflected in Table 5.9. Out of 356 respondents 36.24 per cent admitted the shortage of food staff and 21.91 per cent expressed their worry about shortage of herbs due to depletion of forest cover in the region. It has significant implication over the nature of forest-based activities of the tribes. The process, if continued unabated, certainly will bring total collapse of the traditional knowledge base. And, perhaps at times all these hard earned but unrecorded knowledge system will be lost forever.

Social Inclusion and Exclusion

Social inclusion means the encompassing of the entire population in the performance of the individual function systems. On the other hand, social exclusion is the process through which individuals or groups are wholly or partially excluded from full participation in the society in which they live. The concept of social inclusion and exclusion is a recent development. Since, the social summit in 1994, there has been increasing attention on the usefulness of the concept with regard to poverty, inequality and social justice.

Social exclusion is seen as an institutionalized form of inequality and the failure of society to extend opportunity to all sections of its population and also the social recognition which they need to develop community life (Sonowal, 2008). Thus, social exclusion denotes the following characteristics of a society:

(i) inability to participate effectively in economic, social, political and cultural life;
(ii) alienation from the so-called mainstream society; and
(iii) isolation from major social mechanism, which produces or distributes social resources.

Traditionally, tribal societies are self-sufficient. Self-sufficiency means they need not have to interact with non-tribal societies for their social, cultural and physical existence. This nature of tribal people kept them away from other societies. Tribal groups of Assam-Nagaland Border are excluded group since they are not part of the greater Indian Hindu or Muslim societies. In other words, they may be termed as parallel segments of different domain (Sonowal, 2008).

The Process of Inclusion

The inclusion of tribal societies started during the long historic past. Hindu religious priests and the scholars started giving recognition to tribal Gods and Goddesses by assigning equal status. Events and names concerning Hindu Gods and Goddesses linked with the tribal Gods and Goddesses by framing attractive stories and legends. Thus, the tribal people felt themselves as an integral part of the greater Hindu society. The Ahom, an offshoot of greater mongoloid race, adopted Hinduism as royal religion following Ahom King Suhungmung (1497-1539) who accepted the title "*Swarganarayana*". The Ahom God 'Lengdon' was given status of lord Indraunder the influence of Hinduism (Barua, 2002). Eruption of Moamoria revolt under the leadership of Vaishnavite priest paved the way for decay of Ahom rule (Gogoi, 1991). It also disrupts the religious structure of the society and its impact was pervasive particularly in the areas of Assam-Nagaland Border.

Tribal absorption was prevalent with the advent of Christianity from the time of British annexation of Assam and Nagaland. Christianity entered in this tribal dominanted belt of Assam-Nagaland Border as a charity, working in disadvantaged localities mostly following the total dominance of colonial rule. The absorption process of Christianity was impressive. It associated religion with humanity and sufferings, education and liberal views on man and society. Approximately, the whole of Nagaland came under Christian domain. As such, a section of tea tribes and a sizeable number of plain tribes adopted Christianity in this border belt. In fact, this entire episode of coercive inclusion primarily aimed at establishing the non-tribal domains in tribal dominated areas.

Political and economic perspectives of inclusion was first attempted by incorporating constitutional provisions under articles 16, 335, 340, 341 and 342 which relate to reservation, protection and safeguarding persons belonging to scheduled caste, scheduled tribe and other backward classes. A subsequent provision also included in the Constitution of India to protect the tribal land from large-scale intervention of non-tribal by the formation of tribal belt and block. These special consideration although was provided strictly under several constitutional clauses, the endeavour was not seemed to be affective as tribal unrest on several occasions came up during past few years.

In order to address the social, political, economic, cultural and ecological pursuits of the tribal communities, Government of India provides autonomous status under 6th schedule, a kind of self-rule provision under Constitution of India. The chief objectives of the autonomous status are:

(i) to hand over certain administrative and legal authority in order to improve cultural, social and economic aspects of tribal people;
(ii) to remove material disparities between the advanced and backward section of the society;
(iii) to strengthen the bonds unity between the tribal and non-tribal masses; and
(iv) to emancipate from all types of injustice and explanation.

This run of Constitutional inclusion, however, made no provision to protect and preserve the ecological value of tribal livelihood practice dependent on forest resources. Only a small part, towards the southern side of Assam-Nagaland Border lies within Karbi Anglong Autonomous District Council, Assam.

Consequences of Inclusion

The consequences of inclusion can be summarized as—

(i) Tribal traditional entities and identities were either merged or lost to universal religious domain.

(ii) Invasion of universal religion brought forth a drastic change in social and economic front and as a result the process of detribalization came down to give rise to the problem of identity crisis.

(iii) Religious, political, economic and cultural inclusion change the whole set of perception on ecology and nature. This changed perception insists the tribal to detract themselves from their age old traditional ecological ethics.

(iv) Increasing intervention of non-tribal elements in the tribal dominated areas disrupt the ethical values of the tribals.

(v) Backwardness still found prevalent in the tribal areas of Assam-Nagaland Border which made them feel isolated.

Consequences of Social Exclusion

The process of social exclusion had been therefrom long past. Introduction of modern forestry at the time of colonial rule accelerated the pace of social exclusion by reducing the tribal rights on forest. The Government of post-Independence period virtually had done nothing extraordinary for the cause of tribal rights on forest. Forest conservation policies and the attitude of non-tribal people showed all disregard to the tribal interest which in turn disseminate a sense of social exclusion. A series of movement for autonomy by various tribal groups during 1980s were virtually a product of such social exclusion process.

In order to minimize the social exclusion of the forest tribes, the core committee of World Congress on National Park and Protected Areas (CNDPA) devised few measures to be taken to protect cultural resources associated with forest conservation. Some of these are (IVth World Congress, 1992):

(i) maintaining the life-supporting diversity of ecosystems, species, genetic varieties and ecological processes;
(ii) providing home to human communities with traditional cultures and knowledge of nature; and
(iii) protecting landscapes reflecting a history of human interaction with the environment.

The exclusion of forest dwellers and the tribes from forest areas aggravates the loss of valuable traditional knowledge on plant, animal and microbial species used for food, health and other purposes. As such, eco-friendly rural technology and innovations also disappear along with sustainable agricultural and ecological management systems. It is also observed that a drastic change in value perspectives comes up when a comparison is made between the survivalist compulsion of the tribes of Assam-Nagaland Border with their eco-centric moral attitude towards nature. On the other hand, with the arrival of the latest technology and scientific knowledge accompanied by a consumerist attitude to life, many of the tribal people of new generation hardly feel themselves as a part and parcel of nature. They think that they have every right to exploit the natural resources for their own well-being and luxury. Arrival of consumerist elements like mobile, television, video, internet, fast food culture, luxury wearing, motor bike, car and other household accessories adversely motivate most of the tribal youths. During the survey conducted in the border area, a large number of youths both boys and girls (in the age group of 20-25 years) came into contact. In Napam, a village of Sonowal Kachari at Merapani and Adarsha Mishing Gaon of Janghal block area, 28 youths were approached. Out of them, 21 (accounting for 72%) boys and girls owned mobile handset. The average time of viewing TV programme ranged between 5 to 6 hours per day. Eight of them used Internet regularly primarily devoting time in social networking and 16 of them are ignorant of NWFP or other forest-based activities. This is a very simple picture of upcoming consumer society of the forest-based tribal villages of Assam-Nagaland Border. The growing tendency for consumer based life style will certainly damage the traditional ecological value of the tribal society. It is after all, an impending danger which may erode the entire social value system even in the remote areas like the Assam-Nagaland Border region.

6

Constraints of Development and Probable Solution

6.1 Sorting out of Constraints

Assam-Nagaland Border region presents a significant cultural and ethnic diversity. The ethnic groups also differ in the level of socio-economic development as well as in their behavioural patterns. On the other hand, the forest ecosystem, within which they have been practicing their age-old traditional way of life, has been changing fast over the past few decades. Forests are no longer rich enough to act as support base to their livelihood practices, especially in the plain part of the region. Since, tribals are traditionally attached to the forests they interact more with such ecosystem to pursue their livelihood and forest-based traditions. With the depletion of forest resources, their problems for survival have increased manifold. Even, the tribal mode of life has changed at a faster pace along with the associated socio-cultural and economic consequences. Based on the observations and analysis already done the problems/constraints of the tribal people living in the Assam-Nagaland Border may be sorted out as follows:

1. The entire region with all uniqueness in climatic, vegetative, and ethnic character has distinct topographic structures—hills and plains. Intensified population pressure has slowly impacted the natural environment of the hills and plains. The Hill tribes (the Nagas) who are ethnically different from the plain tribes living in Assam part have been moving down the hills to boost their subsistence economy taking the advantage of both land and forest. The plain tribes also have started moving towards the open patches available in the foothills of the region. Thus, being influenced by social, political and emotional elements of

vested interest both the plain and hill tribal groups have ultimately arrived at the point of confrontation. In fact, this struggle within the same class, i.e. peasantry *vs*. peasantry have now attained a difficult state. A series of conflicts (1989, 1985 and 2013) that took place during last few decades indicate the depth of the problem.

2. The tribal economy, traditionally centre around land and other land-based resources. Even today, land continues to be the mainstay of 90 per cent of the tribal people in this border area of Assam and Nagaland. The land use pattern has changed remarkably in the post-Independence era through conversion of agricultural land into other non-agricultural uses. Construction of railway line, expansion of tea cultivation, various rehabilitation measures, establishment of industries and commercial centres, concentration of land among the big holders etc. have resulted in great pressure on land even to the interior tribal areas and forest belt. Tribal land rights are almost non-existent. The status of tribals with regard to land rights is clear from the Government record. It reads—"the tribal is an encroacher of the land he has been occupying, through the ages. He has no legal rights over land. In Assam the threat of loss of tribal communal land seems to be greater than in other tribal areas of N.E. India" (Nongkynrih, 2009). The total land used for development projects during 1947-2000 works out to be 1,401,184.8 acres. Out of this, 55.71 per cent are common property resources (CPR). Most of the CPR are tribal land, but the state does not recognize their ownership according to the individual ownership-based colonial land laws that the country still continues to follow (Fernandes and Bharali, 2006). Most of the lands occupied by the tribals of Assam-Nagaland Border are with no rights. These are under the jurisdiction of either the Department of Forest and Environment or the Department of Land Revenue. The land ownership pattern in the tribal zones is characterized by community ownership. It is more particularly common among the Karbis, Mishings, Sonowals and the Naga tribes. Nagaland is governed by Article 31 A of the Constitution of India wherein it is stated—"ownership of land and its resources shall apply to the State of Nagaland." Therefore, land ownership creates all kinds of problems relating to land alienation, a vital issue for the plain tribes of the Assam part of the region. A series of movements by the peasantry for land ownership and a series of eviction operations by the forest department covering the whole region gave rise to war like situations. It is thus a vital issue calling immediate attention of the concerned authorities so that the tribes can get relief of the suffocation of the socio-political environment prevailing in the region.

3. The tribals basically depend on agriculture and forest resources for their livelihood. No tribal is interested in the works done in the forest which has seldom any link or any effect on their rights or livelihood. Resentment rose high when tribals were ousted from their land and their right on forests. The degree of external intrusion into the ecosystem society of the tribes was much more pronounced when exploitation of forest resources commenced under the directives of colonial government. With sporadic settlements along the river banks and hamlets in the hills, the densely forested Assam-Nagaland Border region witnessed wanton destruction during 1826-1947. Governments of post-Independence period continued the same practice and implemented the policies on the foundation laid by the colonial government. Analyzing the topographic sheets prepared by Survey of India (1974) it is found that 75.36 per cent (4682.54 km^2 area) of the total area was under forest cover. When this forest area is compared with the 2010 data obtained from satellite imagery (LISS,-III) of IRS Hyderabad, it is found that the forest cover came down to only 44.12 per cent of the total area (6213.35 km^2). It proves a total loss of 31.24 per cent within a span of 36 years. During the colonial era and also in the post-colonial era, the best agricultural lands in the Assam-Nagaland Border region were appropriated for tea planters. A total of 159 tea estates, occupying 72,012.48 hectares of land of this border belt, grabbed a sizeable fertile forest land during the initial period of the colonial regime following the Wasteland Grant Rule, 1838. The later period also witnessed large scale transfer of open forest land to the tea planters. Destruction of forest resulted in depletion of forest resources which created chaos in the forest-based livelihood practice of the tribes living in and around the forest of the Assam-Nagaland Border region. Collapse of tribal traditional practices brought about a tremendous change in the socio-economic profile of the region as a whole. Agriculture and forest-based economy of the tribal turned to be subsistence agriculture under this compulsion of changing forest cover. Tradition, culture, social ethics and ethos, behaviour, habits etc. are now under severe scrutinization with the change of forest cover and depletion of forest resources. It results in identity crisis on the one hand and upsurge of social unrest on the other. In absence of timely intervention into the matter for an amicable solution, it may create unwanted political and social instability in near future. Increasing activity of extremist outfits, i.e. Maoist *Guerilla*, *Adivasi*, National Liberation Army, United Liberation Front of Assam etc. in recent period can be pointed as symptoms of such a predicament.

4. The Johansberg Earth Summit, 2002 primarily emphasized on sustainable development and made an appeal to concentrate all efforts in the use of traditional knowledge base in resource use and management. In the Summit on sustainable development it was argued that the traditional means of resource use and management should be revived in order to mitigate the climatic disaster in the coming future. Indigenous knowledge system thereafter got impetuous in many countries of the world. Government of India also accordingly took steps to revive the traditional practices by organizing Self-Help Group (SHG) in the rural areas of the country. The basic objective of these SHG is to generate self-employment in the rural productive sectors.

The ethnic groups inhabiting the Assam-Nagaland Border and their traditional practices of resource use and management can be used as bases for contextualizing the question of sustainable development. It is important to note that tribal tradition and customs are not cognitive constructs. They emerge out of continuous interaction of people with the natural environment. Continuous interaction between man and nature laid the foundation of all traditions and customs. They are reciprocal to each other. This symbiotic relation between the tribes and the forest had started getting weakened from the time of British occupation of the region. They imposed strict forest laws to exercise exclusive control over commercial benefit out of forests. From British period onwards the forest of Assam-Nagaland Border came under ceaseless removal which in turn jeopardized the forest-based livelihood of the tribal people. Tradition and traditional practices pertaining to forest retarded as such. In the context of sustainable development, revival of the tribal traditional practices and customs becomes necessary. The revival and reshaping of the traditional practices tuning towards sustainable development, demands a positive attitude and timely intervention from the policy-makers and implementing agencies.

5. The adverse consequences of deforestation have been intensely debated during the last two decades. The causes of deforestation and forest degradation are complex. Many scholars identified demographic factors as one of the important causes leading to agricultural expansion, large scale firewood and timber extraction and expansion of associated infrastructure. It has widely been recognized that shifting cultivation in the hills is the chief culprit for deforestation. A long fallow cycle or *jhum* cycle does not cause much depletion of forests and also causes relatively low damage when it takes place in secondary forests. Population pressure is mounting in the areas of Assam-Nagaland Border. To satisfy the food requirement of the growing population it becomes necessary to reduce

the *jhum* cycle. Within a shorter period forest regeneration becomes highly limited. In Mon district, the fallow period was reported to be shortened from 20 to 30 years in 1900 to only 6 years in 2001. Approximately 60 per cent of the total area of Assam-Nagaland Border region is characterized by hilly terrain, of which 90 per cent is shared by Nagaland alone. During the last few decades most of the accessible areas are converted into land for shifting cultivation. As a result, most of the forest resources are degraded. Only 9 per cent of the total area of Nagaland is classified as dense forest as per the State of Forest Report, 2005. Given the rapid population increase and the predominance of shifting cultivation, the hilly section of Assam-Nagaland Border region particularly constitutes a fertile field for the study of the relationship between demographic factors and the fulfilment of subsistence needs (Krug, 2009). As no additional arable land is available for further expansion of shifting cultivation and there exists great limitation for alternative income opportunities, the tribes living in this part is bound to face the fate of impoverishment in near future.

6. The displacement and denial of traditional land rights, rights of self-determination on the part of the tribes of the region may be considered as an important factor for the ongoing tribal unrest. The states have centralized bureaucratic administrative set-up and it has all power to alienate land and natural resources owned by the tribes. Karbi and Naga tribes in the hills and Sonowal Kachari, Thengal Kachari, Tai Khamayang, Tai Turung etc. in the plain part of the Assam-Nagaland Border have been therefrom historic past with all their traditions and customs symbiotically linked with the land and forests. Inadequate government policy, increasing population pressure and in-migration have badly affected the tribal areas in course of time have led to a domain of conflict and unhealthy competition. On the other hand, expanding settlements of immigrants along the disputed boundary, and pressure from indigenous settlers for more land and resources have created chaos among the tribes who basically carry the character of ecosystem people. They spontaneously devised a remarkable range of practices, traditions, rituals, technologies, and social relations in response to the challenges put by their natural surroundings. During the course of survey, many elderly people of the localities referred to the problems they have been facing in performing their age-old rituals and rites, customary laws and traditions. As most of their traditional values and cultural pursuits are closely related to nature, they have been facing hurdles in performing those in the fast deteriorating environment. Large-scale intervention in the tribal land and forests sedentarized the tribal life and economy particularly in the plain tribe occupied areas. The problem is not that acute among the

Naga tribes as most of them adopted Christianity which greatly changed their perception of nature and nature-related traditional practices.

The process of exclusion of majority of population from the mainstream and inadequate and ineffective policies adapted for the tribals caused dissatisfaction among them which needs proper attention for immediate mitigation.

7. Human-induced disturbances such as forest cover change, air pollution, water pollution, soil erosion and loss of productive lands and biodiversity have been increasingly threatening ecosystem productivity. Land cover change can play an important role in environmental changes and continue to encroach more areas in a wider scale. Urbanization denotes changes in land cover, population dynamics, infrastructure, mode of living etc. and also confirms an occupational shift from primary to other sectors. Predominance of activities in sectors other than primary endorses a change in the ecosystem. The Assam-Nagaland Border region has long been free from any significant urban impact. Few townships adjoining the railway line and some forest-based industries mostly in the plain part of the region generated urban growth in the region during the first half of the nineteenth century. Dimapur, Bokajan, Titabor, Mariani, Amguri, Simaluguri, Tuli, Naginamara, etc. are some examples of such township. Besides the weekly markets of the tea estates, a sizeable weekly and fortnightly markets in the border land came up which in fact, compensates the exhausted materials earlier procured from forests or from the locality. Extending limbs of various elements of urbanization engulfed first the peripheral zone of the plain districts of the region which later influenced more interior areas of the region. Merapani, Galeki, Chamaguri, Jamuguri, Tuli, Chunthiya, Tizit, Tengani, Changkhati etc. are few such urban growth centres that came up as a result of continuous influence of the urban belts. Although, the proportion of urban population to the total population is quite low, the rate of increase is very high which ultimately exerts immense pressure on the environment. Forest degradation has been accelerated by population pressure and urban growth. Growing urban influence and the entry of consumeristic attitude through urban cultures act against the traditional fabric of ecosystem societies. It is now apparent in most part of the Assam-Nagaland Border region that it is the external influence that erodes the values of tribal societies, causing anxieties in the tribal minds of this border belt.

8. The depletion of forest has changed the socio-cultural set-up of the tribes living in the Assam-Nagaland Border region as their family structure, house type, dietary habit, kinship have been increasingly under

the influence of market economy. Multi-dimensional change is observed in their social and cultural systems as community-based tradition of life and work is getting replaced by individualism, and the village council system of traditional governance is taken over by *panchayats*, and the traditional tribal religion is taken over by modern world religion. Their perception of nature and ecology as reflected in their folk songs is missing now. All these have a negative impact on their economy, society and culture. Thus, due to depletion of forest and non-availability of required resources in the immediate environment, their socio-cultural set-up is on the verge of rapid change.

9. Another major problem that the tribal people of the region have been facing is inadequate infrastructural facilities. Although the border roads (as regarded by the locals) along with a few roads linking the towns and market centres provide some impetus to the communication facility, majority of the areas are still devoid of better road connectivity. Depletion of forests eroded their traditional practices including the indigenous health care practices. Modern medical facility is yet a distant dream for majority of the people. The local people complained that often they have to carry the sick people on their shoulder or on *thela* for several kilometers to reach the medical centre. School-going children suffer a lot during the rainy months as their schools are located at several kilometers away from home which they have to traverse on foot.

10. The tribal belts and blocks were constituted incorporating Chapter X in the Assam Land and Revenue Regulation, 1886 through an amendment (Assam Act XV of 1947). Clause 160 (2) of the regulation empowered the government to take decision on—"which classes of people would get the protection benefit". The formation of tribal belts and blocks were kept confined to some specific areas of the Brahmaputra valley alone. However, it was not extended to other tribal dominated areas like the Assam-Nagaland Border. The formation of Thengal Kachari Autonomous Council, however, covers only the Thengal Kachari dominated areas. The non-implementation of the Assam Land and Revenue Regulation, 1886 to protect the land rights of the tribals of Assam-Nagaland Border open-up the ways for intervention on land by the people other than the tribals. Dereserving few reserved forests in the border region, the Government of Assam rehabilitates people evicted by flood and river erosion. Land rights of the tribal groups remained unnoticed for long which evoked strong resentment among the tribals of the region against Government negligence. The above mentioned problems are vital and sensitive from ecological point of view as the tribal people of the

Assam-Nagaland Border region have been gradually marginalized. It requires a positive initiative at government level to safeguard the tribes and to keep normalcy in the days to come.

6.2 A Futuristic View on the Existing Scenario

The forests in the Assam-Nagaland Border region are ecologically unique. They provide shelter to diversified tribal groups. Livelihood practices of the tribes primarily revolve around land and forest. They range from primitive foraging and collection of food to shifting and settled cultivation and wage earning in plantation and forestry. However, these activities are land-based in character. The development initiatives to divert activities from primary to secondary or tertiary sectors have not yielded significant results in the tribal dominated border region. It is also seen that a section of the tribal communities having settled or shifting cultivation are drawing their secondary income from food gathering, collection of items like honey, wax, resin, spices, roots, fruits etc.

A systematic analysis on the multiple economic activities of the tribes can help in understanding the interactive roles of cultural, ecological and technological aspects of tribal living and deriving strategies and innovative measures for their development. On the other hand, such an approach will help in bringing out the dynamics of institutionalization among various tribal groups. It is true that the economic pursuits of the tribes have been changing over time and space depending upon the change in the ecological settings of the areas they share. Changes in the existing traditional livelihood strategies of the tribals are brought about by a variety of factors. These include—

1. Contact with the agricultural activities of the non-tribal people around them;
2. Depletion of forest resources and diminishing forest-based activities;
3. Increasing accessibility to the markets and institutionalized economic functions;
4. Development of transport facilities and communication system;
5. Roles played by governmental and non-governmental agencies;
6. Introduction of commercial cropping in adjacent areas and the benefits reaped from it;
7. Conversion from traditional tribal religion to modern world religion.

The change in the socio-economic and ecological scenario is observed in both hills and plains of the region due primarily to four factors: (i) rapid decline in forest cover and forest resources; (ii) growing demographic pressure; (iii) religious conversion and change of ecological perception; and (iv) government policies. In continuation of this pace of change the region in future will obviously portray a picture of uncertainty and poor orientation of traditional eco-friendly practices. The nature of change and the pattern of development, which are prevalent and extensive today in this part of the border belt, is an indicator of probable future orientation of the landscape. It may results in—(i) devastating state of forest ecology owing to encroachment, extensive practice of shifting cultivation and increasing population pressure; (ii) the intra-class conflict, i.e. peasant *vs.* peasant and opening-up of ground for extremist activities in the absence of right kind of government initiatives; (iii) there may arise an ecological disaster with the influx of land grabbing big holders and immigrants, if not properly checked; (iv) further deterioration of values of tribal way of life leading to tribal unrest; (v) consumerism induced by globalization which may disturb the work-culture among the tribes; (vi) dissatisfaction and chaos in the society; and (vii) uprooting and displacement of tribal people due to unhealthy intervention in the tribal way of life.

These are few probable consequences which may develop under the emerging situation concerning the tribes of the Assam-Nagaland Border region.

6.3 Steps Needed to Tackle the Problems

The problems relating to the ecological sustainability as discussed in Section 6.1, however, call for solution in the context of the Assam-Nagaland Border region. The solutions cannot be both pure holistic and pure naturalistic at a time. Holistic approach is, to some extent, anthropocentric where man is regarded as privilege subject, while naturalistic thought is purely bio-centric and man is considered as secondary subject matter. Since, man and nature are in an interwoven state in the Assam-Nagaland Border region as per livelihood and traditional practices, the consideration in identifying the steps needed to tackle the growing problems should be given equal importance for survival of both man and nature so that all the endeavour taken become sustainable. On the other hand, the view of deep ecologists to restore the ecology in its original form is perhaps ambiguous and it may be sometimes disastrous from anthropocentric point of view. As parts of the Assam-Nagaland Border region is already saturated with sizeable population, such an eco-centric approach may cause serious damage to the existing ecological set-up of the region. At these perspectives, steps required to tackle the problems are manifested as:

(i) The border dispute between the State of Nagaland and Assam needs an immediate and amicable solution. Central Government should take initiatives in this regard as the subject of interstate border is not within the jurisdiction of the concerned states. The steps to be taken may be—(a) Government of India should organize tripartite talk taking the two states into confidence; (b) an enquiry commission should be formed incorporating experts from relevant disciplines to identify the boundary line; (c) people of the two states residing in and around the boundary line are to be organized to make them aware of the benefits of harmonious relation; and (d) NGOs and social organizations should be involved to work for a harmonious living among the population groups and with the natural settings.

(ii) Giving proper attention to the issue of land alienation from the tribes, the Department of Land Revenue and the Department of Environment and Forest should work together and the working principle may be: (a) Department of Forest should identify the notified areas and the areas settled by the encroachers and the tribes of forest villages and Taungya villages; (b) forest lands already occupied by the tribal and others also should be identified and allow the dwellers to stay there under some specific terms and conditions; (c) the occupied land should be allotted to the occupants under the wasteland rule, fee simple grant Rule 1838 and Forest Act for the tribal, 2005; (d) the Department of Land Revenue accordingly should come forward to ensure tribal rights over land by issuing notice so that the dwellers can feel secured over their land; and (e) the Department of Forest also should ensure at least the rights of the tribals over collection of NWFP from the forests.

(iii) Formation of tribal belts and blocks are necessary to protect the tribal interest of the region. It is an established fact that the tribals themselves know how to protect their own interest. Governments and other concerned authorities should provide necessary congenial ground to the tribal groups to pursue their interest comfortably. Tribals are best known by their tradition, culture and society. The steps to be taken are: (a) identification of the tribal groups of the region; (b) identification of the concentration zone of the respective tribes; (c) arranging them belt and block wise and providing them all necessary support and space to restore their positive tradition, culture, and society; and (d) formation of monitoring cell involving members from respective tribes to look into the management of the belts and blocks. These steps, if undertaken sincerely and strictly, will make the tribes feel free from the growing identity crisis.

(iv) Restoration of forest ecology is a precondition to revive the tribal traditional practices which are symbiotic with nature and sustainable. Facilities relating to land and forest should be provided in such way that the eco-friendly livelihood practices and social traditions of the tribes become more feasible and operative. The disputed border area along with other forest areas located in the border region can be conserved as miniature biosphere reserves. Afforestation in the degraded forest areas by planting indigenous plant species will enhance biomass generation and the carrying capacity of the forest land. This elongated forested belt along the boundary line between the two states may work in many ways. If declared as biosphere reserve, it will contain two specific zones—buffer zone and core zone. Buffer zone, i.e. the peripheral zone will be the areas of NWFP to be collected by the tribes and the core zone will provide habitats for wild animals. The buffer zone on both sides of the boundary line will serve equally the interest of the hill and plain tribes. Declaration as biosphere reserve means the disputed border land will be no-man's land automatically and hence the question of inter-racial conflict will be irrelevant. The biosphere reserve will also serve the interest of the tribal and help in keeping their identity intact.

(v) Migration of people to the Assam-Nagaland Border is identified as the main cause of increasing population pressure in the area. The main threats caused by migration relate to the land under both open and reserved forest. To check further influx, governments of both the states should take appropriate measures and all necessary steps under the provision of the Forest Conservation Act, 1988 should be properly implemented. Formation of tribal belts and blocks will also check the land transfer process from tribals to non-tribals and will act like a barrier to further influx of population.

(vi) Social, political, cultural organizations should take initiatives so that the tribal groups do not feel isolated. Inclusion of tribal groups in all sphere of activities should be made spontaneous by augmenting the mutual understanding between the tribals and non-tribals. Participatory approach in this respect will be greatly helpful.

(vii) Expansion of the zones of urban influence has created threats to the ecosystem people living in this border region. However, urbanization is a functionally linked process which is not easy to regulate. Therefore, along with the government policies for urban development, participatory initiative for people-centric urban development should also be ensured. In order to make the urban centres eco-friendly some of the steps to be undertaken may be—(a) maintenance of tree cover and environment friendly structure of residential and commercial buildings; (b) proper localization of industrial and manufacturing units; (c) maintenance of ratio between carbon emission and the carbon sink, and proper drainage and sewerage system; (d) restriction in using non-perishable items like plastic, polythene, DDT, chemical pesticides and herbicides; and (e) regular removal of pollutants. For this, it requires an integrated management system to monitor and regulate the overall urban development in the region.

(viii) Most of the tribal people are now aware of the progress and development in the outside world. They now can feel about their state of existence in the context of the nation and the world. Among others, lack of infrastructural facility is a great concern to them. Allotment of special area development fund for the tribal from Central Government, forest infrastructure development fund under the Ministry of Forest and Environment may be made available for eco-friendly infrastructural development in the tribal areas of Assam-Nagaland Border region in particular and for the region as a whole in general. Proper initiatives from both the State Governments and local area development authorities are necessary to procure fund for this purpose.

(ix) People's participation is considered mandatory to have a positive outcome of all endeavours concerning society and environment.

NGO's role in this respect is crucial. It is quite difficult to get everything needed under a bourocratic system of government. On the other hand, the role of people's representative in the government is also vital as all decisions relating to the state welfare are taken by the government, NGOs, clubs, non-political organizations and others concerned with rational development should come forward to make the endeavours aimed particularly at problem-area development a success.

6.4 Approach for Sustainable Development

The concept of sustainable development represents an important progress in the contemporary developmental agenda. It simply points out that not all is well with the prevailing paradigm of development. The highlights of this thinking are the ecological unsustainability of the ongoing mode of development. The term 'sustainable development' got importance with the publication of the World Commission on Environment and Development (WCED) report, Our Common Future in 1987. The principal authority of the report was G. Brundtland. Rio-de-Janeiro Earth Summit (1992) gave it a wide base and appealed to all to follow the line of sustainable development. According to the World Commission, sustainable development is the development that meets the goal of the present without compromising the ability of future generations to meet their own needs (WCED, 1987-88). This pioneering definition implies a view of sustainable development in respect of use of natural resources. It means that the right of future generations to inherit all the ecological and natural resources which the present generation inherited from their ancestors.

A rational and acceptable solution to the growing problem of Assam-Nagaland Border region can be derived from the perspective of sustainable development. The increasing unsustainability of the region is associated with (i) land alienation; (ii) shortage of forest resources; (iii) encroachment of forest land; (iv) increasing population pressure; (v) threat to the existence of tribal tradition and culture; (vi) dismantling of tribal livelihood practices; (vii) inter-state border dispute; (viii) non-availability of required infrastructure; and (ix) loss of biodiversity etc. These problems need a judicious and rational solution with goals of sustainable development. The total area of the region is 6213.35 km^2, out of which 44.12 per cent is under forest (Rs. data, 2010). Majority of the inhabitants belonging to various tribal groups have more or less common livelihood practices. Characterised by multi-cultural traditions, the tribal groups of the region reflect uniqueness in the pattern and essence of socio-economic behaviour except the non-tribal zone in the western margin. The diagnostic features to evaluate the sustainability of the region are (i) the nature and extent of forest cover; (ii) the racial composition of population; (iii) livelihood practices; (iv) tradition-bound life style; (v) topographic diversity; (vi) climate; (vii) soil; (viii) bio-diversity; and (ix) presence of reserved forest. These features are virtually supportive to the concept of bio-sphere reserve. Bio-sphere reserves are sites established by countries and recognized under UNESCO's "Man and the Biosphere" (MAB) programme to promote sustainable development based on local community efforts and scientific management (Dhaliwal and Kukal, 2005). The main characteristics of biosphere reserves are:

(a) Achieving the three inter-connected functions: conservation, development and logistic support.
(b) Out pacing traditional confined conservation zones, through appropriate zoning schemes combining core protected areas with zones where sustainable development is fostered by local dwellers and enterprises with often highiy innovative and participative governance system.
(c) Focusing on a multi-stakeholder approach with particular emphasis on the involvement of local communities in management.
(d) Fostering dialogue for conflict resolution of natural resource use.
(e) Integrating cultural and biological diversity, especially the role of traditional knowledge in ecosystem management.

The characteristics of biosphere reserve as mentioned are identical to the ecological setting of Assam-Nagaland Border area. This region is a rich habitat for many primitive tribes, and harbours plenty of flora and fauna. It provides congenial ground for traditional means of livelihood practice and presents a rich forest cover from grassland to evergreen type under a conducive system of climate, soil and topography. Forest-based livelihood along with settled and shifting agriculture is still predominant in the area. The tribes living in this belt are still happy with their own tradition, culture, rituals, belief system, myths etc. The problems outlined in the previous discussion (Section 6.1) have links with the concept of a biosphere reserve which can favourably rebuild the region removing all the constraints on the way. Problems like border dispute, displacement from forest land, conflict over fertile agricultural land, crisis of tribal identity, threats to traditional livelihood practices etc. could be resolved by creating a biosphere reserve in this belt. Adopting properly the clauses, characteristics and the functions of a biosphere reserve, a sustainable development agenda can be worked out for the region as a whole.

Functions of Biosphere Reserve Proposed to Cover the Assam-Nagaland Border Area

For management purposes and to raise its effectiveness, a biosphere reserve is divided into three functional zones:

(1) *Core Zone*: Strictly protected areas with very little human influence, which are used to monitor natural changes in representative ecosystems and serve as conservation areas for biodiversity (Fig. 6.1). The reserved forests, 11 in number along the interstate boundary covering an area of 1302.65 sq.km of Assam-Nagaland Border can be put under the core zone of the proposed biosphere reserve. The available open forests in addition to the *jhum* regrowth will give the core zone a high impact. This core zone will be an elongated zone extending from one end to the other within the region. Of course, some gaps will remain particularly in the areas like Dimapur, Dayang-Merapani and Nambor South R.F. (Tengani area) where human intervention is already intensive.

(2) *Buffer Zone*: Areas around the core zone where only low impact activities are attended (like collection of NWFP). It is also the area to act as a focal point for research, environmental education and recreation. It is noteworthy that the buffer zone in the proposed scheme for biosphere reserve in the Assam-Nagaland Border will not be extensive in the plain part of the region. However, a distinct and extensive buffer zone will accompany the hilly parts of the region. Districts like Wokha and Mokokchung will provide a strong and extensive base for this buffer zone, while along Dimapur and Mon district area the buffer zone happens to be of smaller extent because of high human intervention and economic activities.

(3) *Transition Zone*: It is the outer zone where sustainable use of resources by local communities is allowed and the impacts can be compared to zones of greater protection.

This zone in the proposed scheme of sustainable development for the Assam-Nagaland Border region is critical as it has witnessed inferences of urban elements. The urban centres located in the western margin of the border region have been working as processing ground for most of the forest-based resources which in turn imposed pressure to extract more than the potential of the forests. The whole set of transition zone obviously requires some rearrangement from management perspectives. Environmental taxation, legal bindings, formation of affective committee on eco-sensitive zone etc. can be part of management principles to scrap the antagonism of environmental protection. On the contrary, the hilly areas of Nagaland part will provide an ideal ground for transition zone with its extensive space and prevailing practices.

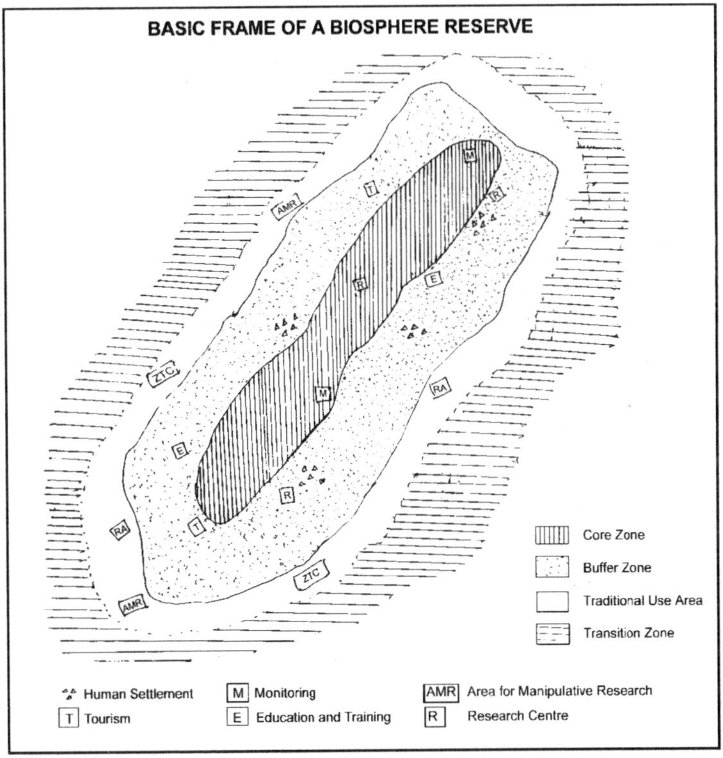

Source: UNESCO, Man and the Biosphere (MAB).

Fig. 6.1: Basic Frame of a Biosphere Reserve.

The Proposed Scheme in Brief

The proposed scheme of biosphere reserve for the Assam-Nagaland

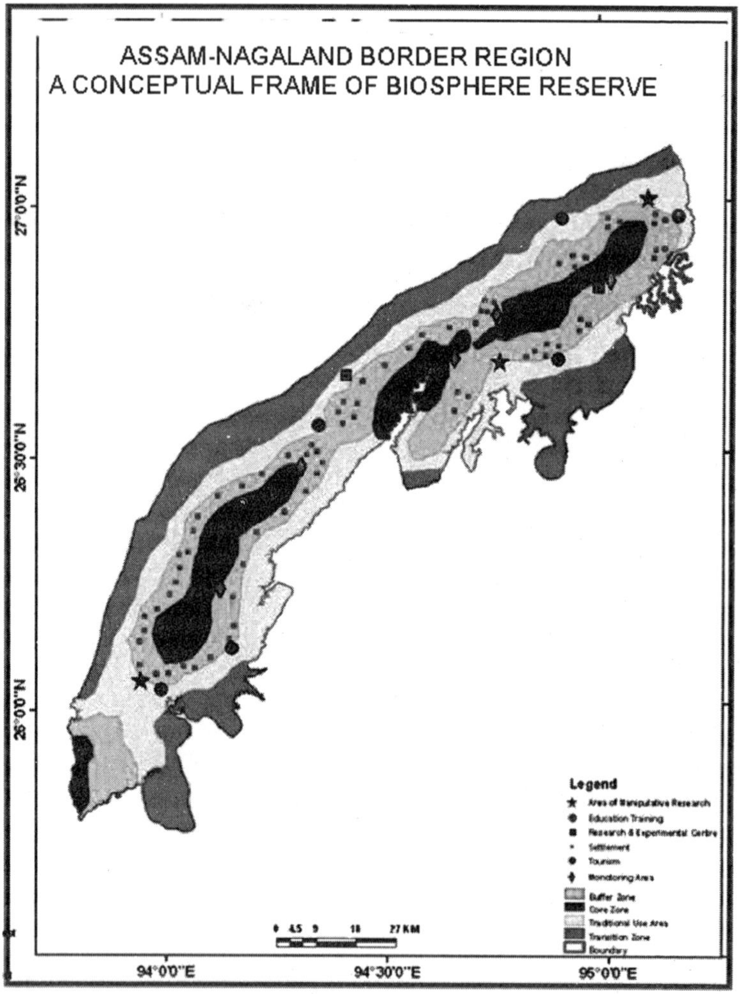

Map 6.1: Assam-Nagaland Border Region: A Conceptual Frame of Biosphere Reserve

Border region is derived on the basis of UNESCO's ideal model for biosphere reserve (Map. 6.1). It incorporates certain strategies/actions as mentioned below:

(i) It is proposed to create 8 monitoring centres and 4 centres for education and training along with 3 tourists and recreation centre for this biosphere reserve.

(ii) Each district will have one monitoring centre and one education and training centre will be located in between two district

(iii) In selecting the tourism and research centre the basic consideration should obviously be the availability of infrastructure, accessibility and availability of materials of tourist attraction.

(iv) The limit of legal protection is not a static line. It will fluctuate with the change of areas of buffer zone. There will be ample scope to extend the limit of legal action with increasing capability of management and monitoring.

(v) The core zone, however, will be constituted by the existing reserved forests plus the nearby areas of secondary regrowth where there is possibility of inclusion. The core zone will be kept free from human settlement as far as possible areas as there are extensive encroachments in parts of the reserved forests.

(vi) The set-up of the entire biosphere reserve will be multi-core and multi-buffer zone with a common demarcation line by the limit of legal action.

(vii) Traditional use area will extend from the buffer zone to the outer areas across the limit of legal action. There will be provision for rehabilitation and for this a specific area is accommodated in the scheme.

(viii) Traditional use areas will be made available as per which are accommodated across buffer zone. Such traditional use areas are kept scattering around the core zone so that it will be possible for the tribes to pursue both agricultural and forest-based practices in a comfortable way. Another important consideration in this regard is the traditional cultural practices which need specific forest environment for their continuity.

(ix) The human settlement areas are kept mostly outside the buffer zone. In cases, the areas where settlements are already there, will remain undisturbed and the inhabitants will be allowed to pursue their practices under certain terms and conditions necessary for the sustainability of the biosphere reserve.

Considering all these criteria and condition, the whole of Assam-Nagaland Border region can be divided into 4 core zones: (i) Singphan-Galeki-Abhaypur core zone, (SGA) (ii) Desoi Chunthiya-Nagabat core zone, (DCN) (iii) Wokha-Dayang-Tengani core zone, (WDT) and (iv) Rangapahar core zone (RCZ). Buffer zones around the core zone are also irregular and in places transition zones thrust upon the buffer zone. On the other hand, buffer zones are not at all free from human settlements. Human settlements are found invading even the core zone like Wokha-Dayang-Tengani and Desoi-Chunthiya-Nagabat.

Important Features of the Scheme

(1) Human settlements will remain undisturbed except the core zone. If feasible, human settlements of the core zone will be rehabilitated in areas fixed for this purpose.

(2) Formation of core zone will help conservation of biodiversity and also open-up the way for further growth checking deforestation and encroachment of forest land.

(3) Constant monitoring and people's active participation in the process of conservation will abolish the illegal timber trade and mining and quarrying. For a spontaneous and assured people's participation the role of research and training centre, village council, local panchayat and also of NGOs will be crucial and imperative.

(4) Plantation of indigenous plant species has to be done in specific areas to reinstate and rebuild the enervated ecosystem. Plantation works in buffer zone will follow the line of agro-forestry and to enlarge the canopy coverage transition zones will be included phase-wise. However, no exotic verities will be allowed within the limit of legal protection.

(5) The land now available for cultivation will remain intact and undisturbed. These will be treated as land under traditional use. Provisions for expansion of area under commercial crops will be curtailed subject to their location. Monitoring centres and biosphere reserve management will be entrusted to justify the quality and quantity of pesticides, herbicides and chemical fertilizers to be used in the areas under commercial crops. All links of drainage and sewerage systems from commercial plantation site to the buffer zone or core zone will be cut off to check further damage to biodiversity.

(6) Change in landholding structure of the inhabitants of the biosphere reserve will not be allowed, while people are the part of the biosphere reserve. Land encroachment and expansion of agricultural areas can be checked as per this clause of the biosphere reserve.

(7) Tribal groups accustomed with the forest-based livelihood strategies will be allowed to collect only the NWFPs. There will be no restriction to performing tribal traditions and rituals in the forest in order to keep the tribal culture vibrant.

(8) As it will under the MAB programme of UNESCO, therefore the administration, management, finance, planning etc. will be under the direct jurisdiction of Government of India. The entire system of the biosphere will be a co-ordinated approach jointly under the concerned State Governments and Central Governments.

(9) Transition zones are the zones of high human-nature interaction. It is the chief economic domain surrounding the buffer zone. Tourism and recreation centres should be established in this belt.

The map (Map. 6.1) is prepared on the basis of the above mentioned characteristics and criteria to set the region as a biosphere reserve. The four core zones are demarcated as per their respective locations. SGA is at the northernmost part of the region, while RCZ occupies the southern end. The DCN and the WDT core zones are placed at the middle of the region. Buffer zones around the core zone are designated as BF_1, BF_2, BF_3 and so on. Transition zones, on the other hand, are denoted by TZ_1, TZ_2, TZ_3 and so on. Monitoring centre (M), Tourism and Recreation centre (TR), Education and Research (ER), Limit of legal action (LLA), Land for traditional use (LTV) and Rehabilitation area (Ra) etc. are shown in places considered to be suitable and effective.

7
Summary and Conclusion

Deforestation is a world-wide phenomenon. Scientists and environmentalists have been expressing sincere concern to the fast deterioration of forest cover everywhere in the world. The causes of deforestation have been debated upon by environmentalists, economists, geographers, government experts and NGOs. But there is no consensus. A number of causes of deforestation like population pressure, agricultural expansion, urbanization, shifting cultivation, fuelwood collection, timber extraction etc. are so far identified which, however, could not provide satisfactory arguments to the people of different fields of interest. The forests of third world countries of Asia, Africa and Latin America are the mere victims of the colonial policies and the policies framed by the subsequent governments of the post-colonial period. Large-scale removal of forest cover in India took place during the colonial era, starting from 1780 to 1947. The primary objective of such deforestation was to enhance revenue accumulation. The lands so deforested were further put to non-forest use like cultivation of food crops, fiber crops, plantation crops and to develop transport and communications to increase the land revenue.

Assam, along with the other states of North-east India successively came under colonial hegemony after 1826. The forest policy was framed by the British colonialists to serve the purpose of colonial exploitation and thus the forests of Assam and other states had to face wanton destruction until 1947. Colonial government made all possible efforts by enacting rules and regulations to exploit the rich forest resources of the region. Through enactment of forest Acts and Regulations (1878, 1894, 1927 and 1935), the British attempted to bring the forests under their control. The Forest Act 1865, Forest Policy, 1894 and Assam Forest Regulation, 1891 were enable to effectively control the extensive forest areas of the region. Continuous and intensive intervention in the extensive forest areas brought all odds to the ecology of the region. As such, extensive forest patch were released by enactment of Wasteland Grant Rules of 1838, Fee Simple Rules of 1826, Revised Fee Simple Rules of 1874 and the New Lease Rules of 1876 for expansion of commercial plantations. The forest policy of post-colonial period framed by the Government in 1952 was indifferent in form and content to the policies of colonial governments, Wasteland Grant Rules, Forest Conservation Policy, Wild-Life Act enacted during the post-Independent period were too flexible to protect the forest and forest resources from elimination.

The Assam-Nagaland Border region, originally a dense forested area extending all along the border of the two states, Assam and Nagaland, has been facing massive deforestation as a consequence of defective forest conservation policies of the Government. In a number of occasions, the reserved forests were deforested through government notification to provide land for cultivation, rehabilitation of erosion and flood affected landless people, construction of roads and railways etc. A numbers of reserved forests were declared dereserved. For example, Janjhi and Kakadonga reserved forests were dereserved by the Government. The period subsequent to the partition of Nagaland (1962) from Assam has been witnessing boundary dispute between the two states which continues to remain unsolved. Instead of sorting out amicable solution to the boundary dispute, people of the two states are encouraged to encroach more and more land along the border areas. It resulted in a series of fierce gun battle causing damage to the life and property of the settlers of the border areas. New settlers in thousand rushed into the area to settle in the land under reserved forests. Under such a population dynamics the entire ecological set-up of the region has changed dramatically. Severe encroachment grabbed reserved forests like Diphu, Rengma, South Nambor (Tengani), Dayang, Tiru hills and Sapekhati. These reserved forests are now virtually non-existent. Not only are the open class forests, a number of reserved forests wiped out from their existence by ceaseless encroachment and deforestation. The history of deforestation in this region is, in fact, a long political history in character and content. The entire Assam-Nagaland Border region is characteristically a tribal dominated zone. The major tribes living therein are Sonowal, Thengal, Mishing, Khamayang, Turung, Karbi, Ao, Angami, Lotha, Sema, Kanyak and Zeliang. Agriculture and food gathering are their mainstay of living. Forests for them were the sources of livelihood, health care, housing and many rites and rituals. They have been living there maintaining a symbiotic relationship with forests. Shifting cultivation although were practiced by the hill tribes, they seldom did severe damage to the forest and wild-life of the region. *Jhum* cycles were as long as to facilitate regeneration of forest and never did anything beyond recoverable limit of the forest. As a whole, ecological balance was well maintained under the traditional culture of the forest tribes.

The advent of the British colonialists and their revenue oriented forestry programme have started disturbing the ecological balance which was till then well maintained by the forest dwelling tribes. Large-scale destruction of forests under the British regime uprooted the livelihood base of the forest tribes. Their age-old traditional rights over forests were humiliated by the introduction of British forestry policies. The Assam-Nagaland Border region occupying an area of 6213.35 km^2 is a vast forested tract with substantial tribal population. Deforestation leads to depletion of forest resources which along with population pressure and increasing greed for forest resources from outside has created an unusual situation for the tribal people living in and around the forest.

The problem as a whole needs proper analysis to formulate measures for an effective solution. A socio-ecological analysis including aspects of political ecology is made in this work to derive a judicious and effective humanitarian solution to the problem of deforestation and its impact on the tribes living in this border area.

The Assam-Nagaland Border region is topographically comprised of both hills and plains. The area is delimited on the basis of few criteria like terrain characteristics, forest cover, vegetation type, climate and human factor. Locationally, the region lies between 25°17′53.57″ N and 27°03′46.8″ N latitude and 93°20′32″ E and 95°18′03″ E longitude. The region is situated at the junction of three separate tectonic belts: the Tibetan at the north, Burmese at the east and the Indian belt at the south-west. The whole region invariably represents similar rock succession except for parts of the elongated Naga thrust. The broad alluvial plain encountered by low hills with tropical monsoon type of climate harbours plenty of flora and fauna. On the basis of the terrain characteristics, the region can be divided into three distinct physiographic units—(i) the open river plain; (i) the low hill zone; and (iii) the intervening built-up plains. The open river plain of this region acts as a threshold zone for varieties of flora and fauna and also the economic activities of the tribes living therein. Numerous rivers flowing down the mountain of Nagaland developed the broad depositional alluvial plains at the base of the hills. Both degradational and aggradational activities of running water are responsible for the formation of the nutrient rich soil layer of the region. Accordingly the soils of this region can be grouped into four major types: (i) entisols, (ii) histosols, (iii) oxisols, and (iv) ultisols. These varying types of soils favour the growth of a variety of plants.

Under all these suitable supporting physical conditions, the region experienced a luxuriant growth of forests of varying types. Several types of forests ranging from deciduous to evergreen type are found in the region because of topographic, climatic and edaphic variations. The major forest types as found in the region are: (i) tropical wet evergreen forest; (ii) semi-evergreen forest; (iii) tropical moist deciduous forest; and (iv) bamboo forest. Evergreen forests dominate the downhill slope of the northernmost part of the region, while the tropical deciduous forests cover most parts of the plain areas of the region. Semi-evergreen forests are scattered and concentrated in the areas of intervening built-up plains and downhill slope of the southern part of the region. On the other hand, bamboo forest has a wide range and spread even up to a height of 200 m. Varieties of bamboo are found all along the Assam-Nagaland Border region. It has a high demand among the dwellers for its easy availability, cheapness and utility. The region as a whole is rich in biodiversity. Being an integrated part of the eastern Himalayan biodiversity hot-spot, the biodiversity of the Assam-Nagaland Border region is characterized by Indo-Malayan and Indo-Chinese linkages. The wildlife diversity of the region is generally studied under two categories. These are—(i) forest ecosystem and (ii) aquatic ecosystem. The wild-life sanctuaries, reserved forests, unclassed state forest etc. are the constituent of the forest ecosystem of the region. The reserved forests constitute the backbone of the forest ecosystem which are endowed with diverse form of flora and fauna. The floristic diversity is represented by numerous species ranging from evergreen type to wet savannah type of vegetation. The forests serve as the source of livelihood for a major section of the people living in the forests and forest fringe areas. The aquatic ecosystem is primarily enriched by innumerable rivers, streams, streamlets along with numerous beels, swamps and marshy lands. Both lotic and lentic ecosystems harbour diverse forms of aquatic life.

The history of human settlement in the region was marked by frequent rise and fall along with the change in the kings and kingdom. References of the Hidimba Rajya, the Kachari Kingdom, the Ahom Kingdom etc., may be cited in the study of the history of human settlement in this region. The entire region was practically not a good ground for human habitation since most of the areas were covered by impenetrable jungles with numerous wild beasts. It was estimated that during the early part of British rule the total inhabitants of old Sibsagar district was 2,00,000. Mills' "Report on the province of Assam" mentioned that the total population of the district was 2,11,477 and the total number of villages was 203. Dispersed pattern and low density of population in the Assam-Nagaland Border region may be related to factors like, (i) concentration of villages in the high land areas; (ii) the dense forests, hostile nature and unhealthy condition of the region did not favour comfortable living of people; (iii) frequent disturbances caused by the Naga recalcitrant in the border region; and (iv) the wild animals made the area hostile for human habitation. The hilly areas of the region, on the contrary, possess the largest part of Nagaland in terms of population size. Higher accessibility provided by its low altitude and gentle slope in comparison to the easternmost part of the state favours the high concentration of settlements. As per the Census of 1981, the total population of this part adjoining Assam was 44,219. The practice of head hunting among the Naga tribes in the past restricted people from settling in the low hill areas. The districts adjoining the border, namely Dimapur, Wokha, Mokokchung and Mon recorded a higher growth of population during the recent decades. Population density of this part increased from 82 persons/km^2 in 1991 to 180 in 2001. Food habit, climatic hazards, excessive labour required to survive in the rugged hills, social custom etc. are some factors which play a determining role in the nature of the demographic structure. Increasing population pressure results from the higher decadal growth of population is estimated to be 60.05 per cent and 71.30 per cent respectively for the period 1981-91 and 1991-01.

The Assam-Nagaland Border region can be divided into three culturally distinct settlement zones: (i) the non-tribal settlement zone; (ii) the plain tribal settlement zone; and (iii) the hill tribal settlement zone. Characterized by small agricultural fields, mixed occupational pattern and better economic development, the non-tribal settlement zone exhibits a high population density. On the other hand, the plain tribal settlement zone is dominated by the plain tribes. The major tribes of this zone are the Thengal Kachari, Sonowal Kachari, Bodo, Mishing, Khaayang, Tai Turung etc. The third zone is mostly inhabited by several sub-tribes of Naga like Ao, Kanyak, Angami, Rengma, Lotha, Sema, Zeliang etc. During last few decades, the Assam-Nagaland Border region has witnessed rapid growth of immigrant Muslim settlements particularly in the plain tribal zone. On the other hand, the growth of a sizeable number of tea tribe settlements, approximately 15 villages in the plain zone becomes significant from the view point of ecological sustainability of the region. It is found that the growth rate of population in the hilly areas is much higher than that of the plain areas. The population growth during 1991-2001 was 16.88 per cent in the plain zone while it was 65.73 per cent in the hills districts.

The border region is virtually dominated by several tribal groups belonging to Burmese-mongoloid stream. Excluding the tea tribes, the percentage share of tribal population in the Assam part is approximately 54.84 per cent and with the addition of the tea tribes its share becomes 68.36 per cent of the total population of the Assam part of the border region. In the Nagaland part of the border, the tribes constitute 89.05 per cent of the total population. During 90s of the twentieth century and the first decade of the twenty first century the influx of traders, workers, agricultural labourers and people engaged in developmental works like PWD, forests, agriculture etc. caused remarkable change in the demographic and social structure of the region.

The tribes namely Tai Turung, Tai Khamayang, Sonowal Kachari, Thengal, Mishing, Ao, Kanyak, Rengma, Lotha, Angami, Karbi etc. are endowed with specific religious culture, traditions and rituals-based mostly on animism, mythism and totemism. Christianity had made its inroad in the areas of tribal dominance during the colonial rule. Most of the hill tribes adopted Christianity under the consistent endeavour of the Christian priests. The Vaisnavite sect of Hindu religion, on the other hand, entered into the areas of plain tribes. The most important aspect of religious conversion in region is that the Christian missionaries tried to nullify the beliefs and other religious practices of the tribal people as superstitions and meaningless. Adoption of Christianity especially by the hill tribes motivated the tribes to give up all their animistic practices. Traditional religious beliefs associated with forests, trees, rocks, rivers etc. got eliminated in due course. Dominance of modern world religion in a region of primitive tribes is quite speculative. Against 10,93,19 Hindu and 3,98,914 Christian population there exists 5,46,096 persons practicing traditional tribal religion in the year 2001.

The Assam-Nagaland Border region primarily possesses three distinct type of traditional dwellings representing three major ethnic groups, (i) Naga, (ii) Karbi, and (iii) Assamese. The traditional houses of the Nagas are of primitive archetype characterized by rectangular courtyard, slanting roof and a decorated frontier. The house-type of the Karbis is of two types: (i) traditional type, and (ii) common rural Assam type. The chief building materials of traditional Karbi house are thatch and bamboo. The house is built on bamboo posts as supporting base and the floor is a raised platform. The house has so many compartments for different uses.

The common Assam type house is a house of thatched roof with mud mixed cow-dung plastered wall. The house is partitioned into several rooms in order to keep provisions for various household functions. The chief building materials are bamboo, thatch, wood and cane. The houses of plain tribes living in the Assam part of the border are of four types: (i) thatched house (*kutcha* house), (ii) semi-*pucca* Assam type, (iii) *pucca* Assam type, and (iv) reinforced concrete. The thatched houses are traditional Assamese dwelling which are well-designed to match the local climatic conditions. The archetype houses are rectangular in shape chiefly made of thatch, bamboo, cane and occasionally wood. Walls are made of crushed bamboo splits and reeds and plastered with a mixture of mud and cow-dung. The Assam type buildings are the products of the colonial rule which have similarities with European architectural design. On the other hand, multi-storied RCC houses have also emerged in the rural landscape but in terms of number these are quite insignificant. The most noticeable aspect of the house type is that there is a sharp change in the building materials. Thatches are replaced by C.I. sheets, whereas bamboo still holds good as building materials. The change in house type is primarily caused by the shortage of locally available building materials. Earlier people constructed their houses with the materials found available at their reach. Large-scale deforestation in the region caused shortages of building materials which pushed the inhabitants for searching alternatives of the traditionally used building materials.

The tribal groups both in the hills and plains primarily depend on cultivation and food gathering practices. They acquire their staple food by practicing cultivation and for other dietary items like vegetable, fish, meat and medicine they merely depend on forest. Depletion of forest resources, however, compelled them to produce some vegetables in their own home gardens. Rice, as a staple food is produced either by practicing shifting cultivation or by settled cultivation. Meat and fish form important dietary items of the tribes of both hills and plains. Each household has its own vegetable garden where they produce their needs. The plain tribes normally include plenty of vegetables in their daily diet along with fish, while the hill tribes prefer meat in their diet and use little vegetables. The vegetables they use are usually procured from the jungles. All the tribes irrespective of their habitats—hills and plains usually take meal three times in a day.

As a bridge of coexistence between the forests and the tribes, the traditional practices have great significance. The tribal people not only collect edible plants, fruits and nuts from the forest, they also collect medicinal plants that they are using traditionally to cure certain diseases. The important herbal items are *Mishmi teeta, bahak teeta, chatiana, bih patal, siju, pategaja, bhomora, arjun, tejmuri, bah gaj, ghila, lochan, dimoru, sonaru, chalkuwari, punonava, koli jamu, bihdhekia, monichal, manimuni, bheveli lata, nefafu, rajghanta, lataguti, saguni lata, satmul, sharpajiva*, etc.

Forests and wildlife are essential ingredients for a balanced ecosystem. Forests have been playing diversified role in the ecosystem including the human society. Prior to the onset of colonial control over forests, the Assam-Nagaland Border region was regarded as an area of extreme greenery and rare beauty. Descriptions of W. Schlich, writings of Mc'Cosh, Allen, Robinson and other contemporaries confirmed the existence of flourishing forest cover in the region. During 1910-11, Sibsagar district including parts of Nagaland and Karbi Anglong possessed 2889 sq.mile of unclassed open forests and 1043 sq. mile of reserved forests. As a whole, the district had 3882 sq. mile forest area out of the district's total area of 4995 sq. mile of the district. In terms of percentage, the forest area covered 77.72 per cent of the district's total area. The Forest Department in Assam was established in 1868 and Gustav Mann was appointed assistant conservator of forest. Assam Forest Reguiation VII of 1891 was approved by the Governor General on 26th December, 1891. As such, a series of Acts and Regulations were derived and enacted to establish control over the forest resources of the region. Establishment of tea estates in large number all along the border districts of the region resulted in large-scale reduction of forest cover. It was followed by wanton destruction of forest by the log businessmen and the newly established plywood and saw mills. The present-day forest cover is represented only by few of the reserved forests and secondary *jhum* regrowth in the region.

On the basis of the Assam Forest Regulations, 1891 initiatives were first taken to bring more and more forest under reserved forest area. As a result of relentless effort made by the Development of Forest, Assam, the area under reserved forest increased from 269 sq. mile in 1875 to 6,514 sq. mile in 1940. During 1879 there were few reserved forests in the region of Assam-Nagaland Border. These were Nambor, Mikir Hills, Daigrung, Obhaypur, Hahchara and Kakadonga. As per the report of the Office of the Chief Conservator of Forest, Assam, and Forest Survey of India, the number of reserved forest during 2006-07 period was only 12 of which 10 were within Assam and 2 in within Nagaland. These reserved forests are: (i) Dayang, (2) Rengma, (3) Diphu, (4) Desoi, (5) Desoi Valley, (6) Tiru hills, (7) Abhaypur, (8) Galeki, (9) Sapekhati, (10) South Nambor,

(11) Singphan, and (12) Rangapahar. The total area under these reserved forests is 1,311.80 sq. km.

Scientific forestry practices started with the coming of Sir Dietrich Brandis, a German forest expert in 1864. Under guidance of Dr. Voeleker, a detailed study was made on the relationship between agriculture and forests. The new forest policy of 1894 was the outcome of such studies. The important features of the forest policy 1894 were: (a) protection and preservation of forests to maintain the climatic and physical condition of the country; (b) commercial management of valuable timbers; (c) demand for cultivable land to be met by forest land; and (d) provisions should be there to use forest land by the local people. As such, many more new Acts and Regulations were enacted to improve the forestry practices in the region. During 1919-1924, Assam alone supplied 34.5 million cubic feet timber, 39.9 million cubic feet fuelwood, 147.8 million pieces of bamboo, 18,203.20 quintals of lac and 2.59 million tons of other forest products. The Assam-Nagaland Border region with its extensive forest cover became the pivot of forestry practices under the colonial administration. Construction of trolley line from Mariani to Kakilamukh, extension of Assam-Bengal Railway through Assam-Nagaland Border region, etc. enhanced the scope for forestry practices. Transportation was considered as great impediment for smooth forestry practices in this region. Rivers were also effectively used to transship the forest products, but it was expensive and required much labour. Bamboo raft, meleng, elephants etc. were used to transship goods from the inaccessible forest areas. The Assam-Nagaland Border region served the forestry practice favourably. During 2006-07, the four plain districts attached to the border produced 417,315 cubic metric ton of industrial timber. In parts of Nagaland, forestry records were not documented well as most of the forest areas were under private or community ownership.

In order to improve the forestry practices the Ministry of Environment and Forests brought out a circular on June 1, 1990. The concept of Joint Forest Management (JFM) or Participatory Forest Management was the subject matter of this circular. At further upper level Forest Development Agency (FDA) was formed accordingly to look after the activities of JFMCs. Under four FDA namely Golaghat, Sibsagar, Jorhat and Karbi Anglong, a total of 70 FJFMCs were formed in the border areas of Assam in 2006. The number of JFMCs in Nagaland part also increased to 85 in 2008.

Social forestry programme financed by Government of India was lunched to incorporate more areas under afforestation measures. During

1984-2005, four mega social forestry parks were established. These are Green park (Jorhat), Rajabari park (Golaghat), Na-Pukhuri park (Sibsagar) and Bio-diversity park (Golaghat). Social forestry programme in Nagaland was not much effective since most of the forest areas are under private ownership.

Deforestation is characteristically a dynamic process. Destruction of forest is not merely an outcome of natural hazards like cyclone, tsunami, earthquake, volcanic eruption, flood etc. Human-induced destruction of forest is much more extensive and penetrative than natural hazards. Deforestation causes extinction of species, loss of habitat, change in climatic conditions, desertification, displacement of people, imbalances in ecology, change in the life style of forest tribes and other forest dwellers. In early days fire was extensively used by the primitive tribes to remove forest cover. However, its effects were confined to a limited area. Forest fires seemed to be devastating in the areas of dry climate. The Assam-Nagaland Border region is characteristically a zone of hot and humid climate with long rainy season and shorter dry months. Fire used to clear *jhum* fields is not found to be devastating to the local environment.

Large-scale removal of forest in India as well as in the Assam-Nagaland Border region started with the coming of the British. To pursue scientific forestry programme, a forest policy was formulated in 1865. It opened-up two ways of exploitation of forest resources: (i) forest areas other than reserved forests came under wasteland category; and (ii) conversion of these wastelands to farmland by way of deforestation. Exploitation of forest resources simultaneously, followed by the introduction of commercial agriculture at the expense of forest land. As a result of the large-scale destruction of forest and forest resources the age-old symbiotic relationship between the forest and the forest tribes was jeopardized. As a result of tribal revolts against the British forest policy came up in different parts of the country. The notable among these are Chaotal Bidroh of Jharkhand, Gudem-Rampa of Tamilnadu, forest Satyagraha of Cuddupah, mass movement of Jagadalpur, Sitarama Raju led movement in the Godavari hills, etc.

The advent of British colonialists in the Indian forest was critical to the rights of the ecosystem people which caused onslaught over the ecological settings of the country. Forest in India primarily were under community ownership. Not only the tribes and forest dwellers, all other communities were also depended on forest produce. Traditions were also related to forest and forest resources which kept them committed to protection of forests around them. Settled agriculture was prominent in the river plains. For these people forests were not only the source of fuel and house building materials but were also important component of their life and culture. Irrespective of caste and community, people living in and around the forests had been maintaining some common ethics related to forest-based activities in order to keep the forest resources undepleted.

Imperial administration in India was started in 1757 immediately after the battle of Plassey. The Forest Act, 1865 was criticized as inefficient by several British forest officials and diplomats. In 1878, a new Forest Act was passed which is known as Indian Forest Act VII of 1878. Implementation of this act curtailed people's right over forest which was enjoined by the people as customary right from historic past. Thus, most of the forest areas were brought under the control of colonial government. In order to make the colonial government comfortable over forest, a forest policy was formulated in the year 1894. The major emphases of this policy were—(i) constitution and conservation of forest and restriction of the privileges of the users; and (ii) management of forest on commercial lines as a source of revenue. As a result of such intention, the rates of gross revenue increased to reach a maximum of approximately 450 times during the period 1870-1920. To pursue the revenue oriented forest policies of the colonial government, a series of acts were amended during the later period. These were 1901 Indian Forest (Amendment) Act; the Repealing and Amending Act, 1914; Devolution Amendment Act, 1920; the Indian Forest (Amendment) Act, 1927, etc.

Construction of railway line and development of transport connectivity were initiated by the British Government to remove the hurdles of transshipment of goods and forest produces. Within a span of 48 years (1852-1900), the extension of railway line reached a length of 65,037.56 km within the country. It tremendously helped them to extract forest resources, primarily the valuable timbers. In 1900, the total deforestation amounted to 286,118 hectares and as such the cultivated land increased to 6.0 million hectares. From 1850 to 1940 the total area deforested under colonial government reached the mark of 30,933.16 sq. km. Assam came under British rule in the year 1826 and in the successive period the whole of North-East India was brought under British administration. The writings of British scholars like Mackenzie (1989), Mc'Cosh (1837), Butler (1841) and Mills (1853) splendidly elaborated the existence of rich biodiversity in this region. The Assam-Nagaland Border region was also a rich stock of green cover with scanty human settlements. Peopling of this region can be summarized as—(i) No traces of early human settlement during prehistoric period; (ii) settlement started in the region 250 years ago; (iii) 27.37 per cent of the settlements came up as a result of Burmese invasion; and (iv) opening of tea gardens and encroachment of forest land by landless peasants started in the later part of twentieth century.

The forest legislation for Assam was first started in the year 1868 under Bengal Forest Department. To augment a smooth management the Department of Forest was separated from the Bengal Forest Department in 1874. Gustav Mann was appointed as Deputy Conservator of forests and under his supervision the Provincial Forest Department was established. Revenue accumulation, as a result, increased sharply from Rs. 2,33,487 in 1881 to Rs. 6,76,944 in 1904. The British Government attempted to bring more and more forest areas under cultivation to acquire land revenue in a recurring manner. In order to bring the forest of Assam under strict management, Assam Forest Regulation VII of 1891 was enacted so that all the forest resources can be brought under proper utilization. It enabled the administration to designate any land a reserved forest through public notification. The Forest Regulation 1891 also made provisions under section 28 to deforest any area with the sanction of the Government of India. The Department of Forest accordingly undertook a series of deforestation measures in parts of Diphu reserved forest and Nambor south reserved forest of the Assam-Nagaland Border region in the subsequent period to make provision for non-forest uses. The colonial Government again derived a new forest act in 1927 in order to ensure total control over forest land and forest produces. The principal aim of this Act was to consolidate law relating to forests, the transit of forest produce and duty on timber and other forest products. It also empowered the State Government to constitute reserved forest on any land and ensure the total property right of the government. The government took initiatives to constitute village forests under the supervision of Panchayats and Mouzadars. This endeavour of the Government failed to draw proper response from the villagers. For the government it was possible to constitute only 11 village forests along the forested tract of the Assam-Nagaland Border region. Imposition of levy on the axe used for cutting timber put pressure on the timber contractors to harvest more trees with their axes to extract more profit from timber cutting.

Dietrich Brandis, who was regarded as the propounder of scientific forestry, took initiatives to survey of the entire forest area of the country. He also classified the trees girth-wise as first, second, third and fourth category. He suggested that the first category trees with more than 6 feet girth should be felled annually.

Extensive uncultivated, unsettled and low forest areas in parts of upper Assam drew attention of the British administration. These unutilized lands were incorporated under wasteland category and initiated to bring them under meaningful utilization. As a result, a new policy to manage the wasteland came up in 1838. Wasteland Grant Rules 1838, Fee Simple Rules, 1826; Revised Fee Simple Rules, 1874; and the New Lease Rule, 1876 were the product of the Government's endeavour for management of wastelands. The wasteland rules were enacted aiming at the vast forest areas of no property rights either of the government or of any individuals. European tea planters in large number came forward to take-up this opportunity to open tea estates in the wasteland areas of upper Assam. There were no inducements for application to limit their urge for the area actually required by them. The total area thus taken up in Sibsagar district was 108,050 acres in 1874. A series of amendments and liberalization of wasteland grant rule was seen in the later period to attract more and more grantees. The purchase value of wasteland even reduced to Rs. 2.8 per acre. As a result the total area allotted to tea planters increased to 337,327 acres in 1900 from 153,57 acres in 1880. Most of the leased wasteland tracts were cultivable waste covered with thick forest. The wasteland leased out for tea cultivation measured 3,45,000 hectares in 1965, which as a result brought tremendous change in the ecological setup particularly in Upper Assam. Notably, 76.39 per cent of the total area of Sibsagar district was cultivable wasteland most of which were leased out to the tea planters. The total area under disposal of the tea garden owners within the Assam-Nagaland Border region measured 72,012.48 hectares as per record of *Tea Area Handbook*, 1991.

Deforestation was not alone confined to the wasteland areas of the region, in many occasions it was extended to the reserved forest area of the Assam-Nagaland Border region. Dereservation of 3418.78 hectares, 66.88 hectares and 2145.54 hectares areas of Panidihing reserved forest by Government notification No. 2807 R of 17.8.1928, GER 92/47/81 of 3.11. 1949 and FOR/Sept/570/68/131 respectively indicate the extent of deforestation in this part of Sibsagar district. Deforestation in south Nambor reserved forest in several occasions strikingly affected the ecological scenario of the area. A series of deforestation drives in the reserved forest areas of the Assam-Nagaland Border opened-up the way for encroachment by the peasantry and the landlords. Continuous encroachment by the Naga and Assamese peasantry on the one hand and enlargement of tea gardens on the other made adversely affected the vast wasteland and forest area of the region. It is, however, clear that the revenue oriented colonial policies brought about a major breakthrough in eliminating the vast forest areas of this part of the Assam-Nagaland Border region.

The process of migration into Assam was a deliberate endeavour of the colonial government. In order to meet the shortage of labour for the tea gardens and to bring the fallow flood-prone areas under cultivation workers from central India and cultivators from Bengal were brought into Assam. The tea garden workers were primarily constituted by socially marginalized group living in the backward areas of Singbhum, Jharkhand, Chotanagper and eastern part of Madhya Pradesh. Recruitment of labour in the tea gardens from the backward, socially and economically marginalized people of Orissa, Bihar, Bengal, Madhya Pradesh etc. continued for long as the area and number of tea estates had been increasing under the initiatives of the colonial administration. As per 1891 census report, the total immigrants in the tea gardens were 423,199 and in 1901 it became 645,100. The workers were mercilessly engaged by the garden managers and compelled them to work in a hazardous situation in the jungles for land reclamation. The Muslim immigrants on the other hand were settled in the areas of central and western Assam to produce crops suitable for those flood-prone areas. Another stream of migration took place from Rajasthan, Punjab, U.P. and Bihar. These migrants took up various jobs like trader, cobbler, mechanic etc. As per 1901 census, the number of migrants from various parts of India was 4,53,876, from Bengal 21,308, from Madras 84,170, from central province and 108,75 from North Western province. The Assam-Nagaland Border region witnessed a huge influx of tea garden workers along with occasional migration of some Rajasthani traders and Hindu Bengali as service holders and small traders.

Continuous deforestation on the one hand and the migration on the other gradually eroded the traditional means of livelihood of the ecosystem people. The tribes living in the forested track of Assam-Nagaland Border have suffered from economic devastation as a result of ecological changes brought about by colonial policies. The invasion of colonialists into the virgin forests brought a major breakthrough in the traditional means of living of the ecosystem people. Capitalist mode of production is not at all conducive for the ecosystem society striving with sustenance economy and traditional production system.

Forested hilly tracts of the Assam-Nagaland Border region extensively experienced shifting cultivation. Most of the Naga and Karbi tribes are accustomed with this practice. This traditional knowledge based agricultural practice had to face hurdles with the advancement of colonial forestry. For the colonialist this production system was wasteful and therefore, the government insisted to stop shifting cultivation in the forested hills of this region. Imposing restrictions on shifting cultivation the government tried to convert the *jhum* lands into areas of settled agriculture so as to generate more revenue. Secondary regrowths seen extensively in the low hill areas of the border region are the regenerated plants in the inter *jhum* cycle period. Forest Survey of India estimated the area of secondary forests at 1011 sq.km. in 2003 in whole of Nagaland. Another major concern of shifting cultivation is the decreasing length of *jhum* cycles which leave no time for regeneration of secondary growth. Tanguya method of cultivation was introduced to prevent shifting cultivation in the hills of this region. Plantation of selected tree crops in the cropland got no response from the *jhumiyas*. As per the Annual Report 1940-41 of the forest department the total number of peasant families engaged in this system was only 950. Efforts to cover up the region by Taungya cultivation failed because of, (i) curtailment of land and property rights of the peasants; (ii) selection of tree crops not as per local demands; and (iii) unwillingness of the peasants to give up their traditional livelihood practice.

The Assam-Bengal railway connecting the Assam-Nagaland Border region was completed by 1903. As the traditional means of transshipment of goods were time consuming, expensive and troublesome and also difficult particularly during the rainy months, construction of railway line was for them a compulsion to ease the way of resource accumulation. Establishment of railway link with the resourceful areas not only made the transshipment easier, but also accelerated the pace of deforestation. During construction a total of 3604.87 acres was deforested. Endowed with hard wood like *Sal* and *Nahar*, Assam forest had to take the burden of railway sleeper supply. During 1928-33, the Forest Department of Assam made agreement to supply 10,000,000 sleepers to facilitate railway construction. Moreover, in order to meet the growing requirement of tea boxes, soft woods were supplied to the plywood and Vanier mills. Within a span of 10 years (1889-1900), the demand for tea boxes increased sharply from 1,19,000 to 4,11,000. A number of sawmills came up to accelerate the pace of tea box production in Sibsagar district and adjacent areas. The process of deforestation got momentum with the coming up of large number of plywood, Vanier and sawmill in and around the Assam-Nagaland Border region.

The tribal and non-tribal communities strictly maintained all social and religious ethics related to flora and fauna. It was during the British period that the government passed orders for killing of wild animals for the safety of workers in forests and tea gardens. In 1859, 18 pounds and 4 shillings was paid as rewards for destruction of wild animals which was increased to 7.18 pounds in 1865. Moreover, reward of 1 shilling were paid for snake killing. Extension of tea garden into the forested belt resulted in shrinkage of forest cover which in turn created shortage of habitats and food for wild animals. All these led to the massive destruction of wild animals.

The principle of "true island biogeography" of Gorman can be used to analyse the changing ecological scenario of the Assam-Nagaland Border region. Large-scale removal of forest for tea cultivation, construction of railway lines, leasing out of the vast wasteland, timber trading, intensive open-cast coal mining etc. caused severe damage to the ecosystem of the region. Shrinkage of forest area caused loss of habitat for the wild animals. Herbivores were the first victim as they suffered from scarcity of food and habitat. Destruction of carnivores came later under this hazardous ecological setting. Decrease in the forest area caused crisis of support base for a variety of life forms. The area once 'super saturated' with variety of species gradually transformed into a deserted state. Reduction in forest area leads to the shrinkage of both flora and fauna. The Assam-Nagaland Border is a genuine representation of Gorman's concept of "true island biogeography".

With all new reality after Independence of India, a revised forest policy to accommodate new aspirations on forest was inevitable. Government of India, *vide* resolution No. 13.1/52-F dated May 12, 1952 introduced a revised forest policy. This policy proposed a classification of forests on a functional basis. These were protection forests, national forests and village forests. As this policy is a revised one of the Forest Policy, 1894, the recommendations remained unchanged. The important recommendations it made was that national forests were to be managed to meet the requirement of defense, communication and industry. As a result, during the first five year (1951-56) a number of development projects like river valley projects, industries and communications and other allied projects were implemented using forests and forest areas. The question of forest conservation rarely got priority in this forest policy.

With the aid and incentives from the government a number of plywood, Vanier and timber industries were established in and around the Assam-Nagaland Border region. Wood Craft, Assam, for instance, was established at Mariani in 1957. Department of Forest issued a permit to this plywood industry sanctioning a collection of 1,00,000 cubic feet timber from the nearby reserved forest namely Desoi, Desoi valley, Tiru hills and Kakadonga. Tree felling with this lone permit continued up to the year 1995. Eventually, the authority of plywood industry did not have a second sanctioning letter from the Department of Forest till 1995. Surprisingly, within a span of 35 years the entire reserved forests were deforested. It is reported that during 1960s and 1970s, the forests of the region supplied the required raw-materials for nearly 175 units of forest-based industries located in and around the border region. Nexus between timber traders and forest officials also was reported by the local people.

Government of India laid down a new forest policy in December, 1988. This policy for the first time emphasized on the need of conservation of forests, restoration of ecological balance and to enlarge the tree cover under a proper management system. From ecological perspectives the importance of the Indian Wildlife (Protection) Act, 1972 and the National Commission on Agriculture, 1976 was undisputable. The formation of joint forest management committee in 1990 to accelerate the pace of forest conservation was a positive step of the Ministry of Environment and Forest. This policy also was criticized for promoting a mechanical type of forest conservation. A controversy was also growing up regarding the Forest Conservation Act, 1980. As a result, the Supreme Court by an order completely banned tree felling in the forest rich North East India and also banned transportation of timbers throughout the region.

It is, however, noticed that most of the unclassed state forests including the reserved forests have already been destroyed. It has created disorder in the ecological settings of the region. The process of deforestation in the Assam-Nagaland Border has passed through three distinct stages: (i) extensive *jhuming* in the hilly parts of the region; (ii) establishment and expansion of tea estates in large number in the forested areas of the plain; and (iii) rehabilitation and encroachment in the reserved forests of the region.

Jhum cycle in the hills has largely been reduced from 15-18 years in the early twentieth century to 5-8 subsequently due to increasing population pressure. Being topographically more accessible the western part of Nagaland witnessed a rapid growth of population and economic activities in the recent time. Nagaland Government is handicapped with no regulation on *jhum* to restrict further extension of this type of cultivation. Forest land accounting for 90.21 per cent is under private ownership. In order to put a control and to enhance the government quota of forest, Nagaland Government recently has taken step to purchase forest land all throughout the state. In 2009, the government completed purchasing of 19,246,73 hectares of forest in the state. Out of the total purchase, 69.61 per cent is from the Assam-Nagaland Border region. Nagaland Forest Act, 1968 failed to protect the forest as it put more emphasis on the regulation of harvesting forest resources to raise state revenue. Through Nagaland Tree Felling Regulation, 2002 and The Biodiversity Act, 2002 along with JFM and Village Forest Committee for implementation of Afforestation Scheme, the Government has at present taken initiatives to rejuvenate its forest cover.

It is also observed that a large section of people belonging to Bodo tribe migrated to Sibsagar and Karbi Anglong during the 60s due to resource scarecity from Goalpara and Kamrup district. Most of them settled in and around the reserved forests of Sibsagar and Karbi Anglong. The post-Independence period also witnessed long peasant movements demanding "land to the landless" and "land to the tiller". These movements took place under the leadership of RCPI and CPI. This peasant up rise came up as a result of (i) destruction of forest-based livelihood by the waves of immigrant settlers; (ii) leasing out of waste land/unclassed state forest for tea plantations; (iii) large-scale trade of forest products causing large-scale deforestation; (iv) establishment of political supremacy through the movements; and (v) occurrence of natural hazards like flood and river bank erosion.

Demand for "land to the landless" and "land to the tillers" got immense popularity. "*Ghiladhari Satyagraha*" organized by Congress Socialist Party during the 1950s of the twentieth century grew stronger. Under the pressure from the agitationists, Government decided to distribute 9,839 *bighas* of village grazing land and 29,174 *bighas* from professional grazing reserves among the landless. In 1965, part of Diphu reserved forest and part of South Nambor reserved forests measuring 820.08 hectares were deforested through government notifications. Thousands of peasants specially belonging to tribal communities rushed into the reserved forest to occupy land. The struggle for land was geared up again under the leadership of Soneswar Borah during the 1970s of the twentieth century. Mr. Soneswar Borah was elected to the Assam Assembly in 1978. People of Ghiladhari and the legislator himself organized "Dayang Vijar Utsab" in which the then Chief Minister Mr. Golap Borbara himself was present as Chief Guest.

Declaration of Nagaland as separate state in 1963 created boundary dispute between Assam and Nagaland. The Government of Assam took initiatives to settle the peasants along the forested border areas to claim its occupation. The Government in the meantime distributed lands measuring 10 *bighas* to each peasant family. In a diplomatic move, the Government of Assam and the Government of Nagaland introduced a system known as "half-a-mile settlement" as a measure to resolve boundary dispute. The debate and conflict over boundary dispute became more strenuous as the Naga extremist outfit geared-up their activities around the border areas. As a result, series of violent gun battles took place during the 1980s onward.

Pressure on the government was mounted as the movement spread all throughout the border areas demanding land for the settlers. The movement organized by Brihattar Tengani Unnayan Sangram Samittee (BTUSS) and Dayang Krishak Mukti Sangram Samittee (DKMSS) became more intensive. Increasing pressure from the peasantry compelled the government to grant land title to the peasants who had settled in the forest before 1980. Amidst all these, the peasantry of the two States—Nagaland and Assam—are more or less engaged in an undeclared war for forest land encroachment.

The tribes living in the Assam-Nagaland Border region are Sonowal Kachari, Thengal Kachari, Mishing, Tai Khamayang, Tai Turung, Bodo, Karbi, Ao, Sema, Kanyak, Angami, Lotha, etc. All these tribal groups are sensitive to their tradition, culture, rites and rituals. Their livelihoods are mostly dependent on land and biological resources. Cultivation and food gathering are their mainstay of their economy. Kinship and social customs are distinctive attributes of these tribal groups in the Assam-Nagaland Border region. Practice like head-hunting once present among the Naga tribes, was associated with variety of social and cultural activities. Totemism is an integral part of tribal tradition. Many tribes and clans claim their origin from their totem. Exogamy, as such, is prevalent and widespread among all the tribes of Assam-Nagaland Border region. Killing totem animals or cutting totem trees for most of the tribes is a great sin and therefore punishable.

Taboo, on the other hand, is characteristically a representation of tribalism and primitiveness. Most of the tribes of Assam-Nagaland Border region have different kinds of taboo. Tabooed animals of Ao community include the tiger, leopard, gibbon, wild dog, civet, squirrel, slow loris, spotted dove, etc. Similarly, the Angami, Lotha, Karbi, Bodo, etc. have their tabooed animals and also tabooed social customs. Tribal societies believe that the taboos are tradition bound and are derived from their experience to keep control over the society and social system.

The presence of Morung, a common tribal institution is important for the tribes of Assam-Nagaland Border region which plays an important role in training and to educating the upcoming youths. In a wider sense, Morung for the younger generation is a club, a public school, a military training camp, a common lodging and meeting place for the village councils. Mishing, Bodo, Thengal Kachari, Ao, Lotha, Sema, Angami, Karbi etc. hold a Morung which is known by different names following their respective dialects. The life of the tribes is governed by the tradition of a customary code of law. These unwritten codes are the base for social administration of all the tribes of this border region. The tribes are loyal to the chieftains or the village heads man. The chiefs of many tribes living in this region enjoy absolute political, economic and religious power. Tribal villages are unique in form and structure and are regarded as functionally a closed system. Villages of Agami, Lotha, Sonowal Kachari, Bodo, Thengal Kachari are big in size, while the villages of Karbi, Mishing, Khamayang, Turung are small. In the rugged hill areas of Nagaland and Karbi Anglong, the villages are relatively small compared to the villages located in the foothills and plains.

The tribes living in the Assam-Nagaland Border region have a well ramified eco-friendly practices which they perform in their own ways. Cultivation, harvesting of crops, storage of crops and other seeds, treatment of pests and diseases of crops, crop protection from wildlife, etc. are maintained with necessary concern for the ecosystem. As such hunting, fishing and food gathering practices are performed judiciously keep in view the sustainability of the environment. Over hunting, hunting of tabooed animals, killing of pregnant and immatured cabs and matting animals are restricted. Food gathering activities are also associated with some strict rules and regulations. Over harvesting is strictly prohibited and destruction of mother seeds is punishable. Big trees, sacred groves, etc. are subject matter to indolate and hence mandatory to conserve it.

Forest and forest resources started getting depleted heavily from the time of colonial rule onwards. As per the topographic sheets prepared by survey of India in 1974, the total forest area of the region measured 4682.54 km^2, which is 75.36 per cent of the total geographical area of the region. Household survey conducted in the area shows that 94.62 per cent of the total people settled in this forested belt could see dense forest, while only 20.33 per cent who settled after 1980 could see dense forest. Forest cover of the border districts of Nagaland (Dimapur, Wokha, Mokokchung and Mon) at present measure 22.24 per cent, 15.58 per cent, 17.93 per cent and 23.32 per cent respectively. The situation of forest cover in the plain districts is also the same with only 20 per cent of the total area of the border districts of Assam part under forest in 2007.

Gradual elimination of community forest management system gives way to both the governmental and non-governmental agencies for free intervention in the forest land which, in turn, causes pressure on the forest resource base. From the period of British regime onwards uninterrupted interventions in the forest by way of enactment of forest policies, laws and regulations, establishing forest-based industries, introducing commercial crops, expanding forest area under government jurisdiction, privatizing community forest area etc. caused severe damage to the forest resource base of the region. As a result production of major forest products and non-wood forest products steadily came down to jeopardize the forest-based livelihood of the tribes living in and around the forest.

It is obvious that under massive depletion of forest resources the dwellers have to change their response from one stimulus to another. Modification of behaviour thus became inevitable to adjust with the changing situation. As the achievement level of their forest-based livelihood got reduced as a result of deforestation, the tribes of Assam-Nagaland Border instead of any kind of *ex-situ* adjustment to balance up their aspiration level, made *in-situ* adjustment by changing their behaviour relating to life and economy. Change in settlement pattern, agriculture practice, disease treatment method, cultural pursuits, etc. are now quite conspicuous among the tribal groups of the region which are, in fact, indicative of behavioural change.

Rampant deforestation in the forest of Assam-Nagaland Border has gradually been demolishing the forest-based economy and practices of the tribes. Enactment of regulations on shifting cultivation during the British period as well as by the Government of Nagaland during the post-Independence period shifting cultivation began to decline and a section of hill tribes adopted settled cultivation. The people of this border belt, once regarded as ecosystem people, now changed their life style and have become more market dependent for their livelihood. Increasing number of markets and expanding urban influence in the border belt subsided the traditional values of the tribes. Removal of the forest cover, establishment of tea estates and expansion of human settlements by encroaching forest land brought a significant change in the house type of the region. The common Assam type cottages with *Ashoka* leaves and thatches as roofing materials have gradually been replaced by CI sheets. Non-availability of required housing materials in the exhausted forest areas of the region compelled the inhabitants to search for alternatives.

The mainstay of the economy of both the plain and hill tribes is cultivation. Shifting and terrace cultivation are typical to the Hill tribes, while the plain tribes are accustomed to permanent cultivation. In the hills, the practice of agro-forestry came up as a result of continuous effort made by the Forest Department under the management of forest development agency (FDA) scheme. The important aspect related to the economy is that the number of people engaged in cultivation has gradually been decreasing in both the hills and the plains as a result of other opportunities growing in the area. It is also noticed that with the decrease of forest cover and forest resources the number of people engaged in food gathering and hunting is also decreasing in a significant way. The friendly relation that they maintained with forests, the culture they developed to keep the forest and themselves living and the knowledge and experiences they gained from their forest based life are getting gradually jeopardized. Under the new situation the bewildered forest tribes have come under total obliviousness to their tradition and culture. As time passes, the positive environmental knowledge base developed the tribes will be lost forever.

Traditionally, tribal societies are self-sufficient. Self-sufficiency means they need not have to depend on the non-tribal societies for their social, cultural and physical existence. This nature of tribal people kept them away from other societies. Accordingly, the tribal groups of Assam-Nagaland Border can be called excluded groups. In other words, they may be regarded as parallel segments of different domain. On the other hand, the exclusion of forest dwellers and the tribes from the forest areas aggravated the loss of valuable knowledge on plant, animal and microbial species used for food, medicinal and other purposes. As such, eco-friendly rural technology and related innovations also slowly disappear along with the changing agricultural and ecological management system.

With the depletion of forest and forest resources, the problems of the tribal people are getting aggravated. Changes in their mode of living during the recent period have resulted in some socio-economic and cultural adversities. Aspiration for more agricultural land resulting from the mounting population pressure in the region has given rise to boundary dispute. A series of conflicts took place during last few decades (1979, 1985 and 2013) between the peasants of Nagaland and Assam. Tribal economy traditionally centres around land and other land-based resources. Ownership over land and other natural resources is a very sensitive issue for them. This land ownership problem particularly in the plain areas of

Assam-Nagaland Border has become a vital issue which created ground for a series of movements in the border areas.

Tribals are best known for their culture, tradition and environment-friendly mode of life. Tradition, culture, social ethics and ethos, behaviour, habits of the tribal people are now under great pressure with the depletion of forest and forest resources. It results in identity crisis on the one hand and upsurge of social unrest on the other. In the absence of timely intervention with a positive attitude by the government and other concerned agencies, there is all potentialities in becoming an abode for extremist activities.

Sustainable development is at present a major concern which seeks to make all developmental works sustainable. Indigenous knowledge system is considered to be vital in a sustainable approach for development. Traditional resource use and management practices adopted by the ethnic groups inhabiting the Assam-Nagaland Border region also can be used towards attaining sustainable development. Depletion of resource base in a tribal setting means erosion of traditional knowledge base of resource use and management. Increasing population pressure in the tribal areas needs proper attention so that the tribal groups can sustain with all necessary support base for their traditional and eco-friendly pursuits. Moreover, growing immigrant settlements along the disputed inter-state boundary and increasing pressure from indigenous non-tribal settlers for more land and resources have created a chaotic situation among the tribes who are basically ecosystem people. Another emerging issue in this tribal dominated border belt is the rapid urbanization and fast penetration of consumeristic culture. For the sake of sustenance of tribal life and practices the process of urbanization needs to be regulated. The entire border region has been suffering from not having adequate infrastructural facilities. As the dwellers are gradually exposed to the modern way of life mainly through print and electronic media, they have started demanding for creation of these facilities. In order to satisfy this kind of demand proper planning for infrastructural facilities should be made keeping in view the ecological and social context of the area. It is time to protect the interest of the tribal groups by creating tribal belts and blocks along with necessary facilities and amenities in this tribal dominated border region. It will certainly reduce the extent of land transfer from tribal to non-tribal and also the growing encroachment of forest land.

A significant change in the existing traditional strategies is brought about by factors like—(i) growing contact with the agricultural activities of the people other than the tribals; (ii) depletion of forest resources and forest-based activities; (iii) increasing access to the markets and institutionalized economic functions; (iv) development of transport and communication systems; (v) role of government and non-governmental agencies; (vi) introduction of commercial cropping in adjacent areas; and (vii) conversion from traditional tribal religion to modern world religion.

At this point of time certain positive measures may be adopted to tackle the problems sustainably. Some of these may be (i) a tripartite talk among the concerned people and agencies should be organized to solve the border dispute; (ii) a working plan should be formulated in co-ordination with the Department of Forest and the Department of Land Revenue for an amicable solution of the problem of forest encroachment; (iii) exploration for formation of tribal belts and blocks wherever required within the region; (iv) restoration of forest ecology should a precondition for revival of helpful traditional practices; (v) formulation of measures to check further influx into the region; (vi) co-ordination of political, social and cultural organisations to augment mutual understanding among the tribal and non-tribal people; (vii) urbanization should be regulated by imposing eco-friendly terms and conditions; (viii) sufficient fund for the development of tribal areas should be provided; and (ix) spontaneous people's participation should be ensured for proper implementation of all these measures.

A rational and acceptable of various problems faced by the Assam-Nagaland Border region can be derived from the perspective of sustainable development. The problem outlined in the discussion have a close link with the concept of biosphere reserve which obviously can rebuild and regenerate the region removing all the constraints on the way to sustainable management of the region in general and of the forest tribes living there in particular. Problems like border dispute, displacement of forest tribes from forest land, conflict over fertile agricultural land, crisis of tribal identity, threats to traditional livelihood practices etc. can be mitigated through creation of a biosphere reserve covering the entire border belt. On the basis of the above summary and findings, the following suggestions towards mitigating the growing ecological crisis among the forest tribes in the Assam-Nagaland Border region are put forth:

1. In order to check further encroachment into the existing reserved forests of the region the governments of Assam and Nagaland should immediately chalk out an integrated working plan viable

and feasible for implementation under the jurisdictions of the Department of Land Revenue and the Department of Forests. Proper attention should be paid to the objective reality in formulating such working plans to restore ecological balance in the region.

2. The long standing border dispute between Assam and Nagaland is another important issue which needs a liberal approach to address amicably. The Central Government being the supreme authority to demarcate inter-state boundary, should take all initiatives with impartial attitudes to mitigate the boundary dispute. Before initiating any step the concerned authority should carefully read the ground reality so that no scope is left for further discontent and disbelief among the inhabitants of the two concerned states.
3. Traditional livelihood practices and locally available forest resources are inter-related. It is necessary to conserve the forest resources for the revival and restoration of sustainable livelihood practices of the tribal people living in the border areas of Assam and Nagaland. Increasing bioresources will enhance the carrying capacity of the forests. The first and foremost consideration in this respect should be massive plantation in the degraded forest areas of the region. Selection of plant species for plantation should be as per the need of the local tribes. The Department of Forest in coordination with the JMFMCs and non-governmental organisations working for the cause of tribal welfare and forest should formulate necessary measures to uphold the forest ecology and the tribal culture in the forested belts of Assam-Nagaland Border.
4. In the process of formation of the proposed biosphere reserve, the concerned authorities must take the people irrespective of their backgrounds—hills and plains into confidence. Without the involvement of the settlers of the border region the formation of biosphere reserve with all necessary ingredients will be in vain. Making a good ground of mutual understanding between the authority of the biosphere reserve and the local inhabitants should be apriority in the process of formation of a biosphere reserve as proposed in an interstate border context.
5. Rapid urban expansion and development of consumeristic life style usually go against the traditional tribal practices and mode

of living. This kind of trend is already visible in the area causing considerable harm to the ecology and economy of the area. If this trend continues uncontrolled, the proposed biosphere reserve would lose its feasibility. Some kind of control with justified rules and regulations shall have to there towards maintaining an environment—friendly situation particularly in the transitional zone of the proposed biosphere reserve. The biosphere reserve as proposed in this work may be a viable answer to the problem of deforestation and consequent degeneration of rural life in this ecologically unique and economically promising region between Assam and Nagaland in North-East India.

Appendix A
A Sample Copy of the Survey Schedule used in the Study

A SCHEDULE FOR COLLECTION OF DATA ON DEFORESTATION AND SOCIO-ECONOMIC CONDITION OF FOREST TRIBES AREA SPECIFICATION: ASSAM-NAGALAND BORDER

Ph.D. Research Topic : **Deforestation and Tribal Life in Assam-Nagaland Border Region: A Political Ecological Analysis**

Name of Institution : Gauhati University
Department of Geography
Guwahati

1. Name of the Village: State: .... District: .... Mouza :......
2. Name of the Chief of Household ....
3. Family Structure: ....

					OCCUPATON			
Sl. No.	Sex	Age	Education	Age of Marriage	Primary	Secondary	Tertiary	Others

4. Landholding Structure:
   (i) Basti Area ....
   (ii) Cultivable Land ....
   (iii) Cultivated Land ....
   (iv) Land leased out/in ....
   (v) Cultivated Land under Forest Area ....

(vi) Own Land ....

(vii) Total Kheraj/Periodic Land ....

5. Cropping Pattern: ....

Crops	Area Cultivated	HYV/TV	Yield	Fertilizer Used	Pesticide/ Chemicals Used	Crop Damaged by Wild Animals	Net Input

6. Other Income Sources:
   (i) Selling of Forest Product:
      (i) Log ....
      (ii) Firewood ....
      (iii) Honey ....
      (iv) Medicinal Products ....
      (v) Animal Flash ....
      (vi) Roots and Fruits ....
      (vii) Others ....
7. Means of hunting animals: Traditional/Modern ....
8. What are the ways you adopt for traditional hunting ....
   ....
9. Do you have fire weapons to perform hunting:
10. Are there sufficient numbers of animals for hunting:
11. If not, why they are found decreasing: Over hunting by locals/increase of poaching/decline in forest cover.
12. Nature of deforestation:
   (a) How long you have been residing here: ....
   (b) Was it a dense forest area: ....
   (c) Who is responsible for deforestation: local people/ Government agencies/Poaching of trees/Natural calamity/Outside log business/clearing forest cover for cultivation.
   (d) Is it your ancestral village: Yes/No
   (e) If not wherefrom you did migrate: ....
   (f) Why did you leave the former one: for better livelihood/ evacuated by Government/frequent animal depredation/ dislocated duc to natural hazards/famine/epidemic/others.

(g) Forest depletion may cause to you: Shortage of foodstuff/ shortage of Traditional herbs/insecurity to forest Dwellers/ frequent appearance of Natural hazards/others
(h) Is forest depletion: harmful/beneficial
(i) Did you observe disappearance of any: Plants/animals
(j) If seen, give the name: ....

13. Housing and housing material:
    (a) Type of house: Thatch bamboo cottage/ Assam type/RCC/Chang ghar/Others
    (b) No. of houses in the family:
    (c) Details of housing materials:

Item	*Annual Requirement*	*Source of Collection*	*Rate*	*Total Expenditure*

14. Food Habit:

Item	*Monthly Consumption*	*Collected/ Purchased*	*Source*	*Total Expenses*

15. Name of specific food item collected from the forest:
    (1) .... (2) .... (3) ....
    (4) .... (5) .... (6) ....
    (7) .... (8) .... (9) ....
16. Name of plant/animal species used as medicines:
    (1) .... (2) .... (3) ....
    (4) .... (5) .... (6) ....
    (7) .... (8) .... (9) ....
17. Ransom paid to officials for collection of forest products: Rs. ....
18. No. of occurrences of animal depredation in a year ....
19. Compensation, incentives by Government or NGO's paid: YES/NO
20. Is the Government incentives or compensation satisfactory as per need: YES/NO

Date: ....
Place: ....

B.N. Goswami
Investigator

Appendix B

Wild Edible Fruits and Plants of Nagaland

Plant Naga	*Fruits Assamese*	*Botanical name*	*Nature of use*
Leribu	Nepal elachi	*Amonumdeal betum Roxb.*	Eaten raw
Okhrashi	Bet	*Calamus floribundus*	Ripe fruit eaten raw
Shikeshi	Jalphai	*Elaeocarpus floribundus*	Fruit eaten raw
Chohroshi	Amlokhi	*Emblica officinalis*	Fruit eaten raw and used to make jams and pickles
Chodoshi	Fig	*Ficusauris cuolata*	Fruit eaten raw and prepared jams
Ovachidoshi	Dimoru	*Ficushi spida*	Leaf eaten as vegetables and fruits eaten raw
Kheloshi	Nunri	*Morus alba*	Ripe fruit eaten raw
Piyeh-shi	Naga tenga	*Myricanagi*	Fruits are eaten raw and used to prepare pickle
Pighilirai Borei	Bhedailata	*Paederia foetida*	Eaten as cooked vegetable
Totsiipa	Titaphul	*Phlogacanthus curviflorus*	Boild with rice and eaten as cooked vegetables
Dziipao	Singa-pat	*Planta goerosa*	Boild and eaten as vegetable
Obiovu	Madhuxuleng	*Polygonum chinese*	Used as cooked vegetable
Lidainipa	Rhodendron	*Rhodadendron arboreum*	Flowers are eaten raw
Zhokhaikhoi	Makria	*Schima wallichi*	Eaten as cooked vegetable
Khekhra	Tikoniboruah	*Smilex ovalifolia*	Half cooked and prepared chutney with dried fish

(*Contd.*)

Plant Naga	*Fruits Assamese*	*Botanical name*	*Nature of use*
Chiivio	Xuhanibon	*Spilanthe spaniculata*	Eaten as cooked vegetable along with dried meat
Ohuphirapr	Pichkati	*Solanumni grum*	Eaten as boiled vegetable
Ehiishikhok	Hatibhekuri	*Solanumtor vumswarts*	Roasted fruits are used to prepare chutney
Houkhusi	Korakholi	*Wendlandiag labra DC*	Used to prepare chutney with dry fish
Kashapro	Ṭara	*Alpinianigra*	Tender shoot and leaves are used as cooked vegetable
Tbophavu	Khutura	*Amaranthus viridis*	Leaves are eaten as vegetable
Levosil	Kainikanchan	*Bauhinia purpurea*	Eaten as cooked vegetables
Khoreio	Maimuni	*Centella asiatica*	Eaten as cooked vegetables and to prepare *sinju*
Haba-vu (Oruo)	Jhilmil	*Chenopodium album*	Eaten as vegetable
Teiba (chiteipa)	Bah	*Chimorobambusa callosa*	Shoots eaten as cooked vegetable
Kokhissii	Tezpat	*Chinnamom umtamala*	Used in curry to give sweet flavour
Peijii-O	Nephaphu	*Clerodendrum*	Used as vegetable
Kodziiapa	Bonhaladhi	*Curcuma argustifilia*	Eaten as cooked vegetable
Kophrehro	Moa-alu	*Dioscorea pentaphylla*	Roasted bulbils are taken
Efochouchoj	Dhekia	*Diplaziume sculentum*	Eaten as cook vegetable
Burmudonia	Saru Manimui	*Eryngium foetidum*	Added to meat curry to give more flavour and used for making chatney

(*Contd.*)

Plant Naga	*Fruits Assamese*	*Botanical name*	*Nature of use*
Shekrabu	Kapur Kachari	*Hedychium coronariumkoening*	Tender shoots eaten as cook vegetable
Esakama	Machandari	*Houttuynia cordata*	Eaten as cooked vegetable and used to make chutney
Papinii	Kathphula	*Lentinu laedodes* (Berk) *peglar*	Whole plant body, fresh or dried form is taken as vegetable item
Shingainisii	Majenkari	*Litsea citrate* (Bl)	Roasted fruits are used to prepare chutney and leaves are used in curry to give more flavor
Huhreshibu	Nuni (Mulberry)	*Morus alba* Linn.	Leaves are eaten as boiled vegetable
Katheimeidokae	Bhatghila	*Oroxylum indicum vent*	Tender-pods are sliced into pieces for making chutney

Source: N.L. Pfoze *et al.* (2011), *Journal of Biodiversity and Environmental Sciences* (Online), http://WULI. Innspub. Net and S.Gogoi, Research Scholar, Taxonomy, Department of Botany, Gauhati University, Guwahati, Assam.

Appendix C
Wild Edible Plants of Assam

Scientific name	*Local name*	*Parts used*	*Disease*	*Methodology*
Abroma augusta L.f. Sterculiaceae	*Utatkambal*	Root	Impotency and weakness	Root juice extracted in watertaken orally
Acacia pennata (L.) Willd. *Mimosaceae*		Bark	Stomach ache	Bark juice is taken orally in water
Acorus calamus L. Araceae	*Boch/Tabiz*	Rhizome	Cough	Taken orally with water
Adhatoda zeyanica Medic. Acanthaceae	*Vahak*	Leaf	Cough/Krimi	Decoction with kali marich/Juice direct use
Ageratum conyzoides L. Asteraceae	*Kangar*	Leaf	Ache on back	Leaf juice applied on affected areas
Ageratum conyzoides L.		Leaf	Stop bleeding	Fresh leaf paste is applied
Aloe barbadensis Mill. Liliaceae	*Shalkuandi*	Pulp	Jaundice	Pulp of 2-3 leaves ground with 50 Gm Talmisri. Taken with 250 ml. milk 6-7 days Leaf
Alstonia schotaris (L.) Br. *Apocynaceae*	*Satiyan gachh*	Stem bark	Malaria and fever	bark of A. scholaris and Andrographis paniculata powdered and taken orally with warm water
Amaranthus spinosus L. Amaranthaceae	*Tanduliya/ Katailichaulai*	Root	Stomach pain	Boil extract of the root is used orally for stomach pain during menstruation cycle.
Artemisia nilagirica (CI.) Pamp. Asteraceae		Leaf	Griping stomach pain	Taken orally
Barleria cristata L. Acanthaceae	*Vahaka*	Stem	Cough	Juice is extracted from stem bark and used orally

(*Contd.*)

Scientific name	*Local name*	*Parts used*	*Disease*	*Methodology*
Belamcanda chinensis DC. Iridaceae	*Ujakanti*	Plant	Menstrual disorder	Juice is extracted from plant and taken orally
Cajanus cajan L. Fabaceae	*Arhar Patta*	Leaf	Jaundice	Fresh juice extract (1 cup) for 3-4 days
Cannabis sativa L. Cannabaceae	*Bhang*	Leaf	Loose motion	Leaf juice extracted and taken orally
Cascabeta thevetia (L.) Lipp. *Apocynaceae*	*Pila Kaner*	Latex	Abortion	Fresh milky latex taken
Centelia asiatica (L.) Urban Apiaceae	*Manimuni*	Plant	Gastric trouble, local drink for good health	Plant mixed with plants of Hydrocotyle javanica made into paste and used as sause and dried cake is prepared
Chenopodium album L. Chenopodiaceae	*Jhitimiti*	Leaf	Digestion/ anemia	Fresh or dried leaves cooked and eaten as vegetable
Chromelaena odorata (L.) King and Rob. *Asteraceae*	*Assam lota*	Leaf	Clotting of blood	Paste prepared and applied on cutted areas
Clerodendrum viscosum Vent. Verbenaceae	*Pakam*	Leaf	Health tonic and Ingredient of local wine.	Mixed with other drugs and made into pills and fermented
Coix lachryma jobi L. Poaceae	*Tapi*	Grains	High pressure	Beaded grains are bore to get relief from high pressure
Costus speciosus (Koen) 5m. Zingiberaceae	*Kushtha/Kebuk*	: Rhizome	Jaundice	Fresh rhizome pasted and kept for a night in water and taken orally.
Cynodon dactyton L Poaceae	*Dunba*	Plant	Pediatric vomiting	Fresh plant of white Durva and paddy straw pasted with water used earthen container piece mixed with carbon ash deposited on the shade roof of fire place. Paste is applied over forehead

(*Contd.*)

Scientific name	*Local name*	*Parts used*	*Disease*	*Methodology*
Eclipta prostrata (L.) L. Asteraceae	*Keyaras*	Plant	Jaundice	Fresh plant juice with milk used orally in empty stomach
Eichornia crassipes Solams Pontederiaceae	*Meteka*	Flower	Stomach trouble	Cooked and eaten as vegetable
Euphorbia ligularia Roxb. *Euphorbiaceae*		Stem	Fingertip pain/ boil	Fingertip is covered in the hole of 2 inch cut piece of stem
Ficus hispida L.f. Moraceae		Fruit	Stomach trouble	Fruit powder eaten with warm water
Ficus racemosa L. Moraceae	*Tajik*	Stem	Bone fracture	Latex of stem is coated on the bamboo strips and tied over the fractured part
Glycyrrhiza glabra L. Leguminosae	*Jashthimadhu*	Stem/ leaf	Throat pain, cough	Fresh stem twig and leaf chewed
Gossypium harbaceum L. Malvaceae	*Shirpak*	Root	Skin disorders in fingers	Paste is locally applied
Hibiscus rosa sinensi L. Malvaceae	*Gokhai Aphun Javaphul*	Flower	Weakness	Flower mixed with Talmisri and taken orally with water
Houttuynia cordata Thunb. Saururaceae	*Masundari*	Roots	Skin disorder	Root is pasted and given in skin disorders
Ipomoea aquatica Forsk Convolvulaceae	*Karmi sag*	Arial plant	Eyesight	Cooked herb washed and cooked, taken as vegetable.
Leucas indica (L.) Br. Lamiaceae	*Drona*	Leaf	Sinusitis, pneumonia, ulcer, menstrual disorder	Leaf juice diluted in water (sinusitis). Cooked and eaten as vegetable in other diseases
Lygodium flexuosum Sw. Schizaceae	*Patifam*	Stem	Fracture in cock/hen	Broken leg tied over with the stem joins the fractured leg
Mcaranga indica L. Euphorbiaceae	*Erapat*	Rhizome	Stomach pain	Warm oil coated leaf placed over the stomach during pain

(Contd.)

Scientific name	*Local name*	*Parts used*	*Disease*	*Methodology*
Michelia champaca L. Magnoliaceae	*Tita champa*	Bark	Malaria	Juice is extracted from stem bark. Powdered bark or decoction is taken orally in water
Mimosa pudica L. Mimosaceae	*Nilajji*	Root	Tooth worm	Paste is applied locally on infected areas
Murray a koeninghii Spreng Rutaceae	*Norsingh Gachh*	Leaf	Acidity/liver tonic	Juice is extracted from leaf and taken orally with water
Nyctanthus arbortristris L. Oleaceae	*Evahgachh*	Leaf	Malaria/fever	Leaf juice or decoction is given orally with water
Nymphea stellata Willd. L. *Nymphaeaceae*		Rhizome	Krimi/worm	Powdered rhizome is taken thrice a day for 4-5 days
Oroxylum indicum Vent. Bignoniaceae	*Bhatgila*	Stem	Malaria	Powdered bark is taken for 5-6 days
Pedilanthus tithimaloides (L.) Poit.	*Atobulo*	Latex	Piles	Local application
Phlogacanthus thyrsiflorus Nees Acanthaceae	*Tita vasaka*	Leaf	Loose motion	Juice is extracted and taken orally with water
Phyllanthus amaras L. Phyllanthaceae	*Bhui amlaki*	Plant	Jaundice	Fresh juice with fresh cold cow milk 1 cup for 5-6 days
Physails angutata L. Solanaceae	*Tumpet*	Fruit/ leaf	Stomach trouble	Leaves and fruits are eaten
Plumaria alba L. Apocynaceae	*Gulcha phul*	Stem	Ear sour/boil	Juice mixed in coconut oil extracted from stem bark
Plumbago zeylanica L. Plumbaginaceae	*Citrok*	Root	Jaundice	Extract of the root is applied in a cotton thread and tied on the upper arm of the patient
Pongamia pinnata (L.) Pierre Fabaceae	*Karanj*	Leaf	Urinary trouble	Juice is extracted from leaf and taken orally

(*Contd.*)

Scientific name	*Local name*	*Parts used*	*Disease*	*Methodology*
Ricinus communis L. Euphorbiaceae	*Erapat*	Leaf	Stomach ache	Pounded leaf applied locally on ache areas
Scoparia dulcis L. Scrophulariaceae	*Mithasem*	Leaf	Digestion, fever and pain	Leaf decoction/paste for cake preparation and taken for getting relief
Sida acuta L. Malvaceae	*Boriar*	Leaf	Bleeding	Leaf paste rubbed on wound
Solanum viarum Dunal Solanaceae	*Katibijwan*	Seed	Tooth worm	Seeds are boiled and steam is applied to remove worms
Sonchus oleraceus L. Asteraceae	*Manishal*	Bark	Liver disorders and kidney stones	Liver disorders and removal of kidney stones
Tabernemontana divaricata Roxb. *Apocynaceae*	*Neelkantha*	Leaf	Pneumonia, cough	Taken orally with water
Zizyphus mauritiana Rhamnaceae	*Bagouri*	Stem	Stomach ache	Powdered bark is taken with warm water

Appendix D
Deforestation and Preparation of Jhum Fields in Border Region

Crop field within tree rows

Illigal sowing of timber in Bahani village

Upper Merapani - a fresh Jhum field

Slash and Burn practice in Akatitto area

Land prepared for Jhum cultivation

A sow mill at Janghal block

Deforested Desoi R.F.

Forest Land encroachment - Desoi valley R.F.

New settlements in Tiru hills R.F.

Bamboo raft over Bhogdoi river

Jhum regrowth - Chanki of Nagaland

Tea Estate in Forest land - Desoi valley R.F.

MFP collection - Bandarchalia village

Tea Estate in Forest land - Desoi valley R.F.

Land encroach by peasants - Dayang

Deforested Diphu R.F.

Murong of Kanyak tribes

A gethering of Ao Youths

Interior part of a house - Ao tribe

Naga youth with their folk dance

Bibliography

A Handbook of Government Notification on Reserved Forests and Protected Areas of Assam, 2010, Office of the Principal Conservator of Forest, Assam, Vol. II, pp. 110-126.

Adam, W.M. (1990): *Green Development: Environment and Sustainability in the Third World*, Routledge, London.

Adhikari, D. and A. Arunachalam: *Secondary Forests: Plea for Ecological Attention and Proper Management*, DVS Publishers, Guwahati, 2010, pp. 80-93.

ALAP (1978): *Assam Legislative Assembly Proceedings*, a statement by Chief Minister Golap Borbora.

——: *Assam Legislative Assembly Proceedings*, a statement of Sri Pradyut Bordoloi, Minister of Forest and Environment, 8th April, 2005.

——(1937): *Assam Legislative Assembly Proceedings*, 14th August.

Allen, B.C., E.A. Gait, H.F. Howard and C.G.H. Allen (2008): *Gazetteer of Bengal and North East India* (compiled), Mittal Publications (photographically reproduced), New Delhi. p. 578.

Annual Report (2011-12): Ministry of Environment and Forest, Government of India.

APR (1874-1955): *Annual Progress Report on Forest Administration in Assam*,. File No. 69/82, 1944-95 (ASD).

Arneil, B. (1996): *John Locke and America: The Defence of English Colonialism*, Oxford, Oxford University Press, pp. 71, 101.

Arnold, D. and R. Guha (ed.) (1995): *Nature, Culture, Imperialism: Essays on the Environmental History of South Asia*, Oxford University Press, New Delhi, p. 2.

ASA: Assam State Archive, Rev.-A, Sept., 14-48, 1975.

ASA: Letter from Bimala Prasad Chaliha to the Ministers of Revenue and Forests, Assam, 17th April, 1954, File No. 222/54, Assam State Archive.

Assam Forest Regulation, 1891, Chapter IV, and Annual Report 1890-91, para 17 and 16, Assam Secretariat Proceedings, Nos.82-99, Revenue A, March, 1897 (ASA).

Assam Land Revenue Manual: 413-8, State Archive.

Assam State Archive: ASF, Nos.41-62, Forest-A, June, 1920.

Athparia, R.P. (2002): "Forest Resource Management by the Karbis of the Hill

Area of Assam: An Analysis" in B. Dutta Ray and K. Alam (ed.) *Forest Resources in North East India,* Omsons Publications, New Delhi, pp. 221-230.

Atkinson, E.T., (1982), *Himalayan Districts of North Western Provinces*, 3 Vols, 1884-86, (Reprint), Cosmo Publications, Delhi, 1982.

Baden-Powell (1874): *Land System of British India*, Vol. 3 (Reprint, 1979), Oriental Publishers, Delhi, p. 172.

Baller, E (1984): *Communism and Cultural Heritage*; Progress Publishers, Moscow, pp. 94-100.

Barooah, N.K. (1970): "David Scott on North-East Frontier of India and in Assam", Article published online—12 October, 2007; Institute of Historical Research.

Barpujari, H.K. (1992): *The Comprehensive History of Assam*, Vol. II, Assam Publication Board, Guwahati, p. 241.

Bartlett, H.H. (1956): Fire, Primitive Agriculture and Grazing in the Tropics, in W.L. Thomas (ed.), *Man's Role in Changing the Face of the Earth*, Chicago University of Chicago Press, pp. 692-720.

Barua, S.L. (2002): *A Comprehensive History of Assam*, Munshiram Manoharlal Publishers Pvt. Ltd., Delhi.

Baruah, D.N. (1989): *Science and Practice in Tea Culture*, Tea Research Association, Calcutta-Jorhat, pp. 18-21.

Baruah, P. (2008): *The Tea Industry of Assam: Origin and Development*, Est. Publishers, Guwahati, p. 29.

Basu, N.G. (1987): *Forests and Tribals*, Manisha, Calcutta, p. 15.

Batten, J.H. (1878a), 'Settlement Report of Garhwal' dated 10.8.1842, *In Official Report on the Province of Kumaun*, 1851' (ed. by H. Batten) Reprint, Government Press, Calcutta.

——(1878b): "Report on Bhabar of Kumaun Proper, dated 10.2.1846. *In Official Reports on the Province of Kumaun,* 1851" (ed. by J.H. Batten), pp. 182-216, Government Press, Calcutta.

Behal, R.P. (1983): "Some Aspects of the Growth of the Plantation Labour Force and Labour Movements in Assam Valley Districts, 1900-47," Unpublished Ph.D. Thesis, J.N.U., Delhi, p. 153, quoted in A.J. Saikia (2011), *Forest and Ecological History of Assam, from 1826-2000*, Oxford University Press, New Delhi.

Behura, B.K. (1999): "Why Conserve Wildlife" in B.D. Sharma (ed.), *Indian Wildlife Resources Ecology and Development*, Daya Publishing House, New Delhi, p. 14.

Bhagabati, A.K., M.C. Kalita and S. Baruah (2006): *Biodiversity of Assam: Status, Strategy and Action Plan for Conservation;* EBH Publishers, Guwahati.

Bhagabati, A.K., A.K. Bora and B.K. Kar (2001): *Geography of Assam*, Rajesh Publications, New Delhi.

Bher Doimari, Date of Interview, 08.09.12, Golakpur (Dayang).

Borah, S. (1978): *Bidrohar Pratiddhani*, Published by S. Borah, Golaghat.

Brandis, D. (1879).: *Suggestions Regarding Forest Administration in India*, Calcutta, Government Printer, para 26 and 27.

Brown, L.A. and E.A. Moore (1970): The Intra-Urban Migration Process: A Perspective; *Geografiska Annaler*, Vol. 5213, pp. 1-13.

Bryant, B.F. (1912): *A Note of Inspection on Some Forests of Assam*, Government Press, Calcutta, Para-2 and Para-14.

Bryant, R.L. (1992): "Political Ecology: An Emerging Research Agenda in Third World Studies" in *Political Geography*, Vol. II, No. 1, pp. 12-36.

BTUSS, (2004): "Gashe Manuhe Jiyai Thakar Sankalpa", a Pamphlet, Published by BTUSS.

Butler, J. (1855): *Travels in Assam*, Manas Publication, New Delhi; pp. 22-23; (reprinted, 1978).

Castells, M., (1977): *The Urban Question a Marxist Approach* (Translated by Alan Sheridan) Cambridge Mass, MIT Press.

Census of India, 1891, pp. 19-22.

Census of India, 1891, pp. 28-29.

Census of India, 1951; Vol. 12, Part II-A, pp. 72-73 and "Report on the Line System Committee", Vol. I, Shillong, 1938, pp. 1-4.

Changkakati, H.C. (1986): "Forestry in Assam" in M. Das Gupta *et al.*, (ed.), *Forestry Development in North East India,* Omsons Publications, New Delhi, pp. 43-44.

Chardin, P.T. De (1959): *The Phenomenon of Man*, Routledge, London, p. 204.

Chattopadhyaya, D. (1959): *Lokayata: A Study in Ancient Indian Materialism*; People's Publishing House, New Delhi, p. 566.

Chaudhuri, B. (2007): "Forest and Tribals: A Historical Review of Forest Policy" in C.K. Paty (ed.) *Forest Government and Tribe*, Concept Publishing Company, New Delhi, pp. 1-17.

Chauhan, R.N. (2009): *Global Forest Resources*, Oxford Book Co., New Delhi.

Choudhury, D. (2008): "Conserving Genetic Heterogeneity in North-East India: Indigenous Knowledge Systems and Opportunities for Sustainable Development" in M.K. Raha *et al.*, (ed.), *North East India: The Human Interface*, Gyan Books Ltd., New Delhi, pp. 147-162.

Circular No. 22-Forest, dated 19th October, 1894 and reviewed by the Inspector-General of Forests, USA.

Circular Resolution of Department of Forest, Nos. 17-105 A, Review of Forest Administration in British India for 1892-93 by the Inspector-General of Forests, USA.

Cleghorn, H. (1860): *Forests and Gardens of South India*. W.H. Allen, London, p. ix.

Colchester, M. (1987): "The Social Dimensions of Government-sponsored Migration and Involuntary Resettlement: Policies and Practice", paper prepared for the *Independent Commission on International Humanitarian Issues*, Geneva.

Confidential Memo, Deputy Conservator of Forests of Sibsagar Division, File No. AFR 222/54,1954, Assam State Archive.

Corlett, R.T. (1995).: *Tropical Secondary Forest, Physical Geography*, Vol. 19, pp. 159-170.

Cornforth, M. (1968): *Materialism and Dialectical Method*; International Publishers (4th revised edition), New York.

Cotton (1911): *Indian and Home Memories*, pp. 260-61, Fisher Unwin, London.

Crosby, A. (1986): *Ecological Imperialism 'The Biological Expansion of Europe'*, Cambridge University Press, Cambridge, p. 134.

D. Vasudha (2006): *Role and Image of Law in India: The Tribal Experience*, Sage Publications, New Delhi.

D. Dowd (2009): *Inequality and the Global Economic Crisis*, Pluto Press, London, pp. 144-45.

D'Zurilla, T.J. and Goldfried (1971): "Problem Solving and Behaviour Modification', *Journal of Abnormal Psychology*, Vol. 78, pp. 107-126.

Dangwal, D.D., "Commercialization of Forest, Timber Extraction and Deforestation in Uttarakhand, 1815-1947", in *Conservation and Society*, Vo. 3, No. 1, pp. 110-133.

Darlong, V.T. (2002): "An Overview of Forest Policies and Legislations *vis-à-vis* Forest Resource Management in North East India" in B. Datta Ray and K. Alam (eds.). *Forest Resources in North East India*, Omsons Publications, pp. 13-38.

Das, H. (1951), Part of Speech in the State Assembly, 10th March, *Assam Legislative Assembly Proceedings*.

Dasmann, F.F. (1988): "Towards A Biosphere Consciousness" in D. Worsteve (ed.) *The Ends of the Earth: Perspectives of Modern Environmental History*, Cambridge University Press.

David, A. (2002): "Disease, Resistance and India's Ecological Frontier, 1770-1947", in J. Scott and N. Bhatt (eds.), *Agrarian Studies, Synthetic Studies at the Cutting Edge*, Oxford University Press, pp. 186-205.

Deogaonkar, S.G. (2004): *Environmental Preservation and Tribal Population in The Dying Earth*, ABC Publication, Calcutta, pp. 473-474.

Derwin, C. (1858): *Origin of Species by Means of Natural Selection*; New American Library, New York.

Down to Earth (2002): T.N. Godavarman Thiramulpad *vs*. Union of India, Supreme Courts of India, Interview between T.N. Godavarman Thirumulpad and Surndranath, C., August, 31. Society for Environmental Communications, New Delhi.

Engel, F. (1954): *Dialectics of Nature*, Foreign Language Publishing House, The University of Michigan.

Evans-Pitchard, E.E. (1951): *Kinship and Marriage Among the Nuer*, Oxford, Clarendon Press, 1951.

Farnandes, W. and Barbora, S. (2008): *Land, People and Politics: Contest Over Tribal Land in Northeast India*, IWGIA, Copenhagen, p. 3.

Flenley, J.R., King, A.S., Tellar, J.T., Printice, M.E., Jackson, J. and Chew, C. (1991) "The Late Quarternary Vegetational and Climatic History of Eastern Island" in *Journal of Quaternary Studies*, Vol. 6, pp. 85-115.

Forde, D. (1934): *Habitat, Economy and Society: A Geographical Introduction to Ethnology*, London, Methuen.

Forest Department, Assam: *A Handbook of Government Notification on Reserved Forests and Protected Areas*, Vol. II, Office of the Principal Chief Conservator of Forests, Guwahati.

Fortes, M. (1949): *The Web of Kinship Among the Tallensi*; London, Oxford University Press.

FPC—Foreign Political Consultations, NAI, New Delhi (Quoted in A.J. Saikia's (2011), *Forests and Ecological History of Assam*, Oxford University Press, New Delhi.

Frankel, O.H. (1984).: Genetic Diversity, Ecosystem Conservation and Evolutionary Responsibility, in F.D. Castri, F.W.D. Baker and M. Hadley (eds.), *Ecology in Practice,* Vol. I, Duslin, pp. 415-27.

Frazer. J.G. (1945): *The Golden Bough*; Abridged Edition, London; p. 45.

Frazer. J.G. (1910): *Totemism and Exogamy*, Vol. I, Macmillan and Co; London p. 53.

Froyed, S. (1953): *Totem and Taboo*; Translated by D. Bug in Bengali; Subarnarekha, Calcutta, p. 2.

Gadgil, M. (1990): *India's Deforestation: Pattern and Processes in Society and Natural Resources,* Vol. 3, Taylor and Francis, U.K., 1990, pp. 131-143.

Gadgil, M. and K.C. Malhotra (1994): "The Ecological Significance of Caste" in R. Guha (ed.) *Social Ecology*. Oxford University Press, New Delhi, p. 37.

Gadgil, M. and R. Guha (1988) "State Forestry and Social Conflict in British India", Vol. 123 (i), *Centre for Ecological Science*, Indian Institute of Science; pp. 141-69.

——(1994): *This Fissured Land: An Ecological History of India*, Oxford, New York, pp. 116-117.

——(1995): *Ecology and Equity: the Use and abuse of Nature in Contemporary India*, Penguin Books, p. 3.

Ganguly, D.N. (1896): *Report of the Indian National Congress*; (private circulation only) Calcutta.

Ghiladhari Satyagraha: A Pamphlet released by Socialist Party (1950), Assam

Ghimire, K.B. and Pimbert, M.P. (2006): *Social Change and Conservation*; Earthscan, London, p. 241.

Gogoi, A. (2011): *Gana Sangramar Dinlipi*, Akhar Prakash, Guwahati, p. 113.

Gogoi, L. (1991): *The History of System of Ahom Administration*, Puthi Pustak, Calcutta.

——(1983): *Beli Mar Gal*, Sribhumi Publishing Co., Calcutta, p. 98.

GoI (1871): "Integrated Wasteland Development Programme," Ministry of Rural Development, Government of India, 1871.

GoI (1952): The National Forest Policy Resolution No. 13-1/52-F, dated 12.5.52, Ministry of Food and Agriculture.

Golledge, R.G. and R.J. Stimson (1987): *Analytical Behavioural Geography*, Croom Helm, London, p. 277.

Gorman, M. (1979): *Island Ecology*, Chapman and Hall, London, 1979.

Goswami, D. (1975): *Upanishad Dhenu*, Chapter V, Part III, pp. 78-81.

Goswami, R.C. (2007): "Social Forestry in Assam" in *ENVIS ASSAM*, Assam Science Technology and Environmental Council, Guwahati.

Goswami, S.D. (1987): *Aspects of Revenue Administration in Assam*, New Delhi, p. 113.

Goudie, A (1981): *The Human Impact on the Natural Environment*, Basil Blackwel Ltd., London.

Gregory, K.J. (1983): *The Nature of Physical Geography*, Arnold, London, p. 191.

Griffiths, S.P. (1967): *The History of Indian Tea Industry*, Weidenfeld and Nicolson, London, pp. 33-38.

Guha, A. (1977): *Planters Raj to Swaraj: Freedom Struggles and Electoral Politics in Assam, 1826-1947*, Peoples' Publishing House, New Delhi, p. 166.

Guha, R. (1984): *A Rule of Property for Bengal: An Essay on the Idea of Permanent Settlement*, Orient Longman, New Delhi.

——(2005): "The Unquiet Woods: Ecological Change and Peasant Resistance in the Himalaya" in *Ramachandra Guha Omnibus*, Oxford University Press, New Delhi, p. 22.

Gustav Mann (1873): *Annual Progress Report on the Assam Forest Administration, from H. Leeds to the Secretary*, Government of Bengal.

H. Cleghorn, *et al.* (1851): "Report of the Committee Appointed by the British Association to Consider the Probable Effects in an Economical and Physical Point of View of the Department of Tropical Forest, *Twenty First Meeting of the British Association, 1851.*

Haeuber, R. (1993): Indian Forestry Policy in two Eras: Continuity or Change, in *Environmental History Review*, Vol. 17, No. I, (Spring, 1993), pp. 49-76.

Handique, R. (2004): *British Forest Policy in Assam*, Concept Publishing Co., New Delhi, p. 24.

Harler, C.R. (1933): *The Culture and Marketing of Tea*, Humphrey Milford, London, pp. 228-247.

Hegel, F. (1817): *Encyclopedia of Philosophical Science*; (English edition), Oxford University Press, London.

Hindu Patriot (188): Editorial, 11th May, 1868.

Horkheimer, M.J. *et al.* (1972): *Dialectic of Enlightment*, Frankfurt School, New York.

Hunter, W.W. (1975): *Statistical Account of Assam*, (reprint), B.R. Publishing, New Delhi, p. 251.

Hussain, J. (2004): "Doyangar Andolan: Kichu Purani Kotha", *Doinik Janambhumi,* 19 June.

Hussain, M. (2011): *Evolution of Geographical Thoughts*; Rawat Publications, New Delhi, (Reprinted).

Ketera Boro, Date of Interview, 08.09.12, Golakpur (Dayang).

Khatowang Kanyak—A retired forest official was interviewed on 25th July, 2012 at his own residence of Hanhchara Naga village located at a distance of 25 km from Nazira of Sibsagar district.

Kikon, D. (2008): "Ethnography of Nagaland—Assam Foothills in North-east India", in W. Fernandes *et al.* (ed.), *Land, People and Politics, Contest over Tribal Land in North-East India,* NESRC and IWGIA, pp. 58-87.

Kniffen, F.B. (1965): "Folk Housing: Key to Diffusion", *Annals of the Association of American Geographers*, Dec., 1965, pp. 549-577.

Kormondy, E.J. (1996): *Concepts of Ecology*; Printice-Hall, New Delhi.

Kosumbi, D.D. (1965): *The Culture and Civilisation of Ancient India in Historical Outline*; Routledge and Kegan Paul, London.

Kraus and Goldammer (2007): "Fire Regimes and Ecosystems: An Overview of Fire Ecology in Tropical Ecosystem in Forest Fires in India", *Workshop Proceedings*, Pillar Human Resource Development, Madurai, February 19th-23rd.

Kumar, B.B. (2009): *The Tribal Societies of India*; Omsons Publications, New Delhi.

Kumar, D. (1984): *The Cambridge Economic History of India*, Cambridge University Press, Vol. II, pp. 10-20.

Lannusosang, T. (1987): "Nagaland: A Study in Social Geography". An Unpublished Thesis, Gauhati University.

Lapatev, I. (1977): *The Planet of Reason*, Progress Publishers, Moscow, p. 41.

Lenin V.I. (1968): *Materialism and Empirio-criticism, Collected Works*, Vol. 14, Progress Publishers, Moscow, p. 46.

Levi-Stauss: "Social Structure" in A.L. Krober (ed.), (1953): *Anthropology Today: An Encyclopedic Inventory*, University of Chicago Press.

M'Cosh, J. (1837): *Topography of Assam*, L.N. Tamuly (ed.), Bhabani edition, 2010, Bhabani Print and Publication, p. 11.

Mackarness, C.G.M. (1932): "Working Plan for the Eleven Forests Reserves in the Lakhimpur and Sibsagar Eastern Circle", Government Press, Shillong.

Mackenjie, A. (1979): *The North East Frontier of India*, Mittal Publications, New Delhi, (Reprinted), p. 140.

Malik, B.B. (2004): *Social Ecology of Forest Resources*; Kalpaz Publication, Delhi, p. 255.

Malinowski, B. (1944): *A Scientific Theory of Culture*, Routledge and Kegan Paul, London.

——(1954): *Science, Magic and Religion and Other Essay*, Anchor Book, New York.

Mann, G.: ARFA, 1874-75, p. 2.

Marsh, G.P. (1864): *Man and Nature*, University of Washington Press, New York.

Marx, K. (1975): "Economic and Philosophic Manuscripts of 1844" in K. Marx and F. Engels, *Collected Works*, Vol. 3, Progress Publishers, Moscow, p. 30.

——(1973): *Collected Works*, Vol. 47, Progress Publishers, Moscow; p. 559.

——(1973): *Introduction to the Critique of Political Economy* (Translated by M. Nicholas) Penguin Books, Harmondosworth, p. 480.

Marx, K. and F. Engels (1975): *Selected Correspondence*, Progress Publishers, Moscow, p. 190.

Medhi, D.K. (1993): "Traditional Medicine in Modern Times: The Place of Herbal and Geo-products in the Life of the People of Assam", in D.K. Medhi (ed.). *Man and Environment in the North East India,* Omsons Publications, New Delhi, pp. 95-111.

Meguine, J. (2000): *Cognitive Behavioural Approaches—An Introduction to Theory and Research,* HMIP, p. 13.

Memorandum on Forest Operations in Assam; August, 1873; Assam State Archives, Guwahati.

Memorandum on the Revenue Administration of Lower Provinces of Bengal, 1873, pp. 121-3; State Archive.

Menon, A. (2004): "Colonial Construction of Agrarian Fields and Forests in the Kohli Hills", in *Indian Economic and Social History Reviewed,* Vol. 41, pp. 315-338.

Mills, A.J.M. (1853): *Report on the Province of Assam,* Assam Publishing House, Guwahati, (reprint, 1984), p. 56.

Mills, J.P. (1973): *The Ao Nagas*, Oxford University Press, London, p. 20.

Monahan, F.J. (1898): *Jute Cultivation in Assam*, No. 814, February 7, 1898, Government Press (Shillong).

Monro, A.V. (1912): *Goalpara Woking Plan*, Part I, Government Press, Shillong, Para 34.

Mukherjee, R.K. (2004): "An Ecological Approach to Sociology" in S. Kothari, I. Ahmed and H. Reifeld (ed.): *The Value of Nature: Ecological Politics in India*, Rainbow Publishers.

Mullick, S.B. (2007): "State Forest Policy and Adivasi Self-Rule in Jharkhand," in, C.K. Paty (ed.), *Forest, Government and Tribe*, Concept Publishing Co., New Delhi, 2007, p. 21.

Nath, M. (2012): *Land Cover Dynamics in the Foothills of Assam-Nagaland Border and its Geo-environmental Impact on the Plains of Assam.* Unpublished Ph.D. Thesis, Gauhati University, p. 363.

Online—www.vanashakti-in (section 39, 41 of IFA) dated 15th July, 2012.

Oriental Times (1999): "Assam-Nagaland Border Dispute", Vol. 2, Issue 9-10. Oxford, Basil Blackwell, p. 228.

P.D. Raturi (1932): *F.P. for Yomuna Forest Division, Tehri-Garhwal State, 1932-33 to 1952-53* (compiled), Meerut, p. 48.

Padhi, S. and N. Panigrahi (2011): "Tribal Movements and Livelihoods: Recent Development in Orissa" *CPRC-IPA working paper*, No. 51, New Delhi, Indian Institute of Public Administration, pp. 1-63.

Parsons, T. (1972): *The Social System*, Amerind, New Delhi.

Peal, S.E. (1982): "The Communal Barracks of Primitive Races", *Science*, Vol. 20, No. 507, The American Association for the Advancement of Science.

Peet, R. and M. Watts, (1996): *Liberation Ecologies, Environment, Development and Social Movements*, London: Routledge, p. 263.

Peet, R. and N. Thrift (2002): *New Model in Geography*, Vol. I, Unwin Hyman, London, p. 11.

Perz, S.G. and D.L. Skole (2003): *Secondary Forest Expansion in the Brazilian Amazon and the Retirement of Forest Transition Theory, Society and Natural Resources* 16, Routledge, UK, pp. 277-94.

Poffenberger, M. (2006): "Forest Sector Review of Northeast India U.C.A." USA, p. x. This paper was commissioned as an input to the study of natural resources, water and the Environment nexus for development and growth in N.E. India, (Online).

Pundir, J.K. (2006): "Sociological Concerns of Ecology and Environment—Some Emerging Issues" in S.K. Chaudhury (ed.), *Culture, Ecology and Sustainable Development,* Mittal Publications, New Delhi, pp. 45-52.

Puyravaud, J.P. (2002): "Standardizing the Calculation of the Annual Rate of Deforestation", in *Forest Ecology and Management ECOS 50, Elsevior Science*, Pondicherry, 593-96.

PWD Notification: No. 13F, *Calcutta Gazette*, 1871.

Ramakrishnan, P.S. (1992): "Shifting Agriculture and Sustainable Development: An Interdisciplinary Study from North-East India", *Man and Biosphere Series*, Vol. 10, UESCO, Partheror Publication, Paris.

Rangarajan, M. (1996): *Fencing the Forest;* Oxford University Press; New Delhi.

——(2001): *India's Wildlife History*, Oxford University Press, New Delhi, p. 8.

Ratzel, F. (1901): *Labansraum;* Downloaded from www.princetonedu/-achuney/tmve/wikilook.

Ray, S. (2011): Historical Review of Growth of Tea Industries in India, *A Study of Assam Tea. Proceedings of International Conference on Social Science and Humanity*, Singapore, 2011, Vol. 5.

Ribbentrop, B. (1989): *Forestry in British India* (Reprint), Indus Publishing Company, New Delhi, p. 104.

Ritter, K. (1817): *Die Erdkunde*; Vorlesungen and, Univ. Berlin.

Rosencranz, A. and S. Lele, (2008): "Supreme Court and India's Forests" in *Economic and Political Weekly,* Vol. XLIII, No. 5, February 2, pp. 11-14.

Rumley, D. and Minghi, J.V. (ed.) (1991): *The Geography of Border Landscapes*, Routledge, New York, p. 19.

Sagreiya, K.P. (2000): *Forests and Forestry*, National Book Trust, New Delhi, pp. 11-12.

Saikia, A. (2012): "Indigenous Control and Sustainability of Common Resources in the Hills of North East India", Online www.ibcperu.org/doc/isis/5154

Saikia, A. (2008): "State Peasants and Land Reclamation: The Predicament of Forest Conservation in Assam," 1850s-1980s, *Indian Economic Social History Review*. On line: http/ier.Sagepub.com

——(2011): *Forest and Ecological History of Assam, 1826-2000*, Oxford University Press, New Delhi, p. 178.

Saldanha, I.M. (1996): "Colonialism and Professionalism: A German Forester in India", *Economic and Political Weekly*, Vol. 31, No. 21, pp. 1265-73.

Sample, E.C. (1911): *Influence of Geographic Environment*; Henry Holf and Company, New York.

Saravanan (2006): Article presented at the "Historical Perspective on the Economic Exploitation of the Forest" (session 27) of the *XIV World Congress of Economic History*, University of Helsingki, 21st-25th August, 2003.

Sarmah, R. (2004): "Atit Suwari" in M. Sarmah (ed.), *Uki*, Souvenir Published by Railway Deka Silpi Samaj, Mariani, pp. 10-14.

Saur, C.O. (1969): *Seeds, Spades, Hearths and Herds*, Cambridge: Mass, MIT Press.

Schmerbeck, J., A. Hiremath and C. Ravidatam, (2007): "Forest Fire in India", *Workshop Proceedings*, Pillar Human Resource Development, Madurai, February 19th-23rd, p. 8.

Sehgal, B. (2010): "The Adibashi Question in India", p. 27 (online).

Sen, P. (2007): "Philosophising Adivasi Ecological Perspectives" in C.K. Paty (ed.), *Forest, Government and Tribe*, Concept Publishing Co., New Delhi, pp. 48-54.

Sen, S.N. (1989): *Ancient Indian History and Civilisation*; New Age International (P) Limited, New Delhi, p. 124.

Shakespear, L.W. (1929): *History of Assam Rifles*, McMillan, London, pp. 37-38.

Sharma, B.D. (1999): "Eco-Conservation of Hill Areas: The Challenges and Proposals" in B.D. Sharma, (ed.), *Indian Wildlife Resources Ecology and Development*, Daya Publishers, p. 162.

Sharma, P. (1994): "Labour Welfare Facilities in Plywood Industries of Assam: A Case Study of M/s. Wood Craft, Assam, Mariani," An Unpublished M.Phil. Dissertation, Dibrugarh University.

Sharmah, R. (1998): "Atit Suwari" in B.N. Goswami (ed.)., *Bachar 25*, A Souvenir Published on the Occasion of Silver Jubilee, Mariani Railway Institute, p. 18.

Singh, A.K.: "Tribal Ecology in India: The Ugly Face of Development" in S.K. Chaudhury, (ed.), *Culture, Ecology and Sustainable Development*, Mittal Publication, New Delhi, pp. 111-122.

Sinha, G.N (2012): "British India's Forestry and Modern Environmentalism", Online, www.sfri.org/images/article, Feb., 4, 2012.

Smirnov, S.N. (1983): "The Development of Material Production and Optimization of Society's Interaction with Nature" in *Philosophy and the Ecological Problem of Civilization*, Progress Publishers, 1983, pp. 122-148.

Smith, (1984): *Uneven development, nature, capital and the production of space*, University of Georgia Press, Georgia.

Sonowal, C.J. (2008): "Indian Tribes and Issue of Social Inclusion and Exclusion", *Journal of 'Steed Tribes Tribals,'* Vol. 6, No. 2, pp. 123-134.

Sorre, M. (1962): "The Concept of Genre-de-vie" in Wagner and Mikesell (eds.): *Readings in Cultural Geography.*" University of Chicago Press, pp. 39-401.

Spate, O.H.K. and A.T.A. Learmonth (1967): *India and Pakistan: Land, People and Economy*; Mithuen and Co. Ltd., London.

Srivastava, A. (2007): "Symbiotic Relationship of Tribals and Forest: Role of Tribals in MFP Marketing in Eastern India" in C.K. Paty (ed.) *Forest Government and Tribe*, Concept Publishing Co., New Delhi, p. 123.

Stebbing, E.P. (1922): *The Forests of India*, Vol. I, London: John Lane the Badley Head Limited, 1922, p. 27.

——(1926): *The Forests of India*, Vol. III, The Badley Head, London, p. 424.

Stewart, O.C. (1956): "Fire as the First Great Force Employed by Man" in W.L. Thomas (ed.), *Man's Role Changing the in Face of the Earth*, Chicago University Press, Chicago, pp. 115-33.

Stracey, P.D. (1949): *Assam's Ecology and Forests*, Government Press, Shillong, p. 17.

Sundel, S.S. and Sundel, M. (1993): *Behaviour Modification in the Human Service: A Systematic Introduction to Concepts and Application*, Sage Publications, New Delhi.

Taher, M. (1993): "Ecological Setting in Assam" in D.K. Medhi (ed.) *Man and Environment*, Omsons Publications, New Delhi, pp. 48-52.

Tea Statistics: Tea Board and Tea Statistics, J. Thomas and Co. Pvt. Ltd.

Thapar, R. (2002): *Early India: from the Origins to A.D. 1300*, University of California Press, California, pp. 111-114.

The Assam Forest Manual, Vol. 8, p. 65.

The Assam Forest Manual, Vol. I, Notification No. 4631R, dated 6th December, 1930.

Tricart, J. and A. Coilleux (1972): *Introduction to Climatic Geomorphology*; Longman, London.

Tripathi, R.S. and S.K. Barik (2003): "Shifting Cultivation in North East India, Proceedings, Approaches for increasing Agricultural Productivity in Hill and Mountain Ecosystem", *ICAR Research Complex*, NEH Region, 2003, pp. 317-322.

Tuan, Yi fu (1971), "Man and Nature", *Commission on College Geography*, Resource Paper 10, 1971.

Tuisam A.S. (1973): "Higher Education for Nagaland," Ph.D. Thesis, University of New York, Buffalo, Mimiographed, p. 13.

Verma, A.K. (2007): "Forest as the Material Basis of the Tribes during Colonial Period," in C.K. Paty (ed.) *Forest Government and Tribe*; Concept Publishing Company, New Delhi, p. 50.

Vidyarthi, L.P. (1903): *The Maler: A Study in Nature-Man-Spirit Complex*, Calcutta Bookland, p. 24.

Viswanath, S.N. (1990): *A Hundred Years of Oil: A Narrative Account of the Search for Oil in India*, Vikas Publishing House, New Delhi, pp. 4-5.

Wallace, R. (1888): *India in 1887 as seen by Robert Wallace*; Oliver and Boyd, Edinburgh, p. 296.

Ward, W.E. (1890): *Introduction to the Assam Land Revenue Manual*, Government of Assam.

Watts, M. (1983): *Silent Violence: Food, Famine and Peasantry in Northern Nigeria*, Berkly, C.A.: University of California Press, p. 226.

Webster's Dictionary, Encyclopedic Edition (1979), J.G. Ferguson Publishing, Chicago, p. 574.

West, P.C. and S.R. Brachin, (1991) (eds.): *Resident Peoples and National Parks: Social Dilemmas and Strategies in International Conservation*, University of Arizona Press, Tucson.

White, G. (1898): *The Natural History of Shelburne*; Thames and Hudson, New York.

White, R.O. (1968): *Land, Livestock and Human Nutrition in India*, F. Fraeger, New York, p. 98.

Whitehead, J. (2010): "John Locke and the Governance of India's Landscape: The Category Wasteland in Colonial Revenue and Forest Legislation", *Economic and Political Weekly*, Vol. XIV, No. 50.

Wilhelm, S. (1873): "Memorandum on Forest Operations in Assam", No. 36, Calcutta, 16th August, 1873, Bengal Government Forest Operation in Assam, File No. 38/45, 1872 (ASA).

William, M. (2006): *Deforesting the Earth: From Prehistory to Global Crisis—An Abridgement*, The University of Chicago Press, p. 11.

Winn, J.J. (1984): The Conserver Ethics and Technological Balance, *Gandhi Marg*, 6.

Woeikof, A. (1901): "De influence de I'hommescer la Terre" in *Annals de Geographie*, Vol. 10, pp. 97-114.

Wolpart, J. (1965): "Behavioural Aspects of the Decision to Migrate," Papers and Proceedings of the *Regional Science Association*, No. 15, pp. 159-169.

——(1966): "Migration as an Adjustment to Environmental Stress", *Journal of Social Issues*, 22; pp. 92-102.

Wood, D. (1995): "Conserved to Death, Are Tropical Forests being over-protected from People?", *Land Use Policy*, Vol. 12, No. 2, pp. 115-35.

Worster, D. (1998): "Doing Environmental History" in Donald Worster (ed.), *The Ends of the Earth: Perspective on Modern Environmental History*, Cambridge, p. 574.

Xaxa, V. (1985): "Tribal Migration to Plantation Estate in North East India: Determinants and Consequences", *Demography India*, 14(I), pp. 70-81.

Zimmerer, K.S. and K.R. Yong, (1998); Nature's Geography: New Lessons for Conservation in Developing Countries in W.M. Adams and J. Hutton (ed.), *People, Parks and Poverty*, University of Wisconsin Press, Madison; p. 149.

"Bhumihin Khetiyokar Satyagraha", *Sadiniya Assomiya*, 10 June, 1950.

"Totemism: General Informations" online (http://nagaland. Nic. In/potential/tourism, htm) Government of Nagaland, Retrieved 2011-12-22.

Index